This edition is issued by
special arrangement with
PICKERING & INGLIS LTD.
the British publishers.

First published	..	..	*1953*
Reprinted ..	..	..	*1963*
,, ..	..	..	*1970*

ISBN 0 7208 0192 3

Printed in Great Britain by Lowe & Brydone (Printers) Ltd., London

KNOW YOUR BIBLE

The Unfolding Drama
of Redemption

THE BIBLE AS A WHOLE

VOLUME I

THE PROLOGUE AND ACT I OF THE DRAMA
EMBRACING THE OLD TESTAMENT

W. GRAHAM SCROGGIE, D.D.

FLEMING H. REVELL COMPANY
OLD TAPPAN, NEW JERSEY

Other Volumes in the Series :

KEY TO
THE UNFOLDING DRAMA OF REDEMPTION

A — Revelation of the Redeeming Purpose	B — Progression of the Redeeming Purpose			C — Consummation of the Redeeming Purpose
PROLOGUE	ACT I	INTERLUDE	ACT II	EPILOGUE
GENESIS i. 1—xi. 9	GENESIS xi. 10 to MALACHI iv. 6	Between MALACHI and MATTHEW	MATTHEW to JUDE	The Book of the REVELATION
1 — From the CREATION to the FALL — i-iii	A DIVINE COVENANT OF LAW EMBODIED IN THE HISTORY AND LITERATURE OF A SEMITIC RACE	JUDAISM AND HEATHENISM PREPARING THE WORLD FOR THE ADVENT OF THE MESSIAH	A DIVINE COVENANT OF GRACE EMBODIED IN THE HISTORY AND LITERATURE OF THE CHRISTIAN CHURCH	1 — A VISION OF GRACE — CHRIST THE LORD OF THE CHURCH — i-iii
2 — From the FALL to the FLOOD — iv-viii. 14	*Scene 1* — THE HEBREW FAMILY Shem to Joseph — Gen. xi. 10-l. 26		*Scene 1* — Introduction of Christianity into the World by JESUS THE MESSIAH — Matthew to John	2 — A VISION OF GOVERNMENT — CHRIST THE JUDGE OF THE WORLD — iv-xix. 10
3 — From the FLOOD to BABEL — viii. 15-xi. 9	*Scene 2* — THE ISRAELITISH NATION Joseph to Zerubbabel — Exod. i-Ezra i		*Scene 2* — Progress of Christianity in the World to the close of the first Century A.D. — Acts to Jude	3 — A VISION OF GLORY — CHRIST THE KING OF THE UNIVERSE — xix. 11-xxii
	Scene 3 — THE JEWISH CHURCH Zerubbabel to Nehemiah — Books of Ezra and Nehemiah and Prophets			

ANALYSIS OF CONTENTS

7

CONTENTS

CONTENTS

CONTENTS

CONTENTS

CHARTS

MAPS

PREFACE

Knowing the Bible

'CHRISTIAN leadership must know its Bible better than any other book'. Bread is baked, not for analysis but for consumption. A house is built, not to be surveyed and criticised but to be inhabited. The Bible is given to us that we might know God, and live the life of His plan for us. In the study of it criticism has its place—criticism Higher and Lower—but into these matters comparatively few can enter, nor is the Bible's chief value affected vitally by the results of such study. It is the people's Book as inheritance, and should be theirs as possession.

Every Christian worker, whether Minister, Sunday School Teacher, Class Leader, Open-air Preacher, or one engaged in any other form of ministry, should have a thorough working knowledge of the Bible in his mother-tongue. It is not enough that we be familiar with great texts, or great chapters; we should know the Bible *as a whole*, and should be familiar with the parts which make the whole; for here is a Divine progressive revelation, in which every part is organically related to every other part; and, consequently, only by knowing the whole Bible can we worthily appreciate its greatness and experience its power.

17

INTRODUCTION

INTRODUCTION

The Synthetical Method of Bible Study

VOLUMES I and II of the author's, 'Know Your Bible',
are *analytical*; I, dealing with the Old Testament, and II,
with the New Testament; but for the vision of the Bible as a
whole this is not enough; the books must be seen to be a Book,
and the details must be apprehended as parts of a sublime
revelation.

This view we speak of as *synthetical*, to distinguish it from
analytical. The words *synthetic*, *synthesis*, and *synthesize* are
widely used to express the idea of putting two or more things
together. In Logic it means the process of reasoning from the
whole to a part; from the general to the particular. In Philosophy
it means the action of proceeding in thought from causes to
effects; from principles to their consequences. In Chemistry it
signifies the formation of a compound by the combination of
its elements. In Physics it connotes the production of a complex
musical sound by the combination of its component simple tones.
In Surgery it refers to the operation of reuniting broken or
divided parts of bones or soft portions of the body. In Biology
it tells of groups formed of members whose structural characters
partake of the characteristics of other often antagonistic groups.

In general, by *synthesis* is meant *the putting together* of parts
or elements so as to make up a complex whole; a constructing
of something new out of existing materials.

By synthetic Bible study is meant, that method whereby the
various parts are viewed together, are seen in their relation to
one another, and are regarded as constituting a whole. It is,
as we have said, the opposite of the analytic method.

In analysis details are separately regarded, but in synthesis
these details melt into the picture of the whole. Analysis moves
from the specific to the general, but synthesis, from the general
to the specific. The analytic is the microscopic method; the
synthetic is the telescopic method. Analysis concentrates on
the infinitesimal, but synthesis concentrates on the infinite.

The synthetic method in geography will lead one to begin with the hemispheres, and from them to move to continents, to countries, to counties, to cities, to towns and villages. The synthetic method in history will require that we begin, not with an event, but with history as a whole, in its three great parts, ancient, medieval, and modern; and after that, we can study its epochs and eras, and finally consider the countless events which constitute the unfolding story.

In like manner, the synthetic method in Bible study demands that we get a mental grasp of the Bible as a whole, eliminating all artificial divisions and arrangements. In this way only can we discern the unity of the Scriptures, and follow the progress of the revelation which they embody. In the Bible, as in biology, the whole is more than the aggregate of the parts. A living body is more than an assemblage of limbs; and the Bible is more than a collection of texts, paragraphs, chapters, or even books; it is a spiritual organism, in which each part is related to, and is dependent on, every other part, the whole being pervaded by spiritual life. That is true of the Bible which Schopenhauer claimed for the system of the universe of knowledge, of which he said: 'It is an architectonic structure, whose parts are organically connected. Each part supports the whole, and is supported by the whole'. Martin Luther used to say that he studied the Bible as he gathered apples. First of all he shook the tree, then the limbs, then the branches, and after that he searched under the leaves for any remaining fruit. In like manner should we approach the Tree of Life, the fruit of which is for 'the healing of the nations'.

This truth may be presented under various figures. The revelation of the Bible begins in a *Garden*, and ends in a *City*, and the record of the slow progress from simplicity to complexity lies between. In *Genesis* are origins; in *Revelation* are issues; and from *Exodus* to *Jude* are processes. The redemptive revelation is *initial* before Christ; is *central* in Christ; and is *final* from Christ. It has a starting-point, a track, and a goal. The Temple of Truth is upreared from its *foundation* to its *consummation* by its glorious *superstructure*, in which are beauty of conception, unity of plan, harmony of parts, and growth towards completion.

To present this view of the Bible is the aim of this book. The method has been tested out in fifty years of teaching in Colleges, Churches, and Bible Schools; and it is hoped that this presentation of it, now embracing the whole Bible[1], may, in spite of its defects, lead not a few to a new interest in, and to a more complete knowledge of, 'the Word of God, which liveth and abideth for ever.'

[1] The Old Testament part was issued in a book called *The Fascination of Old Testament Story*, which is out of print, but which for this volume has been entirely re-written, and to which the New Testament will be added in another volume (D.V.).

THE BIBLE AS A WHOLE.
GENERAL VIEW.

The Books in the Book

IT will be well, first of all, to take a look at the parts which constitute the whole which we call the Bible (ὁ βίβλος, the Book). The units are the separate Books or Writings, and there are 66 of these.

These 66 are divided into two groups, called Testaments or Covenants: one is called Old, Ἡ Παλαια Διαθηκη, meaning first or former, having existed long; and the other is called New, Ἡ Καινη Διαθηκη, with reference to its quality, different from the Old (Heb. ix. 15). The New Testament is also called new in the sense of recent, later than the Old (νεος, Heb. xii. 24). In the Old Testament are 39 of the 66 Books, and in the New Testament are 27 of the total.

Each of these Testaments comprises several groups of Books, which are distinguishable partly by their substance, and partly by their literary form.

The Old Testament groups are generally designated (a) LAW, 5 Books: *Genesis, Exodus, Leviticus, Numbers,* and *Deuteronomy,* known as the *Pentateuch*; (b) HISTORY, 12 Books: *Joshua, Judges, Ruth,* 1-2 *Samuel,* 1-2 *Kings,* 1-2 *Chronicles, Ezra, Nehemiah, Esther*; (c) POETRY and WISDOM, 5 Books: *Job, Psalms, Proverbs, Ecclesiastes, Song of Solomon*; (d) PROPHECY, 17 Books: *Isaiah, Jeremiah, Lamentations, Ezekiel, Daniel, Hosea, Joel, Amos, Obadiah, Jonah, Micah, Nahum, Habakkuk, Zephaniah, Haggai, Zechariah, Malachi.* The designation of PROPHECY here is not quite accurate, as *Lamentations* cannot be so described; *Daniel* is partly historical, and partly apocalyptic; and *Jonah* is the history of a prophet rather than prophecy.

In the Hebrew Bible these 39 Books are arranged in three divisions which are named: 1. TORAH, the Law (5 Books), *Genesis to Deuteronomy.* 2. NEBI'IM, the Prophets (21 Books). These are divided into the *Former Prophets*; the historical Books: *Joshua, Judges,* 1-2 *Samuel,* 1-2 *Kings*; and the *Latter Prophets*;

the prophetical Books more strictly so-called: *Isaiah, Jeremiah, Ezekiel,* and the Twelve Minor Prophets.   3. KETHUBIM, the Writings (Greek, *Hagiographa*: 13 Books).   The Books of this division are separated into three groups which are known as (i) the *Former Writings*: *Psalms, Proverbs, Job*;   (ii) the *Five Megilloth* or Rolls: *Song of Solomon, Ruth, Lamentations, Ecclesiastes, Esther*;   (iii) the *Latter Writings*: *Daniel, Ezra, Nehemiah,* 1-2 *Chronicles*.

In the New Testament there are three groups, which may be designated, (*a*) HISTORICAL (5 Books): *Matthew, Mark, Luke, John, Acts*;   (*b*) DIDACTICAL (21 Books): *Romans* to *Jude*;   (*c*) PROPHETICAL or APOCALYPTICAL (1 Book): the *Revelation*.

These details should be memorized, and for this purpose the following charts may be helpful.

CHART 1

THE BIBLE

THE OLD TESTAMENT ... ... 39 Books						THE NEW TESTAMENT ... ... 27 Books					
HISTORICAL 17		DIDACTICAL 5		PROPHETICAL 17		HISTORICAL 5		DIDACTICAL 21		PROPHETICAL 1	
Legislative 5	Executive 12	Poetry 2	Wisdom 3	Major 5	Minor 12	The Christ 4	The Church 1	Pauline 14	General 7	1	
Genesis Exodus Leviticus Numbers Deuteronomy	Joshua Judges Ruth 1-2 Samuel 1-2 Kings 1-2 Chronicles Ezra Nehemiah Esther	Psalms Song of Solomon	Job Proverbs Ecclesiastes	Isaiah Jeremiah (Lamentations) Ezekiel (Daniel)	Hosea Joel Amos Obadiah Jonah Micah Nahum Habakkuk Zephaniah Haggai Zechariah Malachi	Matthew Mark Luke John	Acts	Romans 1-2 Corinthians Galatians Ephesians Philippians Colossians 1-2 Thessalonians 1-2 Timothy Titus Philemon (Hebrews)	James 1-2 Peter 1-3 John Jude	Revelation	

CHART 2

THE OLD TESTAMENT			
LAW (5)	HISTORY (12)	POETRY-WISDOM (5)	PROPHECY (17)
Genesis Exodus Leviticus Numbers Deuteronomy	Joshua Judges Ruth 1-2 Samuel 1-2 Kings 1-2 Chronicles Ezra Nehemiah Esther	Job Psalms Proverbs Ecclesiastes Song of Solomon	Isaiah Jeremiah (Lamentations) Ezekiel Daniel Hosea Joel Amos Obadiah (Jonah) Micah Nahum Habakkuk Zephaniah Haggai Zechariah Malachi

CHART 3

THE OLD TESTAMENT (Hebrew Arrangement)		
TORAH—LAW (5)	NEBI'IM—PROPHETS (21)	KETHUBIM WRITINGS (13)
Genesis Exodus Leviticus Numbers Deuteronomy	(i) FORMER PROPHETS (6) Joshua Judges 1-2 Samuel 1-2 Kings (ii) LATTER PROPHETS (15) Isaiah Jeremiah Ezekiel Hosea, Joel, Amos, Obadiah, Jonah, Micah, Nahum, Habakkuk, Zephaniah, Haggai, Zechariah, Malachi	(i) FORMER WRITINGS (3) Psalms Proverbs Job (ii) MEGILLOTH, ROLLS (5) Song of Solomon Ruth Lamentations Ecclesiastes Esther (iii) LATTER WRITINGS (5) Daniel Ezra Nehemiah 1-2 Chronicles

CHART 4

THE NEW TESTAMENT		
HISTORICAL (5)	DIDACTICAL (21)	PROPHETICAL (1)
Matthew	(i) PAULINE (14)	The Revelation
Mark	Romans	
	1-2 Corinthians	
Luke	Galatians	
	Ephesians	
John	Philippians	
	Colossians	
Acts	1-2 Thessalonians	
	1-2 Timothy	
	Titus	
	Philemon	
	(Hebrews)	
	(ii) GENERAL (7)	
	James	
	1-2 Peter	
	1-3 John	
	Jude	

A thorough grasp of these particulars will help us to realize
what are the materials which, like many coloured threads, are
wrought into this Cloth of Gold, this Garment of God.

Christ the Sum and Substance of the Bible Revelation

NO more convincingly are the unity and progress of the Biblical revelation demonstrated than in the fact that Christ dominates the whole revelation. This is not imaginative, but real; it is not a wishful theory, but a satisfying fact. The evidence of the fact is manifold, and can be presented in various ways.

For example, His Human Pedigree, His Redemptive Programme, and His Divine Person which are revealed in the New Testament *historically*, are revealed in the Old Testament *prophetically*, not in any general or doubtful manner, but in great and exact detail[1].

In another way also may we see that Christ dominates the whole Biblical revelation, and see also how the presentation of Him, alike in prophecy and history, promises to meet, and does meet, man's deepest needs.

Man the sinner needs someone who will redemptively represent him; he needs someone who will reveal God to him; and he needs someone who, with authority and effect, will rule over him. In other words, man needs a *priest*, a *prophet*, and a *king*: a priest to represent him before God; a prophet to reveal God to him; and a king to take control of, and to rule in and over the whole kingdom of his life.

In vain will man find such an one among his fallen fellows, but in Christ the need is supplied in every respect. Three offices dominate the Old Testament: that of Priest, represented by Aaron; that of Prophet, represented by Moses; and that of King, represented by David. But these were mortal and sinful men, and therefore could not ideally fulfil these several functions, but it is made clear that each of them represented One to come, Who would perfectly fulfil the will of God for man which these three offices disclose. That Aaron pointed to Christ is plainly

---

[1]See the author's *Christ the Key to Scripture*.

30

declared in Hebrews v.; that Moses pointed to Him is affirmed in Deut. xviii. 18; and that David anticipated Him is revealed in various passages, notably Psalm cx. 1; and that which the Old Testament promises, the New Testament presents. That which is needed is supplied. He who was typified appears. What is *longing* in the Old Testament, is *satisfaction* in the New. 'Oh that I knew where I might find Him!', becomes 'We have found Him' (Job xxiii. 3; John i. 45).

Memory may be aided if these facts are viewed as in Chart 5. See also Chart 112.

CHART 5

GOD'S ANSWER TO MAN'S CRY					
OLD TESTAMENT			NEW TESTAMENT		
The Cry of Man			The Answer of God		
The Need	The Office	The Type	The Office	The Antitype	The Writings
Someone to Reveal	Prophet	Moses	Prophet	C H	Gospels
Someone to Represent	Priest	Aaron	Priest	R I S	Acts and Epistles
Someone to Rule	King	David	King	T	Revelation

In the Old Testament Christ is predicted; in the Gospels He is present; in the Acts He is proclaimed; in the Epistles He is possessed; and in the Revelation He is predominant. Christ is the focus of all history, prophecy, and type. Divine revelation converges in Him in the Old Testament, and emerges from Him in the New Testament. Both parts of the Revelation meet in Him; the one part as preparation, and the other, as realization. In this view all parts of the Bible, from books to verses, constitute a divine progressive revelation of redeeming love; God and man meet in the One who is the God-Man.

Redemption in the Bible

THE underlying theme of all the Scriptures is *Redemption*: in the *Old Testament* the *anticipation* of it in type and prophecy; in the *Gospels* the *accomplishment* of it by the death of Christ; in the *Acts* and *Epistles*, the *application* of it to the needs of man; and in the *Revelation*, the *achievement* of it in the subjection of all kingdoms to the rule of God. As running through all British Navy rope there is a thread of some colour according to the dockyard in which it is made, so running through all the Scriptures is the saving purpose, making the whole Bible an Unfolding Drama of Redemption. Into this Drama all the details fit at each stage of its unfolding, so that each and every part of the Bible, whether history, or literature, or type, or prophecy, or law, or grace, is part of the design of God to reconcile to Himself, by the sacrifice of Himself, a fallen and rebellious race.

In the thought of many, a *Drama* is simply a theatrical entertainment, but such an idea misses the essential meaning of the word, and may be destructive of it. What is common to the theatrical and the dramatic is action, but in the former the action is feigned, and in the latter it is real; it is actual, not artificial; it is a living scene, and not a mere semblance.

Human history, regarded as a whole, is a Drama setting forth the struggle of the human mind with life's dark problems, and disclosing the development of alternating human passions and emotions; the conflict of faith and doubt, of joy and sorrow, of hope and despair.

The Unfolding Drama of Redemption

THIS is the theme of the Biblical Writings. They are a record of this struggle, but they are distinguishable from all other such records in that throughout there is clearly discernible a divine purpose and plan, and it is this which gives to history its unity and deepest significance.

Viewing these Writings as a whole, it may be claimed that *the historical unfolding of the redeeming purpose presents a dramatic unity.* The stories make one Story, and the parts make one great Whole.

"Through the ages one increasing purpose runs."

It is when we view the Biblical Writings in this way that we are able to apprehend their incomparable value, and to appreciate the wonder of their congruity and comprehensiveness.

Only in these Writings taken together have we a true perspective of history, and a rational philosophy of life. The Bible so viewed is *a divine progressive revelation made in life, and fixed in literature.*

Whatever our opinions may be on questions of authorship, date, and style of these Writings, the criticism which destroys this fundamental conception cannot be true.

Here are the Writings, whoever wrote them, and whenever they were written. The finished product is what matters, and this product bears upon it the hall-mark of divinity.

This Literature records the progressive fulfilment of a divine design ·which reaches 'from everlasting to everlasting', and all true analysis will fit perfectly into this synthesis.

Of this Drama of Redemption the Earth is the Stage, Man and Nations are the *Dramatis Personae*, and Christ, let it be said most reverently, is the Hero.

Then, there is the developing Plot, the unfolding of an end which is not discernible from the beginning; and that end is the 'salvation' of which 'the prophets enquired and searched diligently . . . searching what, or what manner of time, the Spirit of Christ Who was in them did point to, when He testified beforehand the sufferings of Christ, and the glory that should follow' (1 Peter i. 10, 11).

It is this which makes the Bible the most fascinating book in the world, from whatever standpoint it be viewed, literary, historical, or religious. In what follows, the Drama is outlined in such portions and proportions as to make the mastery of it a comparatively easy task. As already said, the method is from the general to the particular, from the whole to the parts, from synthesis to analysis. Each division with its parts should be mastered in such a way as to prevent a sense of confusion with multiplying details. There will be constant repetition, a doubling back upon outlines to fill in details, which however is not 'vain repetition', but an illustration of the apostolic dicta: 'to write the same things to you, to me indeed is not irksome, but for you it is safe'; 'I have said before'; 'I told you before'; 'as we said before, so say I now again' (Phil. iii. 1; 2 Cor. vii. 3; xiii. 2; Gal. i. 9); and so by 'line upon line; here a little, there a little', the Redemptive Drama unfolds from its mystical beginning to its majestic end.

The Unfolding Drama of Redemption

FIRST SURVEY

THE Plot of the Drama being Redemption, we are shown, first of all, the Revelation of the Redeeming Purpose; then, the Progression of it; and finally the Consummation of it. This embraces everything from *Genesis* to *Revelation*.

The Revelation of the Redeeming Purpose is in *Genesis* i. 1—xi. 9; The Progression of it is in *Genesis* xi. 10—*Jude* 25; and the Consummation of it is in *Revelation* i—xxii.

This survey should be definitely fixed in the mind and contemplated, under whatever figure you please. It indicates clearly that the 66 Books are not a miscellany of unrelated Writings, but are the parts of a sublime Whole.

We must now proceed to give dramatic form to these dominating ideas. The Revelation of the Redeeming Purpose is the Drama's Prologue; the Consummation of it is the Drama's Epilogue; and the Progression of it is unfolded in Two Acts, with an Interlude between them. Act I is presented in *Genesis* xi. 10—*Malachi* iv. 6; the Interlude is what lies between the end of Act I, and the beginning of Act II; and Act II is presented in *Matthew* i. 1—*Jude* 25.

CHART 6

PROLOGUE	ACT I	INTERLUDE	ACT II	EPILOGUE
THE UNFOLDING DRAMA OF REDEMPTION, No. 1				
THE REDEEMING PURPOSE				
REVELATION	PROGRESSION			CONSUMMA-TION
GENESIS i. 1-xi. 9	GENESIS xi. 10 to MAL. iv. 6	MALACHI to MATTHEW	MATTHEW to JUDE	THE REVELATION

This outline should be mastered before proceeding further, as it is the foundation of everything that follows.

The Two Acts

WE should now see that the Two Acts which constitute, with the Interlude, the Progression of the Redeeming Purpose, represent Two Covenants, which, in the Bible, are called The Old, and The New (see under The Books in the Book, pp. 25-29); and, as in every Drama, these Acts are vitally related to one another. The Second is an advance upon the First, and carries the developing Plot forward to its realization.

The First of these Covenants is *preparative*, and the Second is *effective*. The First is a Covenant of *Law*, and the Second is a Covenant of *Grace*. The First is embodied in the history and literature of a Semitic Race, and the Second is embodied in the history and literature of the Christian Church.

Between these Covenants (that is, between the records of them) is the Interlude, in the history and literature of which we are shown that events, both in Judaism and Heathenism, constituted the transition from the Old to the New Economy.

These particulars must now be added to the preceding Plan.

CHART 7

THE UNFOLDING DRAMA OF REDEMPTION, No. 2				
PROLOGUE	ACT I	INTERLUDE	ACT II	EPILOGUE
	Preparative	Between MALACHI and MATTHEW Judaism and Heathenism Preparing the World for the ADVENT OF THE MESSIAH	Effective	
	COVENANT OF LAW		COVENANT OF GRACE	
	Embodied in the History and Literature of a SEMITIC RACE		Embodied in the History and Literature of THE CHRISTIAN CHURCH	
	GENESIS xi. 10 to MAL. iv. 6		MATTHEW to JUDE	

A word must be said here about the terms *Semitic Race*, and *Christian Church*. By the former is meant the descendants of Noah through Shem; and by the latter is meant the aggregate of all believers, that is, of all regenerated men, women, and children throughout this Christian age.

It is of the utmost importance for comparison and contrast to keep in mind the salient features of these Two Covenants.

Each is associated with a mountain, Sinai and Calvary.

Each is represented by a person, Moses and Christ.

Each has its focus in an idea, the Law and the Gospel.

The one is characterised by a prohibition, 'thou shalt not'; and the other, by a promise, 'I will' (Exod. xx. 1-17; Jer. xxxi. 31-34; Heb. viii. 6-13).

Under the one, the command is, 'put off thy shoes from off thy feet'; and under the other, the command is, 'put shoes on his feet' (Exod. iii. 5; Luke xv. 22).

At the inauguration of the one, three thousand souls were slain; and at the inauguration of the other, three thousand souls were saved (Exod. xxxii. 28; Acts ii. 41).

The outstanding ideas of the Drama are *Law* and *Grace*, the *Law* dominating Act I, and *Grace* dominating Act II. These represent two distinct dispensations, and failure to distinguish between them has resulted in much confusion alike in thought and experience.

"The law was given by Moses, but grace and truth came by Jesus Christ" (John i. 17; cf. Col. ii. 16, 17; Gal. iii.).

Under the Law God dealt with one nation only; but under Grace He is dealing with individuals of all nations (Gal. iii. 27-29; Eph. iii. 1-11). Under the Law justification was by *works* (Deut. vi. 25), and so no one was justified; but under Grace justification is by *faith*, and so multitudes are justified (Rom. iii. 20-26; iv; v. 1; Gal. ii. 16).

Long ago Augustine said: 'Distinguish the dispensations, and you will understand the Scriptures'. Consider carefully, then, the Two Acts in the Drama of Redemption; the First making possible the Second, and leading to it (Gal. iii. 24, 25); enabling Paul to say, 'Ye are not under law, but under grace' (Rom. vi. 14).

THE INTERLUDE

Between these Two Acts is an Interlude, of about 400 years duration. We must be careful not to suppose that this pause in the inspired record means a pause in the Divine activity. As there is no break in the redeeming purpose, so there is no break in the preparation for its realization. During this Interlude God was as much and as really imminent in history as He had been before, and was to be afterward. No one can study the world events of this period without realizing that they formed the transition from the Old Economy to the New; that Judaism and Heathenism, in history and literature, were casting up a highway for the coming of the Messiah.

In this period Greece rose to glory, and made the world think in a new way about beauty, and conscience, and retribution, and the soul, and immortality. In this period the Hebrew Scriptures were translated into Greek (the Septuagint, LXX), and so were made available to a multitude of people who otherwise could not have read them. In this period the Jews were widely scattered throughout the world (Diaspora), and so prepared the way for the evangelization of the world in the Gospel age. And in this period Rome became the World Power in the Middle East and West, and so by its political system, and the roads which it built everywhere, it was unwittingly making possible the great missionary enterprise of the Christian dispensation.

The Interlude pause is, therefore, not in the Divine activity, but only in the inspired record of it.

Here, then (Charts 6, 7), in broadest outline is set forth the only true philosophy of history, the human story from the Divine standpoint. This is the frame into which all the details will fit. Take time to be impressed by this development of the redeeming purpose. Slowly, it may seem, but surely, the Divine design was unfolded from age to age.

'God who of old time spake in many parts and in manifold ways . . . has now spoken fully and finally in His Son'.

The first of these facts reaches from the beginning of the Prologue to the end of the Interlude, and the second, reaches from the end of the Interlude to the end of the Epilogue. The words of the one are gathered up and completed in the Word of the other.

PROLOGUE

FROM THE CREATION TO THE FALL
FROM THE FALL TO THE FLOOD
FROM THE FLOOD TO BABEL

The Unfolding Drama of Redemption

SECOND SURVEY

WE must now make the general outline, already given, somewhat more complete, in pursuance of the synthetic method.

THE PROLOGUE
Genesis i. 1—xi. 9

THE REVELATION OF THE REDEEMING PURPOSE

Here are discernible three distinct periods which are indicated by the fact that each ends in human failure. These are:

1. *From the Creation to the Fall.* Gen. i. 1—iii. 24.

2. *From the Fall to the Flood.* Gen. iv. 1—viii. 14.

3. *From the Flood to Babel.* Gen. viii. 15—xi. 9.

A long time is covered by these periods, and each has its own characteristics, but in all three there are two things which dominate, namely, the sin of man and the grace of God. The words Fall, Flood, Babel, tell the one part of the story, and the fact that there was a second and a third period, tells the other part of it. But for the Divine design to redeem the human race, our first parents would have perished at the gates of the Garden.

The *sin of man* indicated the *need* of redemption, and the *grace of God* pointed to the *way* of it.

ACT I

THE PROGRESSION OF THE REDEEMING PURPOSE

PREPARATIVE

GENESIS xi. 10—MALACHI iv. 6

As in every Act there are Scenes, it is of great importance to see clearly what these are in each of the Acts of this Drama. In Act I there are three Scenes:

1. THE HEBREW FAMILY.   Gen. xi. 10—l. 26.
2. THE ISRAELITISH NATION.   Exod. i—2. Kings xxv.
3. THE JEWISH CHURCH.   Ezra. Nehemiah. Prophets.

The Hebrew Family is from Abram to Joseph. The Israelitish Nation is from Joseph to Zerubbabel. The Jewish Church is from Zerubbabel to Nehemiah.

The significance of both groups of words should be considered. The designations *Hebrew*, *Israelitish* and *Jewish* are not synonymous. In point of time the second is later than the first, and the third is later than the second. All Israelites were Hebrews, but strictly speaking, all Hebrews were not Israelites. Again, all Jews were Israelites, but all Israelites were not Jews.

The Jews were the descendants of Judah; the Israelites were the descendants of Jacob, whose name was changed to Israel; and both Jews and Israelites were the descendants of 'Abram the Hebrew' (Gen. xiv. 13). *Hebrew* is the *linguistic* designation; *Israelite* is the *national* designation; and *Jew* is the *religious* designation, which in later times came to be used with considerable latitude (p. 91).

Then, there are the descriptions *Family*, *Nation*, and *Church*. In these terms Old Testament history is summed up. The *Family* expanded into a *Nation*, and the *Nation* contracted into a *Church*. The Family was Hebrew; the Nation was Israelitish; and the Church was Jewish. These descriptions should be accepted in their broad significance, and not pressed too critically (p. 91).

Now let us gather up our analysis thus far.

CHART 8

THE UNFOLDING DRAMA OF REDEMPTION, No. 3	
PROLOGUE	ACT I
Genesis i. 1-xi. 9	Genesis xi. 10-Malachi iv. 6
Revelation of the Redeeming Purpose	Progression of the Redeeming Purpose. Preparative
I CREATION TO FALL Genesis i-iii	SCENE I THE HEBREW FAMILY. ABRAM TO JOSEPH Genesis xi. 10-l. 26
2 FALL TO FLOOD Genesis iv. 1-viii. 14	SCENE 2 THE ISRAELITISH NATION. JOSEPH TO ZERUBBABEL. Exodus i-Ezra i
3 FLOOD TO BABEL Genesis viii. 15-xi. 9	SCENE 3 THE JEWISH CHURCH. ZERUBBABEL TO NEHEMIAH Ezra (Esther), Nehemiah, Haggai, Zechariah, Malachi.

ACT II

THE PROGRESSION OF THE REDEEMING PURPOSE
EFFECTIVE
MATTHEW—JUDE

In this Act there are two Scenes:

1. THE INTRODUCTION OF CHRISTIANITY INTO THE WORLD BY JESUS THE MESSIAH
   MATTHEW—JOHN

2. THE PROGRESS OF CHRISTIANITY IN THE WORLD TO THE END OF THE FIRST CENTURY A.D.
   ACTS—JUDE

For the entire significance of Christianity we must turn to Christ. Judaism was not Christianity, although it was a preparation for it. Christianity has its origin in Christ; it does not and could not go further back. Christ was the Omega of the First Covenant and the Alpha of the Second. In Him one dispensation closed and another opened. He was both a Finisher and an Author; a Goal and a Starting-point.

Thus, He who introduced Christianity into the world, and the way in which He did so, constitute the Fourth of the Five Scenes in the Drama of Redemption (the First in Act II).

The Four Gospels are the record of this Introduction, and they mark the transition from the Old to the New; from what was national to what is universal; from the Israelitish Kingdom to the Christian Church.

The Fifth Scene (the Second in Act II) naturally follows the Fourth. The Christianity introduced so grows and spreads that before the close of the first century of this era it had reached to and established itself in the Capital of the Roman Empire.

No one can read the New Testament intelligently and not feel the thrill of that wonderful movement. What a story of effort and accomplishment, of adventure and reward! What romantic splendour, and what dramatic intensity are here! A power entered into human history which is destined to give to it its last significance, and to bring it to its true goal.

The record of this wonderful movement is given in the *Acts* and the *Epistles*: one historical and twenty-one epistolary Writings. The *Acts* is the record of the progress of Christianity, and the *Epistles* are the product and proof of that progress.

THE EPILOGUE

THE CONSUMMATION OF THE REDEEMING PURPOSE
THE BOOK OF THE REVELATION

Here the unfolding Drama is consummated, and the consummation is recorded in three sublime Visions: a *Vision of Grace* (i.—iii.), in which Christ is seen to be *Lord of the Church*; a *Vision of Government* (iv.—xix. 10), in which He is seen to be *Judge of the World*; and a *Vision of Glory* (xix. 11—xxii.), in which He is seen to be *King of the Universe*.

In the Epilogue the purpose of the Prologue is fulfilled. History has reached its true end in the Will of God. The kingdoms of the world have become the Kingdom of our God and of His Christ. The Crown has been reached by way of the Cross. Tragedy has given place to triumph.

Here, then, is the completion of our second survey.

CHART 9

THE UNFOLDING DRAMA OF REDEMPTION, No. 4	
ACT II	EPILOGUE
Matthew–Jude	The Revelation
Progression of the Redeeming Purpose. Effective	Consummation of the Redeeming Purpose.
SCENE 1 INTRODUCTION OF CHRISTIANITY INTO THE WORLD BY JESUS THE MESSIAH. Matthew–John	1 VISION OF GRACE. CHRIST THE LORD OF THE CHURCH. (i–iii)
SCENE 2 PROGRESS OF CHRISTIANITY IN THE WORLD TO THE END OF THE FIRST CENTURY A.D. Acts–Jude	2 VISION OF GOVERNMENT. CHRIST THE JUDGE OF THE WORLD. (iv–xix. 10)
	3 VISION OF GLORY. CHRIST THE KING OF THE UNIVERSE. (xix. 11–xxii)

To get a complete conspectus of the Drama, as outlined so far, Charts 8 and 9 should be united in one, and the details should be thoroughly mastered, so that one may be able to think through the Bible from start to finish.

THE PROLOGUE

Revelation of the Redeeming Purpose

GENESIS i. 1-xi. 9

WE must now turn to the Prologue for the consideration of it in greater detail. Recall its three Periods (Chart 8, p. 43), and think again of their emphasis on *sin* and *grace*. Each of the Periods is full of detail, and each detail is vitally related to the revelation of the redeeming purpose.

This is confessedly a difficult part of Holy Scripture, and the many questions which it provokes, and the problems which it presents, must be honestly faced by the Bible student; but our object here does not necessitate nor allow of our entering critically into matters historical, literary, theological, scientific, and chronological; or into questions of cosmogony, cosmology, geology, astronomy, evolution, anthropology, and psychology. All of these are important, but they are advanced studies and should follow and not precede a thorough knowledge *of what is said*, however this may ultimately be interpreted and understood.

What is of importance here is not the interpretation of any particular passage or event, but the apprehension of the Divine progressive action towards the realization of an eternal design, either by means of man, or in spite of him.

CHART 10

THE PROLOGUE. REVELATION OF THE REDEEMING PURPOSE. Genesis i. 1–xi. 9

THE FIRST PERIOD	THE SECOND PERIOD	THE THIRD PERIOD
FROM THE CREATION TO THE FALL	FROM THE FALL TO THE FLOOD	FROM THE FLOOD TO BABEL
Genesis i–iii	Genesis iv. 1–viii. 14	Genesis viii. 15–xi. 9
The Creation of the Cosmos (i. 1–ii. 3)	Cain and Abel and their Offerings (iv. 1–15)	Noah and his Family (viii. 15–ix. 29)
The Advent of Mankind (i. 26–31; ii. 4–25)	The Genealogies of Cain and Seth (iv. 16–v. 32)	The Spread of Nations (x. 1–32)
The Probation of Man (ii. 16, 17)	The Great Apostasy and Following Judgment (vi. 1–viii. 14)	The Building of Babel (xi. 1–9)
The Temptation and Fall (iii. 1–24)		

SIN — JUDGMENT — GRACE

ADAM — SETH — ENOCH — NOAH — SHEM

CHART 11

THE PROLOGUE. REVELATION OF THE REDEEMING PURPOSE. Genesis i. 1–xi. 9

THE FIRST PERIOD. Genesis i–iii.

FROM THE CREATION TO THE FALL

CREATION OF THE COSMOS i. 1–ii. 3	ADVENT OF MANKIND i. 26–31; ii. 4–25	PROBATION OF MAN ii. 16, 17	TEMPTATION AND FALL iii. 1–24
(i) The Whole Universe i. 1	(i) Creation of Man Summary Record i. 26–31 Detailed Record ii. 4–7	(i) The Necessity	(i) The Serpent iii. 1–5
(ii) The Earth Planet i. 2–ii. 3	(ii) Adam and the Garden ii. 8–15	(ii) The Means	(ii) The Woman iii. 1–7
	(iii) The Creation of Woman and the Institution of Marriage ii. 18–25	(iii) The Issues	(iii) The Man iii. 6, 7
			(iv) The Lord God iii. 8–24 In Judgment In Grace

THE PROLOGUE

REVELATION OF THE REDEEMING PURPOSE

GENESIS i. 1—xi. 9

THE FIRST PERIOD

From the Creation to the Fall

GENESIS i.—iii.

IN these pregnant and profound chapters four things claim attention. (Chart 11).

1. The Creation of the Cosmos

GENESIS i. 1—ii. 3

(i) THE WHOLE UNIVERSE (Gen. i. 1).

'In beginning God created the heavens and the earth'

The first verse of the Bible has no parallel for sublimity and comprehensiveness. In scope it is declarative, not demonstrative; affirmative, not argumentative; and historical, not philosophical. There is no attempt to prove the Being of God. He is the un-provable Fact upon which all else is built, and only 'the fool' will say, 'there is no God.'

Here the uncreated God is seen creating, and in such a manner that, as Andrew Fuller declared, a child can learn in five minutes from this verse more than all the ancient sages ever knew.

In character the verse is entirely positive, but it rules out all that is false in the thoughts and theories of men about God and the universe.

This simple statement denies at least six false doctrines.

(a) It denies the *Eternity of Matter*. '*In beginning*'. There was, then, a commencement; 'the heavens and the earth' had a 'beginning'; they were not eternal. The antiquity of the universe is beyond human computation; but there was a time when it did not exist.

(b) It denies *Atheism*. The atheist says there is no God, but the Bible begins by declaring His Being. Geology and astronomy may claim a hundred million years for the existence of the universe, but whenever it began *God was there*; He did not begin;

He eternally is. Atheism creates a crop of problems, and solves none.

(c) It denies *Polytheism*. If creation were the work of many gods, the unity of the universe would have to be accounted for, and it can be accounted for only on the hypothesis that God, the One Eternal Mind, created all. *'God created'*.

Both these words, standing as they do at the beginning of all history and revelation, are of profoundest importance.

'God', *Elohim*. This designation, which is plural, occurs 35 times in chapters i. 1—ii. 3, and in the Old Testament over 2,700 times. It certainly does not mean *gods*, and must be something more than a plural of majesty. In the light of the entire revelation in the Bible we must regard this designation of God to be a foregleam of the Divine Trinity (cf. ver. 26).

'Created'. In Genesis i.—ii. three words are used which must be distinguished. *Bara*, which occurs in i. 1, 21, 27; ii. 3; is used exclusively of God, and signifies a distinctively creative act. *'Made'*, *asah*, and *'formed'*, *yatzar*, which occur in i. 7, 16, 25, 31; ii. 2, 3, 7, 8, 19; signify to construct out of pre-existing materials. This distinction is of the utmost importance for an understanding of these first two chapters of the Bible. The idea of evolution can be in *make* and *form*, but not in *create*; so that the bringing into existence of the universe, of animal life, and of human life, was by successive creative acts of God (i. 1, 21, 27). By the word of His power a cosmos was created of orders material, sentient, and moral.

(d) It denies *Pantheism*. This teaches that God and Nature are the same, and so fails to distinguish between mind and matter, right and wrong, good and bad, and utterly confuses things which lie far apart. But this pernicious error finds its answer here: 'God created the heavens and the earth', and as He could not create Himself, He, and 'the heavens and the earth', cannot be the same.

(e) It denies *Agnosticism*. This affirms that it cannot be known whether there is a God or not. But the universe is an effect, and must have had a sufficient Cause; this building must have had an Architect; this design must have had a Designer; this Kingdom must have a King; and this family must have a

Father. Legitimate inference challenges and discredits agnosticism.

(f) It denies *Fatalism*. Reason is against fate and chance. This wonderful universe could not just 'happen'. God has acted in the freedom of His eternal Being, and according to His infinite Mind, and what He willed was and is, and can be nothing else, unless He should will it.

This statement has received detailed attention here because of its unique place and profound importance in relation to the whole Bible.

(ii) THE EARTH PLANET (Gen. i. 2—ii. 3).

Nothing could more clearly indicate the purpose of this Book and of the whole Bible than what follows ch. i. 1.

> 'In beginning God created the heavens and the earth, and the earth . . .'

The interest of the Bible is not in the universe as a whole, but in this earth, which was destined to be the home of mankind, and the scene of his redemption. Where the emphasis of the Bible lies is illustrated by the fact that, whereas chapter i. probably embraces millions of years, chapter iv. relates to a single incident one day in the life of two brothers. And for the same reason the thought passes swiftly from the creation of the universe to a consideration of one little planet in the vast majesty and glory of the Cosmos.

The time between verse 1, and verse 2 is unpredictable. Much depends on whether the first verb in verse 2 is *was*, or *became* (*hayah*). '*And the earth was waste—*'. In Isaiah xlv. 18, it is said:

> 'Thus said Yahweh that created the heavens; Elohim himself that formed the earth and made it; He hath established it, *He created it not waste*'.

There it is declared that God did not create the earth in the condition in which we see it in Gen. i. 2; therefore it must have *become* 'waste and empty', at some time, in some way, and from some cause which is not stated. If this be so, all the time which geology demands may here be found, and verses 2-31 will be the story of how the 'waste and void' earth was fashioned for man's life and habitation prior to the historic period. The object of the record is not to give a scientific account of this work, but to pass in rapid review the process, the crown of which was the creation of man.

Whether or not a break is allowed between verses 1 and 2, the main object of the chapter is clear, namely, to show that man is one with nature, being the crown of it; that he transcends nature, being created in the image of God; and that this earth is the sphere of his probation and redemption, the latter fact emerging later (ii.—iii.). Throughout the chapter what is emphasized is that *God saw*, *God said*, *God did*, and having seen, and said, and done, *God finished* His work, and *rested*.

The following Chart shows the process and progress of God's work.

CHART 12

THE WORK OF THE DAYS		
FIRST	3-5	Day and night appointed.
SECOND	6-8	Heaven and earth appointed.
THIRD	9, 10	Land and sea appointed.
	11-13	Vegetable life appointed.
		Grasses, Herbs, Trees } Self-propagating species.
FOURTH	14-19	Luminaries appointed.
FIFTH	20-23	Creation of life in the sea, and in the air.
SIXTH	24-31	Creation of life on the earth:— Roving .. .. Beasts; Domesticated .. .. Cattle; Creeping .. .. Reptiles; Human .. .. Mankind
SEVENTH	ii. 1-3	The Completion of God's Work, and the Institution of the Sabbath.

It has been pointed out that the words 'formless' and 'empty' (2) are the key to the structure of the chapter, and introduce the system of Hebrew parallelism. The first three days tell of *formlessness*, and the next three of *fulness*, and these days correspond alternately, the first and fourth, the second and fifth, and the third and sixth.

	FORMLESSNESS		FULNESS
First Day	Light (3–5)	Fourth Day	Lights (14–19)
Second Day	Air ⎫ Water ⎭ (6–8)	Fifth Day	Fowls ⎫ Fish ⎭ (20–23)
Third Day	Lands, Plants (9-13)	Sixth Day	Animals. Man (24–31)

Though this record has scientific value, its primary and principal purpose is religious. It is, be it said again, a record of what God *said*, and *saw*, and *did*; and its fundamental truths are unaffected by interpretations and discoveries.

Such, then, is the sweep and scope of this amazing revelation. With poetic grandeur the Divine Being and His activity, with a view to the redemption which He foresaw would be needed, are set forth, and thus the foundation is laid on which the whole superstructure of revelation is to be built.

2. The Advent of Mankind
GENESIS i. 26-31. ii. 4-25

Here are two dominating facts: the *Creation of Man*; and the *Institution of Marriage*. Together these tell us of man's creation, character, commission, constitution, circumstances, connections, and companionship.

(i) THE CREATION OF MAN   (i. 26-31; ii. 4-7).

In chapter i. man comes at the end, *the crown and culmination of creation*, but in chapter ii. he comes at the beginning as the *starting-point of human history*.

In chapter i. 26-31 the reference is to *mankind.*

'God said, Let us make man (*adam*), and let *them* . . . And God created the man (*ha adam*) . . . *male* and *female* created He *them*' (26-28).

But in chapter ii. 4-25 the reference is to two human beings, a man, and a woman. *The man (ha-adam)* in verses 7, 8, 15, 16, 18, 19, 20, 21, 22, 23, is the person ADAM; and in verses 22, 23 is introduced *the woman (l'ish-shah)*; and these two are called *Ish* and *Isha.*

It is evident, then, that in chapter i. 26-31 we have in summary what in chapter ii. is given in detail. In chapter i. the *fact* of man's creation is declared, and in chapter ii. the *process* of it is revealed. To keep this distinction in view will explain much that otherwise would be obscure. Frequently in Scripture the method of the Spirit is first to summarize a passage of particular importance, and then to return to it for detailed analysis and emphasis.

In chapter ii., then, is not a new and contradictory account of man's creation, but a supplementary and circumstantial account. As to the origin of man, it is plainly stated that *he was created* (i. 27), and, as in verses 1, 21, this was an act of origination and not a process of evolution. God *made (asah,* 26) man by *creating (bara,* 27) him.

The created man and woman were created, *as to their nature, in God's image and after His likeness* (i. 26, 27). As the statement cannot refer to what is physical, it must mean that the man and the woman were created rational, moral, and spiritual beings, distinguishing them from all other creatures in the sea, on the earth, and in the air.

The man and the woman were given *a four-fold commission*: the *domination* over the rest of creation (i. 26, 28; cf. Ps. viii); the *multiplication* of their kind, the propagation of the species (i. 28); the *subjugation* of all creatures (i. 28); and the *cultivation* of the earth for the maintenance of themselves and of the lower creation (i. 28-30).

The detailed account of the human creation is given in chapter ii., and is the first of ten *'generations'* in this Book (ii. 4; v. i.; vi. 9; x. 1; xi. 10; xi. 27; xxv. 12; xxv. 19; xxxvi. 1; xxxvii. 2).

The phrase 'the generations of the heavens and of the earth' (ii. 4), followed by the record of how man and woman came to be, indicates that they are of the heavens and of the earth, material and immaterial, physical and spiritual. Adam's body was *formed* (*asah*, not *bara*) of 'the dust of the ground', and 'the LORD GOD (*Yahweh Elohim*, not *Elohim* only as throughout ch. i.) *breathed into his nostrils the breath of lives; and man became a living soul*' (ii. 7). Here the making of man is distinguished from the making of all other creatures, and here is the starting-point of Biblical psychology. The *body* and the *spirit* (*breath*: cf. Job xxxii. 8; Prov. xx. 27; 1 Cor. ii. 11), constituted the *soul*. The *soul* is the middle term in which *body* and *spirit* meet in the unity of personality.

(ii) ADAM AND THE GARDEN (ii. 8-15. Chart 11).

The home of man and his circumstances are described in ii. 8-15. In a garden eastward in Eden, 'the LORD God put the man whom He had formed ... to *dress* it, and to *keep* it' (ii. 8, 15). *Cultivation* and *protection* were his duties in the Garden.

(iii) THE CREATION OF WOMAN. THE INSTITUTION OF MARRIAGE (ii. 18-25).

This is the beginning and foundation of family and social life. 'The LORD God brought the woman unto the man. And the man said: This, now, this at last, this is what I have longed for, bone of my bone, flesh of my flesh; she shall be called *Isha*, because she was taken out of *Ish*' (22, 23).

God did not intend man to live alone, nor did He intend that a man should marry a man, but a woman; and that these should love one another as two men cannot love one another, nor two women. The union of opposite sexes was designed for the propagation of the race, and for the discipline and enrichment of individual life.

This monogamous union was intended to be indissoluble. 'He who made them at the beginning made them male and female, and said: "For this cause shall a man leave his father and mother, and shall cleave to his wife; and they twain shall be one flesh". Wherefore they are no more twain, but one flesh. What, therefore,

God has joined together, let not man put asunder' (Matt. xix. 3-9). Departure from God's original law has plunged countless millions into incalculable sin, suffering, and sorrow.

3. The Probation of Man
GENESIS ii. 16, 17

This is presented in our outline after the institution of marriage, although the prohibition was pronounced before it, because clearly the prohibition applied to the woman as well as to the man (1 Tim. ii. 13, 14; 2 Cor. xi. 3).

(i) THE NECESSITY FOR PROBATION. By probation is meant the state of being under trial, or the act of proving. Because Adam was a man and not a machine, because he had a rational and moral nature, it was necessary that he be tested. He was neither holy nor sinful, but innocent, and as a moral being he was under the necessity to go upward into holiness, or downward into sinfulness, and the choice lay with him. The 'image' of God in which he had been created was a gift and not an attainment. Man was given a will, and the will is the foundation of ethics; nothing is moral which does not proceed from the will. Without the exercise of his will Adam could not become either holy or sinful. Worth or worthlessness is determined by testing. The bridge is tested by the weight; the student is tested by the examination; the soldier is tested by the battle; the metal is tested by the fire; and man's integrity was tested by a prohibition.

(ii) THE MEANS OF PROBATION. 'The LORD God commanded the man, saying, "Of every tree of the garden thou mayest freely eat; but of the tree of the knowledge of good and evil, thou shalt not eat of it".' What this tree was we do not know, but it was made a sign and symbol of the divine law; 'it was a concrete representation of that fundamental distinction between right and wrong, duty and sin, which lies at the basis of all responsibility'; thus it was for the man and the woman a tree of *the knowledge of good and evil*.

The prohibition was far from being a provocation, for man was forbidden the minimum and allowed the maximum (16, 17).

The nature of the test-means is not what matters, but man's attitude towards the expressed will of God. As man's body was strengthened by work (ii. 15), and his intellect by the exercise of it (ii. 19, 20), so now his will was brought into action relative to a specific command. The *knowledge* of the tree was moral, not intellectual. 'The first postulate of morality is the recognition of a higher will'. What man was offered was liberty, but liberty *in* law, not *from* it (*freely, but*, ii. 16, 17).

(iii) THE ISSUES OF PROBATION (ii. 17). Life or death, the reference being to man's body. Whether man would be *physically* immortal, or not, depended on whether he obeyed or disobeyed the Divine command. Physical immortality was not an original endowment, but by the virtue of the Tree of Life was to be the reward of obedience. That *physical* death is meant seems clear from iii. 19, 22, 23; and Rom. v. 12; though some think that 'eternal death' is meant.

4. The Temptation and Fall
GENESIS iii. 1-24

In pursuance of our purpose, we cannot enter upon a detailed exposition of this momentous chapter, but would call attention to its outstanding facts. Perhaps this can best be done by reference to the persons whose parts constitute the story: the Serpent; the Woman; the Man; and the LORD God.

(i) THE SERPENT (Gen. iii. 1-5).

This cunning creature was not the source but the agent of evil; behind and in it was the Devil, who, in the Epilogue of this Drama, is called 'that old serpent', and is still *deceiving* (Rev. xii. 9).

He attacked the woman, not the man (1). The subtilty of this lies in the facts that the woman was created after the man, that she was dependent on him, and that she did not receive the original prohibition, but was told of it by Adam.

He introduced doubt into her unsuspecting mind (1). The concentrated malignity of the Evil One should be noted. If the R.V. marg. be correct, he said: 'Yea, hath God said, "ye shall not eat of *any* tree of the garden?"' (But see ch. ii. 16, 17). This was an attack upon God's goodness.

He ignored God's covenant relationship with man (1). 'Hath God said?', Elohim, the Mighty One. This is the title used throughout ch. i., but when the two individuals are in view (ch. ii.) the title is LORD God, *Yahweh,* throughout the Old Testament, signifying the *covenanting* God. Satan acknowledges *Elohim* (Jas. ii. 19), but ignores *Yahweh.* (The Higher Critical view of this does not explain it; nor does it always harmonize with the facts).

He denied the connection between sin and punishment (4). The LORD God had said: 'In the day that thou eatest thereof thou shalt surely die' (ii. 17). The Devil said: 'Not so'. Throughout all ages this fallacy has persisted in the human mind. It is illustrated by every criminal who thinks he can get away with his crime; and it is implied in the view of many that there was and is no need for the Atonement.

He challenged the Divine veracity (4). He denied what God had affirmed, and in doing so he uttered the first lie; and probably it is to this that Jesus referred when He said: 'When he speaketh a lie, he speaketh of his own; for he is a liar, and the father thereof' (John viii. 44).

He imputed to God a spirit of selfish jealousy (5). 'God doth know', 'but does not want you to know what a gain it would be if your eyes were opened'. Satan's own condition gave the lie to his word, for when he got his eyes opened by disobedience it was not to find that he was like God, but to find out what God was like.

He appealed to the qualities of pride and ambition (5). 'Ye shall be as Elohim', as the Deity. This was the cause of Satan's fall (1 Tim. iii. 6), and he would lead the woman along that ruinous path.

(ii) THE WOMAN (Gen. iii. 1-7).

The steps of her downfall are simply and clearly recorded.

Her unguarded conversation with 'the serpent' (2, 3). If she knew not with whom she was conversing, she should not have been so free with him. If she knew who he was, she should have fled. In any case, the nature of what he said should have excited alarm.

It must be noted, though perhaps not pressed, that she added to the terms of the Divine prohibition. The LORD God did not say, 'neither shall ye touch it' (ii. 17).

She loosened her hold upon God (3). 'God (Elohim) hath said'. Like 'the serpent', she dropped the covenant name *Yahweh*. This cannot be merely incidental (and certainly it is not due to the confusion of two documents), for throughout ch. ii. 4-25, and in iii. 8-24, the name is *Yahweh Elohim*; only in the dialogue between Satan and the woman is *Elohim* used alone.

She looked at the forbidden fruit (6). The ear is one door of access to the soul; the eye is another; and Satan made use of both. She *looked*, as Ham did on his father's nakedness; as Lot did on the well-watered plain, and as his wife did on the smoking cities; as Esau did on the mess of pottage; as Achan did on the bar of gold; as David did on Bathsheba. The woman's was the first look of its kind, and a ruinous look it has ever been. Only a look! but it did not end with a look only!

She longed for that which was forbidden (6). 'She saw . . . that a desire it was for the eyes, and to be desired' (Heb.). Curiosity craved for what was prohibited; looking can easily lead to longing, and in countless instances has done so.

She took of the fruit of the forbidden tree (6). Mark these steps downward: listening, loosening, looking, longing, and laying-hold. The descent downward is a steep gradient. No one begins by *taking* what is forbidden.

She induced her husband to take and eat (6). This indicates, either that she did not realize what wrong she had done, and wished her husband to share her felicity; or, and more likely, she knew what had happened, and definitely tempted her husband to follow her. She became to him what the serpent had been to her. To sin oneself is bad enough, but to lead another into sin is worse.

The primitive temptation is typical of all temptation in its character and comprehensiveness. There are three main lines (1 John ii. 16), and they are all here: 'the lust of the eyes'—'pleasant to the eyes' (6): 'the lust of the flesh'—'saw the tree was good for food' (6): 'the pride of life'—'ye shall be as Elohim' (5). They are all in the temptation of Jesus (Matt. iv. 1-11).

'Lust of the flesh'—'command that these stones be made bread';
'lust of the eyes'—'sheweth Him all the kingdoms of the world,
and the glory of them'; 'the pride of life'—'He shall give His
angels charge concerning thee'. Every temptation is in one or
other of these categories.

(iii) THE MAN (Gen. iii. 6, 7).

The fall of the woman, and the fall of the man

The sin of the woman and that of the man must be distinguished
or the meaning of the facts will be missed. Adam was created
first, and he, not the woman, received from God the prohibiting
command. He, not she, is the head of the race (Rom. v.). She
was beguiled, but he was not (iii. 13; 2 Cor. xi. 3; 1 Tim. ii. 14).
He sinned deliberately, and broke the commandment because he
preferred breaking it to keeping it. Adam looked upon the first
sinner, and then he followed her into sin. The race stood or fell,
not in the woman, but in the man (1 Cor. xv. 21, 22).

The immediate and the ultimate consequences of the Fall

The Immediate and Personal Consequences

The man and the woman immediately became aware of *a
new relation to one another*. 'The eyes of them both were opened,
and they knew that they were naked' (7). This is the beginning
of self-consciousness, and of sex-consciousness.

And they immediately *attempted to put themselves right* in
relation to one another: 'they sewed fig leaves together', and
made themselves girdles (loin cloths, 7). Their first thought
was about themselves and not about God. This is the beginning
of clothes, and what male and especially female vanity has ever
cultivated originated in sin, and but for sin, would never have
been needed.

Then, these two were made aware of the presence of God
and of their altered relation to Him, and they hid from Him (8);
not from a sense of humility, or of modesty, but of guilt and a
fear of punishment. Now they have, what before they had not,
an accusing conscience. Guilt is the sense of righteousness and
the sense of transgression in the same being.

By the Fall there was immediate alienation from God, spiritual disharmony, the predominance of the sensuous over the religious; and this is reflected in the terms used in the Bible to describe sin, *transgression, iniquity, lawlessness,* and other words. Sin put the woman and the man wrong with God.

The Ultimate and Relative Consequences

If there are none such, it is difficult to see why the story of ch. iii. should ever have been told. If the sin of Adam has had no effect upon his posterity, we have no necessary interest in it. But the fact that it is recorded as and where it is carries great implications which it was not necessary at this point to define or detail. What the implications are is clear from all subsequent history, and is plainly declared in Rom. v. 12-21. Here is the doctrine of *original sin,* however much we may dislike it. 'In Adam a person made nature sinful; in his posterity nature made persons sinful'. 'In the first man's sin, the individual ruled the nature; ever since the nature has ruled the individual'. Here also, then, is the doctrine of *heredity.* Also, because the consequence of Adam's sin was *racial,* it was necessarily *penal.* What God said to Adam about the penalty attached to disobedience was applicable also to the whole race. 'By one man, and by his one offence, sin entered into the world, and death by sin' (Rom. v. 12, 19).

(iv) THE LORD GOD (Gen. iii. 8-24).

After the Fall God manifested Himself in two ways: in judgment, and in grace. And these embrace all that the passage tells us.

God's Manifestation in Judgment

God *sought* the guilty pair (8a). This is the first recorded Theophany, though actually not necessarily the first. The language, of course, is figurative. At the beginning of the Old Testament God seeks man, and at the beginning of the New Testament man seeks God (Matt. ii.).

Secondly, God *spoke* to the guilty parties (9-14); and first to *the man* (9, 11). Both heard the LORD, and both hid from Him, but He addresses only the man, and this is another evidence of his priority in status, responsibility, and guilt.

'Where are you?', implying 'why are you where you are?', was not asked for information, but to compel confession. This immediately follows, and it is an acknowledgment of nakedness, fear, and the attempt to get out of God's sight (10).

On this confession follows another question: 'Who told you . . . ?', that is, 'how came you to be self-conscious?' But without waiting for an answer another question is asked, which really is an answer to the former: 'Have you disobeyed my command relative to the tree?' It was disobedience that led to self-consciousness, probably through the loss of a robe of light (Ps. civ. 2). Adam owns up to disobedience, but blames the woman, and by implication, God also. Responsibility is thrown back on the Giver and His gift (12).

God then spoke to *the woman* and asked: 'Whatever have you done?', and she blamed the serpent: 'yes, I ate; but it's not my fault' (13).

God then addressed *the serpent* (14); but He did not, as in the cases of Adam and his wife, ask any question.

Thirdly, God sentenced all concerned, in the inverse order of His approach. His address was to the man, the woman, and the serpent; and the sentences are upon the serpent, the woman, and the man.

The serpent sentenced (14, 15). The reference in verse 14 is to the reptile, and in verse 15 it is to Satan who made the reptile his agent. The serpent was cursed; Satan was finally to be crushed.

The woman is sentenced (16). There are two elements in this; the first relates to her suffering in childbirth, and the second to her submissiveness to her husband. This is not, as in the case of the serpent, a curse, but a veiled promise, for woman was to be the mother of God manifest in the flesh, Immanuel.

The man is sentenced (17-19). God tells Adam (now for the first time without the article) that because he had listened to his wife's voice instead of to the Divine voice, the ground would show that stubbornness and waywardness which he had shown, and he would be an earth-toiler, until his body which came from the earth returned to it.

God's Manifestation in Grace

We have said that the subject of the Prologue (i. 1—xi. 9) is the Revelation of Redemption, but, of course, this presupposes the need for it, and that need is seen in the fact of the Fall.

There could be no redemption where there was no sin, but there could have been sin without redemption. The redemption of sinful man is not of necessity, but of grace. God was not obliged to save the sinner, but He chose to do so, and the revelation of this purpose begins in this chapter.

Redemption is Promised (15)

'I will put enmity between you and the woman, and between your posterity and hers; they shall attack you in the head, and you shall attack them in the heel' (J. Meek).

This is not a promise made to either the man or the woman, but is a curse pronounced on the Devil; in it his fate is sealed. It is the first proclamation of the Gospel, and Satan was the first to hear it. The whole of revelation and history meet in germ in this verse. Here the doom of the Devil and the hope of mankind are proclaimed. From now on there are to be *two seeds*, the serpent's, and the woman's; the children of unbelief, and the children of faith; the line of wrong, and the line of right; those who oppose and those who trust God.

But *the seed of the woman* is pre-eminently Christ, of the line of Abraham, Isaac, and Israel (Gal. iii. 16).

The *bruising* is to be of the *head* of the one seed, and of the *heel* of the other. The wounding in both cases would mean suffering, but in one case it would end in destruction, and in the other, it would not. On the Cross Christ fatally wounded the Devil, and there the Devil's attempt to destroy Christ failed.

This prophetic and symbolic reference to Christ and His Cross carries in it the whole purpose, promise, and power of redemption.

Redemption is Apprehended (20)

After the sentence on the serpent, which evidently the man and the woman heard, Adam called his wife EVE, and the meaning of this is said to be, 'the mother of all living'. He was now the father of all who would die (Rom. v.), but she now became the mother of all who would live.

Those who believe the evidence given in *Matthew* and *Luke* relative to Christ's birth will not have difficulty in seeing in Gen. iii. 15 a hint of the Virgin Birth. Christ was not the 'seed' of the man, but of the woman, by the Holy Spirit.

We are not told what was the reaction of the serpent, or of the woman, to the sentences which were pronounced, but Adam's reaction was one of hope, for he discerned mercy in the judgment.

Redemption is Typified (21)

'Unto Adam also and to his wife did the LORD God make coats of skins, and clothed them.'

It cannot but be that subsequent events throw light on such a statement as this. Adam and Eve were not naked (7), but the provision was not adequate; not *nature* but *sacrifice* was required. This is the first record of blood-shedding, and by it the innocent suffered for the guilty. This Divine act was typical and prophetical of the Sacrifice offered on the Cross which inaugurated the New Covenant (Isa. lxi. 10), as this one does the Old.

But there is yet one thing more.

Redemption is made Possible (22-24).

These verses must raise questions in our minds, but one or two things seem certain. The expulsion from Eden was obviously in judgment, but it was also in grace; indeed, the Economy of Divine Grace began at this point. Wherever the Cherubim are referred to, they are emblems of God's presence to bless, and so they represent His mercy. But there is also the Sword of Flame, and that represents God's judgment upon sin and the sinner.

The Two Trees of ch. ii. 9, reappear here, and however they may be interpreted, it seems that because the guilty pair now had *knowledge of good and evil* they had to be excluded from the *Tree of Life* to prevent them becoming immortal as sinners: 'lest he put forth his hand, and take also of the Tree of Life, and eat, and *live for ever*'. To avert this calamity Adam was driven out of Eden, and, of course, Eve followed him; so what at first looks like the hardest stroke to fall upon these sinners, turns out to be the most gracious and merciful thing that could have happened to them; for death, the penalty of sin, was to become the way of life.

At this point the beginning and the end of the Bible may be compared and contrasted.

CHART 13

COMPARISONS AND CONTRASTS	
GENESIS i–iii	REVELATION xx–xxii
1. COMPARISONS	
The First Rest (ii. 2) The Tree of Life (ii. 9) The River (ii. 10) The Husband (ii. 21–24) The Wife (ii. 21-24) A Garden (ii. 8)	The Final Rest (xxii. 21) The Tree of Life (xxii. 2) The River (xxii. 1) The Lamb (xxi. 9) The Bride (xxi. 9) A City (xxi. 2)
2. CONTRASTS	
Paradise Lost (iii. 6, 23) Satan Victorious (iii. 1–7) The Divine Face Hidden (iii. 8) The Curse Pronounced (iii. 17; iv. 11) The Gates Shut (iii. 24) Death Descending (ii. 17)	Paradise Regained (xxi. 1) Satan Defeated (xii. 10, 11) We "shall see His face" (xxii. 4) The Curse Removed (xxii. 3) The Gates Open (xxi. 25) Death Destroyed (xxi. 4)

In Gen. i. it is the *greatness* of God in *creation* that is revealed (Ps. lxxxvi. 10); in Gen. ii. it is the *goodness* of God in *provision* (Ps. lxxxvi. 5); and in Gen. iii. it is the *grace* of God in *redemption* (Ps. lxxxvi. 15). These three, seen initially in Genesis are seen finally in Revelation xx.—xxii, revealing that all through the chequered history of our fallen race, the Lord has been bringing meat out of the eater, and getting sweetness out of the strong.

THE PROLOGUE

REVELATION OF THE REDEEMING PURPOSE

GENESIS i. 1—xi. 9

THE SECOND PERIOD

From the Fall to the Flood

GENESIS iv. 1—viii. 14

THE Bible is written with a single purpose in view, to make known to man the redeeming love of God, and to present the unfolding of the way of salvation along a chosen Messianic line. Everything in the record is subjected to this purpose. Had it been the intention in these Writings to outline the history of the world, much that is in them would have been omitted, and much that is omitted would have been included, and much that is included would have been elaborated, and much would have been condensed.

It is impossible to say how much time is covered by the First Period of the Prologue, for most of ch. i. is prehistoric, and here astronomy and geology make great claims upon time; but in chapters i. 26—iii. 24 the record relates to a man and a woman, and mainly to the early part of their existence, the time during which they were in the Garden of Eden. The interest here is not scientific but religious; not historical but ethical; not the wonders of the vast universe but the attitude of these two people to the will of God.

And this perspective and emphasis are maintained throughout the Bible. It is not concerned with the rise, course, and passing of mighty Empires such as the Assyrian, Egyptian, Babylonian, Grecian, and Roman, but with the progress of redemption along the chosen line of an obscure race.

God had spoken of 'the seed of the serpent and of the seed of the woman' (iii. 15), and in this Second Period of the Prologue these two 'seeds' come clearly into view; the one in Cain and his posterity, and the other in Seth and his posterity.

The time from Adam to the Flood is as a spasm compared with the uncomputed ages of ch. i.; the Bible's interest is not in stars or strata, but in sinners.

With ch. iii. 24 ends the First of three Periods which form the Prologue to the Drama of Redemption. The man and the woman have failed God, and He had acted towards them in *judgment*, and in *mercy*.

Now the Second Period begins, and the consideration passes from the *individual* to the *family*, and from the *family* to *society*. Chapter iii. tells us of the *origin* of sin; and ch. iv. tells us of its *progress*. Chapter iii. relates to a man and his wife; and chapters iv., v., to three brothers and the posterity of two of them, Cain's and Seth's.

The record of this Period falls into three main parts: Cain and Abel and their Offerings; the Genealogies of Cain and Seth; and the great Apostasy and following Judgment. This Period, then, like the former one, ends in *judgment* mingled with *mercy*.

CHART 14

THE PROLOGUE. REVELATION OF THE REDEEMING PURPOSE. Genesis i. 1–xi. 9

THE SECOND PERIOD. Genesis iv. 1–viii. 14

FROM THE FALL TO THE FLOOD

CAIN AND ABEL AND THEIR OFFERINGS	THE GENEALOGIES OF CAIN AND SETH	THE GREAT APOSTASY AND FOLLOWING JUDGMENT
iv. 1–15	iv. 16–v. 32	vi. 1–viii. 14
(i) The First Home (1, 2)	(i) Cain's Posterity (iv. 16–24)	(i) The Blending of the Seeds (vi. 1, 2)
(ii) The Time of Worship (3a)	(ii) Seth's Posterity (iv. 25–v. 32)	(ii) The Divine Warning (vi. 3)
(iii) The Two Offerings (3, 4a)		(iii) The Prevailing Wickedness (vi. 5, 11–13)
(iv) The Divine Response (4b–7)		(iv) The Divine Resolve (vi. 6, 7, 13)
(v) Murder and Martyrdom (8)		(v) The Godly Remnant (vi. 8, 9)
(vi) The Divine Judgment (9–12)		(vi) The Preparation for Judgment (vi. 13–vii. 10)
(vii) The Cry of Cain (13–15)		(vii) The Punitive Flood (vii. 10–viii. 14)

1. **Cain and Abel and their Offerings**
GENESIS iv. 1-15

(i) THE FIRST HOME (1, 2)

Family life now begins. We are not told how many children Adam and Eve had. There must have been girls and probably other boys, but, in pursuance of the purpose of the Bible, the narrative concentrates on two of the sons, because these respectively start the two lines referred to in ch. iii. 15. Remembering this curse-promise, when the first son was born his mother called him CAIN, *'acquired,'* or *'gotten'*, thinking that in him the promise was fulfilled. But she soon became disillusioned, and when a second son was born she called him ABEL, *vanity.*

Each of these sons chose a line of work; Cain chose agriculture, and Abel chose shepherding. The one is related to ch. iii. 17-19; and the other to ch. iii. 21.

(ii) THE TIME OF WORSHIP (3a)

'At the end of the days'. Probably the Sabbath (cf. ii. 2, 3). The worship of God began at the beginning, in the first family; and, it must be assumed, the first parents taught their children how, where, and when to worship.

(iii) THE TWO OFFERINGS (3, 4a)

'Cain brought of the fruit of the ground a *mincha* (cf. Lev. ii. 1, 3, 12) unto the LORD; and Abel, he also brought of the firstlings of the flock, and of the fat thereof.'

It would seem that both brothers brought 'of the fruit of the ground' (*gam,* also, moreover, cf. iii. 6). Abel was not a ground tiller, but he got corn to offer (Heb. xi. 4). Cain was not a shepherd, but he could have got a lamb to offer. The offerings were not determined by the occupation of the offerers, but by their attitude towards themselves and God.

The produce of the earth was not adequate in the sight of God for clothing for Adam and his wife (iii. 17), and so skins were provided, necessitating blood-shedding (iii. 21). That this has a religious significance seems clear from what is here stated (iv. 4, 5). The parents would teach their children what the LORD had taught them; laying emphasis on the nature of sin, and the necessity for such *covering* as the skins symbolized (*atonement*, *kaphar*, means *covering*: first occurrence Gen. vi. 14, *pitch*. The word *coat* in iii. 21, also means *cover*, though not the word *kaphar*).

The difference, then, between the two brothers as worshippers was not vocational, but spiritual. Both had received the same instruction, and witnessed the same example, but, whereas Abel worshipped according to God's will, Cain worshipped according to his own will. To use terms which belong to a later time, Cain was *religious*, but Abel was *Christian*. Abel believed that guilt demanded blood-shedding, but Cain did not acknowledge his guilt.

(iv.) THE DIVINE RESPONSE (4b-7)

The LORD accepted Abel's offering, probably by fire (Lev. ix. 24); but He rejected Cain's. This should have led Cain to inquiry and self-examination; but, on the contrary, it stirred in him fierce resentment. However, instead of immediately judging him, the LORD expostulated with him (7). What He said may mean:

> 'If you do well, will you not be accepted? And if you do not well, it is because sin is lying at the door like a crouching beast, ready to spring on you; and to you is sin's desire, but you should rule over it.'

Or,

> 'If you do not well, even then there is a sin-offering ready at hand for use as a propitiation. And not only so but Abel, your brother, will submit himself to you as the first-born, and you shall exercise your right of authority over him'.

In either view, in what the LORD said warning and promise meet. But it was of no avail.

(v) MURDER AND MARTYRDOM (8)

Cain was the first murderer, and Abel was the first martyr, and each is at the head of a very long line. Cain *did* wrong because he *was* wrong; because he hated when he should have loved (1 John iii. 11, 12).

In Cain we see envy, wrath, and murder; the beginning, middle, and end of a wicked man's life (1 John iii. 15). Cain, who would not shed a lamb's blood by the will of God, shed his brother's blood in defiance of law human and divine. The seed of the serpent is revealing itself.

(vi.) THE DIVINE JUDGMENT (9-12)

'Where? What?' These two questions were asked, not for information, but to bring home to Cain's conscience his crime. Like a wild beast caught in a net, he twists and turns, but to no purpose, for he is caught.

Then follows the judgment:

'You are cursed; doomed to fruitless toil, and to weary wandering.'

The serpent, the devil, and the earth had been cursed, but this is the first curse pronounced upon a human being.

(vii.) THE CRY OF CAIN (13-15)

There is no confession here, but only complaint. Cain cries out, not against his sin, but against his sentence. Yet still mercy is mingled with judgment, and the Divine rejection is accompanied with the Divine protection of Cain; the murderer must not be murdered. With this, 'Cain went out from the presence of the LORD'.

This story greatly clarifies the redemptive idea, and advances the formulation of the doctrine of atonement by blood-shedding. Rationalism and revelation confront one another, and it is rationalism which we see condemned and doomed. Those who in our time think that there is a way to God other than by Calvary, are followers in 'the way of Cain' (Jude 11).

2. The Genealogies of Cain and Seth
GENESIS iv. 16—v. 32

This section is of great interest and importance.

(i.) CAIN'S POSTERITY (iv. 16-24)

The LORD told Cain that he would be 'a fugitive and a vagabond in the earth' (12), and when the guilty man 'went out from the presence of the LORD', it was to dwell 'in the land of Nod', which means *wandering, exile, vagrancy*. The posterity of Cain is traced briefly for six generations, and the record shows that they were utterly irreligious.

The only event recorded in the first five generations is that Cain built a city, and called it after his first son Enoch, *initiated, begun.* But what was it that was *begun?* The glorification of polygamy and murder (19, 23). The former had been forbidden (ii. 24), and the latter had been condemned (iv. 9-12).

Cain's posterity were progressive in industry and the arts. Here we read of architecture, weaving, manufacture, agriculture, music and poetry, but it was all divorced from true religion, and only ministered to pride, indulgence, and the ambition to be rich. The industries and arts are valuable as allies of true religion, but divorced from it they are potentials of much evil.

(ii.) SETH'S POSTERITY (iv. 25—v. 32)

Another son was born to Adam and Eve, and because they regarded him as taking the place of murdered Abel they called him SETH, *compensation*, or *appointed.*

If Abel can be regarded as a type of the Lord in His death, Seth will typify Him in His resurrection.

It would appear that all the other children went in the way of Cain. In respect of numbers the seed of the serpent has always been more numerous than the seed of the woman; faith, truth, and righteousness have never been dominant in this world. This fact is reflected in Seth calling his son Enos, *Enosh, frail mortal man.*

And now follows what is of momentous importance for the seed of the woman in all ages:

'*Then it was begun (Heb.) to call on the name of the* LORD' (26).

This may mean one of two things, and probably it means both, namely,

(*a*) the re-establishment of religious worship, which Cain and his line had abandoned; or (*b*) that they separated themselves from the ungodly around them, by the formation of a distinct religious community, a church. These ideas are so closely related as to be virtually inseparable. This action on the part of Seth's posterity reveals their awareness of the necessity for an uncompromising attitude towards irreligion, and devotion to the revelation of the LORD which they had received. Abel's faith was theirs, and so his form of worship was theirs, for it is along this line that the altars were built.

In ch. v. is the second of the ten 'generations' of Genesis, and it is 'the generations of Adam' *in the line of Seth*, for ten generations. Cain's line is not in view here, but reappears in ch. vi.

After a reference to the creation of the race in Adam and Eve (1, 2), there is a brief and monotonous summary of a millennium and a half of life, telling only of births, marriages, children, and deaths. This indicates again the object of the Bible record, namely, to spot-light those events only which disclose the redeeming purpose of God, and trace its progress; and in pursuance of this object the light is focussed on the seventh from Adam in each of the two lines. The seventh in Cain's line was *Lamech*, a polygamist and murderer; and the seventh in Seth's line was *Enoch*, of whom it is said that 'he pleased God'. Lamech walked in the way of Cain, but Enoch 'walked with God'. The distinction is clean-cut, and the lines move in opposite directions. Here are the Church and the World, separated from one another by deep moral dissimilarity determined by their respective relation to God. What always matters is not *that* people live and die, but *how* they do so; and so the Bible is not a book of annals, but of attitudes.

Adam was created 'in the likeness of God' (1), but his posterity were begotten 'in his own likeness' (3), the likeness of his own fallen nature; yet along this line redemption was to come. The line is thin but strong through *Seth, Noah, Shem, Abram, Isaac, Jacob*, and *Judah* to *Jesus* the Redeemer.

3. The Great Apostasy and following Judgment

GENESIS vi. 1—viii. 14

This is the third part of the Second Period of the Prologue, and the story concentrates, not on the Apostasy, but on the Judgment; and it does this because in the Judgment is redemptive mercy.

(i.) THE BLENDING OF THE SEEDS (vi. 1, 2)

Sin is as a spreading leprosy. An individual first fell a victim to it, then, a family, and now, the whole of society. By *apostasy* is meant the abandonment, in practice at least, of principles and beliefs once professed.

Cain's posterity had no true principles or beliefs to abandon, but Seth's posterity had, and it was they who apostatized.

'The sons of God (Sethites) saw the daughters of men (Cainites) that they were fair; and they took them wives of all that they chose'.

The first great failure was by *disobedience* (ch. iii.), and this one, the second, is by *compromise*. The seed of the woman and the seed of the serpent commingled. The line of demarcation which was drawn in ch. iv. 26 is now almost entirely erased; the distinction between the Church and the World fails, and by this the World did not gain, but the Church lost. It has always been so. Whenever God's people have compromised the Faith, lowered the standards, and lost their first love, a period of spiritual decline and of judgment has set in. Revivals are just returns to abandoned articles and attitudes.

(ii.) THE DIVINE WARNING (vi. 3)

Every time of probation must issue in approbation, or reprobation; the result of every Divine test must be either commendation, or condemnation (cf. Parable of the Talents; and of the Pounds: Matt. xxv. Luke xix.). The test of Abel issued in approbation; and that of Cain, in reprobation. The early history of the Sethites also was approved (iv. 26; v. 24); but their later history was disapproved, because they apostatized. God's Spirit continued to strive with them, but they were warned that He would not do so indefinitely. The suspension of judgment was an act of mercy.

(iii.) THE PREVAILING WICKEDNESS (vi. 5, 11-13)

The appalling condition of things is summed up in a few terrible words, words which bellow and burn: *wickedness, evil imagination, corruption,* and *violence*; and these sins were *great, widespread* 'in the earth', *continuous,* 'only evil continually', *open* and *daring,* 'before God', *replete,* 'filled', and *universal,* 'all flesh'.

Looking at the whole situation from ch. iv. we may discern seven distinct stages of growth in wickedness: (1) the birth of children in the parents' fallen likeness (v. 3; i. 26); (2) the refusal of Cain to acknowledge himself a sinner (iv. 3); (3) the exhibition of Cain's hatred of God in the murder of Abel (iv. 8); (4) the progress of civilization without God (iv. 17-24); (5) the obliteration of the line between the two 'seeds' (vi. 2; iii. 15);· (6) universal wickedness of heart (vi. 5); and (7) open violence and corruption (vi. 11, 12).

(iv.) THE DIVINE RESOLVE (vi. 6, 7, 13)

God's nature never changes, but He changes His attitude and action according to changing moral conditions in men; hence 'dispensations', methods changing with changing man. The immutability of God's character is the reason for the vicissitudes in His methods towards men. *He* does not change, but His *procedure* does (Num. xxiii. 19; 1 Sam. xv. 11, 29; 2 Sam. xxiv. 16; Mal. iii. 6; Jas. i. 17). Because God is righteous He must judge.

(v.) THE GODLY REMNANT (vi. 8, 9)

Here occurs the third of the ten 'generations' of Genesis (vi. 9). In the first family there was one who was true, Abel; and Seth who replaced the murdered man, was so personally and morally. Yet his posterity apostatized, though not all of them. Had *all* become corrupt, and been destroyed by the flood, history would have ended, and the promise of ch. iii. 15 would never have been fulfilled. Never in history has there been a time when God had *no one* whom He could trust and use. There has always been a faithful line, though often a thin one.

The qualifications which make possible such distinctions are seen in NOAH, of whom seven things are said. He was *righteous*, upright, virtuous, straight (vii. 1); he was *perfect*, characterized by moral integrity; he was *pious* for 'he walked with God', as did Enoch; he was *courageous*, 'a herald of righteousness' (2 Pet. ii. 5); he had '*godly fear*', and '*faith*', by which he became 'an heir of *righteousness*' (Heb. xi. 7).

(vi.) THE PREPARATION FOR JUDGMENT (vi. 13—vii. 10)

The righteous were not to be destroyed with the wicked, for Noah had 'found *grace* in the eyes of the LORD' (vi. 8). This is the first occurrence of the word, and it means *favour*; and not without interest is it that it has the same letters as the name Noah, only reversed (eh-n, N-eh). But though the *word* occurs now for the first time, the *quality* which it expresses has already been shown to Adam, Eve, Abel, Seth, and Enoch. It is *grace* that prepares for *judgment*.

God tells Noah to 'make an ark', giving him a detailed description of what would be needed (vi. 14-16). He tells him that He intends to send a flood of waters to destroy all flesh (17), but that with *him*, the covenant already made with man (i. 26-30) will be established (18). The depravity of man cannot destroy the decrees of God. Instruction is then given as to the selection of creatures of earth and air, enough to preserve the species (19, 20). Food also is to be taken, sufficient for the duration of the Flood (21), and into this Ark Noah and his wife, and his three sons and their wives, eight persons, are to enter (10, 18).

Noah obeys all these commands, and a week's notice is given of the Flood which is to last for about six weeks (vi. 22—vii. 10).

The Ark foreshadowed Him who was to save His people through and from judgment (1 Pet. iii. 20, 21). Christ is the ultimate Sacrifice (ch. iv.) and Shelter (chs. vii., viii), and thus the promised redemption is illustrated and advanced.

(vii.) THE PUNITIVE FLOOD (vii. 10—viii. 14)

Our present purpose is not affected by critical questions, and certainly not by sceptical views of this record. The *fact* of a Flood is not as confidently denied to-day as it used to be, for there is much evidence outside the Bible of such an event. As the *purpose* of it was the destruction of the human race, it is not necessary to assume that the Flood was literally universal, but rather, that it was co-extensive with the race; the moral purpose determining its *extent*.

All that the narrative requires us to believe is that the whole race perished, except eight people; and calculations have shown that there could be well over 1,000,000 people alive at the time.

The Flood consisted in 'all the fountains of the great deep being broken up, and the windows of heaven being opened' (vii. 11); that is, waters from above and below met to submerge the earth. It *rained* for nearly six weeks (vii. 4, 12), and after the rain ceased the waters were upon the earth for 110 days, making 150 days in all (vii. 24), at the end of which time 'the earth was dry' (viii. 14).

This is an astounding event! After over 1,600 years of human history the race was so utterly corrupt morally that it was not fit to live; and of all mankind only four men and four women were spared, because they did not go with the great sin drift.

Man in Eden disobeyed God, but Society out of Eden defied Him. The first sin brought expulsion, but the second brought destruction. Progress in the sciences and arts no more saved that world than far greater progress in these things has saved our world from two ghastly wars (1914-1918; 1939-1945). Civilization without true religion has been man's curse from the beginning, and will be to the end (Rev. xviii).

CHART 15

THE PROLOGUE.   REVELATION OF THE REDEEMING PURPOSE.   Genesis i. 1–xi. 9

THE THIRD PERIOD.   Genesis viii. 15–xi. 9

FROM   THE   FLOOD   TO   BABEL

NOAH AND HIS FAMILY	THE SPREAD OF NATIONS	THE BUILDING OF BABEL
viii. 15–ix. 29	x. 1–32	xi. 1–9
(i) The Momentous Emergence (viii. 15-19)	(i) The Line of Japheth (2–5)	(i) The Plan of Confederacy (1–4)
(ii) The Family Sacrifice (viii. 20)	(ii) The Line of Ham (6–20)	(ii) The Punishment by Confusion (5–9)
(iii) The Divine Intention (viii. 21, 22)	(iii) The Line of Shem (21–31)	
(iv) The New Era (ix. 1–7)	(iv) JOB (?)	
(v) The Covenant Renewed (ix. 8–11)		
(vi) The Sign of the Covenant (ix. 12–17)		
(vii) The Persistency of Evil (ix. 18–29)		

REVELATION OF THE REDEEMING PURPOSE
GENESIS i. 1—xi. 9

THE THIRD PERIOD

From the Flood to Babel
GENESIS viii. 15—xi. 9

Chronology

IT may be well at this point to say a word about the chronology of the PROLOGUE age, that is, from the Creation to Babel. Our present survey of the Bible Revelation is independent of chronological calculations, and only occasional references are made to the subject in the interests of general guidance. (See Note A, Bible Chronology, pp. 136-138).

Whatever the dates may be the truth remains that all history is dominated by two facts, namely, man's sin, and God's grace, and the very *raison d'être* of history is the purpose of God to conquer sin by saving the sinner. And so we turn to the Third Period of the Prologue.

Twice man failed God, and twice God judged man, but He did not abandon him. The destruction of 'all flesh', except Noah and his family, was necessary for its preservation. Only out of death could there come new life. The Grave of the Old World was the Cradle of the New.

The record of this Third Period is in three parts: Noah and his Family; The Spread of Nations; and The Building of Babel.

1. Noah and His Family
GENESIS viii. 15—ix. 29

(i) THE MOMENTOUS EMERGENCE (viii. 15-19)

Briefly but graphically the story is told of the new beginning. It is summed up in three words: *go-out* (16); *bring-out* (17);

went-out (18, 19). After being water-borne for a year, eight people, with birds, cattle, and reptiles stepped out upon a mountain of Ararat (4).

At the first beginning there were two people, a man and a woman, one pair; at the second beginning there were eight people, four men and four women, four pairs; and between these beginnings many hundreds of thousands of people had died naturally or violently. Here, then, is the new embryonic race.

(iii) THE FAMILY SACRIFICE (viii. 20).

The first act of the delivered family was one of worship and dedication. This is the first *altar* mentioned in history, though not necessarily the first to be built; and on it burnt-offerings of beasts and birds were presented to the LORD, betokening sinfulness, and the need of atonement (cf. iii. 21; iv. 4).

The creatures offered were *clean,* and for this purpose *odd* clean ones had been taken into the Ark, whereas of *unclean* creatures there were only pairs (vii. 2). This is the first reference to a *burnt-offering,* and the last reference is in Heb. x. 8. The word means *ascending,* a holocaust which *goes up in smoke.* The new beginning was well begun.

(iii) THE DIVINE INTENTION (viii. 21, 22)

When the LORD *smelled an odour of satisfaction,* 'He said in His heart', that is, *to Himself*; and without doubt what He resolved He communicated to Noah.

Three things in this resolve should be carefully considered.

(a) That there shall not be another visitation such as the one which had just ended. 'I will not again add to the curse of the soil . . . nor again smite every living thing as I have done'. This resolve is repeated in ch. ix. 11.

(b) That forbearance will be shown to man because of his *inherited depravity*; *'from his youth'*, which implies, says Rashi, 'that from the moment the embryo bestirs itself to have an independent existence the evil inclination is given to it'. The race, except Noah and his family, had been destroyed because of their personal and practical moral corruption; not because of 'original sin'; and such corruption would be visited in the future, but not by a Deluge.

(c) That the orderly constitution and course of nature would henceforth be conserved.

(iv) THE NEW ERA (ix. 1-7)

Noah is now *blessed*, and commissioned as Adam had been at the beginning (i. 28); but three important differences are observable. (*a*) Man's rule over the lower creation is now based on their *fear* of him (2). (*b*) Man is now permitted to eat animal food (3). (*c*) Man is placed under human as well as under Divine law in respect of blood-shedding (5, 6). Here capital punishment is instituted, and it has never been abrogated.

These differences in the new beginning are traceable from that day to our own, and in all parts of the earth.

(v) THE COVENANT RENEWED (ix. 8-11)

'I am causing-to-stand My covenant with you, and with your seed after you; *and with every living creature*'. While the reference implies an antediluvian covenant (vi. 8), it certainly embraces also, and has special reference to, the covenant just made with Noah (viii. 21, 22). The root of the Covenant is the curse-promise of ch. iii. 15, in which we see that it is a covenant of Redemption through Judgment.

(vi) THE SIGN OF THE COVENANT (ix. 12-17)

As the rainbow is a natural phenomenon, appearing at a time of rain, it is not necessary to suppose that it was first seen at this time, but it was now dedicated by God to be the sign and seal of His promise never to send another Flood.

The eminent suitability of the sign is discernible in at least three respects: its *beauty*, lovely to look at; its *universality*, not confined to any locality; and its *perpetuity*, not something occasional and rare. In *Ezekiel* the *bow* is likened to 'the glory of the LORD' (i. 28), and in the *Revelation* it is 'round about the throne', and 'a strong angel' has one 'upon his head' (iv. 3; x. 1).

(vii) THE PERSISTENCE OF EVIL (ix. 18-29)

This bit of the record is in sad contrast to that which has preceded it. Only eight people were accounted by God worthy to survive the judgment which fell upon the whole human race; but they also were sinners. They took sin into the ark, and they brought it out in themselves.

6

The salient facts here are that Noah got drunk; that Ham saw his father drunken and naked, and told Shem and Japheth; that these two sons, without looking, covered their father's nakedness; and that in consequence Canaan, Ham's son, was cursed, and Shem and Japheth were blessed. Canaan may have been the real perpetrator of the crime, and this would account for him being cursed, and not Ham. This is the second curse on a human being (cf. iv. 11), and it fell on his posterity also, the Canaanites.

2. The Spread of Nations

GENESIS x. 1-32

This is a record of great importance historically, politically, geographically, genealogically, and biographically. It does not pretend to be a complete record, but the *selection* is in keeping with the design of the whole Biblical story. The *scope* of the record is seen in the words *lands, tongues, families, nations* (5); and the *method* is that which is characteristic of this Book of Genesis, namely, first of all to dispose of lateral material, and then to concentrate on the main material in the unfolding redemptive purpose.

It is stated in ch. ix. 18, 19, that Noah's three sons are *Shem, Ham,* and *Japheth,* and that by them the whole earth was to be overspread. But in this chapter (x), the order is reversed, Japheth's sons coming first, and Shem's sons coming last; the reason being that Shem's is the line of the woman's 'Seed', and so it is reserved for detailed consideration (x. 21-31; xi. 10-26), the lines of Japheth and Ham having been disposed of.

Here is the fourth of the ten 'generations' of *Genesis* (x. ,1). Seventy peoples are detailed; fourteen in the line of Japheth; thirty in the line of Ham; and twenty-six in the line of Shem. The number *seventy* is evidently symbolical (cf. Gen. xlvi. 27; Exod. i. 5; Deut. x. 22; xxxii. 8, 9).

Regarding the division of the earth among the three sons, it may be said generally that Europe was given to Japheth, Africa to Ham, and Asia to Shem. (See Map 1, p. 85).

The following table simply presents the details given in Gen. x., and 1 Chron. i. 4-23, without comment.

CHART 16

THE POST-DILUVIAN SPREAD OF NATIONS

GENESIS X. 1-32: 1 CHRONICLES i. 4-23

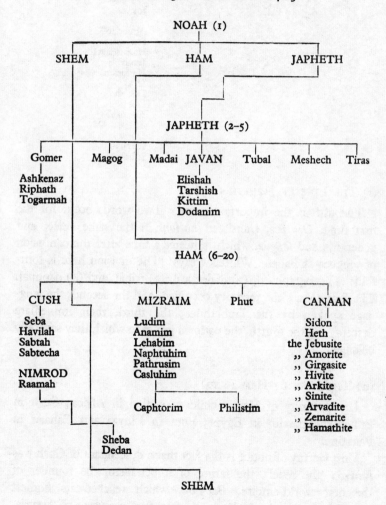

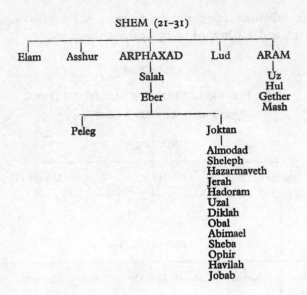

(i) THE LINE OF JAPHETH (2-5)

The fifth is the important verse. Two words occur for the first time, *Gentiles*, translated *nations* in the same verse, and generally; and *tongue*, which indicates a time after the confusion of tongues at Babel. Whitelaw says: 'The division here is four-fold: (1) geographical, (2) dialectical, (3) tribal, and (4) national. The first defines the territory occupied, and the second, the language spoken by the Japhethites; the third, their immediate descent, and the fourth, the national group to which they severally belonged'.

(ii) THE LINE OF HAM (6-20)

The posterity of Ham's children settled in Africa; Cush in Ethiopia; Mizraim in Egypt; Phut in Libya; and Canaan in Palestine.

Most worthy of notice is the fact that a descendant of Cush was *Nimrod* 'the rebel', the father of imperialism, the founder of the first world-empire, *Babylon*, which reached its highest imperial glory under Nebuchadnezzar, the conqueror of Assyria, and the builder of Nineveh (11). Four cities of his Babylonian

The Distribution of the Nations: The Posterity of Noah's three sons, Shem Ham and Japheth (Gen. X)

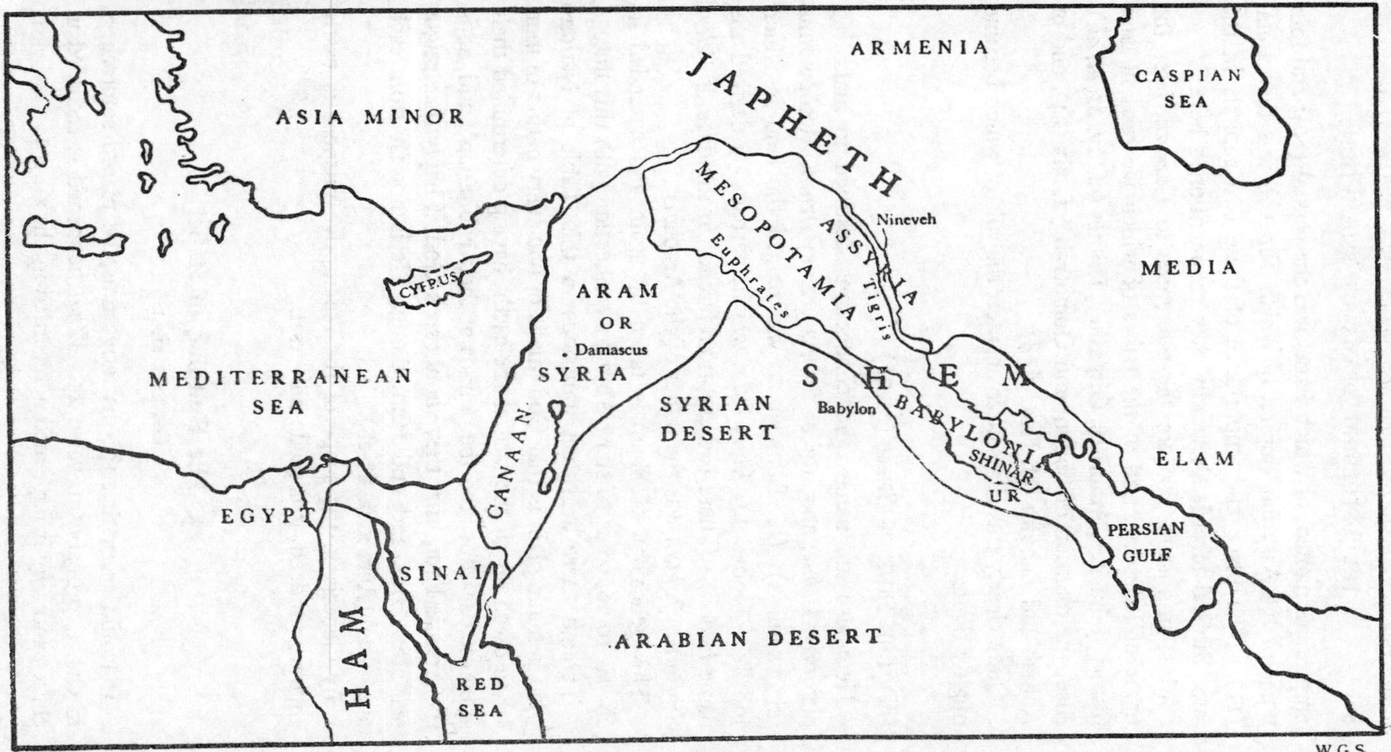

MAP I

Copyright

W.G.S.

85

empire are named, of which Babel was the capital (10); and four cities of his Assyrian empire, of which Nineveh was the capital (11). The place and importance of these two capitals in the later Biblical records show why they are mentioned here.

Most important also are the references to *Canaan*, later the name of Palestine, and of the tribes of which we read in later history, Jebusites, Amorites, Girgasites, Hivites (cf. xv. 21, *et. al.*). Also, the mention of Sodom and Gomorrah (cf. xix. 24), and of Admah and Zeboim (cf. Hos. xi. 8).

Quite clearly this is a source chapter, the rills of which become mighty rivers.

(iii) THE LINE OF SHEM (21-31)

Here also are names and connections destined to make big history—*Asshur*, ancestor of the Assyrians; *Aram*, Mesopotamia (cf. xxviii. 2); *Uz*, from whom was named the land in which Job lived (Job i. 1); *Eber*, from which, perhaps, is derived the name *Hebrew*. There is a cryptic reference to the days of *Peleg*, *division*. *Joktan* was the father of the Arabians.

This genealogy of Shem is taken up again and extended in ch. xi. 10-26, so as to show Abram's connection with this line.

Though there are great omissions in this Table of Nations what is made plain is that God 'made of one every nation of men for to dwell on all the face of the earth, having determined their appointed seasons, and the bounds of their habitation'; and, adds the Apostle Paul, 'that they should seek God, if haply they might feel after Him, and find Him, though He is not far from each one of us' (Acts xvii. 26-28).

By Genesis x. the scope of the redemptive purpose is vastly enlarged; indeed, it is made universal.

3. The Building of Babel
GENESIS xi. 1-9

It would seem that this narrative must be placed somewhere in ch. x., probably in verse 25. *What* happened is recorded in ch. x., and *why* it happened is recorded in ch. xi. 1-9.

The story is told with amazing brevity, but the picture is perfectly clear. These nine verses divide into four, and five. In the four we are told of the plan of confederacy; and in the five, of the punishment by confusion.

(i) THE PLAN OF CONFEDERACY (1-4)

Verse 1 says that 'the whole earth used only one language, with few words', (or, 'one kind of words'). What that language was we cannot tell.

Verse 2 says that there was a great trek 'from the east', and that this host of nomads came upon 'the plain of Shinar', that is, Babylonia (x. 10), and they 'settled there'; and from what follows it is clear that they intended to remain there. But this is not what God intended them to do (cf. 1, 28; ix. 1, 7, 9), so that their purpose reveals a spirit of rebellion. They said: 'Let us build ourselves a city with a tower'. City-building began with Cain (iv. 17). But the special evil of this projected city is that it was to have in it 'a tower whose top shall reach the heavens (thus making a name for ourselves)'. This purpose is a disclosure of proud ambition, open rebellion against God, and false security. Their folly was as stupendous as their motive was sinful. The Flood had destroyed sinners, but not sin.

(ii) THE PUNISHMENT BY CONFUSION (5-9)

'Then the LORD——' And He said: 'They are just one people, and they all have the same language. *If this is what they can do as a beginning*, then nothing that they resolve to do will be impossible for them' (J. Meek). One people, one language, one purpose! If God had left them to do as they intended, what would have been the course of human history? But they that dash themselves against the Divine Will only destroy themselves. Human sin is no match for Divine sovereignty.

'Come, let us go down, and there make such a babble of their language that they will not understand one another's speech'. 'That was why its name was called *Babel*, because it was there that the LORD made a babble of the language of the whole earth' (J. Meek).

The punishment of the people was also a providence, and the dispersion was a way of deliverance.

For the third time did man fail God, and for the third time God, while judging man, did not utterly destroy him, but preserved a line which led to Calvary and universal redemption.

This, then, is the Prologue of the Unfolding Drama of Redemption, the Epilogue of which reveals a finished 'City, whose Builder and Maker is God'. The tragic beginning will have a glorious end.

GENESIS THE BOOK OF BEGINNINGS

GENESIS means *Beginning*; and in the Prologue of the Unfolding Drama (i. 1—xi. 9) are the beginnings of: the universe; day and night; heaven and earth; seeds; vegetation; periods of time; beasts, cattle, fowl, and fish; man and woman; the sabbath; rain; gardens; rivers; ores; covenants; marriage; nomenclature; temptation; sin; self-consciousness; fear; lies; judgment; recrimination; punishment; curse; grace; sorrow; blood-shedding; cherubim; hope; family life; offerings of worship; hatred; anger; murder; death; cities; polygamy; nomads; music; mechanics; invention; poetry; feuds; prayer; piety; social wickedness; violence; apostasy; giants; altars; preaching; drunkenness; nations; laws; and languages.

With the complete Prologue now before us, we are able to see how the curse-promise of ch. iii. 15 was being fulfilled in the Primeval Age.

CHART 17

THE TWO SEEDS. Genesis iii. 15	
The Woman's Seed	**The Serpent's Seed**
Mediated Revelation	Godless Civilization
Leading to the Redeeming LAMB Rev. v. 6, 9, 12; xvii. 13, 14	Leading to the Rebel BEAST Rev. xiii; xvii. 13, 14
ABEL SETH ENOCH NOAH SHEM	CAIN LAMECH JAPHETH HAM NIMROD

ACT I

SCENE 1

THE HEBREW FAMILY

ABRAHAM

ISAAC

JACOB

JOSEPH

THE UNFOLDING DRAMA OF REDEMPTION

ACT I

THIS Act, which shows the Progression of the Redeeming Purpose, is Preparative to Act II which is Effective. The record of it is in *Genesis* xi. 10 to *Malachi* iv. 6; and it embraces Three Scenes:

THE HEBREW FAMILY. Genesis xi. 10—l. 26.

THE ISRAELITISH NATION. Exodus i.—2 Kings xxv: and contemporary literature.

THE JEWISH CHURCH. Ezra. Esther. Nehemiah; and contemporary literature.

See Charts 8 and 18.

The words Hebrew, Israelitish, and Jewish should be distinguished (p. 42).

HEBREW (Gen. xiv. 13, and often) may be derived from *Eber* (Gen. x. 21), or may come from a word which means the *crosser*, referring to Abram having *crossed* the Euphrates. At any rate, it is the earliest of the appellations of the posterity of Shem.

ISRAELITISH, that is, of *Israel*, the name given to Jacob at the Jabbok (Gen. xxxii. 28), and meaning, *prevailed*, having *power with God* (EL). Of Jacob's posterity it occurs over 2,500 times in the Old Testament.

JEWISH. The first reference to *Jews* in the Old Testament is in 2 Kings xvi. 6. Strictly speaking, a *Jew* is a descendant of *Judah*; and it is important to notice that the word occurs only in the later history of the nation.

It may be said, then, that *Hebrew* is racial; *Israelitish* is national: and *Jewish* is tribal.

The other three words also should be carefully considered. A *Family* expands into a *Nation*, and contracts into a *Church*. That is the history of Abram and his posterity in the Old Testament dispensation.

The presentment of Act I is in two forms, *History* and *Literature*. The literature is presented in a frame of history, and there is considerably more of the former than of the latter. Everything from *Job* to *Malachi* is literature; and to these Writings must be added *Deuteronomy*. *Ruth* is both history and literature; and *Leviticus* is neither, being legal and ceremonial. So then, 23 of the O.T. Writings are *literature*; 14 are *history*; 1 is both; and 1 is neither.

History and Literature are always vitally related, each throwing light on the other; and for an understanding of the Old Testament (and, of course, of the N.T. also) the literature must be read in its historical setting, as far as that may be known. These particulars should be well fixed in the mind.

CHART 18

ACT I		
SCENES	HISTORY	LITERATURE
1 HEBREW FAMILY	Genesis xi. 10–l. 26 1 Chronicles i. 32–ii. 4	(Job ?)
2 ISRAELITISH NATION	Exodus. Numbers. Joshua. Judges. Ruth. 1–2 Samuel 1–2 Kings 1–2 Chronicles	(Leviticus). Deuteronomy. Ruth. Psalms. Proverbs. Ecclesiastes. Solomon's Song. Isaiah. Jeremiah. Lamentations. Hosea. Joel. Amos. Obadiah. Jonah. Micah. Nahum. Habakkuk. Zephaniah.
3 JEWISH CHURCH	Ezra. Esther. Nehemiah	Ezekiel. Daniel. Psalms. Haggai. Zechariah. Malachi.

JOB

The word JOB refers, first of all, to the man whose name it was, and then to the Book which is so-called. The time when the man lived, and the time when the Book was written must not be confounded.

The author of the Book is unknown. It has been attributed to Job himself, and to Elihu, Moses, Solomon, Heman, Isaiah,

Hezekiah and Baruch. The guessed-at period of the Book ranges from before the time of Abraham to after the Exile. Such widely different views will no doubt continue to be held; but, without dogmatism, we place the person Job in the patriarchal age, and not unlikely, before the time of Abraham. Some think he was a Gentile, and others, that he was of Shemitic stock.

The historical allusions of the Book are ancient, e.g., the Pyramids (iii. 14); the cities of the Plain (xviii. 15); and the Flood (xxii. 16). On the other hand, there is complete absence of reference to any of the great events of Israel's history such as, the Exodus, the passage of the Red Sea, the giving of the Law on Sinai, the Conquest of Canaan, the times of the Judges and the Kings of Israel.

The scene of the story is connected with the land of Edom. Uz, Teman, and Eliphaz are names connected with Idumaean chiefs. References to the war horse, the hippopotamus, and the crocodile, well suit a dweller in Idumaean Arabia.

In form the Book is a poetical treatment of historical facts. Its dramatic cast is made the vehicle for conveying the moral instruction which it was the writer's object to give. Its subject is the Mystery of Suffering, or the Problem of Pain; and, as the following Chart shows, the subject is treated elaborately and ideally, by 'a writer of the highest genius'.

The lessons of the Book are many, and are of abiding interest and importance. It is shown that there is a providential government of the world; that though the punishment of the wicked may be delayed, it is never ultimately evaded; that the sufferings of an individual are not necessarily the consequence of the sufferer's sin; that goodness does not exclude suffering; that theories must be tested by facts; and that notwithstanding unmerited suffering God is just and good.

CHART 19

THE BOOK OF JOB

PROLOGUE	THE PROBLEM OF SUFFERING				EPILOGUE
	THE DRAMA				
i-ii	iii-xlii. 6				xlii. 7-17
	LAMENTATION OF JOB	DISCUSSION of the FRIENDS	INTERVENTION of ELIHU	REVELATION of JEHOVAH	
	iii	iv-xxxi	xxxii-xxxvii	xxxviii-xlii. 6	
Before Job's Trial i. 1-5	Why was I born? 1-10	First Cycle iv-xiv	Introduction xxxii. 1-5	Jehovah xxxviii-xl. 2	Jehovah's Wrath and Witness xlii. 7-9
The First Assault i. 6-22	Why did I not die? 11-19	Second Cycle xv-xxi	To the Friends xxxii. 6-22	Job xl. 3-5	Job's Prayer and Prosperity xlii. 10-17
The Second Assault ii. 1-10	Why do I live? 20-26	Third Cycle xxii-xxxi	To Job xxxiii	Jehovah xl. 6-xli	
The Coming of Job's Friends ii. 11-13			To the Friends xxxiv	Job xlii. 1-6	
			To Job xxxv-xxxvii		

ACT I

SCENE 1—THE HEBREW FAMILY

GENESIS xi. 10—1. 26.   I CHRONICLES i. 32—ii. 4

JOB   ?

Abram to Joseph

WITH the exception of nine verses, forty of the fifty chapters of Genesis relate to the stories of four men—ABRAM, ISAAC, JACOB, and JOSEPH. The Prologue period (i. 1-xi.9) covers an uncalculated age, and from the creation of Adam to the Flood appears to have been over sixteen hundred years, yet the Patriarchal period is only three-hundred-and-sixty-one years (p. 139c).

It is perspective and proportion that matter here. Including the original creation, millions of years are compressed into ten chapters and nine verses, but only a few centuries are covered in the next forty chapters.

This is not history as we commonly understand it, but it is revelation. That which commands the stage and demands attention is the revelation and progress of God's redeeming purpose. The emphasis is not on the material, but on the moral and spiritual. The vast universe is of no significance save as the home of rational and moral beings, and in all the vastness of this universe this little earth planet is the focus of interest and action as being the home of mankind. A chapter (i) is given to creation, but also a chapter is given to the story of two brothers (iv.).

In like manner ancient civilizations are merely named in one chapter (x), but one man's history, Abram's, occupies fourteen chapters (xi. 10—xxv. 11), for in the purpose of God Abram counted for far more than all these civilizations, because he was the chosen nexus for redemption between God and all the ungodly.

This *elective* and *selective* process is clear throughout the Book of Genesis. Adam had two sons, Cain and Abel, the place of murdered Abel being taken by Seth. In the record Cain is disposed of, and *Seth* is chosen. Jared had sons and daughters, but only *Enoch* is chosen. Lamech had sons and daughters, but only *Noah* is chosen. *Noah* had three sons; Japheth and Ham are disposed of, and *Shem* is chosen. Terah had three sons; Haran and Nahor are disposed of, and *Abram* is chosen. Abram had two sons; Ishmael is disposed of, and *Isaac* is chosen. Isaac had two sons; Esau is disposed of, and *Jacob* is chosen. Jacob had twelve sons, and of these *Judah* is chosen for the continuance of the Messianic line, the line of redemption. And so, for the long period which *Genesis* represents, only ten men constitute the line of revelation and redemption—

ADAM, ABEL, SETH, ENOCH, NOAH, SHEM, ABRAM, ISAAC, JACOB, and JUDAH; and of these CHRIST came, the Redeemer of mankind.

In Genesis x. are the beginnings of the Scythians, the Medes, the Greeks, the Ethiopians, the Egyptians, the Babylonians, the Canaanites, the Hittites, the Elamites, the Assyrians, and the Syrians; but not in the line of any of these was redemption to come, but in the line of the *Hebrews*, and within this race by means of selected persons.

The first of the Hebrew Family descended from Shem (xi. 10) is ABRAHAM, and because of his great importance in world-history we must consider him in greater detail than will be necessary in the cases of Isaac, Jacob, and Joseph.

It will be well here just to glance at the time-factor of this First Scene.

The aggregate ages of the Patriarchs is 612 years: Abram, 175; Isaac, 180; Jacob, 147; Joseph, 110. But these lives overlap, and the time from Abram's birth to Joseph's death is 361 years.

Isaac was born when Abram was 100 and was 75 when Abram died, and as the total age of Isaac was 180 years, he lived 105 years after his father's death.

Jacob was born when Isaac was 60, and as Isaac was 180 at death, Jacob was then 120 years old, and lived for 27 years after his father's death.

Joseph was born when Jacob was 91, and so was 56 when Jacob died; and thereafter he lived for another 54 years.

The duration, therefore, of the Patriarchal period, Abram to Joseph, Genesis xi. 27—l. 26, was

$$175 + 105 + 27 + 54 = 361 \text{ years (Chart 22, p. 131).}$$

This period begins in Ur in *Chaldea*, and ends in Goshen in *Egypt*, and most of the time between was spent in *Canaan*. Look at this on Map 1, p. 85.

ACT I

SCENE 1   THE HEBREW FAMILY

Abraham

His Personal History.

THE CALL.   *Faith Awakened.*
A Chosen Man.   A Planned Life.   A Sad Departure.
A New Start.   A Victorious Path.

THE COVENANT.   *Faith Disciplined.*
Its Occasion and Character.   Its Sign.   Its Scope.
Its Immutability.   The Reception of it.   The Compromise of it.
Its Renewal.   Its Confirmation.   Its Fulfilment.

THE CROSS.   *Faith Perfected.*
Mount Moriah.   Machpelah.
Rebekah.   The End.

His Profound Significance.

HIS PLACE IN THE HISTORY OF RELIGION.
Abraham and God.
Abraham and his Life.
Abraham and the World.

HIS PERSONAL CHARACTER AND WITNESS.
His Faith as Character.
His Faith as Testimony.

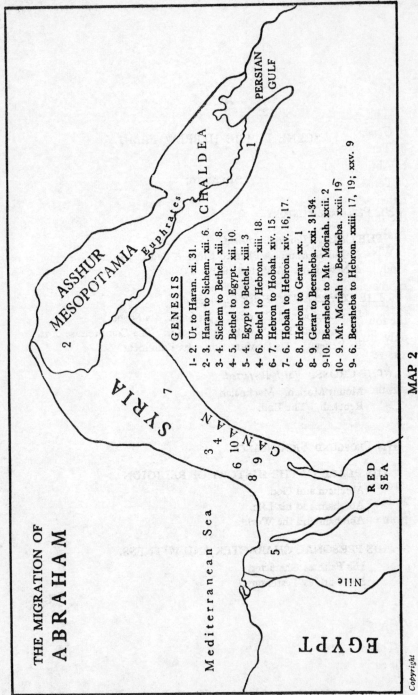

THE MIGRATION OF
ABRAHAM

Mediterranean Sea

MESOPOTAMIA
ASSHUR

Euphrates

CHALDEA

PERSIAN GULF

SYRIA

CANAAN

RED SEA

Nile

EGYPT

GENESIS

1- 2. Ur to Haran. xi. 31.
2- 3. Haran to Sichem. xii. 6.
3- 4. Sichem to Bethel. xii. 8.
4- 5. Bethel to Egypt. xii. 10.
5- 4. Egypt to Bethel. xiii. 3.
4- 6. Bethel to Hebron. xiii. 18.
6- 7. Hebron to Hobah. xiv. 15.
7- 6. Hobah to Hebron. xiv. 16, 17.
6- 8. Hebron to Gerar. xx. 1
8- 9. Gerar to Beersheba. xxi. 31-34.
9-10. Beersheba to Mt. Moriah. xxii. 2
10- 9. Mt. Moriah to Beersheba. xxii. 19
9- 6. Beersheba to Hebron. xxiii. 17, 19; xxv. 9

MAP 2

Copyright

ABRAHAM

Genesis xi. 10—xxv. 10

'The generations of Shem', the fifth of the ten 'generations' of *Genesis*, is given in ch. xi. 10-26. This leads to 'the generations of Terah', the sixth of the ten, and this long section is the story of Abraham.

Terah, Haran, and Nahor are of no significance, save as the father and brothers of Abram. It would be difficult to exaggerate the importance of this man, who is acknowledged alike by Jews Arabs, and Christians.

What must be clearly seen is that, *a world* having turned from God, He left it and chose *a man*, through whom He would ultimately, by Christ, reach the lost *world*.

Abram, therefore, marks a new beginning in history. He is the founder and father of what is called the Jewish Race; and the only man who was ever called 'the friend of God' (2 Chron. xx. 7; Isa. xli. 8; Jas. ii. 23).

We shall first of all outline his story, and then consider the significance of it.

1. The Personal History of Abraham

This falls quite naturally into three parts, which may be named, the Call, the Covenant, and the Cross. The first tells of the *awakening* of his faith; the second, of the *disciplining* of it; and the third, of the *perfecting* of it. These parts are distinguished from one another by the words 'after these things' (xv. i.; xxii. 1).

1. The Call   Genesis xi. 27—xiv. 24
ABRAHAM'S FAITH AWAKENED

(i) A Chosen Man

This man was descended from Shem through Terah (xi. 10-26). His early home was in Ur of the Chaldees (xi. 28), the inhabitants of which were of a peaceful disposition, and devoted themselves to science and art. They were idolators, worshipping the celestial bodies, chiefly the moon, from which fact, it would seem, the place took its name, as the Moon-god was called Hurki. The Semites, who migrated from the north, probably for pastoral reasons, were not immune from these heathen practices, but themselves became idolators (Josh. xxiv. 2, 15). There is no evidence, however, that Abram himself ever worshipped false gods.

Abram seems much further removed from our normal standards than is Jacob for instance, but he was a sinner, like the rest of us, and possessed of like passions; and if he rose high, he also fell low.

He was a typical Bedouin Arab, manifesting their characteristics, and following their customs. He was a dweller in tents (xi. 9); and a slave owner (xii. 5; xiv. 14); he was easily cowed in the presence of danger (xii. 11-20; xx), and was a polygamist (xvi). Among his people he was a Chief or Sheikh, readily distinguishable by his cloak of brilliant scarlet, by the fillet of rope which bound the loose handkerchief round his head, and by the spear with which he guided the march of his dependents. But though Abram was a true representative of his own people and tribe, he was essentially different from them, as his story shows.

(ii) A Planned Life

The evidence of God in Abram's life is abundant. God called him out of Ur, giving him no promise (Acts vii. 2-4). He later called him out of Haran, giving him rich promises (Gen. xii. 1-5). He separated him from Lot, and gave him Canaan for an inheritance (xiii). He promised him a son to perpetuate his name (xv). He sealed His promise with signs—circumcision and changed names (xvii). He fulfilled His promise in the gift of Isaac (xxi); and by sacrifice He led him into deep and rich spiritual experience (xxii.).

It would appear that God's call of Abram came first by *circumstance*, the trek of the family from Ur to Haran (xi. 31); and then by *revelation*, giving him a promise which embraced himself, his family, the nation of which he was the father, and the whole human race (xii. 1-3).

The Patriarch's response to the Voice of God was instant, and surely unique. 'He went out not knowing whither he went' (Heb. xi. 8); and the completeness of his obedience is indicated by iteration: he *departed, went forth, passed through, removed,* and *journeyed* (Gen. xii. 4-9). His sense of vocation carried him forward, not without retreats, until at 175 years of age he died fully assured of 'the city which hath the foundations, whose architect and maker is God' (Heb. xi. 10).

(iii) A Sad Departure

It has just been said, *not without retreats,* of which there were two (xii. xx.). The first backsliding is briefly and graphically told (xii. 10-20). Temporal circumstances became a test, and precipitated a crisis. In sad contrast to Abraham's great faith at the beginning, is his great fall now. He acted without praying; he planned his own course; he feared the ungodly; he tampered with the truth; he played the coward; he exposed to gravest danger the mother of the promised seed; he became the victim of his own intrigue; he suffered the humiliation of a heathen's censure; and he and all his were expelled from Egypt; and in ch. xx the old sin is repeated.

(iv) A New Start

We should thank God that wherever there has been a back move there can be a move back (Joel ii. 25). Abram went *back to the beginning* (xiii. 1-4). Spiritual progress had been at a standstill while he was in Egypt. There he built no altar, nor called on the name of the LORD; but now he returns to the place of blessing. Famine had damaged his fidelity and his faith, but at Bethel, the *House of God,* he recovered both.

But as return was not enough, Abram went *forward into freedom* (xiii. 5-13). The narrative reveals that the path of freedom was the path of separation. The Egypt experience had damaged the whole family; but while, in the issue, it melted Abram, it hardened Lot, whose backsliding seems to have been permanent. Circumstances showed that the uncle and the nephew must separate. Opposite moral elements cannot dwell together in harmony. But the circumstances which called for separation, called also for faith. At that time Lot was Abram's only heir, and to say good-bye to him must have been like bidding farewell to all prospect of the fulfilment of the promise of a perpetual line. But faith, while not contrary to reason, is more than reason, and has its roots deeper down in the soil of ultimate reality. Lot had *sight*, but Abram had *faith*, and we know who it was that won.

In the next place, we see Abram *viewing the inheritance* (xiii. 14-17). The path of separation and faith might have seemed to Abram as one of definite loss, but, in reality, it was one of wonderful gain. He lost a part, Sodom, but he gained the whole, North, South, East, and West. He stepped out into a richer, fuller life.

In this new start which began with a return to the *House of God*, Bethel (3), we see the Patriarch *entering into possession* of the promised inheritance. He went to live at Hebron, which means *fellowship*, and there, as everywhere else in the path of God's will, he built an altar, and called on the name of the LORD. The *inheritance* was all that God gave to him. The *possession* was that much of it which he took.

In this part of Abram's life, here spoken of as *The Call*, there is one more chapter (xiv), in which we see that his was—

(v) A VICTORIOUS PATH

It is a chapter which tells of Abram's contact with Kings: the Kings of the East (1-16); the King of Salem (17-20); and the King of Sodom (21-24)); and the occasion of it all was the capture of Lot, whom Abram rescued.

These contacts reveal Abram in three aspects. (*a*) His *magnanimity in rescuing Lot*, after the latter's selfishness in choosing his possession (xiii. 10, 11). (*b*) His *acknowledgment of spiritual blessing* outside of his own experience of God. (*c*) His *dignified independence of a heathen King* in the matter of the spoil of battle. Behind each of these, and accounting for them is the *faith in God* which had been awakened in him at the time of his Call. When Divine revelation was met by human apprehension, the redeeming purpose of God took a leap forward in history.

What a world turned its back upon, a single man set his face towards. Henceforth carnality and spirituality, sight and faith, selfishness and sacrifice were to be seen in ever sharper contrast.

2. The Covenant Genesis xv.—xxi.

ABRAHAM'S FAITH DISCIPLINED

'After these things'. What things? All that had gone before, but with special reference to ch. xiv. Abram's faith had been fully awakened; now it had to be disciplined; and how this was done is recorded in the next seven chapters, the subject of which is God's Covenant with the Patriarch.

(i) THE OCCASION AND CHARACTER OF THE COVENANT

The powerful King of Elam had been vanquished, but he had escaped, and might rally his army and fight again. The King of Sodom may have been offended by Abram's independence and seeming discourtesy, so that, in the event of an attack from the North, it was not likely that he would render the Patriarch any assistance.

And further, Abram was now eighty-five years of age, and he had no family. Were he attacked and slain, there was no son to succeed him, and his property would fall into the hands of others. The outlook was dark, and, it may be, that Abram had doubts as to whether it had paid him to be true to God and his conscience.

It is 'after these things' that the LORD revealed Himself to His servant, and He did so in keeping with his need. Did the Patriarch tremble at the thought of Chedorlaomer? The LORD said: 'Fear not, Abram, I am thy *Shield*'. Had Abram refused the spoils of battle at the hand of the King of Sodom? The LORD said: 'I am thy exceeding great *Reward*'. Did Abram fear that all he had would, in the event of his death, be left to a foreigner (xv. 2, 3)? The LORD said: 'Your seed will be as numerous as the stars' (xv. 4, 5).

Here, then, are the phases of a critical experience: Abram looking *outward*; *upward*; and *onward*. Looking outward all was *night*; looking upward, all was *bright*; and looking onward, all was *right*. A dark prospect gave way to a sure protection and the promise of an innumerable posterity.

(ii) THE SIGN OF THE COVENANT

Bible covenants are between man and man, and between God and man. The latter are sometimes conditional, and sometimes unconditional, as in this case. God's great Covenants were with Noah, Abram, Levi, and David.

In the present instance the seal of the Covenant was a ritual act (xv. 9-11), which later became a form of agreement between contracting parties (Jer. xxxiv. 18, ff.). It was a covenant made by blood-shedding, by suffering and sacrifice.

(iii) THE SCOPE OF THE COVENANT

God had promised Abram and his posterity an inheritance (Acts vii. 2-5), and here the boundaries of it are defined (xv. 18-21). Their portion was to be the land which lay between the Nile and the Euphrates, and included some of the peoples named in ch. x. (15-19).

(iv) THE IMMUTABILITY OF THE COVENANT

When a covenant made by ritual was mutual, both parties passed between the severed pieces of that which was slain (Jer. xxxiv. 18, ff.). But this Covenant was unconditional, and so, only 'a flaming torch', emblem of the Divine presence, 'passed between those pieces' (xv. 17).

Had Abram been a contracting party the Covenant might never have been fulfilled; but God's purpose to send Christ, the promised Seed, was not dependent on the fidelity of man; the Covenant was established by God alone in blood and fire.

(v) THE RECEPTION OF THE COVENANT

'And he believed in the LORD; and He counted it to him for righteousness' (xv. 6).

This is one of the greatest verses in the Bible, one of its foundation stones, one of its seed plots, one of its fountain heads. Of fourteen words (A.V.), three occur for the first time in the Bible, and these pass into the warp and woof of theology. They are, *believed, counted,* and *righteousness.* This response of Abram is referred to three times in the New Testament, and in each instance one of the three words is prominent. In *Galatians,* it is *faith* (iii. 6); in *Romans,* it is *counted* (iv. 3); and in *James,* it is *righteousness* (ii. 32). It becomes more and more evident why God chose Abram, and how He prepared and used him in the fulfilment of His redeeming purpose.

(vi) THE COMPROMISE OF THE COVENANT

This is the second black passage in Abram's story (cf. xii. 10-20 and xx). Abram believed that God would give him a son, but it had not been explicitly revealed who would be his mother. It is through 'faith and patience' that the promises are inherited. Abram had the *faith,* but not the *patience.* The sin of ch. xvi. was instigated by Sarai, and executed by Abram. Reflection might well have led him to see in Sarai's suggestion a sinful temptation, for it would have taken his thoughts back to Egypt, where he should never have been. Hagar's presence was a result of the visit to Egypt, and therefore should have been suspect. And as this sin had its root in a previous one, so has it had its fruit in a race which, for thousands of years, has been known as *wild ass men* (xvi. 12), the Bedouin Arabs; and at the present time Ishmael's posterity and Israel's are in conflict with one another.

Abram's faith had been awakened, but it much needed to be disciplined. Subjection to God's will always means economy of time, and self-will always means a waste of time. Abram was eighty-six years old when Ishmael was born, and, according to the record, he was ninety-nine before God again spoke to him—thirteen years of grieved silence (xvi. 16; xvii. 1)!

(vii) THE RENEWAL OF THE COVENANT

Each communication of God with Abram added something to what had been said before. After thirteen years of silence

He reveals Himself as *El Shaddai*, the Mighty God, and He emphasizes by repetition that the Covenant is between Him and Abram. It was repeated to Isaac and Jacob, but the revelation was made to Abram.

At this point the name *Ab-ram*, father of elevation, is changed to *Ab-raham, father of a multitude*; and *Sarai, princely*, is changed to *Sarah, princess*, or *fruitful* (5, 15). This is the first announcement that Sarah is to be the mother of the promised 'seed' (19,21).

It had been said that Abram would be the father of 'a great nation', that his seed would be 'as the dust of the earth', and 'as the stars of heaven'; and now is added, 'many nations', and 'kings shall come out of thee'; and the covenant is to be 'everlasting'.

The Seal of the Covenant is to be circumcision (9-14), now for the first time enjoined, and it is to indicate that the chosen people were separated unto God.

Abraham was now ninety-nine years of age, and Sarah was ninety, and the idea that they would have a child made Abraham laugh (17), as later Sarah laughed (xviii. 12); but *his* laugh indicated delight, and *hers*, doubt; but when the promised son came, he was called *Laughter, Isaac*.

(viii) THE CONFIRMATION OF THE COVENANT

This is seen in chs. xviii—xx. The LORD visits Abraham and repeats that the son who had been promised would be his child by Sarah. He then takes the Patriarch into His counsels about Sodom, and hears his intercession for Lot. Then, when again Abraham exposes Sarah to grave danger (xx, cf. xii), the LORD preserves her for His revealed purpose.

(ix) THE FULFILMENT OF THE COVENANT

Twenty-five years after the call of Abraham God fulfilled to him His promise and gave him a son, *Isaac*. Abraham's other son was not Sarah's, and was not the fulfilment of the promise, and so ch. xxi, which tells of the coming of Isaac, tells also of the going of Ishmael.

3. The Cross Genesis xxii. 1—xxv. 10

ABRAHAM'S FAITH PERFECTED

The awakening and disciplining of this man's faith were means to an end, and that end was his perfect surrender to all the will of God. This was the crown of his faith, and it was reached by the cross.

The story here is brief, but it is profoundly significant: the experience on Mount Moriah (xxii); the purchase of Machpelah (xxiii); the provision for the maintenance of the line of the promise (xxiv); the handing over of everything to Isaac (xxv. 1-10). After a day of chequered experience, Abraham's sun sets in glory.

1. MOUNT MORIAH. Genesis xxii.

This chapter records the supreme act of Abraham's life, for therein we are shown how he responded to the severest test to which a man can be subjected.

(i) THE TERMS OF THE COMMAND

What? A burnt offering. *Who?* Thy son; thine only son; Isaac; whom thou lovest. *When?* Now. *Where?* Upon one of the mountains in the land of Moriah. *Why?* That was not revealed then.

Isaac would be about twenty-five years of age, and for twenty-five years Abraham had waited for him to be born, so that Isaac had been in his heart for fifty years; yet now God tells the father to slay the son; and in this case the son was the first of a line which was to be as the stars, and as the sand for multitude. Abraham might well have asked: 'If I sacrifice Isaac, what becomes of the covenant?'

(ii) THE MEASURE OF THE OBEDIENCE

This answered to each part of the command, and was absolute. Early in the morning, Abraham set out with Isaac for the mountain to which God had promised to guide him, with wood for the burnt offering. On the mountain he built an altar, laid the wood on it, bound Isaac and put him on the wood, took a knife, and lifted it to plunge into his son. Has there ever been a more tragic hour, save one, in all history?

(iii) THE SECRET OF THE VICTORY

Because Abraham believed God, he obeyed Him. Faith was the root of his obedience, and obedience was the fruit of his faith. He told the young men from whom he parted on the way, that *he and Isaac* would return to them (5); yet he intended to sacrifice his son. But so truly did the father believe that his son would live, that he expected God to raise him from the altar after he was slain (Heb. xi. 19). This is faith far in advance of the faith of his posterity, who had no idea of a resurrection of the dead (cf. Job xiv. 14). In his will Abraham had sacrificed Isaac before they reached the mountain; the sword had pierced his heart, but he held on to God and the covenant.

(iv) THE WITNESS OF THE LORD

When the Devil *tempts*, it is that the tempted may fall; but when God *tests*, it is that the tested may stand. Abraham was tested, and he stood. To this fact 'the Angel of the LORD', the Second Person of the Trinity, bore him testimony. '*Now I know that thou fearest God*'. '*Thou hast not withheld thy son, thine only son from Me*'. The place of renunciation became the place of provision; and He who was to Abraham, first LORD, and then, EL SHADDAI, now becomes JEHOVAH-JIREH (14).

(v) THE RENEWAL OF THE PROMISE

What the LORD had said fifty years before (ch. xii. 1-3), is now repeated (15-18). Abraham's posterity would, for number, be as the stars and as the sand, and through them all the nations of the earth would be blessed. That promise has been fulfilled, both literally and spiritually.

(vi) THE LINE OF THE PROMISE

The genealogy in verses 20-24 is given to introduce Rebekah, who was to become Isaac's wife, and the mother, second in succession, of the chosen race.

2. MACHPELAH. Genesis xxiii.

The death of Sarah was sorely felt by Abraham and Isaac, but this is passed over in a few words. The purpose of the chapter is to show how Abraham began to possess the land which God had promised should be his. While he lived all that he possessed of the inheritance was a field in which there was a cave which he used as a grave. But it was *his*, and, without doubt, Abraham saw in this small portion the promise of the whole. The foci of the Covenant were the son and the soil; he had the one, and now he began to possess the other.

3. REBEKAH. Genesis xxiv.

The object of this long chapter of sixty-seven verses is not to tell a lovely story, though it is that, but to show how Abraham made sure that the promised line was safeguarded.

'Swear that thou wilt not take a wife for my son of the daughters of the Canaanites. But go unto my country, and to my kindred, and take a wife for my son Isaac" (3, 4).

The Canaanites had been cursed (ix. 25), and the Covenant could not be fulfilled in their line. Abraham, therefore, arranged that someone should be found who was of the family of his brother Nahor who had settled in Mesopotamia. This is another evidence of the Patriarch's faith in the Divine purpose and promise, and of his obedience to the Divine will and command.

4. THE END. Genesis xxv. 1-10

The thing of importance in this brief statement is that, while Abraham is not indifferent to his obligations to the many members of his family (6), he makes it quite clear that Isaac is his heir, and he leaves to him his estate (5).

'Then Abraham gave up the spirit, and died in a good old age, an old man, and full (satiated (8))'.

Thus ends the life of one of the greatest men that God ever made.

II The Profound Significance of Abraham

We have outlined this man's story, and from this it is possible and necessary to form an estimate of his significance. This will lead us to consider his place in the history of religion, and his personal character and witness.

1. ABRAHAM'S PLACE IN THE HISTORY OF RELIGION

What were this man's relations to God, to life, and to the world?

(i) ABRAHAM AND GOD

There were certain theological elements in Abraham's faith which made his life and mission what they were. One of these was his consciousness of and confidence in the *Divine Unity*. The Patriarch's forebears were idolators, and he was brought up in a heathen land, yet he was the first great monotheist. He believed in one only God, the LORD, Who revealed Himself to him, and with Whom he had fellowship.

Another element in Abraham's faith was his sense of the *Divine Justice*. It was his belief that a good and omnipotent God could not do that which was evil. He would distinguish between the righteous and the wicked, and not engulf them all in a common fate. It was this belief which lay behind his intercession for Lot in Sodom. 'Shall not the Judge of all the earth do right?' (xviii. 25).

A third element in this man's faith was his assurance of the *Divine Presence*. Believing that God was with him and was leading him, he passed from land to land, he reared his altars for sacrifice beneath the open sky, he shunned the tumult of cities and sojourned in the broad and silent spaces of the wilderness.

These are great beliefs, and without them the race could not have survived.

(ii) ABRAHAM AND HIS LIFE

How did he understand his own life? What was the significance of it to him? How, in his consciousness, was it related to God and the future? In his story we find the answers to these inquiries.

His God was his Saviour. He exulted as he anticipated the day when the Messiah should come Who would be the fulfilment of all the promises made to him, and in Whose provision made on Mount Moriah he discerned the Sacrifice that would save. 'Your father Abraham rejoiced to see my day; and he saw it, and was glad' (John viii. 56).

His God was his Guide. The LORD had said to him, 'Get thee out', and 'he went out, not knowing whither'. Abraham's life was planned by God, except where he took charge of it himself. There were three backward movements in his story: when he went from Bethel to Egypt (xii); when he took Hagar to be a wife (xvi); and when he again jeopardised Sarah (xx.). But the trend of his life was forward: from Ur to Haran; from Egypt to Bethel; from Bethel to Hebron; and from Hebron to Mount Moriah; and all the way he believed that God was guiding him. Also it was this consciousness which led him and his to be circumcised; to separate, first from Lot, and then from Hagar and Ishmael; to buy a plot in Canaan; and to make sure that the promised line should be secure by Isaac's marriage. Abraham believed that his was a Divinely-appointed path, and he followed his Guide.

His God was his Hope.

> 'He looked for the city which hath the foundations, whose architect and maker is God'.

This was the longing and hope of this nomad Sheikh. He was not looking merely for a place, or for a land, but for a City of God, a stable and eternal dwelling-place, where no more would tents be put up and pulled down, but where, on foundations, he and all God's people would forever rest.

Of Abraham's life-journey, salvation was the start, guidance was the track, and immortality was the goal.

(iii) ABRAHAM AND THE WORLD

He was made aware of *God's world purpose* to bless 'all the nations of the earth'. This purpose is kept clearly in view throughout God's dealings with Abraham, and throughout the whole revelation of the Old Testament.

Further, to Abraham was made known *God's selective method*. The world was to be reached through his posterity, that is by Christ, *the promised Seed*, Who said, 'I, if I be lifted up, will draw all men unto Myself', The missionary enterprise did not originate with the Christian era; the purpose is eternal, and the movement began with the call of Abraham, who came to realize that he was *God's chosen man*. Long before he breathed his last at Hebron, he was fully aware of his significance to God, a significance which was rooted, not in his essential greatness, but in God's abounding grace. But it was because of his believing and obedient acceptance of God's grace that the Patriarch became the 'friend of God', the father of the faithful, and the founder of the religion of Israel.

2. ABRAHAM'S PERSONAL CHARACTER AND WITNESS

The word *faith* does not occur in the Old Testament, but the quality is exhibited there, and nowhere more clearly and wonderfully than in Abraham. The objects of faith are the future and the unseen, and its office is to give present existence to future things, and vital reality to unseen things (Heb. xi. 1).

In Abraham is this faith first radiantly manifest. It was the motive principle of his life; and he exhibited it on its two sides, as faith to endure, and as faith to achieve; the one being seen in his waiting for Isaac, and the other, in his offering up of Isaac.

And it is by his faith that Abraham witnesses to the world. The world is guided by sight, but Abraham was not. The world says, get and keep, but Abraham teaches that the only way to keep is by giving what you get. The world stakes everything on the present, but Abraham staked everything on the future. The world turns to God as a last resource, but Abraham started with Him. The world's kind of life, and Abraham's, lie poles asunder, but it is Abraham's that wins. Most people die without ever having truly lived, but Abraham being dead yet lives. If God is of value to a man, that man is of value to God, and of how much value depends on the completeness of his self-surrender.

CHART 20

SYNOPSIS OF ABRAHAM'S LIFE. Genesis xi–xxv.

1. Names

AB-RAM, Father of elevation. Genesis xi.-xvi.	AB-RAHAM, Father of a multitude. Genesis xvii–xxv.

2. Titles

FRIEND of God. James ii. 23	FOUNDER of Israel. Genesis xii. 2	FATHER of Christians. Gal. iii. 29

3. Periods

(1) From the Call in Chaldea to the Settlement in Canaan.	Genesis xi. 31-xiii. 18
(2) From the Settlement in Canaan to the Birth of Isaac.	Genesis xiv. 1-xxi. 21
(3) From the Birth of Isaac to the Death of Abraham.	Genesis xxi. 22-xxv. 10

4. Age

75 Years. Ch. xii. 4 Aged 75	11 Years. Ch. xvi. 3 Aged 86	14 Years. Ch. xxi. 5 Aged 100	75 Years. Ch. xxv. 7 Aged 175
¾ Century	½ Century	¼ Century	¾ Century

5. Spiritual History

THE CALL. Genesis xi.-xiv.	THE COVENANT. Genesis xv-xxi.	THE CROSS. Genesis xxii-xxv.
Faith Awakened	Faith Disciplined	Faith Perfected

6. Progress of Revelation

1	2	3	4	5	6	7	8	9
Acts vii. 2-4	Gen. xii. 1-3	xii. 7	xiii. 14	xv. 1	xvii	xviii	xxi	xxii

Genesis / 7. Keys to Chapters

Genesis	Key
xi	Genealogy
xii	Bethel-Egypt
xiii	Separation
xiv	Rescue
xv	Revelation
xvi	Hagar
xvii	Covenant
xviii	Intercession
xix	Sodom
xx	Abimelech
xxi	Isaac
xxii	Moriah
xxiii	Machpelah
xxiv	Rebekah
xxv	Journey's End

ACT I

SCENE 1   THE HEBREW FAMILY

Isaac

The Submissive Son
The Devoted Husband
The Indulgent Father

Jacob

THE SUPPLANTER IN BEERSHEBA
The Birthright
The Blessing

THE SERVANT IN PADAN-ARAM
Deceived
Deceiving

THE SAINT IN HEBRON
Discipleship
Discipline

THE SEER IN EGYPT
Two Sons in Prophecy
Twelve Sons in Prophecy

Joseph

THE STORY OF JOSEPH

The Princely Son.	Trained
The Patient Sufferer.	Tested
The Powerful Sovereign.	Triumphant

JOSEPH AND JESUS

ISAAC

Genesis xxi. 1—xxviii. 5; xxxv. 27-29

It will be helpful, first of all, to get Isaac's chronological setting in the record. There are ten important dates.

AGE	ISAAC'S YEARS, 180
0-1	Born. Abram was 100. Sarai was 90: xvii. 17; xxi. 5
25	Probably, when he went with Abram to Mt. Moriah: xxii.
37	When Sarah died: xvii. 17; xxiii. 1. Abraham was 137: xxi. 5.
40	Married Rebekah: xxv. 20
60	When Esau and Jacob were born: xxv. 26. Abraham 160.
75	When Abraham died: xxi. 5; xxv. 7. Jacob was 15.
137	When Jacob left home: xxviii. 5. Jacob was 77.
151	When Joseph was born: xxx. 22-25
168	When Joseph was sold into Egypt: xxxvii.
180	When he died: xxxv. 28, 29. Jacob was 120. Joseph was 29.

Though we have given the story of Abraham in some detail, because of the unique place he occupies in history and religion, we are not, in this First Scene of Act I, concerned with details of the course and character of each of the Patriarchs, but would see that each is a link in a chain of purpose, and it is this fact which gives to each his place in history.

Regarded personally, Isaac is not particularly interesting, his life being unromantic and undistinguished. Three things give him a place in history: his being the submissive son of Abraham, the faithful husband of Rebekah, and the indulgent father of Esau and Jacob. The man before him, and the man after him are great, in different degrees, but Isaac himself is in no sense great. Only once do we read of him building an altar to God (xxvi. 25). Only once do we read of him praying (xxv. 21). Only once are we told that 'he called on the name of the LORD' (xxvi. 25). And only once is it recorded that God appeared to him and spoke with him (xxvi. 2-5). It is this last fact that places Isaac in the Covenant purpose of God. But even here, what God said to him is not a *revelation*, but a repetition of a revelation which already had been given to Abraham (xxvi. 3).

*'Sojourn in this land, and I will be with thee, and will bless thee;
for unto thee, and unto thy seed, I will give all these countries, and I
will perform the oath which I sware unto Abraham thy father; and I
will make thy seed to multiply as the stars of heaven, and will give
unto thy seed all these countries; and in thy seed shall all the nations
of the earth be blessed; because that Abraham obeyed my voice, and
kept my charge, my commandments, my statutes, and my laws'* (Gen.
xxvi. 3-5).

'Isaac is unheroic, and far nearer than Abraham to the level
of ordinary humanity. He shrinks from death, and does not
scruple much about the means he uses to escape from it. He
is devoid of any stern sense of the duty of veracity. He likes
'creature comforts', and unduly favours the son who provides
them for him. No formal eulogy is bestowed upon him, either
in Genesis, or in the rest of Scripture. The Apocryphal writers,
who delight in lauding the worthies of early times, pass him over
almost in silence' (Rawlinson).

The one thing in Isaac's life which stirs our admiration is
his amazing act of submission and self-abnegation on Mount
Moriah. He was then old enough and strong enough, to have
resisted the attempt of his father to bind him, but, at twenty-five
years of age, when a young man clings to life and reaches to the
future, Isaac consented to die. That is the one elevation in the
landscape of his story. For the rest, the land is flat and drab.
He was gentle, affectionate, patient, sensitive, peace-loving, and
God-fearing, as were many others in Israel's history; but Divine
Providence made him one of *the* Patriarchs, of whom there were
but three (Exod. iii. 6, 15, 16, and often). Others were 'patriarchs'
but only to these three was the Covenant revealed and repeated
(1 Chron. xvi. 15-18).

What is important in Isaac's story is soon summarized. He
was the necessary link between Abraham the root of the nation
of Israel, and Jacob the father of the twelve sons, whose posterity
constituted that nation.

He was the first 'child' of Abraham, as contrasted with the first
'seed', Ishmael (Rom. ix. 7). He, therefore, marks the point of
divergence between the *natural* and the *covenant* lines (Gen.
xvii. 17-21).

He was inspired to forecast the courses, respectively, of his two sons and their descendants (Gen. xxvii. 27-29, 39, 40; Heb. xi. 20). He was typical of the promised Messiah (a) in that he was predicted long before he was born (cf. Gen. xii. 7; xv. 4; Isa. vii. 14): (b) in that he was supernaturally begotten (cf. Gen. xviii. 12-14; Heb. xi. 11; Rom. iv. 19; Matt. i.): (c) in that he was the 'only' son of the Covenant (cf. Gen. xxii. 2; John iii. 16); contrast Abraham's son of the 'flesh' (Gal. iv. 29), and his sons by Keturah (Gen. xxv. 1-4): (d) in that he was the sacrificial lamb (cf. Gen. xxii; Isa. liii. 7): and (e) in that he was made the type of Abraham's spiritual posterity, as contrasted with his posterity under the Law, the nation of Israel (Gal. iv. 21-31).

In these facts and features, rather than in his personal character, we must see the real value of Isaac's life.

JACOB
Genesis xxv. 19—l. 13

A few dates in Jacob's life will help us to get the chronological perspective.

AGE	JACOB'S YEARS. 147
0–1	Born. Gen. xxv. 26. Also Esau. Abraham, 160. Isaac, 60
15	Abraham died at 175. Gen. xxv. 7. Isaac, 75
40	Esau married. Gen. xxvi. 34.
77	Left home for Padan-aram. Gen. xxviii. 5. Isaac, 137
84	Married to Leah and Rachel. Gen. xxix. 21-30; xxx. 1, 22–26; xxxi. 38-41
91	Joseph born. Gen. xxx. 25; xxxi. 38-41
97	Returned to Canaan. Isaac, 157. Joseph, 6
108	Jacob returned to Hebron
108	Joseph sold into Egypt. Gen. xxxvii. Isaac, 168
120	Isaac died, 180. Joseph, 29
130	Went to Egypt. Gen. xlv. 6; xlvii. 9. Joseph, 39
147	Died. Gen. xlvii. 28. Joseph, 56

The Abraham mountain dipped down to the Isaac plain, and now that plain moves up again to the Jacob height. Abraham's place in history and religion is necessarily unique, as he was the

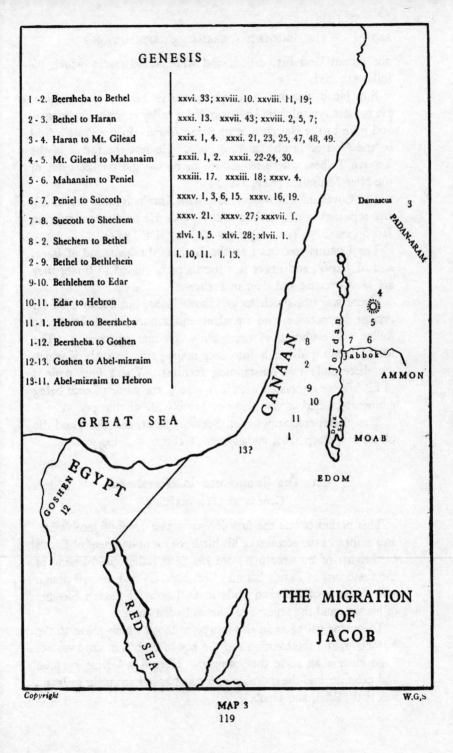

GENESIS

1 -2.	Beersheba to Bethel	xxvi. 33; xxviii. 10. xxviii. 11, 19;
2 - 3.	Bethel to Haran	xxxi. 13. xxvii. 43; xxviii. 2, 5, 7;
3 - 4.	Haran to Mt. Gilead	xxix. 1, 4. xxxi. 21, 23, 25, 47, 48, 49.
4 - 5.	Mt. Gilead to Mahanaim	xxxii. 1, 2. xxxii. 22-24, 30.
5 - 6.	Mahanaim to Peniel	xxxiii. 17. xxxiii. 18; xxxv. 4.
6 - 7.	Peniel to Succoth	xxxv. 1, 3, 6, 15. xxxv. 16, 19.
7 - 8.	Succoth to Shechem	xxxv. 21. xxxv. 27; xxxvii. 1.
8 - 2.	Shechem to Bethel	xlvi. 1, 5. xlvi. 28; xlvii. 1.
2 - 9.	Bethel to Bethlehem	l. 10, 11. l. 13.
9-10.	Bethlehem to Edar	
10-11.	Edar to Hebron	
11 - 1.	Hebron to Beersheba	
1-12.	Beersheba to Goshen	
12-13.	Goshen to Abel-mizraim	
13-11.	Abel-mizraim to Hebron	

Damascus 3

PADAN-ARAM

CANAAN

Jordan

Jabbok

AMMON

GREAT SEA

8

2

9

10

11

1

7 6

5

4

Dead Sea

MOAB

13?

EDOM

EGYPT

GOSHEN

12

RED SEA

THE MIGRATION OF JACOB

Copyright

W.G.S

MAP 3
119

one whom God first called, and who blazed tracks which his followers trod.

But Jacob also has a unique place in history and religion. He is more typical than Abraham, has a wider range of experience, and gave to the chosen race its name *Israel*. In the Psalter God is 'the God of Jacob' (xlvi., *et. al.*). He was the father of the Twelve Tribes, whose names are to be written on the gates of the New Jerusalem (Rev. xxi. 12).

The Covenant which God made with Abraham (xii.; xv.; xvii.), and repeated in part to Isaac (xxvi. 3-5), He finally confirmed to Jacob (xxviii. 3, 4, 13-15; xxxv. 11, 12; xlviii. 3, 4).

The LORD is spoken of as 'the God of Abraham, and of Isaac, and of Jacob', and never is a fourth name added to these; they are *the* Covenant and Pilgrim Fathers.

There was not much to say about Isaac, but Jacob is of far greater importance, and we shall endeavour, though briefly, to follow the evolution of this man's spiritual experience. The life of Jacob is divisible into four main parts, in each of which are discernible two outstanding features. These four periods of his life are associated with four places, the name of each being eminently suited to the phase of Jacob's life of that period.

The phases are, Supplanter, Servant, Saint, and Seer; and the places are, Beersheba, Padan-aram, Hebron, and Egypt.

1. The Supplanter in Beersheba
Genesis xxv. 19—xxviii. 9

This period covers the first seventy-seven years of Jacob's life, and embraces the account of his birth; of his obtainment of Esau's birthright; of his securing from his aged father the blessing of the firstborn; of Esau's hatred of his brother, and his evil design against him; of Rebekah's advice to Jacob; of Isaac's blessing of his son, and the sending of him to Padan-aram.

The principal parts in this story are those which relate to the *birthright*, and the *blessing*, and the key to both is in ch. xxv. 23: 'The elder shall serve the younger'. Here is a Divine purpose and promise, and the meaning of it must have been plain to Isaac, Rebekah, Esau, and Jacob.

(i) THE BIRTHRIGHT (xxv. 29-34)

What followed was rooted in that knowledge. Though Esau was the elder of the two brothers, God purposed that Jacob should take precedence over him. The birthright included temporal and spiritual blessings; it carried with it a double portion of the paternal inheritance, and constituted the possessor of it the spiritual head of his people.

Both Esau and Jacob knew this; but Esau was indifferent to it, and Jacob coveted it. The wrong was not in Jacob getting the birthright, for God intended that he should do so, but in the way he obtained it. As Abram had tried to force the fulfilment of a divine purpose by marrying Hagar (xvi), so did Jacob, by buying the birthright from his brother.

God's purposes must be fulfilled in God's time, and in God's way.

(ii) THE BLESSING (xxvii.)

Deception followed cunning. What Jacob had stolen from his brother, he must secure from his father. Isaac and Rebekah were well aware of the prediction (xxv. 23), but the attitude of each of them to it was wrong. Isaac planned that Esau should have the blessing (1-4); and Rebekah plotted to get it for Jacob (6-10). Something can be said for each of the four persons in this drama, and much must be said against each; and in the background of it all is God.

A right thing was purposed by these four people in a wrong way. Each was to blame, and each suffered. Isaac was deceived; Esau was robbed; Rebekah lost her favourite son for ever, for the last time we hear of her is when he left home (xxviii.); and Jacob was exiled for twenty years. 'The way of transgressors is hard'.

All this makes necessary the severe disciplining of Jacob, if he is to become the man God wanted him to be for the carrying forward of His redeeming purpose.

2. The Servant in Padan-aram
Genesis xxviii. 10—xxx. 43

When Jacob was seventy-seven years of age he left Hebron for Haran about 450 miles away, in a straight line North East, where Terah had settled and died, and where his posterity through Nahor now lived. He was sent thither that he might marry in the family and not out of it, as Esau had done (xxvi. 34, 35). This showed Isaac's regard for the Covenant which God had made with Abraham, and repeated to himself, and it is important as indicating how the chosen line was safeguarded.

Yonder, in exile from the land of promise, Jacob spent twenty years of his life, nearly one-seventh of the whole.

On the outward journey he halted at *Bethel*, and on the inward journey he halted at *Peniel*, and each place, because of what happened there, has become spiritually famous.

(i) BETHEL (xxviii. 10-22)

It was here that Jacob had his first spiritual experience, and we may believe that that experience was the equivalent of what we call conversion. In a dream he saw that earth and heaven are connected (12), and he heard the Voice of God. The importance of the revelation now vouchsafed to him cannot be exaggerated.

> The LORD is the God of his father and grandfather. The land on which he was lying was given to him and his posterity. His seed would be innumerable, and would spread abroad to all quarters of the earth; and in that seed all families of the earth would be blessed.
>
> Jacob was assured of the Divine presence and protection, and of the certainty of the Divine promise (13-15).

Jacob's response to this revelation follows (16-22), in which is the first vow recorded in Scripture (20). The sentiment expressed is not an elevated one, but it does indicate that Jacob wanted to return home sometime, though not at once (21).

(ii) PADAN-ARAM (xxix., xxx.).

Here Jacob remained for twenty years (xxxi. 41), during which time he married Leah and Rachel, and together with their handmaids Bilhah and Zilpah he begat eleven sons and some daughters.

Two words sum up this twenty years, *deceived* and *deceiving*. Laban deceived Jacob in the matter of his daughters, and Jacob deceived Laban in the matter of the flocks. Craftiness was met by craftiness, and two sharpers pitted their wits against one another and, from a worldly point of view, Jacob did well (xxx. 43).

But this state of things could not continue. At Padan-aram Jacob could never be made a fit agent for the carrying on and out of the purpose of God. He had learned only one lesson in the Divine School, and there were others awaiting him, but he could not learn them where he was. To some extent Jacob seems to have realized this, and he expressed the desire to return home after the birth of Joseph, six years before he actually left Haran (xxx. 25). No man who had had Jacob's experience at Bethel could remain for ever in Mesopotamia. Conversion does make a difference in one, though he may for a time smother and silence his convictions.

3. The Saint in Hebron
Genesis xxxi.—xlv.

This description requires two safeguards, one in respect of each of the words used. In much of the story of these chapters Jacob is anything but a *saint*; and of the thirty-three years between his leaving Haran and going down to Egypt, only a part of the time was spent at *Hebron*, less than two-thirds of it. Yet, in extenuation of the description, it may be said that here was *a saint in the making*, and that from the time that Jacob left Haran *his goal was Hebron*, though he took long to get there.

We are here not so concerned with his story in detail, as to trace the way in which God guided him, and fitted him for the advancement of His redeeming purpose. This purpose would have advanced more rapidly if those whom God had chosen had not delayed it by wilfulness and sinfulness. The delaying passages are; chs. xii. 10-20; xvi.; xx.; xxvi. 6-10; xxvii—xxx; xxxiii., xxxiv.; a sad total!

(i) FROM HARAN TO HEBRON (xxxi. 1—xxxv. 26)

When God appeared to Jacob at Bethel, as he was on his way to Padan-aram, the Patriarch vowed that *he would come again to his father's house in peace* (xxviii. 21); and when, after twenty years, the LORD appeared to him at Padan-aram, he said: 'Return to the land of thy fathers, *and to thy kindred*; and I will be with thee' (xxxi. 3, 13; xxxii. 9). 'To the land', meant Canaan; and 'to thy kindred', meant Hebron, where Isaac was living. It is clear, then, that God told Jacob to go back to Hebron, and that Jacob had promised to do so.

Turning his back on Padan-aram, and facing Canaan, he found himself between two enemies, Laban behind him, and Esau in front of him, and from these there was neither retreat nor escape. With the enemy behind him he made a covenant in Mount Gilead (xxxi. 25, 44-55), and he then gave his attention to the one in front of him (xxxii.).

At a ford called *Jabbok*, about midway between the Sea of Galilee and the Dead Sea, on the East of Jordan, Jacob, having sent all his company forward, was *'left alone'* at *night*, and there *'a man wrestled with him until daybreak'*. This Wrestler, Who was the Angel of the LORD, crippled Jacob in the struggle, but the Patriarch clung to Him, refusing to let go until he received a blessing. Then occurred the second major spiritual experience of Jacob's life: his name was changed from *Jacob*, 'supplanter', to *Israel*, 'prince of God'; and the Patriarch named the place *Peniel*, the 'face of God' (xxxii. 24-32). *Bethel* and *Peniel* are, then, the two great landmarks in Jacob's life; the first marking his *conversion*, and the second, his *consecration* (see Chart 21). He had lost twenty-years of spiritual opportunity and privilege, but now he is facing the goal and not fleeing from it.

But attitude and action did not at once harmonize. After Peniel the returning prodigal should have obeyed God's command, and fulfilled his own vow; and have gone at once to Bethel and Hebron. But it was about ten years before he did this, after leaving Haran; years which for him, and his family, were disastrous.

As indicating his want of faith in God, notwithstanding Peniel, mark Jacob's timid and fawning approach to Esau (xxxiii. 1-11); his promise to follow Esau to Seir, without having any intention of doing so (xxxiii. 12-17); his settlement at Succoth, east of Jordan, building a house for his family, and so preparing for a lengthened stay (xxxiii. 17); and his removal into Canaan, but only "to pitch his tent before the city of Shechem", belonging to the Hivites, one of the Canaanite nations, and to buy from them 'a parcel of ground' (xxxiii. 18-20). His building an altar there could not atone for his disobedience, or save him from the consequences of his unfaithfulness (xxxiv.). No Christian is clever enough to dodge the consequences of his backsliding. Chapters xxxiii. 17—xxxiv. 31, need not and should never have been written.

After all this loss of power and waste of time Jacob had to do what God had commanded, and what he had vowed to do; he had to go back to Bethel. For years after re-entering the land Jacob had been within thirty miles of Bethel, yet did not go to it. The 'prince of God' had been most unprincely; but God came to him again, and said: 'Arise, go up to Bethel, and dwell there'. This he did; and again God appeared to him, confirming his new name *Israel*, and reaffirming the covenant which He had made with Abraham and Isaac (xxxv. 1-15). And here again, after thirty years, Jacob 'set up a pillar' (14; cf. xxviii. 22), and offered upon it the first drink offering of which we read in Scripture.

But Bethel was not the goal. Isaac was at Hebron, the home of his father (xiii. 18), and thither Jacob and his family went (xxxv. 27-29). The journey from Shechem to Hebron had been a sorrowful one, marked by two deaths, Deborah's, and Rachel's, and by the sin of his son Reuben; but it was the right road for Jacob, for now he was in the will of God for him.

(ii) AT HEBRON (xxxv. 27—xlv. 28)

Most of this record is about Joseph, but it is important to realize that in the year Jacob returned to Hebron Joseph was sold into Egypt (xxxvii. 14); that Isaac lived for twelve years after his son's return; and that Jacob lived in Hebron for twenty-two years, and then went down to Egypt.

His experience at Hebron was in respects a sad one. Almost at once he lost his beloved son Joseph, and for over twenty years he mourned him as dead; and after about twelve years he lost his father. This was the snapping of a great link with the past, and it must have released a flood of memories; and also it was probably at Isaac's funeral that Jacob saw Esau for the last time.

The twenty-two years at Hebron, which means *fellowship*, was a time of *discipleship* and *discipline*. He would think of his grandparents, and parents; of Leah and Rachel; of the birthright and the blessing which he stole; of the experience he had at Bethel when he left home; of the regrettable twenty years at Padan-aram; of the Peniel experience on the way home; of the reconciliation with Esau; of his foolish and costly delay on his way back to Bethel; of his reunion with his aged father; and of God's patience with him, and goodness to him through all the years.

These memories and experiences ripened him into sainthood, and made him more worthy of his name *Israel*. But the end was not yet. He had still a ministry to perform, and in some respects it was the greatest of his life.

4. The Seer in Egypt
Genesis xlvi. 1—l. 13

'He that is now called a prophet was beforetime called a seer' (1 Sam. ix. 9). A *seer* is one who *sees*, and it was in Egypt that Jacob saw things which are still in process of fulfilment. The words spoken about Joseph's two sons, and his own twelve sons, are prophetic programmes; 'sketches of the tribes in their grand characteristics rather than predictions of special events, or of the history of Israel as a whole' (Edersheim). 'Round his dying bed the powers of the world to come arrayed themselves, and there fell on him the breath of clear exalted prophecy. From the shadows of his own coming end, his eye ranged along the ages until, in prophetic insight, he saw the Conqueror of death' (Hastings).

Jacob's dying words mark the close of the Patriarchal dispensation. The first patriarch had developed into a family, and the family was now beginning to develop into a nation, and so it was eminently suitable that the last of the patriarchs should look back, and look on; should review the past, and predict the future. With Jacob the First Scene of Act I of the Drama of Redemption ends. The story which began with the call of Abram, and ends with the death of Jacob, shows when, how, and by whom the foundations of the People of Israel were laid.

The Prologue made the story possible and necessary, and the Advent of the Messiah made it glorious. The Hebrew family which began with one name, ends with seventy (xlvi. 27), or, according to the LXX, seventy-five (Acts vii. 14).

This record of 361 years tells of the providential training of the patriarchs for their part in the fulfilment of the Divine purpose to redeem the world, and a comparison of the beginning and the end of it will show how that purpose was advanced, and how Israel was being prepared to be the repository and instrument of it.

CHART 21

JACOB. Genesis xxv. 19–l. 13

SUPPLANTER	SERVANT	SAINT	SEER
Beersheba	Padan-aram	Hebron	Egypt
77 Years	20 Years	33 Years	17 Years
xxv. 19–xxviii. 9	xxviii. 10-xxx. 43	xxxi–xlv	xlvi. 1–l. 13
	B E T H E L Conversion	P E N I E L Consecration	
Birthright Blessing	Deceived Deceiving	Discipleship Discipline	Two Sons in Prophecy Twelve Sons in Prophecy

Wives, Handmaids, and Children			
LEAH	RACHEL	BILHAH	ZILPAH
Reuben Simeon Levi JUDAH Issachar Zebulun Dinah	JOSEPH Benjamin	Dan Naphtali	Gad Asher

JOSEPH

Genesis xxx. 22-24; xxxvii.—l.

Joseph was not one of *the* patriarchs, and to him the Covenant was not renewed, though he inherited it; yet as much space is given to him in Genesis as to Abraham, fourteen chapters. There are several reasons for this, the chief being, because his story is necessary for the completion of Jacob's story; because he is the link between the family and the nation, between Canaan and Egypt, and between a nomad and a civilised mode of life; and also because he is the most perfect anticipation of Him who was to be *the* Seed of the woman, and the fulfilment of all Messianic prophecy.

(i) The Story of Joseph

This falls naturally into three parts: *Joseph the Princely Son*— xxxvii. 1—xxxix. 20; *Joseph the Patient Sufferer*—xxxix. 21— xli. 36; and *Joseph the Powerful Sovereign*—xli. 37—l. 26. First trained; then tested; and finally triumphant.

Prof. Richard Moulton says that this is 'the masterpiece for all literature of the simple story', but we are not here concerned with it as a story, but as an integral and vital part of a plan which has for its end the fulfilment of the Covenant which God made with Abraham. That plan was often advanced by what was tragic, and sometimes by what was definitely wicked in the actions of men.

We cannot say whether or not Jacob would ever have gone to Padan-aram if he had not had occasion to flee thither, but his going was a flight from possible murder. Yet there were born to him all but one of the twelve sons who were to become tribes, and to form a nation.

The action of Joseph's brethren in selling him to the Ishmael- ites cannot be defended on any ground; yet the result was a contact with Egypt which proved to be a place both of preservation from the Canaanites, and of education for the part which Israel was to play in the history of the world to the end of time; and when God made Jacob go down to Egypt, He said: 'I will *there* make of thee a great nation' (xlvi. 3).

The centuries of Israel's servitude in Egypt had been predicted, though *Egypt* was not named, lest man's free volition should be interfered with (xv. 13, 14); and the fulfilment of this prophecy was initiated by the sin of Joseph's brethren. 'Out of the eater came forth meat, and out of the strong, sweetness'.

Joseph apprehended this overruling providence when he said to his fear-stricken brethren, before and after Jacob's death:

'Be not grieved nor angry with yourselves, that ye sold me hither; for God did send me before you to preserve life' (xlv. 5).

'God sent me before you to preserve you a posterity in the earth, and to save you alive by a great deliverance' (xlv. 7).

'As for you, ye meant evil against me; but God meant it for good' (l.20).

Truly He made the wrath of man to praise Him.

The imprisonment of Joseph was a crime, due to the passion of an unscrupulous woman (xxxix), yet it led to his becoming Prime Minister of all Egypt (xli.), and this position led to all that followed in the fortunes of his family (xlvi.—l.).

At every turn we see God turning the wickedness of man to account for the fulfilment of His redeeming purpose and promise.

(ii) JOSEPH AND JESUS

As God's method in fulfilment of His purpose to send into the world a Redeemer was to choose and discipline Abraham and his posterity, it is not irrelevant here to see that Joseph, more than any other character in Bible story, typified Him, and to note in what respects.

There are scores of parallels between Joseph's history and that of the Messiah, but it will suffice for our present purpose if a few of these are named, to justify the claim that Jacob's much-loved son foreshadowed the Son of God's love.

1	The beloved Son	Gen. xxxvii. 3	Matt. iii. 17
2	Hated by his brethren	Gen. xxxvii. 4, 5	John xv. 25
3	His Kingship rejected	Gen. xxxvii. 8	Luke xix. 4
4	Conspired against	Gen. xxxvii. 18	Matt. xxvii. 1
5	He was stripped	Gen. xxxvii. 23	Matt. xxvii. 28
6	Sold for silver	Gen. xxxvii. 28	Matt. xxvi. 15
7	Went into and came out of Egypt	Gen. xxxvii. 36	Matt. ii. 14, 15
8	Two others were bound with him, one of whom was saved, and the other destroyed	Gen. xl.	Luke xxiii. 32-43
9	Without sin: in his conduct; in His nature	Gen. xl. 15	John viii. 46
10	Released by the King	Ps. cv. 20	Acts ii. 24
11	Perfect wisdom	Gen. xli. 39	Col. ii. 3
12	All power given unto Him	Gen. xli. 55	Matt. xxviii. 18
13	To be obeyed	Gen. xli. 55	John ii. 5
14	Served all nations	Gen. xli. 57	Isa. xlix. 6
15	Not known by his brethren	Gen. xlii. 8	John i. 10, 11
16	Made known through an interpreter	Gen. xlii. 23	John xvi. 13, 14
17	A fruitful bough	Gen. xlix. 22	John xv. 5
18	All of God	Gen. xlv. 8	Acts ii. 23

This, then, is the Book of Genesis, supplying the Prologue to the Unfolding Drama of Redemption, and Scene 1 of Act I. In these is found implicitly all that is afterwards revealed. Here are profound truths concerning *God*, His nature, designs, activities, and methods; concerning *man*, his creation, responsibility, sinfulness, and hope; concerning the *human race*, its unity, vanity, and divisions; concerning *life*, individual, domestic, social and tribal; concerning *Providence*, the immanence of God in the affairs of men, and the way in which He uses both their willingness and waywardness; concerning *redemption*, in promise, and symbol; and concerning *destiny*, the necessary connection between character and fate.

All these are *big* things, and only the Bible deals with them in a big and authoritative way.

CHART 22

THE PATRIARCHS. Genesis xi. 10-l. 26

ABRAHAM 175 years xi. 10-xxv. 10	From the Call in Chaldea to the Settlement in Canaan xi. 27-xiii. 18	From the Settlement in Canaan to the Birth of Isaac xiv. 1-xxi. 21	From the Birth of Isaac to the Death of Abraham xxi. 22-xxv. 10	
ISAAC 180 years xxi-xxxv	From his Birth to his Marriage with Rebekah xxi-xxiv	From his Marriage to his Settlement at Beersheba xxv-xxvi	From his Settlement at Beersheba to his Death xxvii-xxxv	
JACOB 147 years xxv. 19-l. 13	From his Birth to his Departure from Home xxv. 19-xxviii. 9	From his Home-leaving to his Covenant in Gilead xxviii. 10-xxxi	From his Covenant in Gilead to his Descent into Egypt xxxii-xlv	From his Descent into Egypt to his Burial at Hebron xlvi-l. 13
JOSEPH 110 years xxx. 22-l. 26	From his Birth at Haran to his Arrival in Egypt The Son. His Training xxx. 22-24; xxxvii	From his Arrival in Egypt to his Promotion to Premiership The Sufferer. His Testing xxxix-xli. 36	From his Promotion to the end of his life The Sovereign. His Triumph xli. 37-l. 26	

CHART 23

THE BOOK OF GENESIS. No. 1

THE UNFOLDING DRAMA OF REDEMPTION

Revelation of the Redeeming Purpose			Progression of the Redeeming Purpose			
i. 1–xi. 9			xi. 10–l. 26			
THE PROLOGUE			ACT I. SCENE I. THE HEBREW FAMILY			
ANTEDILUVIAN		POSTDILUVIAN	PATRIARCHAL			
BABYLONIA (?) or ARMENIA (?)			PALESTINE: xi. 10–xxxvi, xxxviii		EGYPT: xxxvii, xxxix–l	
i–iii	iv–viii. 14	viii. 15–xi. 9	xi. 10–xxv. 10	xxi–xxxv	xxv. 19–l. 13	xxx. 22–l. 26
Creation to Fall	Fall to Flood	Flood to Babel	ABRAHAM	ISAAC	JACOB	JOSEPH

CHART 24

THE BOOK OF GENESIS. No. 2

	1	2	3	4	5	6	7	8	9	10
1 Generations	Heaven Earth	Adam	Noah	Sons of Noah	Shem	Terah	Ishmael	Isaac	Esau	Jacob
	ii. 4–iv. 26	v. 1–vi. 8	vi. 9–ix. 29	x. 1–xi. 9	xi. 10–26	xi. 27–xxv. 11	xxv. 12–18	xxv. 19–xxxv. 29	xxxvi. 1–xxxvii. 1	xxxvii. 2–l. 26

2 Beginning and End

The Beginning — The End

In Eden. ii. 8 — In Egypt. l. 26

A Creation. i. 1 — A Coffin. l. 26

Two People. i. 27 — Seventy-five People. Acts vii. 14

3 Line of the Revelation

ADAM	NOAH	SHEM	ABRAHAM (CH. 22)	ISAAC	JACOB	JOSEPH

4 Messianic Covenant

iii. 15, iii. 21, vi. 18, viii. 21, 22, ix. 8–17, ix. 26, 27, xii. 1–3, xiii. 14–17, xv., xvii, xviii. 9–15, xxii. 15–18. xxv. 23, xxvi. 3, 4, xxviii. 10–15. xxxii. 12, xxxv. 9–13, xlvi. 1–4, xlviii. 3, 4, 21. xlix. 8–12.

5 Revelations of God

ADONAY. Blesser. xviii. 3
ADONAY JEHOVAH. Covenant LORD xv. 2
ANGEL OF ELOHIM: of Strength. xxi. 17
ANGEL OF JEHOVAH, the Covenant God. xvi. 7
EL. Mighty. xxxv. 1
EL-BETH-EL. God, God of Bethel. xxxv. 7
EL-ELOHE-ISRAEL. Almighty God of Israel. xxxiii. 20

EL. ELOHIM. Almighty Strength. xlvi. 3
EL ELYON. Most High God. xiv. 18
EL ROI. God of Vision. xvi. 13
EL SHADDAI. Almighty God. xvii. 1
EL combinations: iv. 18(2); v. 12; xii. 8; xvi. 11; xvii. 19; xxxii. 28, 30, 31
ELOHIM. God of Strength. i. 1
EL OHIM of the heavens, and of the earth. xxiv. 3

JEHOVAH. Covenant LORD. iv. 6
JEHOVAH ELOHIM. Covenant LORD of Strength. ii. 5
JEHOVAH the Everlasting EL. xxi. 33
JEHOVAH JIREH. The LORD will provide. xxii. 14
JUDGE of all the earth. xviii. 25
MIGHTY ONE of Jacob. xlix. 24
SHADDAI. Almighty. xlix. 25
SHILOH. Rest-Giver. xlix. 10

133

NOTES

NOTE A

BIBLE CHRONOLOGY

IT is fortunate that for our subject, The Unfolding Drama of Redemption, the matter of chronology is not of vital importance. The study of Bible Chronology presents many difficulties, and these are reflected in the results of chronologers, no two of whom agree. *Anno Mundi* reckoning can be entirely ruled out, because no one with any show of reason can say when the creation of Genesis i. 1 was, except that it must have been unimaginable millions of years ago.

But there remain two other methods of reckoning, *Anno Hominis*, and B.C. The former begins with the creation of Adam and works forward to the birth of Christ, following carefully every chronological reference in and to the Old Testament period. This is the method adopted by MARTIN ANSTEY in his remarkable book *The Romance of Bible Chronology* (1913), in which he claims that there is an 'exact chronological relation of every dated event recorded in the Old Testament', making possible 'a Standard Chronology'. By this method of reckoning from man's creation to B.C. 1 is a period of 4042 years.

The other method is the commonly adopted B.C. one, that is, reckoning from the birth of Christ backwards, assuming that Christ was born four years (possibly five) before the era called *Anno Domini*. According to this reckoning various results are reached, the creation of man being placed at 5411 (Hales), 4004 (Ussher), 3901 (Mack), and at other and longer time-distances from the birth of Christ.

For the pre-Abrahamic ages there are three different reckonings, the Hebrew, the Samaritan, and the Septuagint, which complicate the matter somewhat; and the supposition that thousands of years before Abraham there were civilizations in the valleys of the Euphrates and the Nile, still further adds to the problem of chronology.

In the present work, therefore, dates are employed only as a general guide, and are subject to modification if necessary, and the B.C. method employed is based on Ussher's reckoning.

There are a few dates which may be regarded as certain, such as 722 when the Northern Kingdom of Israel ended; 586 when the Jewish Monarchy ended; 536 when, with the permission of Cyrus, a large number of Jews returned from Babylonian captivity; 516 when the Temple of Zerubbabel was completed; 458 when Ezra returned to Canaan; 445 when Nehemiah returned; and other dates can be arrived at by reckoning from these backward and forward.

But in tracing the Unfolding Drama of Redemption dates are of very minor importance, except as they indicate how, through long centuries, grace battled with man's sin, and finally triumphed.

NOTE B
THE CHRONOLOGY OF THE BOOK OF GENESIS

THERE are, as we have said, two ways in which O.T. Chronology can be calculated: from Christ backwards, B.C.; or from Adam forwards, *Anno Hominis*. The record of this Book reaches from the creation of Adam to the death of Joseph, and the date-references in it show that this is a period of 2369 years. We shall divide this period into three parts.

CHART 25

A. FROM THE CREATION OF ADAM TO THE FLOOD: 1656 YEARS						
Name	Age at Birth of Son	After Birth of Son	Age at Death	Reference	An. Hom. Date	B. C. Ussher
Adam	130	800	930	v. 3–5	930	3074
Seth	105	807	912	v. 6–8	1042	2962
Enos	90	815	905	v. 9–11	1140	2864
Cainan	70	840	910	v. 12–14	1235	2769
Mahalaleel	65	830	895	v. 15–17	1290	2714
Jared	162	800	962	v. 18-20	1422	2582
Enoch	65	300	365 (trs.)	v. 21–24	987	3017
Methusaleh	187	782	969	v. 25–27	1656	2348
Lamech	182	595	777	v. 28–31 v. 32; vii. 6	1651	2353
Noah	600 to the Flood —— Gen. vii. 6 1656		950	ix. 28, 29	1656	2348

B. FROM THE FLOOD TO THE CALL OF ABRAM: 427 YEARS

Name	Age at Birth of Son	After Birth of Son	Age at Death	Reference	An. Hom. Date	B. C. Ussher
Shem	Gen. xi. 10 2(100)	500	600	xi. 10, 11	2158	1846
Arphaxad	35	403	438	xi. 12, 13	2096	1908
Salah	30	403	433	xi. 14, 15	2126	1878
Eber	34	430	464	xi. 16, 17	2187	1817
Peleg	30	209	239	xi. 18, 19	1996	2008
Reu	32	207	239	xi. 20, 21	2026	1978
Serug	30	200	230	xi. 22. 23	2049	1955
Nahor	29	119	148	xi. 24, 25	1997	2007
Terah	130	75	205	xi. 26; xii. 4	2083	1926
Abram	75 at time of Call			xii. 4	2083	
	427					1921

C. FROM THE CALL OF ABRAM TO THE DEATH OF JOSEPH: 286 YEARS

Abram	From Call to Death Age at Death, 175	100	xii. 4 xxv. 7	2083–2183 2183	1921–1821
Isaac	Death of Abram to Death of Isaac Age at Death, 180	105	xxxv. 28	2288	1821–1716
Jacob	Death of Isaac to Death of Jacob Age at Death, 147	27	xlvii. 28	2315	1716–1689
Joseph	Death of Jacob to Death of Joseph Age at Death, 110	54	l. 26	2369	1689–1635
		286			

From the Creation of Adam to the Death of Joseph=1656+427+286=2369 Years.

It should be observed that this 2369 years is not the time from the creation of the world, *Anno Mundi*, but from the creation of Adam, *Anno Hominis*. The creation of the world must have been many millions of years before the appearance of man.

NOTE C

THE CHILDREN OF ISRAEL THAT WENT DOWN INTO EGYPT

Gen. xlvi. 26   'All the souls that came with Jacob into Egypt, which came out of his loins, besides Jacob's sons' wives, all the souls were *threescore and six*.'

Gen. xlvi. 27   'All the souls of the house of Jacob which came into Egypt were *threescore and ten*.'

Deut. x. 22   'Thy fathers went down into Egypt with *threescore and ten* persons.'

Acts vii. 14   'Jacob and all his kindred, *threescore and fifteen souls*.'

Here three different figures are given for what appears to be the same event, but these are not irreconcilable. In the 66 are not included Jacob himself, Joseph, Manasseh, and Ephraim, the latter three being already in Egypt; but these four *are* included in the 70 souls, for they were of 'the house of Jacob'.

As to the 75, to Gen. xlvi. 20, the LXX adds: 'And there were born unto Manasseh and Ephraim, whom his concubine the Aramitess bare him, Machir; and Machir begat Gilead. And the sons of Ephraim, the brother of Manasseh, were Shuthelah, Tahath; and the sons of Shuthelah, Eden'. This addition is taken, no doubt, from Num. xxvi. 29, 35; 1 Chron. vii. 14, 20.

Stephen, in Acts vii. 14, quoted from the LXX, and added to the 70 of Gen. xlvi. 27, the five grandsons of Joseph, named above; or to the 66, of Gen. xlvi. 26, these five grandsons, and Jacob, Joseph, Manasseh, and Ephraim; and in this way these varying numbers are harmonized.

NOTE D

THE DURATION OF ISRAEL'S SOJOURN IN EGYPT

THE duration of Israel's stay in Egypt has not been determined, and probably never will be, for the dates of Egyptologists and of Biblical chronologers vary greatly, and the references to the matter in the Bible are not determinative. These references are as follows.

EXODUS xii. 40, 41

THE HEBREW TEXT.

'Now the sojourning of the Children of Israel, which they sojourned in Egypt was 430 years.'

THE SEPTUAGINT TEXT.

'The sojourning of the Children of Israel, which they sojourned in Egypt, *and in the land of Canaan,* was 430 years.'

THE SAMARITAN TEXT.

'The sojourning of the Children of Israel, *and of their fathers,* which they sojourned in the land of Canaan, and in the land of Egypt, was 430 years.'

If the Hebrew text is correct, the reckoning must begin from the descent of Jacob into Egypt (Gen. xlvi.).

If the other two texts are correct, the reckoning must commence from the entrance of Abram into Canaan (Gen. xii.).

The alternatives, therefore, are a *short* period, and a *long* period.

1. THE SHORT PERIOD.   Septuagint and Samaritan Texts

	Years
From the entrance of Abram into Canaan to the birth of Isaac (Gen. xii. 4; xvii. 1, 21)	25
From the birth of Isaac to the birth of Jacob (Gen. xxv. 26) ..	60
Jacob, when he went down into Egypt, was (Gen. xlvii. 28) ..	130
	215

This leaves 215 years from Jacob's going down into Egypt, to the Exodus (Gen. xlvi. 28; Exod. xii. 40. 41).

Reckoned backwards:—

The Plagues	0-1
Moses in Midian (Acts vii. 30)	40
Moses at Court (Acts vii. 23)	40
From birth of Moses to death of Joseph	64
From death of Joseph to death of Jacob	54
Jacob's sojourn in Egypt	17
	215

2. THE LONG PERIOD. The Hebrew Text and References

Gen. xv. 13 'Thy seed shall be a stranger in a land that is not theirs, and shall serve them; and they shall afflict them 400 years.'

Acts vii. 6 'His seed should sojourn in a strange land, and they should bring them into bondage, and entreat them evil 400 years.'

Exod. xii. 40, 41 'The sojourning of the Children of Israel, which they sojourned in Egypt was 430 years.'

According to these references the reckoning must be as follows.

Years

From the descent of Jacob into Egypt, to the death of Joseph (Gen. xlvi. 28; l. 26)	71
From the death of Joseph to the birth of Moses	278
From Moses' birth to his flight into Midian	40
From Moses' flight to his return to Egypt	40
From the return to Egypt to the Exodus	0-1
	430

The details of the 400 and 430 years are as follows.

Years

	400	430
From Abram's Call to his marriage with Hagar (Gen. xii.-xvi.)		10
From this marriage to the birth of Ishmael		-
From the birth of Ishmael to the birth of Isaac (Gen. xvi.-xxi.)		14
The weaning of Isaac (Gen. xxi. 8, 10)		5
From the weaning of Isaac to Jacob's descent into Egypt (Gen. xxi.-xlvii.)	185	185
		215
From Jacob's descent into Egypt to the Exodus .. (for the details see under The Short Period)	215	215
	400	430

For discussions of these reckonings see *The Speaker's Commentary,* Vol. 1; Hastings' *Dictionary of the Bible,* vol. 2; *International Standard Bible Encyclopædia,* vol. 1; Anstey's *The Romance of Bible Chronology,* vol. 1; *The Cambridge Companion to the Bible; The Dated Events of the Old Testament,* by W. J. Beecher.

NOTE E

CHART 26

THE GENEALOGIES OF GENESIS

1. ADAM'S POSTERITY

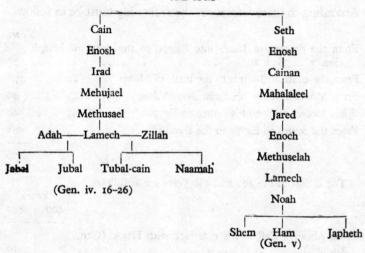

ADAM

Cain   Seth

Enosh   Enosh

Irad   Cainan

Mehujael   Mahalaleel

Methusael   Jared

Adah——Lamech——Zillah   Enoch

Jabal   Jubal   Tubal-cain   Naamah   Methuselah

(Gen. iv. 16–26)   Lamech

Noah

Shem   Ham   Japheth
(Gen. v)

2. JAPHETH'S POSTERITY

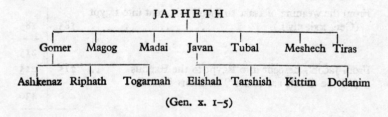

JAPHETH

Gomer   Magog   Madai   Javan   Tubal   Meshech   Tiras

Ashkenaz   Riphath   Togarmah   Elishah   Tarshish   Kittim   Dodanim

(Gen. x. 1–5)

3. HAM'S POSTERITY (Gen. x. 6–20).

4. SHEM'S POSTERITY

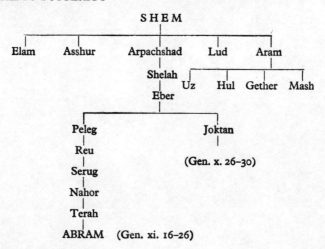

SHEM

Elam — Asshur — Arpachshad — Lud — Aram

Shelah

Eber

Uz — Hul — Gether — Mash

Peleg

Joktan

Reu

(Gen. x. 26–30)

Serug

Nahor

Terah

ABRAM (Gen. xi. 16–26)

5. TERAH'S POSTERITY

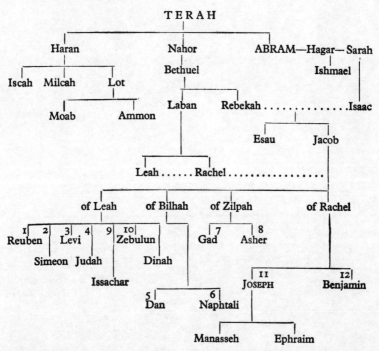

TERAH

Haran — Nahor — ABRAM—Hagar—Sarah

Iscah — Milcah — Lot — Bethuel — Ishmael

Moab — Ammon — Laban — Rebekah .... Isaac

Esau — Jacob

Leah ...... Rachel ....

of Leah — of Bilhah — of Zilpah — of Rachel

1 2 3 4 9 10
Reuben Levi Zebulun — Gad 7 — Asher 8

Simeon Judah — Dinah

Issachar

11
JOSEPH

12
Benjamin

5 6
Dan Naphtali

Manasseh — Ephraim

(Gen. xi. 26-29; xxii. 20-24; xxix. 31-35; xxx. 1-24; xxxv. 16-20, 23-26; xii. 51, 52).

143

ACT I

SCENE 2

THE ISRAELITISH NATION

PERIOD A
THE AGE OF THE THEOCRACY

ISRAEL IN EGYPT

ISRAEL IN THE WILDERNESS

SCENE 2. THE ISRAELITISH NATION

Exodus i.—Ezra i.

Joseph to Zerubbabel

NOTE D on pages 139-141, shows what uncertainty exists as to the length of time covered by Exodus i. But chronology does not affect our purpose in this survey, which is to trace in the drama of history the Divine purpose to redeem mankind.

However, it may be well to say that notes of time which we may make are based, without dogmatism, on the assumption that the 430 years of Exod. xii. 40, 41; Gal. iii. 17, are dated from the call of and promise to Abram in Gen. xii. 1-3; and xv. 13-18; which means that from Abram's call to Jacob's descent into Egypt (Gen. xii.-xlvi.) was 215 years, and that from the descent into Egypt to the Exodus was 215 years. If this be correct the gap between Genesis l., and Exodus ii., that is, from the death of Joseph to the birth of Moses is a period of 64 years; long enough to allow of the *family* (Gen. xlvi.) becoming a *nation* (Exod. i.) of perhaps $2\frac{1}{4}$ million souls.

Scene 1 of Act I has traced the redeeming purpose in the call of an individual and his posterity for two generations. That family became a nation, and the record of this nation, from the descent into Egypt of Jacob to the return under Zerubbabel from Babylonian captivity, embraces the major part of the Old Testament.

It is of the utmost importance that the main outline of this long period be accurately drawn and kept steadily in mind as one reads and studies, so that the Writings of the period may be placed where they belong in the outline.

The history of Israel as a nation falls into three distinct parts which are represented by the words *Theocracy, Monarchy,* and *Dependency.*

The first refers to the rule of *the Divine King*; the second, to the rule of *native kings*; and the third, to the rule of *alien kings*

The first reaches from the descent into Egypt to the rise of Saul; the second, from the rise of Saul to the captivity of Zedekiah; and the third, from the captivity of Zedekiah to Zerubbabel.

The duration of the first is more than six centuries; of the second, over five centuries; and of the third, half a century; making together eleven and a half centuries.

In detail the Writings which belong to these periods will be noted as we proceed: but, summarily, the records are found in Genesis xlvi—1 Samuel vii; 1 Samuel viii—2 Kings xxv; and 2 Kings xxv—Ezra i. The following chart should be memorized.

CHART 27

SCENE 2. THE ISRAELITISH NATION. Exodus 1–Ezra 1		
A	**B**	**C**
The Theocracy	**The Monarchy**	**The Dependency**
Rule of the DIVINE KING	Rule of NATIVE KINGS	Rule of ALIEN KINGS
Descent into Egypt to Saul	Saul to Zedekiah	Zedekiah to Zerubbabel
Over 600 years. Gen. xlvi–1 Sam. vii	Over 500 years. 1 Sam. viii–2 Kings xxv	50, years. 2 Kings xxv–Ezra i
1706–1095 B.C.	1095–586 B.C.	586–536 B.C.
Over eleven and a half centuries		

PERIOD A

THE AGE OF THE THEOCRACY

FROM THE DESCENT OF JACOB INTO EGYPT TO THE RISE OF SAUL.

Genesis xlvi.—1 Samuel vii.   B.C. 1706-1095.   Over 600 Years.

THIS world was created by God and belongs to Him. He only Who made mankind can rule them. But He made man rational, moral, and responsive; able to submit to, and to rebel against, the Divine rule. In Eden Adam and Eve rebelled. After Eden the human race rebelled, and all except a family were destroyed. This family grew into a second race, and it too rebelled, and was scattered over the earth.

Then God called a man out of heathendom; revealed to him His redeeming purpose; and made a covenant with him. This man was Abraham, the first of *the* Patriarchs, the father of the Hebrews, and the founder of Israel. God confirmed to his son and grandson, Isaac and Jacob, the covenant which He had made. When this family grew to be seventy-five souls, Divine providence led them from Canaan to Egypt (Gen. xlvi.), and the Book of *Exodus* begins by stating this fact (i. 1-6).

They were in a strange land, as had been predicted (Gen. xv. 13, 14), but they were God's people, and He had promised that, after protracted suffering, He would deliver them from Egypt, and bring them back to Canaan, the land of their inheritance. They were as yet an unorganized and subject people, without kings, priests, or prophets, but they were God's people, and He was their Ruler.

This rule, mediated through a succession of men whom God chose, continued to the time of the rise of Saul, a period of over 600 years from the descent into Egypt. It was during this period that the Israelites were delivered from Egyptian bondage, were constituted a nation, were led through the wilderness of Sinai to Canaan; entered, conquered, and possessed the land, and for over 300 years were under Judges whom God raised up to deliver them from oppression. This long period falls into three parts, and each of these is again divisible. We have said that the record of this period is in Genesis xlvi—I Samuel vii, and it reveals God as the King of Israel. Slowly, but quite clearly the redeeming purpose unfolds. The three parts of this period are as follows:

CHART 28

A. THE THEOCRACY		
ISRAEL IN EGYPT	ISRAEL IN THE WILDERNESS	ISRAEL IN THE LAND
215 Years Genesis xlvi– Exodus xii. 36	40 Years Exodus xii. 37– Joshua ii	356 Years Joshua iii– I Samuel vii
1706–1491 B.C.	1491–1451 B.C.	1451–1095 B.C.

The first of these parts, *Israel in Egypt,* is reckoned from the descent of the patriarchal family into Egypt (Gen. xlvi); and embraces 215 of the 430 years of Exodus xii. 40, 41 (see p. 140. Note D). This period is in two parts: Exod. i. covering 135 years, from the descent into Egypt to the birth of Moses; and chs. ii.—xii. 36 covering exactly 80 years.

The events of this comparatively short period are momentous, for by them the redeeming purpose of God takes a great leap forward.

But before going further into detail, it will be well to get a conspectus of the Book of Exodus, which covers a period of 145 years—from the death of Joseph to the construction of the Tabernacle, 1635—1490 B.C.

CHART 29

THE BOOK OF EXODUS

Subjection i-xii. 36 — 144 Years	Emancipation. xii. 37-xix. 2 — 2 Months	Revelation. xix. 3-xl — 9½ Months
ISRAEL IN EGYPT	**ISRAEL FROM EGYPT TO SINAI**	**ISRAEL AT SINAI**

ISRAEL IN EGYPT — Subjection i-xii. 36 — 144 Years

PERSECUTION OF THE PEOPLE. i. 8-22

- National Expansion (1-7)
- Cruel Exaction (8-14) / Purposed Extinction (15-22)

PREPARATION OF A SAVIOUR. ii. 1-iv. 28

- Moses the Prince in Egypt (ii. 1-15a)
- Moses the Shepherd in Midian (ii. 15b-iv. 28)

PLAN AND PROGRESS OF REDEMPTION iv. 29-xii. 36

- 1st Movement Exploratory (iv. 29-vii. 13)
  - First Appearance of Moses before Israel and Pharaoh (iv. 29-vi. 8)
  - Second Appearance of Moses before Israel and Pharaoh (vi. 9-vii. 13)
- 2nd Movement Evidential (vii. 14-x. 29)
  - PLAGUES
    1. Blood
    2. Frogs
    3. Lice
    4. Beetles
    5. Murrain
    6. Boils
    7. Hail and Fire
    8. Locusts
    9. Darkness
- 3rd Movement Executive (xi. 1-xii. 36)
  - 10th Plague Death of the Firstborn (xi. 1-10)
  - Institution and Observance of the PASSOVER (xii. 1-36)

ISRAEL FROM EGYPT TO SINAI — Emancipation. xii. 37-xix. 2 — 2 Months

TO THE RED SEA — xii. 37-xiv. 14

- Rameses. Succoth. Etham. Pi-hahiroth. The Sea

THROUGH THE RED SEA — xiv. 15-xv. 21

- Passage of the Israelites — xiv. 15-22
- Overthrow of the Egyptians — xiv. 23-31
- The Song of Moses and Miriam. — xv. 1-21

FROM THE RED SEA — xv. 22-xix. 2

- Marah. Elim. Wilderness of Sin. Rephidim. Mount Sinai

ISRAEL AT SINAI — Revelation. xix. 3-xl — 9½ Months

THE WILL OF GOD DISCLOSED — xix. 3-xxxi

- The Law — xix. 3-xxiv
- The Tabernacle — xxv-xxvii.
- The Priesthood — xxviii, xxix
- The Service — xxx, xxxi

THE WILL OF GOD CONTEMNED — xxxii-xxxiv

- The Great Transgression. — xxxii. 1-6
- The Divine Displeasure. — xxxii.7-xxxiii
- The Law and the Covenant Renewed — xxxiv

THE WILL OF GOD FULFILLED — xxxv-xl

- The Tabernacle Constructed, — xxxv-xxxix. 31
- The Tabernacle Completed, — xxxix. 32-xl. 33
- The Tabernacle Consecrated. — xl. 34-38

(Leviticus and Numbers i. 1-x. 10 continue the record of Israel's Encampment at Sinai, and add 7 weeks to the 9½ months: Exod. xl. 17; Num. i. 1; x. 11,12)

We must now consider separately the three parts of the Theocratic Period.

CHART 30

ISRAEL IN EGYPT		
Persecution of the People	Preparation of a Saviour	Plan and Progress of Redemption
Exod. i. 8-22	Exod. ii. 1-iv. 28	Exod. iv. 29-xii. 36
ISRAEL and PHARAOH	MOSES and GOD	GOD and PHARAOH
64 Years	80 Years	0-1 Year
1635-1571 B.C.	1571-1491 B.C.	1491-1490 B.C.

That which dominates in this part of the story is the idea of *deliverance*. The *need* of it is seen in the misery of the people; the *agent* of it is provided in the person of MOSES with whom was associated his brother *Aaron*; and the *crisis* of it is precipitated by a succession of plagues, the last of which was, for the Israelites, a *passover*.

The connection between these three things must be obvious. A deliverer would be of no use if there was no need for deliverance; and the need and agent would be of no use if the act was not consummated; but here are all three.

ISRAEL AND PHARAOH

In ch. i., history is greatly compressed. In a score of verses we are told of the *national expansion* (1-7), the *cruel exaction* (8-14), and the *purposed extinction* of Israel (15-22).

Divine providence and human perverseness are in conflict: God multiplying the Israelites, and Pharaoh trying to exterminate them; just as in our time the Divine and the diabolical are bidding for the souls of men; but these powers are not commensurate, as the issue shows.

MOSES AND GOD

In chs. ii. 1—iv. 28 is put on record two-thirds of the life of one of the greatest men of all time, MOSES, the Prince, the Shepherd, and the Deliverer.

Forty years in Egypt and forty years in Midian prepared him for forty years in the Wilderness. In the first period he saw his importance; in the second, he discovered his impotence; and in the third he witnessed God's omnipotence.

With the coming, preparation, discipline, and ministry of Moses the redemptive purpose was greatly advanced.

His call was as definite as Abraham's, 430 years before, but it was to a very different task. Abraham's *faith in God* distinguished him, but Moses' *distrust of himself* is outstanding. When God called him, he offered five excuses in an attempt to evade the task. He pleaded *no fitness* (iii. 11), *no message* (iii. 13), *no authority* (iv. 1), *no gift of speech* (iv. 10), and *no inclination* (iv. 13).

But God met him at every point, promising His *presence* (iii. 12), His *Name* and *covenant* (iii. 14-22), His *power* (iv. 2-9), His *enabling* (iv. 11, 12), and His *instruction* (iv. 14-16).

At 'the back of the wilderness' Moses received two great revelations of God: of *His Preserving Presence* (iii. 1-10), and of *His Eternal Being* (iii. 14); and both revelations are related to Israel His People.

The burning bush represents Israel, and the 'flame of fire' Egyptian persecution. The people were not consumed by the persecution (ch. 1), because the '*Angel of the LORD*' was in their midst; not protecting them from suffering, but preserving them in it, and through it. This '*Angel of the LORD*' is the 'I Am That I Am' of the second revelation. A critical moment had arrived both in history and theology.

'EHYEH 'ASHER 'EHYEH is the self-existent, unconditioned, eternal, changeless God; the *I Am Because I Am*, the *I Am Who Am*, and the *I Will Be That I Will Be*.

GOD AND PHARAOH

In chs. iv. 29—xii. 36 a drama is enacted the parties of which are God, Egypt, and Israel. The object of it is three-fold: to reveal the power of God over His enemies; to demonstrate that Israel belonged to God and not to Pharaoh; and to establish the faith of Israel in God.

There are three distinct movements. The first is *exploratory*

(iv. 29—vii. 13); the second is *evidential* (vii. 14—x. 29); and the third is *executive* (xi. 1—xii. 36).

(*i*) The *exploratory movement* (iv. 29—vii. 13) tells of the approach to the subject of deliverance, and consists of two appearances of Moses before Israel and Pharaoh (iv. 29-vi. 8; and vi. 9-vii. 13). The effect of this approach is varied, as is seen in the reactions of Pharaoh, Israel, and Moses; but the total result is an advance towards the object in view.

(*ii*) The *evidential movement* (vii. 14—x. 29) is in a series of *plagues*, which were a clash between two Powers, one Divine, and one human; a conflict between two religions, one true, and one false; a struggle for the supremacy of heaven, or of earth; of a Saviour or of a 'Serpent' (iv. 1-5).

The struggle was protracted and the battle swayed to and fro, but the devil was defeated by the Deliverer. These plagues were something more than devices to reduce Pharaoh's power of resistance; they were attacks upon the religion of the Egyptians, and upon their many gods. They are in a trinity of triplets, with a final movement which is both a curse and a blessing, a plague and a passover. The details of the plagues are summarized in Chart 31, which should be carefully studied.

CHART 31

THE PLAGUES ON EGYPT

(i) SERIES	(ii) NO.	(iii) PLAGUE	(iv) REF.	(v) ATTACK	(vi) FEATURES	(vii) EFFECT
I Inflicted by Aaron. vii. 19. viii. 5. viii. 16	1	BLOOD	vii. 14-25	On the Idol River	Announced. vii. 15 In the morning	Hardened. vii. 22
	2	FROGS	viii. 1-15	On the Goddess Hekt (with frog head)	Announced. viii. 1	Hardened. viii. 15
	3	LICE	viii. 16-19	On Seb, the Earth God	Unannounced. viii. 16 Defeat of Magicians	Hardened. viii. 19
II Inflicted by Jehovah viii. 20-24. ix. 3-6. On Egyptians only viii. 23. x. 23. Inflicted by Moses ix. 8, 10	4	BEETLES	viii. 20-32	On the Sacred Scarabaeus	Announced. viii. 20 In the morning	Compromise. ix. 25-28
	5	MURRAIN	ix. 1-7	On Apis, the Sacred Bull	Announced. ix. 1	Hardened. ix. 7
	6	BOILS	ix. 8-12	On Typhon, the Evil Genius	Unannounced. ix. 8 Defeat of Magicians. ix. 11	Hardened. ix. 12
III Inflicted by Moses ix. 22. x 12. x. 21. On Egyptians only viii. 23. x. 23. Protection for God-fearing Egyptians. ix. 20, 21	7	HAIL & FIRE	ix. 13-35	On Shu, the Atmosphere	Announced. ix. 13 In the morning	Hardened. ix. 35
	8	LOCUSTS	x. 1-20	On Serapia, protector from locusts	Announced. x. 1	Compromise. x. 8-11
	9	DARKNESS	x. 21-29	On Ra, the Sun God	Unannounced. x. 21 Defeat of Pharaoh x. 28, 29	Compromise. x. 24
IV Birthday, and Doomsday	10	DEATH OF FIRST-BORN	xi. 1-xii. 36	On all Gods	THE PASSOVER	CAPITULATION xii. 29-36

(*iii*) The *executive movement* (xi. 1-xii. 36) is distinct and distinctive. It was vastly more than a plague on Egypt, being the first institution of the people now about to become a nation, the first sacrifice which was Divinely founded and directed.

The central fact and feature of *the Passover* was the slain lamb, and that lamb pointed forward to 'the Lamb of God', the shedding of Whose 'precious blood' was to make atonement for sin.

Here are, the Anticipation of the End (xi.); the Institution of the Feast (xii. 1-28); and the Visitation upon Egypt (xii. 29-36); and in these events another great advance is made in the Unfolding Drama of Redemption.

The second part of the Story of the Theocracy here emerges. In the first part we see *Israel in Egypt* (Gen. xlvi.—Exod. xii. 36), and here we see *Israel in the Wilderness* (Exod. xii. 37—Josh. ii.). The first part covers nearly a century and a half (Chart 30); but this part covers less than half a century; to be exact, forty years (Deut. viii. 2—Chart 28).

As our object throughout this study is rapid review, and not detailed examination, it will be enough to outline this crowded story with sufficient fulness for us to trace the development of the redeeming purpose in the history of the new-born nation. The following chart presents this outline.

CHART 32

ISRAEL IN THE WILDERNESS

FROM EGYPT TO SINAI	THE ENCAMPMENT AT SINAI	FROM SINAI TO SHITTIM
Exodus xii. 37-xix. 2	Exodus xix. 3-Numbers x. 10	Numbers x. 11-Joshua ii
To the Red Sea xii. 37-xiv. 14	The Revelation of the LORD Exod. xix. 3-25	The Story of Israel on the March Num. x. 11-xxxvi. 13
Through the Red Sea xiv. 15-xv. 21	The Constitution of the Nation Exod. xx-Lev. xxvii	A Review and Preview of Israel's History Deuteronomy
From the Red Sea xv. 22-xix. 2	The Preparation for the Journey Num. i. 1-x. 10	Israel Planning to Enter the Promised Land Joshua i-ii
2 months	11 months, 19 days	over 38 years

CHRONOLOGICAL REFERENCES

Exodus xii. 2-6, 40-42; xvi. 1; xix. 1, 2; xl. 17. Numbers i. 1; x. 11, 12; xiv. 33, 34; xxxii. 13; xxxiii. 38; Deuteronomy i. 3; Joshua i. 11; v. 6

157

1 FROM EGYPT TO SINAI

Exod. xii. 37—xix. 2

In the three movements of the journey from Egypt to Sinai, *to*, *through*, and *from* the Red Sea, there are nine stages, and the events of this journey, which occupied about two months, should be noted, because they show, as does all Old Testament history, the weakness and sin of man, on the one hand; and the strength and grace of God, on the other hand.

The shame of this part of the story is the incorrigible unbelief and discontent of the Israelites; and the glory of it is the faithfulness and patience of the LORD. This is manifested in a sixfold manner: in *redemption* (xii. 37—xiii. 18); in *guidance* (xiii. 19-22); in *salvation* (xiv.—xv. 21); in *provision* (xv. 22 —xvii. 7); in *victory* (xvii. 8-16); and in *government* (xviii.).

CHART 33

STAGES AND EVENTS OF THE JOURNEY FROM EGYPT TO SINAI			
Stages	Places	Refs.	Events
1	Rameses to Succoth	xii. 37-xiii. 19	Instructions for the future
2	Succoth to Etham	xiii. 20-22	Guidance of the pillar of cloud and fire
3	Etham to Pi-hahiroth	xiv. 1-14	The Egyptians pursue. The Israelites murmur. Moses reassures
4	Pi-hahiroth through the sea	xiv. 15-xv. 21	The command to advance. The passage through the Sea. The destruction of the Egyptians. The Song of Moses and Miriam
5	Red Sea to Marah	xv. 22-26	Complaint of the people. Cure of the waters. Covenant of the LORD
6	Marah to Elim	xv. 27	Twelve springs of water, and seventy palm trees
7	Elim to Wilderness of Sin	xvi	The Israelites murmur. Provision of quails and manna
8	Wilderness of Sin to Rephidim	xvii, xviii	The Israelites murmur. Water from the rock. Conflict with Amalek. Defeat and fate of Amalek. The arrival of Jethro, Moses' father-in-law, with Moses' wife and two sons. On Jethro's advice Elders are appointed to judge Israel
9	Rephidim to Sinai	xix. 1, 2	Encampment at the Mount, two months after leaving Egypt

THE WANDERINGS OF ISRAEL FROM EGYPT TO CANAAN

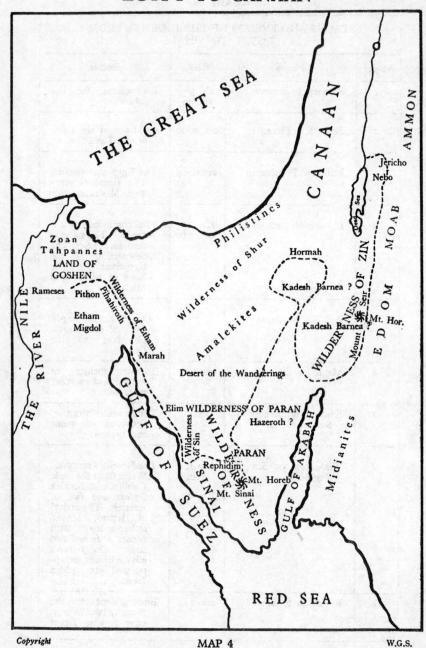

THE GREAT SEA

CANAAN

AMMON

Jericho
Nebo

Dead Sea

MOAB

Philistines

Wilderness of Shur

Hormah

Zoan
Tahpannes
LAND OF
GOSHEN

Kadesh Barnea ?

WILDERNESS OF ZIN

Seir of Edom

Rameses

Pithon

Pihahiroth

Wilderness of Etham

Kadesh Barnea ?

Mt. Hor.

EDOM

Etham
Migdol

Mount

Amalekites

THE RIVER NILE

Marah

Desert of the Wanderings

Elim WILDERNESS OF PARAN

GULF OF SUEZ

Hazeroth ?

GULF OF AKABAH

Wilderness of Sin

PARAN

Midianites

WILDERNESS

Rephidim

Mt. Horeb

Mt. Sinai

OF SINAI

RED SEA

2 THE ENCAMPMENT AT SINAI
Exod. xix. 3—Num. x. 10

A brief glance at this part of the record must impress us with its profound importance. These fifty-eight chapters and a few verses represent a period of *less than one year*; probably the most important year in all history, but certainly the greatest up to that time, marking, as it does, 'a decisive epoch in the history of the human race' (Kalisch).

This is the *theological* period of Israel's history; a time, not so much of *events* as of *lessons*; not so much of *doing* as of *listening*. The period is characterized not so much by history as by legislation; what is ethical and religious takes precedence over all other interests. The details relative to the Tabernacle and the Priesthood are of value only on account of their spiritual significance. The whole complex legislative system is religious in its origin, operation, and outcome.

In no other year of Israel's history was such a great revelation vouchsafed to them. What in that year was ordered and ordained gave colour and direction to the whole course of Israel until the Messiah came; and ever since, in Christianity, it has had its fullest interpretation.

Let us first of all get a survey of the whole record, and then we shall comment a little on the various parts. Read the text of these parts, and memorize Chart 34.

CHART 34

THE ENCAMPMENT AT SINAI. Exodus xix. 3–Numbers x. 10, cf. Chart 32

Record: 58 Chapters		Duration: 11¾ months
REVELATION OF THE LORD	CONSTITUTION OF THE NATION	PREPARATION FOR THE JOURNEY
Exodus xix. 3-25	Exodus xx-Leviticus xxvii	Numbers i. 1-x. 10
Declaration of Purpose xix. 3-8	ISRAEL'S LAWS The WILL OF GOD Unfolded Exodus xx-xxiv	Organization of the Camp i-iv
Sanctification of the People xix. 9-15	ISRAEL'S LIFE The Way to GOD Appointed Exodus xxv-xl	Legislation for the People v-vi
Manifestation of Jehovah xix. 16-25	ISRAEL'S LIBERTY The WALK WITH GOD Conditioned Leviticus	Provision for the Service vii. 1-ix. 14
		Anticipation of the March ix. 15-x. 10

(i) THE REVELATION OF THE LORD (Exodus xix. 3-25). Chart 34.

Next to the birth and mission of Jesus Christ, the existence and institutions of the Hebrew People are the most important events in universal history. It is not surprising therefore, that, as preliminary to the formation of the Israelites into a nation, there is a *Revelation of the LORD*.

This revelation consists in three things. First, in a *declaration of His purpose* (3-8). Israel would be His 'peculiar treasure', a precious possession, as no other nation would be; and they would be 'a kingdom of priests', and 'a holy nation', *if* they obeyed His voice, and kept His covenant (5).

Though they promised to obey (8), Israel, by its unfaithfulness, forfeited these privileges, which are now transferred to the Church of God (1 Peter ii. 9).

The second factor in the revelation is *the sanctification of the people* (9-15). Necessarily this was external and instant, but it was symbolic of what was to be internal and progressive.

The third factor is *the manifestation of Jehovah* (16-25).

'This was a real Theophany, in which amid the phenomena of storm and tempest, and fire and smoke, and thick darkness, and heavings of the ground as by an earthquake shock, first the loud blast of a trumpet sounded long, commanding attention, and then, a clear penetrating voice, like that of a man, made itself heard in distinctly articulated words, audible to the whole multitude, and recognized by them as superhuman, as "the voice of God".' (Rawlinson. cf. Deut. iv. 11, 12, 33; Heb. xii. 18-21).

(ii) THE CONSTITUTION OF THE NATION (Exodus xx.—Leviticus xxvii.). Chart 34.

These forty-eight chapters are the heart of the Theocracy, and the foundation of Israelitism; for the Will of God is unfolded in Israel's laws; the Way to God is appointed for Israel's life; and the Walk with God conditions Israel's liberty.

I ISRAEL'S LAWS: THE WILL OF GOD UNFOLDED
(Exod. xx.—xxiv.)

This section is in three parts:
(1) The Revelation of the Law.
   The Ten Commandments (xx. 1-17).

(2) The Regulation of the Law.
   The Book of the Covenant (xx. 18—xxiii. 33).

(3) The Ratification of the Law.
   The Solemn Ceremonies (xxiv.).

Beneath what necessarily was local and temporal in these instructions the injunctions are of age-long authority and application.

(1) The Revelation of the Law

THE TEN COMMANDMENTS (Exod. xx. 1-17; Deut. v. 1-21).

The Revelation of the Law began with what is called the *Decalogue*, or *Ten Words*. These assume that all duties are owed either to God, or to man. Duties to God belong to *religion*, and duties to man belong to *morality*, and their common denominator is *love* (Matt. xxii. 37-40). These laws are authoritative, fundamental, universal, comprehensive, systematic, obligatory, and eternal.

Those which are related to religion come first, because true morality is rooted in religion, and true religion issues in and safeguards morality. When man is rightly related to God, he cannot be wrongly related to his fellow men. Piety is productive of probity. A man's outlook will be right whose uplook is right,

And these laws are related to our thoughts, words, and deeds. in the First Table; and to our deeds, words, and thoughts, in the Second Table, and so embrace all our modes of emotion and expression, both internal and external.

The following chart indicates the main features of the Decalogue and is designed to show its profound and far-reaching importance.

CHART 35

(I) ISRAEL'S LAWS. THE WILL OF GOD UNFOLDED.
Exodus xx. 1-xxiv. 18

(1) The Revelation of the Law. The Ten Commandments
Exodus xx. 1-17. Deuteronomy v. 1-21

FIRST TABLE. Exod. xx. 3-12	SECOND TABLE. Exod. xx. 13-17
RELIGION	MORALITY
Laws concerning Man's Relation to God	Laws concerning Man's Relation to Man
God to be Loved Matt. xxii. 37, 38	Neighbours to be Loved Matt. xxii. 39, 40
Filial Relations. Piety	Fraternal Relations. Probity
Upward-looking aspects of life	Outward-looking aspects of life
Thought (3-6) Word (7) Deed (8-12)	Deed (13-15) Word (16) Thought (17)
"THE LORD THY GOD"	"THOU SHALT NOT"

PLAN.   Introverted Parallelism

(a) Internal (3-7)
(b) External (8-12)
(b) External (13-16)
(a) Internal (17)

THE INTERNAL IN RELIGION (3-7)	THE EXTERNAL IN MORALITY (13-16)
(i) The Unity of God (3) Against Polytheism	(vi) The Sanctity of Life (13) Against Murder
(ii) The Spirituality of God (4-6) Against Image-worship	(vii) The Sanctity of Marriage (14) Against Adultery
(iii) The Majesty of God (7) Against Profanity	(viii) The Sanctity of Property (15) Against Theft
	(ix) The Sanctity of Character (16) Against Slander
THE EXTERNAL IN RELIGION (8-12)	
(iv) The Worship of God (8-11) Against Secularism	THE INTERNAL IN MORALITY (17)
(v) The Representatives of God (12) Against Irreverence	(x) The Sanctity of the Heart (17) Against Covetousness

(2) **The Regulation of the Law**

THE BOOK OF THE COVENANT (Exod. xx. 18—xxiii. 33).

This is a division of the Book of Exodus, complete in itself, and it is called *The Book of the Covenant* (xxiv. 7). It was *written* by Moses (xxiv. 4), and is the first portion of Holy Scripture that ever existed as such. Its terms were told to the people, who promised to do all that it commanded (xxiv. 3), and in ratification thereof blood was sprinkled on the *altar*, and on the *people* (xxiv. 5-8). The laws of this Book are civil, social, and religious, numerous and varied. The following is a summary of the Covenant.

I THE DIVINE PREREQUISITES (xx. 18-26)
    1 The Solemnity of Worship (18-21)
    2 The Object of Worship (22, 23)
    3 The Altar of Worship (24-26)

II THE DIVINE PRECEPTS (xxi. 1—xxiii. 19)
    1 The Rights of PERSONS (xxi. 1-32)
      (i) Concerning Slavery (1-11)
      (ii) Concerning Smiting (12-27)
      (iii) Concerning Goring (28-32)

    2 The Rights of PROPERTY (xxi. 33—xxii. 15)
      (i) Concerning Neglect (xxi. 33-36)
      (ii) Concerning Theft (xxii. 1-6)
      (iii) Concerning Deposits (xxii. 7-15)

    3 The Rights of PIETY (xxii. 16—xxiii. 19)
      (i) Concerning Proper Conduct (xxii. 16-31)
      (ii) Concerning Common Justice (xxiii. 1-9)
      (iii) Concerning Sacred Seasons (xxiii. 10-19)

III THE DIVINE PROMISES (xxiii. 20-33)
    1 The 'Presence' with Israel (20-23)
    2 The Prospect before Israel (24-33)

There are some seventy regulations in this Book, and although they are local and temporary in detail, they are world-wide and abiding in principle, and reveal the care of God for people, *beginning with slaves* (xxi. 1-11).

And now follows:

(3) The Ratification of the Law

THE SOLEMN CEREMONIES (xxiv.)

I   The LORD Announces His Will (1, 2)
II The People Accept the Covenant (3-8)
III The Leaders Ascend the Mount (9-18)

The record relating to the constituting of Israel a Nation tells of their *laws*, and *life*, and *liberty*, and these respectively tell of the *will of God*, the *way to God*, and the *walk with God* (see Chart 34).

Having outlined the Laws, we must now consider the Life of Israel.

(II) ISRAEL'S LIFE: THE WAY TO GOD APPOINTED
(Exod. xxv.—xl.)

Sixteen chapters are given to this subject, a fact which shows the importance of it, and it includes three of the four great events at Sinai: the *Revelation of the Law*; the *Institution of the Tabernacle*; the *Ordination of the Priesthood*; and the *Prescription of the Offerings*.

The second of these four receives so much notice in our present section (Exod. xxv.—xl.), that it appears in *Leviticus* simply as a fact; but the other three, relating to *Law*, *Priesthood*, and *Offerings*, are considerably developed in that Book, as we shall see.

It should be borne in mind that the whole record from Exodus xix. to Numbers x. 10, belongs to the year of Encampment at Sinai.

These chapters (xxv.—xl.) fall into three parts:

(1) The Divine Provision for Israel (xxv.-xxxi.)
(2) The Grievous Perversion of Israel (xxxii.-xxxiv.)
(3) The Ultimate Performance through Israel (xxxv.-xl.)

(1) THE DIVINE PROVISION FOR ISRAEL (xxv.-xxxi.)

(*i*) The Institution of the Tabernacle (xxv.-xxvii.).
(*ii*) The Ordination of the Priesthood (xxviii., xxix.; Lev. viii.-x.).
(*iii*) The Regulation of the Service (xxx., xxxi.).

(1) The Divine Provision for Israel (xxv.-xxxi.).

(i) THE INSTITUTION OF THE TABERNACLE
(xxv-xxvii).

The *Tabernacle* dominates the Book of Exodus from ch. xxv., instructions concerning it being given seven times: xxv.-xxvii, xxix. 42-xxxi. 11; xxxv. 4-19; xxxv. 20-xxxvi. 7; xxxvi. 8-xxxviii. 31; xxxix. 32-42; xl. 1-11; xl. 16-38 (see p. 174).

Its Names

This dominance requires of us special attention. The Structure is called the *Tabernacle* (xxv. 9). because there God dwelt in the midst of His people; the *Tent of Meeting* (xxix. 44), because there God met with His people; and the *Tabernacle of Testimony* (xxv. 21), because there the Tables of the Law were kept.

Its Origin

God delivered the Tabernacle to Moses when he was on Mount Sinai, and instructed him minutely as to its form and purpose. "See", saith He, "that thou make all things according to the pattern shewed thee on the Mount". This word *pattern* means type or model, and conveys the thought that Moses looked upon a model of the Tabernacle as God was instructing him. Certain it is that in no particular of its construction was he left to his own ideas; the whole was a direct and complete revelation, as was the giving of the Law at the same time, and in the same place.

Its Form

THE STRUCTURE

    The Court, 100 cubits by 50.

    The Tabernacle, 30 cubits by 10.

        The Holy Place, 20 cubits by 10.

        The Holiest of All, 10 cubits by 10.

    The Tent over the Tabernacle.

    The Covering over the Tent.

THE FURNITURE

    In the Court.

        The Brazen Altar.

        The Laver.

In the Holy Place.
>   THE GOLDEN LAMPSTAND.
>   THE TABLE OF SHEWBREAD.
>   THE ALTER OF INCENSE.

In the Holiest of All.
>   THE ARK.
>   THE MERCY-SEAT AND CHERUBIM.

This wonderful Structure was placed in the midst of the Camp, and was at once the personal, social, political, and religious centre of the people. Every piece of the Tabernacle furniture, as, indeed, the entire Tabernacle, is of profound spiritual significance, the full meaning of which is found only in the New Testament.

The Brazen Altar tells of *Regeneration*; the Laver of *Purification*; the Lampstand of *Illumination*; the Shewbread of *Sustentation*; the Altar of Incense of *Intercession*; the Ark of *Representation*; and the Mercy-Seat and Cherubim of *Consecration*; all of which are to be found, and found only, in Christ Jesus, the Word who 'became flesh and *tabernacled* among us' (John i. 14).

CHART 36

PLAN OF THE ENCAMPMENT

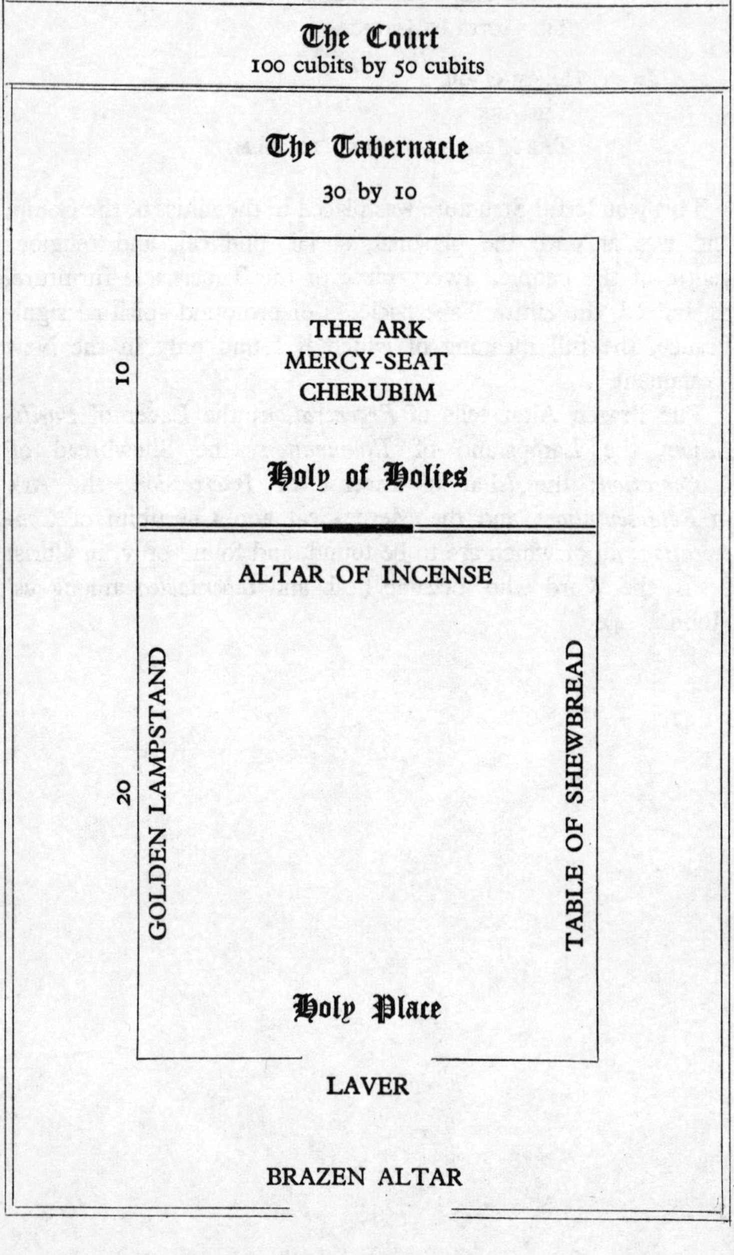

The Court
100 cubits by 50 cubits

The Tabernacle
30 by 10

THE ARK
MERCY-SEAT
CHERUBIM

Holy of Holies

10

ALTAR OF INCENSE

GOLDEN LAMPSTAND

20

TABLE OF SHEWBREAD

Holy Place

LAVER

BRAZEN ALTAR

It will be seen that this Chart is not drawn to scale, but only to give a visual idea of the structure and furniture of the Tabernacle.

Its History

It appears first of all at Sinai, where the instructions, given to Moses seven times, were executed a fortnight short of twelve months from the time that Israel left Egypt (xl. 2, 17).

During the wanderings of the people through the wilderness, and throughout the different stages of their conquests in the land, the Tabernacle accompanied them, and when the inhabitants of Canaan were subdued by them, it was located in Shiloh, the place chosen by the LORD (Josh. xviii. 1). In this place it was found over 450 years later (1 Sam. i. 3), and the people were still going there to sacrifice; but its days were then drawing to a close. The Israelites fetched the Ark from its resting place when they went to battle against the Philistines (1 Sam. iv.), and it never again returned to the Tabernacle.

About 110 years later, when Solomon built the Temple, this Tent of Meeting between God and Israel, which had existed for about 600 years, disappeared altogether.

Its Significance

The spiritual truth for which the Tabernacle stood may be said to be two-fold, namely,

        (a) the fact of God's approach to man, and

        (b) the way of man's approach to God;

and as the Tabernacle is a type of Christ (John i. 14), we have reason to look for the counterparts of the type in His life and death; and these we find.

The fact of God's approach to us is by Christ's incarnation, preparation, and ministration; and the way of our approach to God is by His crucifixion, resurrection, and ascension (2 Cor. v. 19).

(ii) THE ORDINATION OF THE PRIESTHOOD
(Exod. xxviii., xxix.; Lev. viii.-x.)

The entire idea of priesthood, true or false, is rooted in the human consciousness of sin and the need for mediation. In man's religious character, using the word 'religious' in its simplest meaning as pointing to man's sense of dependence on God, we find the first occasion for priesthood apart altogether from revelation.

The priestly caste and system were not peculiar to Israel, but were to be found in all the surrounding countries. In Gen. xli. 45, we read that Joseph married the daughter of an Egyptian priest, and in ch. xlvi. 22, 26, that he specially recognized the priestly caste. Also in the land of the Ammonites, and the Moabites, in the Valley of Hinnom, and on Olivet, priests were at work, sacrificing not only innocent beasts, but also men, women, and children.

We need not be surprised at this function of priesthood, because the necessity for it lies in the very constitution of the human soul. Man's conception of sin may and does vary greatly according to his intelligence and light, but whatever view is held, the instinct of worship, and the conscious need of mediation are universal. The consciousness, divorced from a knowledge of the truth, has ever led to the institution of corrupt forms of priesthood. The function itself is good and necessary, however corrupt may become the form and practice of it.

Effectual priesthood was the exclusive privilege of a chosen line, represented by Abel, Noah, Abraham, Israel, and the spiritual 'seed'; and the Scriptures which reveal and record this, also show most fully the need for it.

The idea of priesthood is progressive. In the *Pre-Mosaic age* if was *Family priesthood*, the head of each family being the priest. In the *Mosaic age* it was *State priesthood*. The office was the prerogative of one only of the twelve tribes of Israel, the tribe of Levi, and it was handed down from father to son, and this continued to the end of the Jewish dispensation.

Ordained priesthood in Israel did not begin until after the deliverance from Egypt, and it takes place with the Law, the Tabernacle, and the Offerings, which were the privileges of a redeemed people.

And now, in this *Christian age*, there is *Church priesthood*, every believer being a priest, and the whole Church 'a kingdom of priests' (1 Peter ii. 9; Rev. i. 6). A class of priests in the Christian Church is an anomaly and an anachronism.

Nor is there within the Church, as there was in Israel of old, any distinction in the priesthood, such as 'high priest', and 'priest'. There is only one High Priest, the Lord Himself, and in Him are fulfilled both the Aaronic and Melchisedecan priesthoods of intercession and benediction.

THE PRIESTS

CLOTHING, CONSECRATION, AND COVENANT
(Exod. xxviii., xxix.)

THE CLOTHING OF THE PRIESTS (xxviii.)

AARON (4-39)
  Garments for glory and for beauty (1-4)
  The materials of the garments (5)
  The Ephod and its Girdle (6-8)
  The stones, ouches, and chains (9-12)
  The Breastplate with the Urim and the Thummim (13-30)
  The Robe of the Ephod (31-35)
  The Golden Plate and Mitre (36-38)
  The Tunic and Girdle (39)
  For other details see ch. xxxix. 1-31.

AARON'S SONS (40-43)

THE CONSECRATION OF THE PRIESTS (xxix. 1-37)

  Requirements for sacrifice (1-3)
  The Ablutions (4)
  The Investiture of Aaron (5, 6)
  The Anointing of Aaron (7)
  The Investiture of the Priests (8, 9)
  The Consecration Offerings (10-34)
      Sin Offering (10-14)
      Burnt Offering (15-18)
      Peace Offering (19-28)
      Other details (29-34)
      Repetition of the Ceremonial (35-37)

THE COVENANT WITH THE PRIESTS (xxix. 38-46)

      The Daily Sacrifice (38-42)
      The Divine Promises (43-46)

(iii) THE REGULATION OF THE SERVICE (xxx, xxxi.)

Supplementary Instructions

These instructions are, for the most part, related to matters which have already been dealt with, and should be read in their proper settings.

The Altar of Incense (xxx. 1-10; setting, ch. xxv., after ver. 22).
The Atonement Money (xxx. 11-16; setting, ch. xxv., after ver. 3).
The Brazen Laver (xxx. 17-21; setting, ch. xxvii., after ver. 8).
The Anointing Oil (xxx. 22-33; setting, ch. xxix., after ver. 7).
The Holy Perfume (xxx. 34-38; setting, end of ch. xxvii.).
The Chosen Workmen (xxxi. 1-11).
The Sanctity of the Sabbath (xxxi. 12-18).

(2) THE GRIEVOUS PERVERSION OF ISRAEL (xxxii.-xxxiv.). See p. 167.

(*i*) The Great Transgression (xxxii. 1-6).
(*ii*) The Divine Displeasure (xxxii. 7-xxxiii.).
(*iii*) The Renewal of the Covenant (xxxiv.).

(3) THE ULTIMATE PERFORMANCE THROUGH ISRAEL (xxxv.-xl.)

These chapters reiterate the details to be followed in the construction of the Tabernacle, and, as we have said, (p. 168), there is a sevenfold repetition:

The Instructions Given (xxv.-xxvii; xxix. 42-xxxi. 11)
The Materials Needed (xxxv. 4-19)
The Materials Supplied (xxxv. 20-xxxvi. 7)
The Making of the Parts (xxxvi. 8-xxxviii. 31)
The Assembling of the Parts (xxxix. 32-43)
The Setting up of the Structure (xl. 1-11)
The Completion and Consecration of the Work (xl. 16-38)

Summarily, the last six chapters of this Book tell of the construction (xxxv.-xxxix. 31), the completion (xxxix. 32-xl. 33), and the consecration (xl. 34-38) of the Tabernacle. For other details see pp. 168-170.

(III) ISRAEL'S LIBERTY: THE WALK WITH GOD
CONDITIONED
(Book of Leviticus)

The Book of Leviticus does not advance the history of the Israelites, but it does increase greatly their knowledge of themselves as sinners in need of God's mercy; of God's requirements of them; and of the provision for their acceptable approach to Him.

Detailed exposition of this Book, profitable as that would be, does not fall within our present scheme, but we must see here what contribution it makes to the Unfolding Drama of Redemption.

Israel's liberty could be known and enjoyed only in fellowship with God, and Leviticus reveals the ground, the condition, and the product of this fellowship.

Spiritually this is one of the richest books in all the Bible, and to know it mentally and experimentally is a liberal education in divinity.

The *Tabernacle* is in this Book, not descriptively, but simply as a fact, the description having been given in *Exodus*.

The *Law* also is here, but to the Decalogue and Book of the Covenant of *Exodus*, many other laws are added, chiefly ceremonial, dietary, and seasonal (xi.—xxv.).

The *Priesthood* also is here. For the creation and description of this Office we must go to *Exodus*, but here other details are added, and the seriousness of disobedience is illustrated (viii.—x.).

The *Offerings* here receive a great development of statement (i.—vii.), and the reason for this should be obvious.

The Passover Sacrifice (Exod. xii.) represents Christ as the Lamb of God (1 Cor. v. 7, 8), and in the sacrifice of Himself on the Cross all the need of man is met for both life and life abundant (John x. 10). The Passover told of the virtue of Christ's atoning Sacrifice, but it did not, and of course could not then, unfold the doctrine of that Sacrifice. All that the *sinner* needs to know is what virtue the fact has; but the *saint* needs to know much more than this, indeed all the content and implications of the Passover. The *fact* of the atonement is in Exodus, and the *doctrine* of it is in Leviticus; just as the *fact* is in the Gospels, and the *doctrine* in the Epistles.

Leviticus is in two main divisions: the first (i.—x.) treating of *the way to God*; and the second (xi.—xxv.), of *the walk with God*. The first sets forth *privilege*; and the second, *practice*. The first tells of the *work of the Son for us*; and the second, of the *work of the Spirit in us*. The first is *judicial*; and the second is *experimental*. The first is *objective*; and the second is *subjective*. The first shows *what God is and does*; and the second, *what we should become and do*. The first reveals a *creed*; and the second, a line of *conduct*. The first tells of our *standing*; and the second, of our *state*.

In each of these divisions are two parts, and these are presented in a moral order. Firstly, *Oblation*; secondly, *Mediation*; thirdly, *Separation*; and fourthly, *Sanctification*; or, in other words, sacrifice, priesthood, purity, and holiness. The following Chart shows how each of these is developed.

CHART 37

THE BOOK OF LEVITICUS

Division I. Chapters i-x		Division II. Chapters xi-xxv	
PART 1. Chs. i-vii	PART 2. Chs. viii-x	PART 3. Chs. xi-xvi	PART 4. Chs. xvii-xxv
OBLATION	MEDIATION	SEPARATION	SANCTIFICATION
SACRIFICE	PRIESTHOOD	PURITY	HOLINESS
(i) The Revelation of the Offerings. (i. 1-vi. 7)	(i) Consecration of the Order (viii)	(i) The Requirement (ix-xv)	(i) The Requirement (xvii-xxiv)
(a) BURNT (i)			Holiness in our
(b) MEAL (ii)		(a) Law of Food (xi)	(a) Daily Meals (xvii)
(c) PEACE (iii)	(ii) Inauguration of the Office (ix)	(b) Law of Childbirth (xii)	(b) Social Conduct (xviii-xx)
(d) SIN (iv. 1-v. 13)		(c) Law of Leprosy xiii-xiv. (33-59)	(c) Priestly Relations (xxi, xxii)
(e) TRESPASS (v. 14-vi. 7)	(iii) Transgression of the Ordinance (x)	(d) Law of Purification (xiv. 1-32)	(d) Public Worship (xxiii)
		(e) Law of Issues (xv)	(e) Entire Life (xxiv)
(ii) The Ritual of the Offerings (vi. 8-vii)		(ii) The Provision (xvi)	(ii) The Provision (xxv)
(a) BURNT		Atonement	Jubilee
(b) MEAL		Behind	Before
(c) SIN		The Cross	The Coming
(d) TRESPASS		The Power	The Prospect
(e) PEACE		Concerning the Covenant (xxvi)	Concerning Vows (xxvii)

Though the ritual of this Book is typical, local, and temporary, its doctrinal value, which is historical, universal, and abiding, cannot be exaggerated.

The *Offerings* represent the doctrinal content of the Passover, and both they and it tell of Christ crucified, a propitiation for the sins of the world (1 John ii. 2).

The simple truth in Exodus xii is that all who are sheltered by the blood of the slain Lamb are delivered from judgment, and from bondage. The complex truth of Leviticus i—vii is that that slain Lamb meets all that is required by a righteous God, and all that is needed by redeemed man.

When the significance of the five Offerings is understood, it will be seen that they can be viewed in two orders: that of *revelation*, from God to man, which is the order in *Leviticus*— Burnt, Meal, Peace, Sin, and Trespass; and that of *experience*, from man to God, which is the reverse of the former—Trespass, Sin, Peace, Meal, and Burnt.

These divide into two, one, and two, and typify the efficacy and sufficiency of Christ's death for such a situation as this world presents.

The first two are *dedicatory*, and tell of the complete acceptance of Christ, Who was *perfect in death*, the Burnt Offering (i), and *perfect in life*, the Meal Offering (ii).

The third, the Peace Offering (iii) is *eucharistic*, and tells of peace with the Father, and with the saints.

The fourth and fifth are *expiatory*: the Sin Offering telling of iniquity (iv. 1—v. 13); and the Trespass Offering, of injury (v. 14—vi. 7).

Each of these Offerings has a Godward and a manward aspect; and they are all referred to frequently in the Scriptures.

Then, the doctrinal value of the *Sacred Seasons* is great, in the light of later references to them in the Scriptures of both Testaments. They are called 'the set feasts of the LORD' (xxiii. 2, R.V.), and there are nine of them.

The Weekly Sabbath (xxiii. 3). The Passover, and Feast of Unleavened Bread (xxiii. 4-8). The Sheaf of Firstfruits (xxiii. 9-14). The Feast of Pentecost (xxiii. 15-21). The

Feast of Trumpets (xxiii. 23-25). The Day of Atonement (xxiii. 26-32; xvi). The Feast of Tabernacles (xxiii. 33-36, 39-43). The Sabbatical Year (xxv. 1-7). The Year of Jubilee (xxv. 8-55).

In all this the Drama of Redemption is moving steadily towards its *dénouement* in the life, death, and resurrection of Jesus Christ. The third and last part of the *Encampment at Sinai* is,

(iii) THE PREPARATION FOR THE JOURNEY (Numbers i. 1-x. 10), Chart 34.

The Israelites are still at Mount Sinai (Exod. xix. 1, 2). Laws have been given to them; Priests have been ordained; Sacrifices have been prescribed; and the Tabernacle has been constructed. Very soon they are to strike camp, and resume the march towards the promised land.

The final preparations are recorded in Num. i. 1—x. 10; and here there are four sections telling of the: Organization of the Camp (i.—iv.); Legislation for the People (v., vi.); Provision for the Service (vii.—ix. 14); and Anticipation of the March (ix. 15—x. 10).

ORGANISATION OF THE CAMP (i.-iv.)

The detailed precision in all this is noteworthy. The some two million people in the wilderness were not a mob, but an orderly camp with its centre in the Tabernacle, and its glory in the Ark of the Covenant in the Holy of Holies.

We are not here concerned with all the details, but it will be well to get a clear view of the encampment (Chart 38).

LEGISLATION FOR THE PEOPLE (v-vi.)

This relates to two things: *Purification* (v.) relative to Leprosy (1-4), Trespass (5-10), and Jealousy (11-31); and *Devotion* (vi.), relative to the Law of the Nazarite (1-21), and the Blessing of Israel (22-27).

THE TABERNACLE ENCAMPMENT

Perhaps the following explanatory note will be of use. The Tabernacle consisted of the two compartments, the Holy Place, and The Holiest of All, both of which were covered. Around the Tabernacle was the

Court. Outside and around the Court were the Levitical families, three of them on each of the South, West, and North Sides. On the East Side were the places of Moses, Aaron, and the Priests.

Outside of all these were the people; three of the Twelve Tribes on each side, N.S.E.W., with the Tribe that had the standard in the centre on each side.

Under the names of the Levitical families on the S.W.N. sides are two numbers. The larger one is the number of the males from a month old. The smaller one is the number of those appointed to serve from 20-50 years of age. The total of the former is 22,300; and of the latter, 8,580.

Other totals. The men of war on the South side, 151,450; on the West side, 108,100; on the North side, 157,600; and on the East side, 186,400; the grand total being 603,550.

The letter C means cubits, and F means feet. By these figures it is easy to see the dimensions of the various parts of this Structure, each cubit being eighteen inches.

The Bible text does not describe the banners of the leading tribes, but Jewish tradition says that they were the living creatures of Ezekiel's vision (i. 10), namely the lion, the man, the ox, and the eagle. Jewish tradition says also that the colours of the standards were the same as of the precious stones in the high-priest's breastplate, blood-red, dark-red, hyacinth, and bright yellow.

CHART 38

THE CAMP OF ISRAEL AT SINAI

Numbers i.-iv.

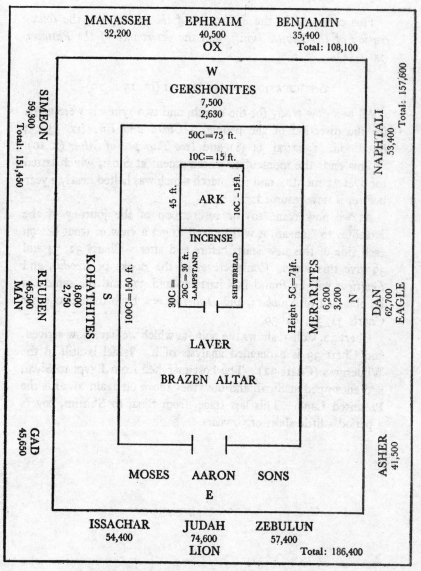

MANASSEH 32,200   EPHRAIM 40,500   BENJAMIN 35,400

OX   Total: 108,100

W

GERSHONITES 7,500 2,630

50C=75 ft.

10C=15 ft.

45 ft.

ARK

10C – 15 ft.

INCENSE

SHEWBREAD

30C = 30 ft.

20C = 30 ft.
LAMPSTAND

100C=150 ft.

S

KOHATHITES 8,600 2,750

SIMEON 59,300 Total: 151,450

REUBEN 46,500 MAN

GAD 45,650

Height: 5C=7½ft.

MERARITES 6,200 3,200

N

LAVER

BRAZEN ALTAR

NAPHTALI 53,400 Total: 157,600

DAN 62,700 EAGLE

ASHER 41,500

MOSES   AARON   SONS

E

ISSACHAR 54,400   JUDAH 74,600   ZEBULUN 57,400

LION   Total: 186,400

1. Of the Kohathites, Gershonites, and Merarites the larger figure is the number of the males from a month old. The smaller figure is the number of those appointed to serve, from 30 years old to 50 (cf. Num. iv. 3, 23 et al; viii. 24; 1 Chron. xxiii. 27). The totals respectively are 22,300; 8580.

2. The men of war, grand total = 603,550.

3. The cubit (C) = 18 inches.

PROVISION FOR THE SERVICE (vii.—ix. 14)

This consisted in the *dedication of the altar* (vii.), the *consecration of the Levites* (viii.), and the *observance of the Passover* (ix. 1-14).

ANTICIPATION OF THE MARCH (ix. 15-x. 10)

All was now ready for the march, and two symbols were given for the direction of the people, a *Cloud and Fire* (ix. 15-23; Exod. xiii. 21, 22; xl. 34-38), and *Two Trumpets of Silver* (x. 10).

This ends the momentous encampment at Sinai, which lasted for over 11 months, and the march which was halted nearly a year before, is now resumed.

As we now come to the resumption of the journey of the Israelites to Canaan, it will be well to get a view of what lies on each side of this new start, before and after. Charts 32, 34 and 39 give this view. Conspectuses of the Books of *Exodus*, and *Leviticus* will be found in Charts 29 and 37; and the same can be obtained of *Numbers*, and *Deuteronomy*, by bringing together Charts 32, 34, and 39.

Chart 32, Col. 3, shows the point at which we have now arrived, and Chart 39 is a detailed analysis of it. Israel is still in the Wilderness (Chart 32). The host marched from Egypt to Sinai, and encamped at Sinai, and now they move on again towards the Promised Land. This last stage, from Sinai to Shittim, covers a period a little short of 39 years.

CHART 39

FROM SINAI TO SHITTIM		Numbers x. 11-Joshua ii
THE STORY OF ISRAEL ON THE MARCH	REVIEW AND PREVIEW OF ISRAEL'S HISTORY	ISRAEL PLANNING TO ENTER THE PROMISED LAND
Numbers x. 11-xxxvi. 13	Book of Deuteronomy	Joshua i, ii
DISAFFECTION ON THE JOURNEY (x. 11-xiv)	ORATIONS OF MOSES IN THE LAND OF MOAB (i-xxx)	
Divine Direction in the Path. x. 11-36. Sinful Discontent with the Provision. xi, xii Fatal Disbelief of the Promises. xiii, xiv.	*First Oration.* i. 1-iv. 43. Story of the Wanderings.	Inward Preparation. i. Faith in Principle.
THE APOSTASY AT KADESH.	*Second Oration.* iv. 44-xxvi. Repetition of the Sinaitic Law. iv. 44-xi. 32. The Book of the Covenant. xii-xxvi.	
INTERRUPTION OF THE JOURNEY. xv-xix. Legislation. xv, xviii, xix. Revolt xvi, xvii.	*Third Oration.* xxvii, xxviii. God's Purposes concerning Israel.	Outward Preparation. ii. Faith in Practice.
CONTINUATION OF THE JOURNEY. xx-xxxvi.	*Fourth Oration.* xxix, xxx. A Covenant in the Land of Moab.	
TO THE PLAINS OF MOAB. xx-xxi. Death of Miriam, and of Aaron. The Smitten Rock. The Brazen Serpent.	CLOSING EVENTS OF MOSES' LIFE. xxxi-xxxiv. Four Solemn Charges. xxxi. 1-29. Song of Moses. xxxi. 30-xxxii. 47. Blessings on the Twelve Tribes. xxxii. 48-xxxiii. Moses' Death on Pisgah. xxxiv.	
IN THE PLAINS OF MOAB. xxii-xxxvi. THE PARABLES OF BALAAM. xxii-xxiv.		

3. FROM SINAI TO SHITTIM

Numbers x. 11—Joshua ii.

The record of this consists of the *Story of Israel on the March* (Num. x. 11-xxvi. 13); a *Review and Preview of Israel's History* (Deuteronomy); and *Israel Planning to Enter the Promised Land* (Josh. i., ii.); the whole representing a period of from thirty-eight to thirty-nine years (Chart 32).

The section, *The Story of Israel on the March* (Num. x. 11-xxxvi. 13) is in three parts (Chart 39, Col. 1).

> Disaffection on the Journey (x. 11-xiv.).
> Interruption of the Journey (xv.-xix.).
> Continuation of the Journey (xx.-xxxvi.).

In the first part of this Book the record is of *Array*; in the second, of *Advance*; in the third, of *Retreat*; and in the fourth, of *Return*.

(1) DISAFFECTION ON THE JOURNEY (x. 11-xiv.)

The first division, the Advance from Sinai to Kadesh, is of solemn importance (Num. x. 11-xiv.) It occupied from two to four months, though it was a journey of only *eleven days* (Deut. i. 2), and makes plain the incorrigibility of the people, notwithstanding all that God had done for them, and promised to them.

There are here three sections: Divine Direction in the Path (x. 11-36); Sinful Discontent with the Provision (xi. xii.); and Fatal Disbelief of the Promises (xiii. xiv.).   Chart 39.

(i) *Divine Direction in the Path* (x. 11-36).

The Divinely-appointed order of the march should not be overlooked (x. 11-28).   Chart 40 shows the movement from back to front.

CHART 40

THE ORDER OF THE MARCH

ASHER   DAN   NAPHTALI

MANASSEH   EPHRAIM   BENJAMIN

The Sacred Furniture

carried by the

KOHATHITES

GAD   REUBEN   SIMEON

The Tabernacle

carried by the

GERSHONITES & MERARITES

ISSACHAR   JUDAH   ZEBULUN

With these Tribes and Levites, in the above order, were the people who belonged to the respective Tribes, about two million, whose camps occupied about three square miles. The Gershonites and Merarites arrived at the next camping place in time to erect the Tabernacle before the Kohathites arrived with the Furniture; and so there was no confusion, and no delay.

In front of the Tabernacle were three Tribes; between the Tabernacle and the Furniture were three Tribes; and behind the Furniture were six Tribes, as before it there were six, carefully guarding things so precious. Right in the centre of the central bloc was the Ark of the Covenant. "And it came to pass, when the ark set forward, that Moses said: 'Rise up, LORD, and let

Thine enemies be scattered, and let them that hate Thee flee before Thee!' And when it rested, he said: 'Return, O LORD, unto the many thousands of Israel".' (35, 36).

(ii) *Sinful Discontent with the Provision* (xi., xii.)

Here are to be noted the *complaint because of the way*, at TABERAH (xi. 1-3); the *lusting because of the food*, at KIBROTH-HATTAAVAH (xi. 4-34); and the *sedition because of the leader* at HAZEROTH (xi. 35-xii.).

(iii) *Fatal Disbelief of the Promises* (xiii., xiv.).

What happened at KADESH constituted one of the greatest crises in the whole history of Israel. That place, the exact locality of which is not known, marked the terminus of their first journey, the beginning of their wanderings, and the starting-place of their final march; a place only second in importance to SINAI.

The tragic story is quickly told: the mission of the spies (xiii. 1-25); the report of the spies (xiii. 26-33); and the apostasy of Israel (xiv.). The importance of ch. xiv. is very great.

(2) INTERRUPTION OF THE JOURNEY (xv.—xix.)

Here are two legislative sections (xv. and xviii., xix.), and one narrative section (xvi., xvii.). The *legislative* section relates to the future, and is indicative of the purpose of God to bring the people into the land, and to fulfil His covenant with them, in spite of all their sin.

The *narrative* section is a fresh illustration of their sin; nothing less than a revolt against the Aaronic Priesthood. The costly challenge (xvi.), and God's convincing choice (xvii.) are here recorded.

During this period, Israel's history as a *theocracy* was in abeyance, and for thirty-eight years their advance was suspended; for those who rebelled at Kadesh had excommunicated themselves, and were to perish in the wilderness.

'While the general impression left upon us by these passages is dark indeed, it is hopeless to look for anything definite or precise as to the moral and religious condition of the people at this time. A similar obscurity hangs over their movements and proceedings. We have nothing to guide us except the probabilities of the case, and a list of stations which really tells us nothing. It is only reasonable to suppose that the marching orders issued at Sinai fell *ipso facto* into abeyance when the short, swift, decisive march for which they were designed came to an abrupt conclusion. We have no authority for supposing that the host held together during these years of wandering which had no aim but waste of time, and no end but death. The presumption is that they scattered themselves far and wide over the wilderness (itself of no great extent), just as present convenience dictated. Disease and death, and all those other incidents revived in full force which make the simultaneous march in close array of two million people an impossibility. No doubt the headquarters of the host and nation, Moses and Aaron, and the Levites generally, remained with the Ark, and formed, wherever they might be, the visible and representative centre of the national life and worship. It is of the movements of this permanent centre which contained in itself all that was really distinctive and abiding in Israel, that Moses speaks in ch. xxxiii., and elsewhere; and no doubt these movements were made in implicit obedience to the signals of God, given by the cloudy pillar (ch. ix. 21, 22).

'It is quite possible that while the Ark removed from time to time, some portion of the people remained stationary at Kadesh, until the "whole congregation" (ch. xx. 1) was reassembled there once more. If this were the case, the peculiar phraseology of Deut. i. 46, as compared with the following verse, may be satisfactorily explained'. (Pulpit Commentary, *Numbers*, pp. 180, 181).

(3) CONTINUATION OF THE JOURNEY (xx.—xxxvi.)

TO THE PLAINS OF MOAB (xx., xxi.)

The new generation of Israelites returned to *Kadesh*, where the old generation had been thirty-eight years before. There MIRIAM died. The people complained of lack of water; and MOSES, smiting the rock he was told to speak to, was sentenced to exclusion from the promised Land. From there the messengers of Moses requested of the Edomites that the Israelites might pass through their land, and were refused (xx. 1-21).

They journeyed to *Mt. Hor*, and there AARON died, and Canaan-ites were destroyed (xx. 22-xxi. 3). Then they *compassed the land of Edom*, and on the way the people complained of the journey, the lack of water, and nothing but manna; and a plague of fiery serpents was sent upon them. A brazen serpent was made, typical of the Lord Jesus (John iii. 14, 15), and all who beheld it lived (xxi. 4-9). Then they journeyed through *the coasts of the East*, defeating Sihon of Ammon, and Og of Bashan (xxi. 10-35).

IN THE PLAINS OF MOAB (xxii.-xxxvi.)

A narrative here of some length, and of great importance, relates to the prophecies of BALAAM (xxii.-xxiv.), in favour of the Israelites, and against the Moabites.

These utterances, without doubt, are Messianic in character, and were given to Balaam by divine inspiration. They are called *parables*, and there are seven of them (xxiii. 7, 18; xxiv. 3, 15; 20, 21, 23). The whole narrative is 'a sacred drama wherein characters and events of the highest interest are handled with consummate art.'

Through this man's evil counsel (xxxi. 16) the Israelites fell into idolatry and licentiousness, and in the plague which followed 24,000 people perished (xxv.).

A second census was taken (xxvi., cf. i.); and sundry laws were decreed (xxvii.-xxx.). The Midianites were defeated (xxxi.); and two tribes and a half, Reuben, Gad, and half Manas-seh, were promised inheritance east of the Jordan (xxxii.).

An itinerary is given of the journeyings of Israel from Rameses to the Jordan (xxxiii.). It would seem that the places named in verses 18-36 are those to which the people went during the period of their *wanderings*.

Final instructions are given in view of the conquest of Canaan (xxxiii. 50- xxxvi. 13), and here the Book of *Numbers* ends.

The geography of Israel's journeyings and wanderings falls into three distinct parts: *from Egypt to Sinai* (Exod. xii. 36—xix. 2); *from Sinai to Kadesh* (Num. x. 11—xiv.); and *from Kadesh to Shittim* (Num. xxi.; xxxiii.), Chart 32.

In the first of these stages the places named are Rameses,

Succoth, Etham, Pi-hahiroth, the Red Sea, Marah, Elim, Wilderness of Sin, Rephidim, and Sinai (see Chart 33).

In the second of these stages the places named are Taberah (xi. 3), Kibroth-Hattaavah (xi. 34), Hazeroth (xi. 35), the Wilderness of Paran (xii. 16), Kadesh (xiii. 26).

In the third of these stages many places are named in two lists (chs. xxi. and xxxiii.). These lists appear to have been drawn from different sources, and they appear at points to be in disagreement, but we do not know enough about this part of the story to say that they are in disagreement.

One thing at any rate is clear, namely that the people were at Kadesh *twice*, and that the second visit was separated from the first by about 38 years. On the second visit they went on to Mt. Hor, where Aaron died; and then, by a number of places to Shittim in the plains of Moab (xxxiii. 37-49), where Moses died, and where the wanderings ended.

The events of the 40 years from the exodus to the entrance into Canaan are many, and are of inestimable importance. What has already been written, and the charts, show this; but again attention must be called to the following:

The Oppression of the Israelites. The Passover. The Exodus. The Miracle at the Red Sea. The Encampment at Mount Sinai. The Giving of the Law, Moral, Civil, and Ceremonial. The Erection of the Tabernacle. The Order of Priests appointed. The Organization of the Camp for Worship, Work, and War. The Cloudy and Fiery Pillar. The Rebellions of the Israelites. The Crisis at Kadesh. The Wanderings in the Wilderness. The Prophecies of Balaam. The Orations of Moses. The Death of Aaron, and of Moses.

CHART 41

NUMBERINGS OF ISRAEL'S MEN OF WAR

First	B.C. 1490	Second	B.C. 1452
Exod. xxx. Num. i		Num. xxvi	
*46,500	REUBEN		43,730
*59,300	Simeon		22,200
*45,650	Gad		40,500
74,600	JUDAH		76,500
54,400	Issachar		64,300
57,400	Zebulun		60,500
*40,500	EPHRAIM		32,500
32,200	Manasseh		52,700
35,400	Benjamin		45,600
62,700	DAN		64,400
41,500	Asher		53,400
*53,400	Naphtali		45,400
603,550			601,730

It should be observed that during the 38 years of wandering in the Wilderness those capable of bearing arms decreased by 1,820 (see totals). Also, it should be noted that the numbers of five tribes (asterisks) decreased, and of seven, increased. The greatest decrease was in Simeon (37,100), and the greatest increase was in Manasseh (20,500).

CHART 42

INCREASES AND DECREASES OF THE MEN OF WAR

TRIBE	FIRST CENSUS	SECOND CENSUS	DECREASE	INCREASE
REUBEN	46,500	43,730	2,770	
SIMEON	59,300	22,200	37,100	
GAD	45,650	40,500	5,150	
JUDAH	74,600	76,500		1,900
ISSACHAR	54,400	64,300		9,900
ZEBULUN	57,400	60,500		3,100
EPHRAIM	40,500	32,500	8,000	
MANASSEH	32,200	52,700		20,500
BENJAMIN	35,400	45,600		10,200
DAN	62,700	64,400		1,700
ASHER	41,500	53,400		11,900
NAPHTALI	53,400	45,400	8,000	
	603,550	601,730	61,020	59,200

In the Book of *Deuteronomy* are four Orations which Moses delivered in the plains of Moab (i.—xxx.), and a review of the closing events of his life (xxxi.—xxxiv.), Charts 39, 43.

The first oration is the *Story of the Wanderings* (i.-iv. 43). The second is a *Repetition of the Sinaitic Law*, much elaborated (iv. 44-xi.); and a great many *Special Laws* (xii.-xxvi.). The third is a *Revelation of God's purposes concerning Israel* (xxvii-xxviii). The fourth is *A New Covenant* (xxix, xxx).

In the closing events are *Four Solemn Charges* (xxxi. 1-29); the *Prophetic Song of Moses* (xxxi. 30-xxxii. 47); and his *Blessings upon the Twelve Tribes* (xxxii. 48-xxxiii.).

Then, in an appendix, we read of the death of this great man Moses—leader, lawgiver, ruler, and prophet.

CHART 43

THE BOOK OF DEUTERONOMY

FIRST ORATION	SECOND ORATION	THIRD ORATION	FOURTH ORATION	CONCLUSION
i. 1–iv. 43	iv. 44–xxvi. 19	xxvii–xxviii	xxix–xxx	xxxi–xxxiv
REVIEW OF ISRAEL'S WANDERINGS AND GOD'S LONGSUFFERINGS	REPETITION AND EXPOSITION OF THE LAW	REVELATION OF THE DIVINE WILL FOR ISRAEL	RETROSPECT AND PROSPECT IN A NEW COVENANT	RECORD OF THE CLOSING EVENTS OF MOSES' LIFE
Preface i. 1–5	Preface iv. 44–49	Instructions for the Land xxvii	In the Wilderness xxix. 1–9	Four Solemn Charges xxxi. 1–29
From Horeb to Kadesh i. 6–46	PART A THE SINAITIC LAW v–xi	Consequences of Obedience and Disobedience xxviii	In the Land xxix. 10–21	The Prophetic Song of Moses xxxi. 30–xxxii. 47
From Kadesh to Heshbon and Bethpeor ii–iii	Recital of the Decalogue v. 1–21		In Captivity xxix. 22–29	The Final Events xxxii. 48–xxxiv. 12
Exhortations to Obedience iv. 1–40	Discourse on the Decalogue v. 22–xi. 32		In the Land Again xxx. 1–10	Psalms xc–xci
Historical Note iv. 41–43	PART B xii–xxvi SPECIAL LAWS		The Final Appeal xxx. 11–20	
	Concerning Religion xii. 1–xvi. 17			
	Concerning Government xvi. 18–xx			
	Concerning Private and Social Life xxi.–xxvi. 15			
	Conclusion xxvi. 16–19			

MOSES

The greatest character in history so far is ABRAHAM, who was born 2,008 years after the creation of Adam. The next very great character is MOSES, who was born 425 years after Abraham's birth. In round figures Abraham lived 2000 B.C.; and Moses, 1600 B.C.

Because of the importance in history of Moses, this is the place for a brief outline of his story.

(A) A REVIEW OF HIS TIME AND LIFE

FIRST PERIOD. Exod. ii. 1-15. Forty Years

MOSES THE PRINCE IN EGYPT

1 His Childhood and Youth (1-10)
   Birth and Concealment: 1-4
   Rescue and Adoption: 5-10
   Education and Illumination: Acts vii. 22-25

2 His Early Manhood (11-15a)
   Murder of an Egyptian: 11, 12
   Resentment of his Brethren: 13, 14a
   Fear and Flight from Egypt: 14b-15a

SECOND PERIOD. Exod. ii. 15-iv. 28. Forty Years

MOSES THE PASTOR IN MIDIAN

1 His Domestic and Pastoral Life (ii. 15b-22)
   Arrival at Midian: 15b.
   Defence of Reuel's Daughters: 16-20
   Marriage with Zipporah: 21, 22

2 His Divine Call and Commission (ii. 23-iv. 28)
   Continued Cruel Oppression of Israel: ii. 23-25
   Call of Moses to the Work of Deliverance: iii. 1-10
   Excuses of Moses and God's Replies: iii. 11-iv. 17
   Submission of Moses to God's Will: iv. 18-28

THIRD PERIOD. Exod. iv. 29-Deut. xxxiv. Forty Years

MOSES THE PROPHET IN THE WILDERNESS

1 From Egypt to Sinai (Exod. iv. 29-xix. 2)
   The Conflict with Pharaoh: iv. 29-xii. 36.
   The Journey to the Mount: xii. 37-xix. 2

13

2 The Sojourn at Sinai (Exod. xix. 3-Num. x. 10)
   The Constitution of the Nation: Exod. xix. 3-Lev. xxvii.
   The Disposition of the Camp: Num. i.-x. 10

3 From Sinai to Shittim (Num. x. 11-Deut. xxxiv.)
   From the Mount to Kadesh-Barnea: Num. x. 11-xix.
   From Kadesh to the Plains of Moab: Num. xx.-Deut.

(B) An Estimate of His Work and Worth

I. HIS MANIFOLD MISSION
   1 THE LEADER. Ps. lxxvii. 20
   2 THE LAWGIVER. John i. 17
   3 THE RULER. Acts vii. 35
   4 THE PROPHET. Hos. xii. 13

II. HIS GREAT EQUIPMENT
   1 Educational   2 Political
   3 Military   4 Disciplinary
             5 Religious

PSALMS XC.—XCI.

The title of Ps. xc. attributes it to Moses, and Ps. xci. is anonymous. Professor R. Moulton points out that these two Psalms are expansions of two lines in the final Blessing of Moses (Deut. xxxiii. 27):

'THE ETERNAL GOD IS THY DWELLING PLACE,
AND UNDERNEATH ARE THE EVERLASTING ARMS'

Psalm xc. develops the first of these lines; and Psalm. xci.. the second.

'*Lord, Thou hast been our dwelling place in all generations*' (xc. 1).

'*He will deliver thee*' (xci. 3, 11, 14, 15).

Nowhere else in the history of Israel are these two Psalms more appropriate than at this point, and it may safely be assumed that Moses wrote them at the end of his leadership of this people.

In Num. xxv. 1, we read that Israel went to *Shittim*, and in Josh. iii. 1, we read that they removed from there, and with this removal the Story of *Israel in the Wilderness* ends (Chart 32).

Throughout this forty years God is revealed as ruling over and over-ruling the chequered course of His people, and as advancing His redeeming purpose in spite of their sin. While His love for them is illustrated in their history, it is not actually named till Moses speaks of it in his second oration (vii. 7, 8), a passage which is the key to the whole history of Israel.

Now that we have come to the end of the Pentateuch, it may be well to see the connection between its several books, for this will show the progress of the redeeming purpose.

CHART 44

CONNECTION OF THE BOOKS GENESIS TO DEUTERONOMY	
1. GENESIS and EXODUS	
GENESIS	**EXODUS**
Divine purpose revealed.	Divine programme exhibited.
Human effort and failure.	Divine power and triumph.
Word of promise.	Work of fulfilment.
A people chosen.	A people called.
God's electing mercy.	God's electing motive and manner.
Revelation of nationality.	Realization of nationality.

2. EXODUS and LEVITICUS	
EXODUS	**LEVITICUS**
Brought nigh to God.	Kept nigh to God.
The fact of Atonement.	The doctrine of Atonement.
Begins with sinners.	Begins with saints.
God's approach to us.	Our approach to God.
Christ is the Saviour.	Christ is the Sanctifier.
Our guilt prominent.	Our defilement prominent.
Reveals God as Love.	Reveals God as Light.
Brought into union with God.	Brought into communion with God.
Offers us pardon.	Calls us to purity.
Delivered from Satan.	Dedicated to God.
The Passover.	The Offerings.
God speaks out of the Mount.	God speaks out of the Tabernacle.

| 3. LEVITICUS and NUMBERS ||
LEVITICUS	NUMBERS
The believer's worship. Treats of purity. Our spiritual position. Our condition within. Is ceremonial. The Sanctuary is prominent. Our privileges. Fellowship with God. The Priests. Access to God.	The believer's work. Treats of pilgrimage. Our spiritual progress. Our conduct without. Is historical. The Wilderness is prominent. Our responsibilities. Faithlessness to God. The Levites. Service for men.

| 4. GENESIS–NUMBERS and DEUTERONOMY ||
GENESIS to NUMBERS	DEUTERONOMY
The human story Outward facts. Experience of God's ways. Course of Israel's history. Divine performances.	The spiritual significance. Inward spirit. Revelation of God's love. Philosophy of Israel's history. Divine principles.

Anticipating a little we carry the connection on to Judges.

CHART 45

| CONNECTION OF THE BOOKS DEUTERONOMY TO JUDGES ||
| DEUTERONOMY and JOSHUA ||
DEUTERONOMY	JOSHUA
Prospect set before. Vision for faith. Israel's inheritance. The call to conflict. Faith in principle. The actual and the ideal. Possibility.	Experience entered into. Venture of faith. Israel's possession. The clash of arms. Faith in action. The ideal becomes actual. Realization.

JOSHUA and JUDGES	
JOSHUA	**JUDGES**
The Heavenlies	The Earthlies.
The Spirit.	The Flesh.
Song of joy.	Sound of sorrow.
Victory.	Defeat.
Progress.	Decline.
Faith.	Unbelief.
Freedom.	Bondage.

The period of the Judges ends at 1 Samuel vii.; and there, strictly speaking, the Theocracy ends (Chart 28).

In the Theocratic period, following *Israel in Egypt*, and *Israel in the Wilderness*, is *Israel in the Land* (Chart 46).

But only a part of Israel's history in the Land is in this period, about three-and-a-half centuries of it; and the other part falls in the period of the Monarchy, and extends to over five hundred years.

ACT I

SCENE 2

THE ISRAELITISH NATION

PERIOD A

THE AGE OF THE THEOCRACY

ISRAEL IN THE LAND
UNDER JOSHUA
UNDER JUDGES

ISRAEL IN THE LAND, UNDER JOSHUA

(The Book of Joshua)

CHART 46

ISRAEL IN THE LAND. Joshua–1 Samuel vii.

UNDER JOSHUA. Book of Joshua.			UNDER JUDGES. Judges, Ruth, 1 Samuel i-vii.	
ENTERING THE LAND.		i. 1-v. 12	FROM JOSHUA TO JUDGESHIPS.	i. 1-iii. 6
The Preparation.	i, ii		Retrospective	i. 1-ii. 10
The Passage	iii, iv		Prospective	ii. 11-iii. 6
The Purification.	v. 1-9			
The Passover	v. 10-12			
CONQUERING THE LAND.		v. 13-xii	THE PERIOD OF THE JUDGESHIPS,	iii. 7-1 Sam. vii.
The Central Campaign.		v. 13-ix. 27		
The Southern Campaign.		x.	The Succession of the Judges.	iii. 7-xvi.
The Northern Campaign		xi.	The Times of the Judges.	xvii-xxi, Ruth
The Entire Campaign.		xii.	The Last of the Judges.	1 Sam. i-vii.
POSSESSING THE LAND		xiii-xxiv.		
Distribution of the Land among the Tribes.		xiii-xxi.		
Dispute about an Altar on the Border.		xxii.		
Discourse and Death of Joshua.		xxiii, xxiv.		

See the author's *The Land and Life of Rest*

This Book covers a quarter of a century (B.C. 1451-1426), and it swiftly tells a fascinating story. This is in three distinct parts, and these mark both the progress of Israel's history, and of God's purpose.

First, we are told of

ISRAEL ENTERING THE LAND (i. 1-v. 12)

For this, *preparation* was made by exhortation and action; preparation inward (i), and outward (ii). The people were exhorted to obedience, and to courage; to obedience promoting courage, and to courage expressing obedience.

Spies were sent forward to view the situation and report. Over thirty-eight years before, twelve spies were sent, but only two advised advance, and now, only two are sent.

The next two chapters (iii., iv.) tell of the *passage* into the land, and the two stages were, *into* Jordan (iii.), and *over* Jordan (iv.). The priests, carrying the Ark, went first, and were followed by the people. The miracle which was performed on the Red Sea was performed on the Jordan also. The one passage meant separation from Egypt, and the other meant entrance into Canaan; the one told of redemption, and the other, of dedication.

The distance from Shittim to Gilgal was six or seven miles; and Micah bids the people *remember* what happened from the one place to the other (vi. 5, R.V.). The twelve stones set up in the Jordan indicated the end of their pilgrimage, and the twelve set up over Jordan indicated the beginning of their possession of the promised land.

But before the host could engage the enemy two things were necessary. The males who had been born in the wilderness had not been circumcised, and so Joshua's first act in the land was one of *purification* (v. 1-9). And the second was the observance of the *Passover* (v. 10-12), the first to be observed in the land; and probably the first since the multitude left Mount Sinai (Num. ix.). The one ceremony reminded them of their covenant relation to God, and the other, of their mighty deliverance from bondage.

At Gilgal the manna ceased, and the people ate of the old corn of the land (v. 11, 12).

The typical significance of all this is not entered into here, as it would involve too great a digression, but it should not be overlooked, for behind and beneath the historical facts are spiritual realities, as the New Testament plainly declares (John vi.; 1 Cor. v. 6-8; x. 1-12).

The next division of the Book tells of

ISRAEL CONQUERING THE LAND (v. 13-xii.)

Immediately previous to the march of the host upon Jericho, Joshua received a vision of the LORD as Captain (v. 13-15). It will be found that every manifestation of God under the Old Covenant was adapted to the conditions and requirements of the people at the time it was given. He appeared as Lawgiver to Moses the legislator, and as Captain of the host to Joshua the soldier; and to both He said, 'Remove your sandals, for you stand on holy ground.' The *rod* was the symbol of Moses' ministry, but the *sword*, of Joshua's.

The record which follows shows that the conquest of the land was carried out according to a well-defined plan. There were three distinct campaigns, central, southern, and northern, and in each there was a crisis action.

THE CENTRAL CAMPAIGN (vi.-ix.).

By attacking the towns in the centre, a wedge was driven between Israel's enemies in the South and North, making it impossible for them to unite.

The details relate to the capture of JERICHO (vi); the sin of Achan, accounting for Israel's defeat at AI (vii); the subsequent destruction of Ai (viii. 1-29); the writing and reading of the law in Mount Ebal (viii. 30-35); and the craftiness of the Gibeonites (ix.). These incidents were full of valuable instruction for the newcomers, and still are, for us. The secrets of victory at Jericho were faith, courage, and obedience; and the causes of defeat at Ai were covetousness, disobedience, and self-confidence. In ch. viii. are lessons on trying again, and the value of strategy in holy warfare. With ch. viii. 30-35 should be read Deut. xxvii., xxviii. The passage emphasizes the supremacy of God's will, and the only acceptable way of approach to Him. The soldier's first building was not a fortress, but an alter.

The Israelites were outwitted by the Gibeonites because they 'asked not counsel at the mouth of the LORD' (ix. 14). The cost of prayerlessness, and fidelity to promise (18-20), are two of the lessons here.

THE SOUTHERN CAMPAIGN (x.).

The army now turned southward, and made a circuit of the towns, mercilessly destroying as they went. The battle of BETHHORON was the outstanding feature of this campaign, as the taking of Jericho and Ai was of the central campaign. This engagement, says Dean Stanley, 'is one of the most important in the history of the world'; and it is in connection with it that the sun was made to stand still at the bidding of Joshua.

Throughout the narrative great emphasis is laid on the necessity that Israel's foes were to be 'utterly destroyed', that none were to be spared, a statement which is used of command or accomplishment no fewer than twelve times in this chapter.

At Bethhoron, Makkedah, Libnah, Lachish, Eglon, Hebron, and Debir the Israelites were victorious, 'from Kadesh-barnea even unto Gaza, and all the country of Goshen, even unto Gibeon' (41).

THE NORTHERN CAMPAIGN (xi.).

This was the third great stage of the conquest, and it was not easy (18). The focus of the struggle was the lake of MEROM where a number of kings and peoples were assembled against Israel, but Joshua attacked them before their preparations were complete and totally routed them (1-14). After this great victory Joshua turned upon and destroyed the Anakim of the north, and with this, brought to a conclusion his conquest of the land (15-23).

In ch. xii. is a review of the conquest, the precision, value, and lessons of which should be carefully marked. First is victory on the east of Jordan, Moses leading (2-6); then on the west of Jordan, Joshua leading (7, 8); and then the three stages of the western conquests; the central (9), the southern (10-17), and the northern (18-23), and the grand total (24). This summary was designed for the remembrance and gratitude of the Israelites in time to come.

CONQUERING THE LAND

The Central Campaign. Chs. vi.-ix.
    Crisis: JERICHO, AI.

The Southern Campaign. Ch. x.
    Crisis: BETHHORON.

The Northern Campaign. Ch. xi.
    Crisis: MEROM.

The Entire Campaign. Ch. xii.
    East. West.
    Central. Southern. Northern.

The final division of the Book treats of

ISRAEL POSSESSING THE LAND (xiii.—xxiv.)

There is here much more than a mere recital of place names. The distribution of the conquered land among the tribes was not determined by caprice, but by principles which all could appreciate, such as the capacity of the holder (xvii. 16; xix-9, 47); the rights of conquest (xvii) 14, 17, 18); providence (xiii. 6; xiv. 2); request (Num. xxxii. 1-5); privilege (xxi. 3); claim (xv. 19); and faithfulness (xiv. 13, 14).

It is also made clear that what might have been fully possessed was not, because of indolence (xviii. 3), or indifference (xvi. 10; xvii. 12), or inability (xv. 63; xvii. 12).

For the possessors provision was made in the Cities of Refuge for sin unwittingly committed; three on the east of Jordan, Bezer, Ramoth, and Golan; and three on the west of the River, Kedesh, Shechem, and Hebron.

See the author's *The Land and Life of Rest*

THE TRIBAL ALLOTMENTS

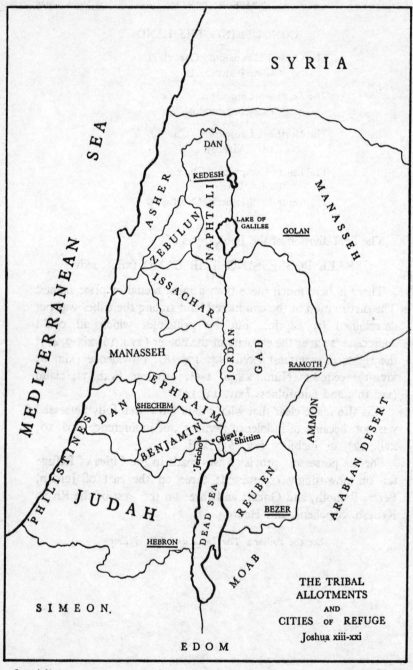

SYRIA

SEA

DAN

KEDESH

MANASSEH

ASHER

ZEBULUN

NAPHTALI

LAKE OF
GALILEE

GOLAN

ISSACHAR

MEDITERRANEAN

JORDAN

GAD

MANASSEH

RAMOTH

EPHRAIM

SHECHEM

BENJAMIN

Gilgal • Shittim

Jericho

AMMON

DAN

PHILISTINES

JUDAH

DEAD SEA

REUBEN

ARABIAN DESERT

BEZER

HEBRON

SIMEON.

MOAB

THE TRIBAL
ALLOTMENTS
AND
CITIES OF REFUGE
Joshua xiii-xxi

EDOM

W.G.S.

MAP 5

ISRAEL IN THE LAND, UNDER JUDGES
(Judges—Ruth—1 Samuel i.-vii.)

The age of the Theocracy lasted for over 600 years; from the going down of the patriarchal family into Egypt (Gen. xlvi. 5-7) to the election of Saul as King (1 Sam. viii.). This age is in three well-defined periods as follows (Charts 27, 28):

ISRAEL IN EGYPT: 215 years: Gen. xlvi.—Exod. xii. 36.
      B.C. 1706-1491.

ISRAEL IN THE WILDERNESS: 40 years. Exod. xii. 37-Josh. ii.
      B.C. 1491-1451.

ISRAEL IN THE LAND: 356 years: Josh. iii.—1 Sam. vii.
      B.C. 1451-1095.

Under Joshua: 25 years: Josh. iii.—Jud. iii. 6.
      B.C. 1451-1426.

Under Judges: 330 years: Jud. iii. 7—1 Sam. vii.
      B.C. 1426-1095.

Some chronologers think that certain of the Judgeships over-lapped, and so they considerably reduce this period; but it is interesting to note that the time-references in the Book of Judges and Paul's reference in Acts xiii. 20 agree. The figures are:—

Years of Servitude		
8+18+20+7+18+40	=	111
(iii. 8, 14; iv. 9; vi. 1; x. 8; xiii. 1)		
ABIMELECH'S USURPATION (ix. 22)		3
Years of Rest		
40+80+40+40+23+22+6+7+10+8+		Total
40+20	= 336	450 Years
(iii. 11, 30; v. 31; viii. 28; x. 2, 3; xii. 7, 8, 11, 14; 1 Sam. iv. 18; vii. 2)		

It should, however, be pointed out that there is another rendering of Acts xiii. 19, 20, which makes the 450 years refer to the period previous to the Judges (see R.V.), so that the chronology of JUDGES is still an open question.

The period of the Judges was one of unsettled and uncertain rule between the leaderships of Moses and Joshua, on the one hand, and the beginning of the Monarchy by the appointment of Saul as king, on the other hand.   The record of this period is compressed into thirty-two chapters of our Bible (Judg. i.— I Sam. vii.) in a succession of romantic incidents.   The nation had no king, and no succession of prophets; neither had it any fixed capital, sanctuary, or government.   All was occasional, irregular, and uncertain, religious and moral conditions being in a state of fluidity.   The two outstanding features of this period are the sinful incorrigibility of the people, and the persistent mercifulness of the LORD.

For a general survey of the whole period Charts 46 and 47 should be carefully studied.

Before the *Succession of the Judges*, which is the major part of the story, is a *Prelude*, which looks back to the times of Joshua, and on to the history which follows; and after the story of *the Succession* three incidents are recorded which reflect *the Times* of the whole period.   The first incident (xvii.-xviii.) tells of prevailing *infidelity*; the second, of prevailing *immorality* (xix-xxi); and the third, of *piety and purity* in some in spite of prevailing conditions (*Ruth*).

These incidents break the sequence of the *Succession of Judges*, by being placed between the Judgeship of Samson, and those of Eli and Samuel.   This arrangement of the story is neither accidental nor artificial, for it is evident that the last two Judgeships differed from all those which preceded them, each being linked with another office; Eli's, with that of *priest*, and Samuel's, with that of *prophet* (I Sam. i. 9; Acts xiii. 20); and in this brief record (I Sam. i.-vii.) we discern the *Transition* from one order of things to another; from the *Theocracy* to the *Monarchy*.

PERIOD OF THE JUDGES
ISRAEL'S ENEMIES

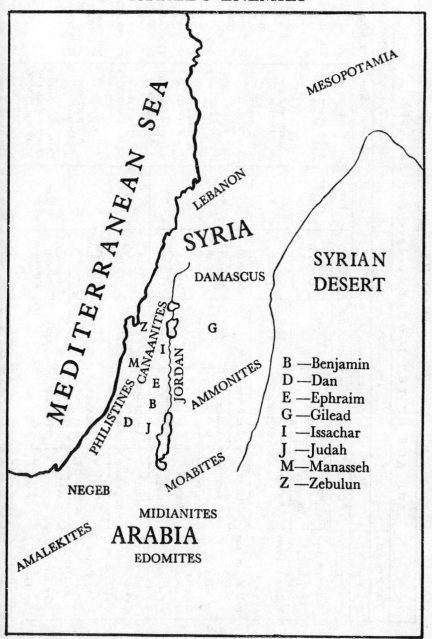

MESOPOTAMIA

MEDITERRANEAN SEA

LEBANON

SYRIA

DAMASCUS

SYRIAN DESERT

G

Z

CANAANITES

I

M

JORDAN

E

B

PHILISTINES

D

J

AMMONITES

B —Benjamin
D —Dan
E —Ephraim
G —Gilead
I —Issachar
J —Judah
M—Manasseh
Z —Zebulun

NEGEB

MOABITES

MIDIANITES

ARABIA

AMALEKITES

EDOMITES

CHART 47

THE AGE OF THE JUDGES. Judges i — 1 Samuel vii.

THE PRELUDE (i. 1-iii. 6)	THE SUCCESSION (iii. 7-xvi. 31)					THE TIMES (xvii-xxi. Ruth)	THE TRANSITION (1 Samuel i-vii)
	CYCLE	ENEMY	SERVITUDE	JUDGE	REST		
I RETROSPECTIVE i. 1-ii. 10	FIRST iii. 7-11	Mesopotamia	Years 8	OTHNIEL	Years 40	**1** A STORY OF APOSTASY	**I** The Judgeship of ELI
Failure of Israel i. 1-36	SECOND iii. 12-30	Moabites	18	EHUD	80	Micah and the Danites xvii-xviii INFIDELITY	i. 1-iv. 22 — 40 Years
Rebuke of the Angel ii. 1-5	THIRD iii. 31-v. 31	Philistines / Canaanites	20	SHAMGAR / DEBORAH BARAK	40		Philistine Defeat of Israel; and Capture of the Ark
Days of Joshua Recalled ii. 6-10	FOURTH vi. 1-viii. 32	Midianites	7	GIDEON	40	**2** A STORY OF REVENGE	**2** The Judgeship of SAMUEL v-vii
2 PROSPECTIVE ii. 11-iii. 6	FIFTH viii. 33-x. 5	Usurpation of ABIMELECH	Usurpation 3	TOLA JAIR	45	A Levite and the Benjamites xix-xxi IMMORALITY	20 years
The Period ii. 11-23	SIXTH x. 6-xii. 15	Ammonites	18	JEPHTHAH IBZAN, ELON ABDON	31	**3** A STORY OF DEVOTION	Religious Revival in Israel, and defeat of the Philistines
The Enemies iii. 1-6	SEVENTH xiii-xvi	Philistines	40	SAMSON (during servitude)	(20)	Ruth the Moabitess. Ruth i-iv PIETY and PURITY	

THE PRELUDE TO THE JUDGES

(Judges i. 1—iii. 6)

The purpose of this Prelude is to prepare the ground for the subsequent narrative, and it indicates that, in all likelihood, the narrative existed before the Prelude was written.

It is in two distinct parts, the one being *retrospective* (i. 1-ii. 10), and the other, *prospective* (ii. 11-iii. 6). The one looks back, and the other looks forward; the one is reflective, and the other is anticipative; the one points to past failure, and the other, to future failure.

In *Unfolding the Drama of Redemption* it had to be shown that God is sovereign, and that sin is idolatry. This Book, more than any other in the Bible, presents these two facts together and in relation to one another. Israel had been called of God to be a separate people. They were commanded not to enter into league or covenant with other peoples; not to intermarry with them, and to abominate their gods (Deut. vii. 1-11; xii. 1-3); and they were warned of the consequences of disobedience (Deut. xxvii. 15). This Book of Judges is a detailed commentary on these passages in Deuteronomy.

The first part of the Prelude (i. 1-ii. 10) shows that Israel failed to separate themselves from the heathen; and the second part (ii. 11-iii. 6), shows that the consequence of this was idolatry, which brought upon them the wrath of God.

RETROSPECTIVE (i. 1-ii. 10).   Sins of Omission.

The Failure of Israel (i. 1-36). The Rebuke of the Angel (ii. 1-5). The Days of Joshua Recalled (ii. 6-10). Chart 47.

So evident is it that this part of the Prelude belongs to the time of Joshua that the opening statement 'after the death of Joshua it came to pass', must be regarded as referring to the whole Book, or, it may be, the text is corrupt, and *Joshua* is put instead of *Moses*.

Judges	Joshua	Judges	Joshua
i. 10–15	xiv. 6–15; xv. 13–19	i. 27–36	xvi. 10; xvii. 11–13
i. 19	xvii. 16	i. 29	xvi. 10
i. 20a	xiv. 9	i. 36	xv. 3
i. 20b	xv. 14	ii. 3	xxiii. 13
i. 21	xv. 63	ii. 6–10	xxiv. 28–31

Judah came nearer to doing God's will than any other of the tribes (i. 1-20); and the failure of Benjamin, of Manasseh, of Ephraim, of Zebulun, of Asher, and of Naphtali, is emphasised in the condemnatory declarations that they *did not drive out* their enemies, but allowed them to *dwell among them*, albeit as *tributaries* (i. 21-36).

PROSPECTIVE (ii. 11-iii. 6).   Sins of Commission.

This part of the Prelude supplies the key to the seven cycles of narrative which follow.

The outline may be summarized in four words, *rebellion, retribution, repentance*, and *rest*; or *sin, servitude, supplication*, and *salvation*.   In the story these words represent the phrases, 'the children of Israel did evil in the sight of the LORD'; 'the anger of the LORD was hot against Israel, and He delivered them into the hands of spoilers that spoiled them, and He sold them into the hands of their enemeies round about'; 'Israel cried unto the LORD'; and 'the LORD raised up judges' (ii. 11-23).   These phrases or their equivalents, occur seven times (iii. 7-11; iii. 12-30; iii. 31-v. 31; vi. 1-viii. 32; viii. 33-x. 5; x. 6-xii. 15; xiii.-xvi).

THE SUCCESSION OF THE JUDGES
(Judges iii. 7—xvi. 31)

Here, as we have said (p. 210, Chart 47), are seven cycles of narrative, each constructed on the frame indicated—*sin, servitude, supplication, salvation*.   These are amazingly graphic accounts, which, no doubt, are contemporary with the events narrated. It is not unlikely that the tribes kept records of their fortunes, and the compiler of the Book seems to have brought some of these together within the frame indicated.

Many questions which one could ask about these records may have to remain unanswered, but certain features which are clear should be observed.

1. In every case, in the main division of the Book, the trouble was due to *idolatry*. The emphasis on this fact makes it clear that the message of this Book is, 'Keep yourselves from idols'.

For the references to idolatry see ii. 2, 3, 11, 13, 17, 19; iii. 6, 7; vi. 10; viii. 27, 33; x. 6, 10, 13, 14, 16; xvii. 3, 4, 5; xviii. 14, 17, 18, 20, 27, 30, 31; xxi. 25. The idolatry of the Israelites varies according to the religion of the people whose gods they worshipped, but in every case it was a denial of the Divine sovereignty, of their national calling, and of all their covenant obligations.

2. Attention should be given to the identity of Israel's enemies, and to the quarters from which they arose. The enemies were: Mesopotamians, Moabites, Amalekites, Canaanites, Midianites, Ammonites, and Philistines, seven in number. Chart 47.

The 'land of Israel' (1 Sam. xiii. 19) reached from Mt. Hermon in the North to Kadesh-barnea in the South, and from the Mediterranean to the Jordan, and included the territory on the east of Jordan occupied by Reuben, Gad, and half Manasseh.

In relation to all this territory the *Mesopotamians* were in the far North East, beyond Syria. The *Moabites* and *Ammonites* were on the East of Jordan. The *Canaanites* were in the North West of 'the land'. The *Philistines* were due West, on the Mediterranean seaboard. The *Amalekites* were in the peninsula of Sinai; and the *Midianites* occupied Arabia. From this it will be seen that the Israelites were attacked from every quarter (see Map 6).

3. It should be observed also that the deliverers or judges came from at least eight of the tribes: from *Judah*, Othniel, Ibzan, and probably Deborah; from *Benjamin*, Ehud; from *Naphtali*, Barak; from *Manasseh*, Gideon; from *Issachar*, Tola; from *Zebulun*, Elon; from *Ephraim*, Abdon; from *Dan*, Samson; from *Levi*, Eli and Samuel; and Jephthah and Jair were Gileadites (see Map 6 and Chart 47).

4. Of the thirteen Judges—Shamgar, Barak, and Abimelech were not such—we know almost nothing of five of them; *Tola*, *Jair*, *Ibzan*, *Elon*, and *Abdon*. Jair and his family were evidently of considerable means and influence (x. 3-5); and the references to Ibzan, and Abdon, relate to their families (xii. 8-10, 13-15).

This leaves eight Judges, two of whom, *Othniel* and *Ehud*, are of importance, but for very different reasons, and six, *Deborah*, *Gideon*, *Jephthah*, *Samson*, *Eli*, and *Samuel*, who are of great historical and religious interest and importance.

OTHNIEL (iii. 7-11), was the nephew and son-in-law of Caleb (i. 12-15; Josh. xv. 16-19). 'The Spirit of the LORD came upon him', and by the LORD (10) he delivered Israel from eight years of Mesopotamian servitude.

EHUD (iii. 12-30), delivered Israel from eighteen years of Moabite servitude, but it does not say that he did so by 'the Spirit of the LORD'. There is no word of commendation of his horrible stratagem. When he said to Eglon that he had 'a message from God' for him, he lied.

SHAMGAR (iii. 31; v. 6; x. 11). Like Barak, this man was a soldier, but not a judge. From ch. v. 6 it is clear that he was contemporary with Deborah and Barak. He checked the first onslaught of the Philistines of which we read in this period, and the way in which he did so shows that he had ingenuity and courage.

DEBORAH (iv., v.). After having been 'mightily oppressed' by the Canaanites for twenty years, Israel 'cried unto the LORD', and He raised up Barak to deliver them, and Deborah to judge them. Strangely enough Barak is named in Heb. xi. 32 among the heroes of faith, but not Deborah, though in Judges she is seen to be the greater character (iv. 8, 9). She was the only woman Judge, was a wife, a prophetess, a poet, and a person of great public spirit and courage. Hers is the third great Song so far in the Bible, the first being that of Moses at the Red Sea (Exod. xv.), and the second, his farewell Song in Deut. xxxii.

The tragic passage in this story is that which relates how Jael, disregarding all laws of hospitality and humanity, murdered

Sisera the captain of Jabin's army.   Deborah praises this ghastly
deed in the words:

> Most blessed of women may Jael be,
> The wife of Heber the Kenite;
> Of bedouin women most blessed!
>
> Water he asked; milk she gave;
> In a lordly bowl she brought him curds.
>
> She put her hand to the tent-pin,
> And her right hand to the workman's mallet;
> And she struck down Sisera,
> She crushed his head;
> She shattered and smashed his temple.
>
> At her feet he sank, he fell, he lay prone;
> At her feet he sank, he fell;
> Where he sank, there he fell slain.
>
> (Translation by Dr. T. J. Meek)

This terrible act added nothing to the overthrow of the Canaanites, which already had been accomplished by the LORD in the
army of Israel (iv. 14-16; v. 19-22); but perhaps some mitigation
of the deed may be found in the understanding that a man
incurred death who entered the tent of an Arab woman.

GIDEON (vi. 1-viii. 28).   This man is the most heroic of all the
persons brought before us in the Book of Judges.   He is the only
one of them to whom the *Angel of the LORD* appeared.   In the
Old Testament there are over eighty references to the Angel
Who, undoubtedly, is the Second Person of the Holy Trinity,
and of these, twenty are in the *Judges*.   Of these twenty, seven are
connected with Gideon; ten are connected with Manoah and his
wife, and of the other three, two are in the Prelude (ii. 1, 4)
and one is in Deborah's Song (v. 23).

That this Angel directly and visibly appeared to Gideon to
call and commission him, places him uniquely among the Judges.

In addition to this, he is one of four only on whom the Spirit
came (vi. 34), the others being Othniel, Jephthah, and Samson.

Commissioned to deliver Israel from their seven years oppression by the Midianites, Gideon's story may be divided into five
parts: the Call; the Preparation; the Rout; the Aftermath;
and the Sequel.

THE CALL (vi. 1-24)

The Midianites were wild nomads who raided their neighbours to steal their crops and cattle (1-6). Greatly impoverished, the Israelites cried to the LORD, Who sent to them an unnamed prophet to rebuke them for their past rebellion (7-10). While Gideon threshed wheat for his family in Ophrah, a little town on the south-western border of Manasseh, the Angel of the LORD called him to be the deliverer of his people, and authenticated the call by consuming by fire a 'present' which Gideon had brought to Him; and at the place he built an altar, and called it JEHOVAH-SHALOM, 'the LORD is peace' (11-24).

> 'Once for the least of children of Manasses
>   God had a message and a deed to do,
> Wherefore the welcome that all speech surpasses
>   Called him and hailed him greater than he knew;
> Asked him no more, but followed him and found him,
>   Filled him with valour, slung him with a sword,
> Bade him go on until the tribes around him
>   Mingled his name with naming of the Lord.'

(F. W. H. Myers)

THE PREPARATION (vi. 25-vii. 15)

Judgment must begin at the house of God (1 Pet. iv. 17), and so, with the help of ten men, Gideon by night destroyed the altar and grove of Baal at Ophrah, and he was given the name *Jerubbaal*, 'let Baal plead' (vi. 25-32).

As the opposing hosts gathered, Gideon wanted further assurance that he was called to this great task, and thus was given to him the sign of the dew on the fleece, and on the ground (vi. 33-40). Gideon was then told that his army of 32,000 was too large, and so, by two tests, he got rid of 31,700; 22,000 of whom *dreaded*, and 9,700 of whom *delayed*; and he was left with 300 men who *dared* (vii. 1-8).

A dream which Gideon heard a Midianite relate one night on the margin of the camp completed his preparation for the great venture (vii. 9-15).

THE ROUT (vii. 15-22)

What happened is briefly and graphically told. The 300 men were divided into three companies; each was given a trumpet, and an empty water pitcher, in which was hidden a lighted torch. These came down on three sides of the enemy camp in the middle of the night, and, at a given signal, they blew the trumpets, smashed the pitchers, revealing the torch lights, and shouted, as Jewish warriors could, 'the Sword of the LORD, and of Gideon'. This immediately caused panic, and the Midianites fled, but to be met by the swords of Gideon's warriors (vii. 15-22).

> Who ordered Gideon forth
>   To storm the invader's camp,
> With arms of little worth,
>   A pitcher and a lamp?
> The trumpets made his coming known,
>   And all the host was overthrown.

Before Gideon, it was over 200 years since the Midianites attacked Israel (Num. xxxi.), and after him, they are never mentioned again in Scripture as enemies.

THE AFTERMATH (vii. 23-viii. 21)

The rout was followed up by the slaughter of the kings and princes of Midian, and the punishment of the men of Succoth and of Penuel, who had refused to help Gideon and his men in the hour of their need.

THE SEQUEL (viii. 22-32)

Here are two incidents which stand in sharp contrast to one another. The first is to Gideon's credit, and the second is not.

Kingship Declined (22, 23)

An attempt was now made to depart from the Theocracy and establish a Monarchy—which was actually done about 200 years later—but Gideon resolutely declined, and firmly upheld the Theocracy in the words, 'the LORD shall rule over you'. This is the highest level to which he rose; but, alas, he at once fell from it to the common level of his time.

Idolatry Promoted (24-27)

The thought of idolatry was not in Gideon's mind when he collected the spoil of gold ornaments, and with them made an ephod to keep for use in Ophrah, but idolatry was the actual result, for 'all Israel went thither a whoring after it: which thing became a snare unto Gideon, and to his house'. This is a sad end to an outstanding career, and solemnly warns us of the peril of success, and of the folly of employing wrong means to fulfil right intentions.

If Gideon's story had ended with his victory over the Midianites he would still be regarded as one of the greatest of the men of old, but

> 'The grey-hair'd saint may fail at last,
> The surest guide a wanderer prove':

and as the poet continues:

> 'I have seen
> (The) bark, that all the way across the sea
> Ran straight and speedy, perish at the last,
> E'en in the haven's mouth'.

He who had so valiantly destroyed idolatry in Ophrah left his people at last very much as he had found them (vi. 25-27; viii. 27).

Of course it was not Gideon's *intention* to encourage idolatry, but it *was* the consequence of his action; and we are all responsible not only for the courses we pursue, but largely for the consequences which follow our courses.

When Gideon was introduced he was poor and humble (vi. 15), and when he passed from the scene he was rich and confident. He had many wives, a concubine, and seventy-one sons, besides daughters, no doubt, and he was buried 'in a good old age' in the family sepulchre.

ABIMELECH (viii. 29-ix. 57). There is now a break of three years in the succession of the Judges (ix. 22). What Gideon refused, his bastard son secured (viii. 31), when he got the men of Shechem to make him king (ix. 6). This wicked man slew sixty nine of Gideon's legitimate sons, and only one, Jotham, escaped (ix. 5).

From the summit of Gerizim, the Mount of the Blessings, Jotham utters the first of the only two fables found in the Bible (cf. 2 Kings xiv. 9). In form and substance it is of great significance (ix. 8-15). In Indian and Greek fables the *dramatis personae* are *animals*, but in these two Hebrew fables they are *trees*.

Treedom wanted a king, and invited in succession the *olive*, the *fig*, and the *vine*, which all refused; but the *bramble* accepted. Abimelech, of course, was the bramble, and the curse of Jotham on him and on those who made him king (ix. 20) was fulfilled. During. this unlawful and lamentable reign Baal was again worshipped (viii. 33). For the second time a *woman* brought deliverance, but all we know about her is that she made one successful shot at Abimelech's head; and thus died 'the first tyrant of the Jewish nation'. So from this story we learn that even in this life ingratitude, treachery, and cruelty are visited with retributive justice.

TOLA, JAIR (x. 1-5). These two men judged Israel, one for 23 years, and the other for 22 years after the death of Abimelech. They are types of the undistinguished and unsung people who do their duty, die, and are buried. They who make the most noise in the world are not necessarily the greatest people. There can be fame without notoriety; the fame, not of exploits, but of honesty.

JEPHTHAH (x. 6-xii. 7). Ch. x. 16-18 is a historical summary, and the story of Jephthah in xi.-xii. 7 follows on naturally from x. 17, 18, although it appears to be from a different source (cf. xi. 4, 5 with x. 17, 18).

Jephthah himself, of irregular birth, was a wild lawless freebooter living in the land of Tob. When the Ammonites came against Israel in the east of Jordan the Elders of Gilead sent and invited Jephthah to become their captain, and generously he agreed, but with a bargain. His remonstrance with the King of the Ammonites is noteworthy (xi. 12-28), and indicates that he had caution as well as courage.

At this point two things demand attention, the advent of the Spirit upon him, and his vow (29-31), but these are entirely

unrelated. The reference to Jephthah in Heb. xi. 32 relates to
the former, but not to the latter.

The view has been, and still is, held by some that Jephthah
did not kill his daughter, but that she was appointed to perpetual
virginity. This question might be resolved if we knew exactly
what 'lament' means in ch. xi. 40. The word really signifies
'to talk with', and in v. 11, is translated 'rehearse'. This favours
the view that the daughter did not die as vowed; but the sense
of the record in ch. xi. 31, 39 looks the other way, and for the
making of such a vow, and the carrying of it out, there can be no
justification whatever. God was no party to it, and therefore
Jephthah need not have been.

What emerges glory-crowned from this horrible thing is
the heroism of the daughter.

> 'Since our country, our God,—oh, my sire!
> Demand that thy daughter expire;
> Since thy triumph was brought by thy vow—
> Strike the bosom that's bared for thee now!
>
> When this blood of thy giving hath gush'd,
> When the voice that thou lovest is hush'd,
> Let my memory still be thy pride,
> And forget not I smiled as I died'.
>
> (Byron)

The proud, ambitious, and quarrelsome Ephraimites (cf. xii.
1-6, and viii. 1-3) paid dearly for their insult to the Gileadites
(xii. 4). And after this Israel had rest for thirty-one years.

IBZAN, ELON, ABDON (xii. 8-15). These three appear to
have been only civil, not military, Judges, and all we know of
them relates to what is social and domestic (9, 14).

SAMSON (xiii.-xvi.). The story of Samson is given more space
than that of any other Judge, not because he was the best of them,
but because of certain circumstances and features of special
importance, of which the following should be noted.

That the period of subjection is twice as long as the next
longest in the whole story of the Judges. In Deborah's
time the Canaanites oppressed Israel for *twenty* years, but
the Philistine oppression lasted for *forty* years.

That whereas Othniel, Ehud, Deborah and Barak, Gideon, and Jephthah delivered Israel from the oppression of their enemies, Samson did not deliver them from that of the Philistines. The twenty years of his Judgeship was *during* and not *after* the Philistine oppression.

That whereas other Judges were raised up in times of crisis to deliver Israel from their enemies, Samson was dedicated to his task from before his birth (xiii. 5).

That of the seven references in the Book of the Judges to 'the Spirit of the LORD', four occur in connection with Samson (xiii. 25; xiv. 6, 19; and by implication in xvi. 20).

That of the twenty-three references in this Book to 'the Angel of the LORD', or 'of God', thirteen are found in ch. xiii. in connection with the birth of Samson. Undoubtedly the Angel is the Second Person of the Holy Trinity, and so these appearances are Christophanies. Seven of the remaining references are in the story of Gideon.

That of all the Judges Samson was the only Nazarite.

That Samson alone of all the Judges entered into fateful and fatal relations with the enemy.

That of Samson only is it related that he was forsaken of the LORD (xvi. 20).

That Samson only of all the Judges died in captivity, and left Israel in servitude to the Philistines.

That Samson's history connects directly with the Judgeship of Eli, and the story of Samuel.

The story of Samson is neither mythical nor mystical, it is neither romance nor allegory, but very sad history; a story of solemn import to both careless and thoughtful people. It is made up of fourteen incidents which reveal the man as largely an adventurer and a joker. His glorious start had a gruesome end, and between are the steps from the one to the other.

The incidents referred to are: marrying a Philistine woman; killing a lion with his hands; propounding a riddle; slaying thirty Philistines, and taking their clothes to fulfil a promise; catching 300 foxes, tying them together in pairs tail to tail, placing a firebrand in the tails of each pair, setting the firebrands on fire, and driving the foxes into the standing corn; smiting the Philistines with a great slaughter; snapping the cords wherewith his arms had been bound; killing a thousand Philistines with the jawbone of an ass; carrying away at midnight the gates of Gaza; breaking seven green catgut strips with which he had been bound; severing ropes by which he had been bound; carrying away the shuttle and warp in which, as woof, his hair had been woven; allowing his head to be shaven, and so breaking the Nazarite vow; and, finally, bringing down in ruins the amphitheatre in which thousands of Philistines were gathered to worship Dagon their god, killing them all, and himself also.

We do not read of Samson praying until at the end he asked God that he might die with the Philistines. Thus ended a life which, viewed personally, was inconsequential.

> Straining all his nerves he bow'd
> As with the force of winds and waters pent,
> When mountains tremble, and two massy pillars
> With horrible convulsion to and fro,
> He tugg'd, he shook, till down they came and drew
> The whole roof after them, with burst of thunder,
> Upon the heads of all who sat beneath—
> Lords, ladies, captains, counsellors, and priests,
> Their choice nobility and flower . . .
>
> .   .   .   .
>
> Samson with these unmix'd, inevitably
> Pull'd down the same destruction on himself.
>
> (MILTON, *Samson Agonistes*)

But a question arises here which relates, not to Samson only, but to other of the Judges also; and that is the light in which they are represented in Hebrews xi. 32, where Gideon, Barak, Samson, and Jephthah are mentioned as being heroes of faith. We shall fail to understand this reference unless we clearly distinguish two things, namely, the personal character of these men, and God's providential use of them. It will be noticed that in Hebrews no judgment is passed on the character of these men, but only on what they did, consciously, or unconsciously, to advance the divine purpose for and through Israel.

Barak refused to go to battle with the Canaanites unless Deborah went with him.

Gideon asked for repeated signs; he had 'many wives'; and he set up what came to be an idolatrous shrine in Ophrah.

Jephthah made a rash vow, and in fulfilment of it murdered his daughter (but see page 219, 220).

Samson became a fornicator. These details do not represent the whole story of any of these men, but they are there, and are as far removed from faith as anything could well be. But all this, notwithstanding, God made use of these men, and to the degree in which they were conscious of His presence and purpose, and were responsive to them, it can be said that they were actuated 'by faith'.

THE TIMES OF THE JUDGES
(Judges xvii.—xxi. Ruth)

The three incidents on record in these chapters do not advance the history of the Judges, but they are selected to indicate the moral conditions in Israel. The main narrative tells of troubles which came upon them from *without*, but here we learn of troubles which arose from *within*.

MICAH AND THE DANITES (xvii.-xviii.).

The first story is one of *apostasy*, and shows how rife in Israel was *infidelity*. The trouble all along had been idolatry, and this is a concrete example of it. Mark the references to this evil in xvii. 3, 4, 5,; xviii. 14, 17, 18, 20, 24, 27, 30, 31.

A LEVITE AND THE BENJAMITES (xix.-xxi.).

The second story is one of *revenge*, and shows how deeply the people were sunk in *immorality*. It is a horrible story, and but illustrates the fact that where there is irreligion, or false religion, immorality is not far away.

Though these two stories form an appendix to this Book, they are, both by their style and by the actual order of the events which they relate, its natural preface, and Josephus adopts this arrangement.

RUTH THE MOABITESS. The Book of Ruth.

The third story is one of devotion, of *piety*, in contrast to the first story; and of *purity*, in contrast to the second.

In the ancient editions of the Hebrew Scriptures this story is always joined to the Book of Judges.

Prof. R. Moulton has said that 'if the chief distinction of the Idyl be its subject matter of love and domestic life, then in all literature there is no more typical Idyl than the Book of Ruth.' The story tells of how a blighted life was made, through the struggle of devoted love, to bloom again; and in it is an immortal passage which has become for all time the formula of personal devotion.

> Intreat me not to leave thee,
> And to return from following after thee;
> For whither thou goest, I will go;
> And where thou lodgest, I will lodge;
> Thy people shall be my people,
> And thy God, my God;
> Where thou diest will I die,
> And there will I be buried;
> The LORD do so to me,
> And more also,
> If aught but death part thee and me.

In Judges is war, but here is peace. In Judges is cruelty, but here is kindness. In Judges is idolatry, but here is the worship of the true God. In Judges is villainy, but here is virtue. In Judges is lust, but here is love. In Judges is disloyalty, but here is devotion. This story is like a pure lily in a miasmal pond.

To the UNFOLDING DRAMA OF REDEMPTION this Book makes two great contributions: one historical, and the other spiritual. *Historically* it connects the period of Theocracy with the period of Monarchy by showing the ancestry of David, Israel's greatest king (iv. 18-22); and *spiritually* it reveals the inclusive character of the Gospel.

Notwithstanding Deut. xxiii. 3-6; Ezra ix. 1; Neh. xiii. 1-3, 23-27; Mahlon, the elder son of Elimelech and Naomi, married a Moabite woman, and later, Boaz, who was related to Elimelech, married her, and she became the great grandmother of David. Like Melchisedec, Rahab, and others outside of the chosen race, Ruth's inclusion in the family of Israel anticipates the time when Gentiles and Jews alike were to share in the blessings of the Gospel.

Viewing the Book of Judges as a whole, we see, on the one hand, the incorrigible sin of man; and, on the other hand, the amazing mercy of God. The record is designed to teach us that while none should presume, none need despair.

Here we see the tribes slowly moving from Theocratic government to something less ideal. They had attempted to make Gideon king, and had actually crowned Abimelech. The Book ends with the words: 'In those days there was no king in Israel: every man did that which was right in his own eyes'. But a great change would take place 'ere long, and a visible kingdom was already within sight.

THE LAST OF THE JUDGES
(1 Samuel i—vii)

The period of the Judges and the Theocratic Age run into the first Book of Samuel to chapter seven. The last of the Judges in the Book of this name, is Samson, but there are two others, *Eli* and *Samuel*, the record of whom is separated from the main story by the two appendices in Judges, and the Book of Ruth. The Judgeships of these two differ in important respects from those of their predecessors, and they constitute a period of transition from Theocracy to Monarchy (p. 208).

1 THE JUDGESHIP OF ELI (i. 1-iv. 22)
SUMMARY
(*i*) The Families of Elkanah and Eli Contrasted
(i. 1-ii. 26)
(*ii*) The Doom of Eli and his House Predicted and Confirmed
(ii. 27-iii. 21)
(*iii*) The Defeat of Israel by the Philistines, and Capture of the Ark
(iv. 1-11a)
(*iv*) The Doom of Eli and his House Fulfilled
(iv. 11b-22)

2 THE JUDGESHIP OF SAMUEL (v.-vii.)
SUMMARY
(*i*) The Ark in Exile, and Judgments on the Philistines
(v. 1-12)
(*ii*) The Return of the Ark, and its Settlement at Kirjath-jearim
(vi. 1-vii. 1)
(*iii*) Religious Revival in Israel, and the Defeat of the Philistines
(vii. 2-12)
(*iv*) Summary of the Period of Samuel's Judgeship
(vii. 13-17)

15

The stories of Eli and Samuel in the first seven chapters of *Samuel* are so interwoven as scarcely to allow of their being considered separately. Our present purpose does not lead us into much detail, but we should grasp the salient facts and features of the closing years of a period which has lasted, probably, for over four centuries.

Priesthood goes back to the time of Aaron, and prophethood to the time of Moses, but up to now kinghood had not been an office in Israel; but it had been anticipated as later we shall see. It is worthy of notice, then, that Eli was not only or primarily a Judge, but a Priest; and Samuel was not only or primarily a Judge, but a Prophet, so that in each case civil and religious functions were united. The priestly *order* began with Aaron, but the prophetic *order* began with Samuel. We see, then, in the story of Eli, and in the first part of Samuel's story, a vital link between the past and the future, and a period of transition from one order of things to another.

These few chapters (i.—vii.) are full of historical colour, and there is one literary gem (ii. 1-10). The *dramatis personae* are: Elkanah, Hannah, Peninnah, Eli, Hophni, Phinehas, Samuel, 'a man of God', Eli's daughter-in-law, Ichabod, Abinadab, Eleazar, and Samuel's sons Joel and Abiah. The *foreigners* are the Philistines, and the Amorites.

The *places* in the story are: Ramah, Shiloh, Eben-ezer, Aphek, Ashdod, Gaza, Askelon, Gath, Ekron, Beth-shemesh, Kirjath-jearim, Mizpeh, Shen, Beth-car, Bethel, and Gilgal.

Other details relate to a poem, offerings, Samuel's ephod and yearly coat, 'the lamp of God', 'the ark of God,' revelations, battles, Dagon, golden emerods, golden mice, 'a new cart', 'two milch kine' and their calves, 'strange gods', Ashtaroth, Baalim, fasting, and a thunder storm.

The period represented is sixty years; the forty years of Eli's judgeship, and the twenty of Samuel's.

The chief characters are, of course, *Eli* the old priest, and *Samuel* the young prophet.

ELI

This man must have been a great grief to God, as is everyone who fails to rise to great opportunity. He was strong in one thing only, and that was *weakness*. We know nothing of the first fifty-eight years of his life, and the last forty do him no credit (iv. 15). How he came to be appointed Judge we do not know, but alike in that office and in the priesthood he was undistinguished. Indeed, he was not the rightful high priest, and must, by means now unknown, have usurped the office, and the illegal line continued for about a century. According to 1 Chron. vi. 4-12; Ezra vii. 3; Neh. xi. 11, the proper succession was through Eleazar, but it was broken in favour of the line through Ithamar. Surely we may assume God's displeasure with him from the fact that 'the word of the LORD was rare in those days; there was no open vision' (iii. 1). In strange contrast was his treatment of Hannah and of his sons. Francis Quarles has forcefully stated this:

> When barren Hannah, prostrate on the floor,
> In heat of zeal and passion did implore
> Redress from Heaven, censorious Eli thought
> She had been drunk, and check'd her for her fault;
> Rough was his censure, and his check austere;—
> Where mildness should be used we're oft severe.
>
> But when his lustful sons, that could abuse
> The House of God, and ill God's offerings use,
> Appeared before him, his indulgent tongue
> Compounded rather than rebuked the wrong.
> He dare not shoot for fear he wound his child;—
> Where we should be severe, we're oft too mild.

Eli's end was tragic. As he sat in Shiloh near the highway, old and blind, awaiting news of the battle of Israel with the Philistines, a messenger came and told him that his sons were dead, and that the Ark was captured. On hearing about the Ark, he fell from his seat and broke his neck. His concern for the Ark does reveal his deep attachment and reverent love for the symbol of his faith; but that evidence came too late.

His sons, Hophni and Phinehas, were villains, whose outstanding characteristics were immorality and profanity. How far this was due to a want of paternal discipline in early years we cannot say for certain, but there is reason for thinking that it was so. We must remember, however, that this could not be attributed to Samuel, yet his sons, Joel and Abiah, were bad men. (viii. 1-3).

The disaster at Shiloh, due to the barbarous cruelty of the Philistines, could not be forgotten, and references to it were made centuries later.   A Psalm says of God,

> That He forsook the Tabernacle at Shiloh,
>> The tent which He placed among men;
> And delivered His strength into captivity,
>> And His glory into the enemy's hand.
> He gave His people over also unto the sword;
>> And was wroth with His inheritance.
> The fire consumed their young men;
>> And their maidens were not given to marriage.
> Their priests fell by the sword;
>> And their widows made no lamentation
>
> (lxxviii. 60-64)

And in the time of Jeremiah, when another and a worse disaster confronted Judah, priests, prophets, and people resolved that he should die because he declared that the judgment of Shiloh would be repeated: 'Then will I make this house like Shiloh, and will make this city a curse to all the nations of the earth'.   They indignantly asked: 'Why hast thou prophesied in the name of the LORD, saying', 'this house shall be like Shiloh?' (Jer. xxvi. 6-9).

HANNAH

In this age of spiritual decline Hannah, like Ruth before her, stands out in shining contrast.   Dean Stanley has well said: 'She was herself almost a prophetess and Nazarite (i. 15; ii. 1). She is the first instance of silent prayer.   Her song of thanksgiving is the first hymn, properly so called,—the direct model of the first Christian hymn of "the *Magnificat*", the first outpouring of individual as distinct from national devotion, the first indication of the coming greatness of the anointed King (ii. 10; the first mention of the *Messiah*), whether in the divine or human sense'.

Her wonderful song (ii. 1-10), after a brief introduction (1) is in three parts: I. The Character of God (2, 3); II. The Method of God (4-8); III. The Purpose of God (9. 10).

Hannah's song is the only poetry of any distinction between Deborah and David.   It is characterized by insight and foresight, for, beyond anticipating the coming change from Judge to King, she reached on to Jehovah's final King, the Divine Messiah; and the mother of the Messiah based her great Song on this noble woman's inspiration.

Hannah was one in a long line of famous mothers whose sons have made history—Sarah, Ruth, Mary, Eunice, Monica, Susannah Wesley, and others. Well did Lord Shaftesbury say: 'Give me a generation of Christian mothers, and I will undertake to change the face of society in twelve months.'

SAMUEL

. . . occupies a unique place in the history of Israel. He was the last and the best of the Judges; and he was the first of the *Order* of the Prophets. He stood at the end of one long period of Israel's history, and at the beginning of another long period. He was one of very few in history who were called and empowered by God to see one age out, and another in. Such a person was *Moses*, who guided the Israelites from a state of slavehood to one of nationhood. Such was *Jeremiah*, who saw the end of the Jewish Kingdom, and the beginning of the Jewish Church. Such was *Paul*, who proclaimed the end of Judaism, and the rise of Christianity. And such was *Samuel*, who was used of God to pilot Israel from the Theocracy to the Monarchy. Two ages, each of about 500 years, met in Samuel, one terminally, and the other germinally. He stood between the old and the new order; between the past and the future. Samuel is one of the greatest of great men, and the record of him though comparatively brief is very instructive. His influence lay not in military exploits, nor in diplomatic skill, nor in political shrewdness, but in his wonderful integrity, and his splendid loyalty.

To him was committed almost the hardest task ever given to man, Moses perhaps excepted, that of guiding his country safely through a period of transition, when new conditions brought new needs, and when the nation was spiritually at its lowest. The Judges had failed, as the record of Samson shows. The priesthood had failed, as Eli and his sons prove. The army was ineffective, as their defeat by the Philistines makes clear (ch. iv.). But through this dark and dangerous period of Israel's history, this simple, strong, spiritual man led the people to a place of dignity and power. Beside his moral and spiritual strength Samson's physical power is of little account. At the end of his days he could challenge the people to say if any of his dealings with them had been corrupt, and they affirmed that his claim was just and true. Truly he 'wore the white flower of a blameless life'. He was asked from God, given by God, dedicated to God, and he lived for God.

Samuel's life falls into two distinct parts, up to the beginning of the Monarchy, when Saul was crowned king (i.-vii.); and from that point to the day of his death (viii.-xxv. 1). The most of what we know of him falls in the first of these two parts. Chapter i. tells of his birth, and as early in the record as chapter viii. 1, he is an old and greyheaded man (2).

Few stories are so simply beautiful as that of Samuel's child-ministry (i.-iii.). And very impressive are the references to his gradual growth, consistently devout and devoted. Connect i. 24-28; ii. 11, 18, 21, 26; iii. 1-18, 19-21; iv. 1a; vii. 3-12; viii. 1; ix. 18, 19; xii. 1-3.

Out of Samuel's conscious call and loyalty to it emerged the three things for which he has ever been, and ever will be, remembered.

1 His part in the transition from the Theocratical to the Monarchical government of Israel (viii.-x.).

2 His founding of the Order of Prophets. There were prophets before his time, such as Moses, and Deborah, but he was pre-eminently 'The Prophet', and 'The Seer' (iii. 20; ix. 11, 18, 19; 1 Chron. ix. 22; xxix. 29; Acts iii. 24; Heb. xi. 32); and he brought into being what has been called *Schools of the Prophets*, centres in which young men were taught what God was pleased to reveal, and also singing, accompanied by musical instruments (iii. 1, 21; x. 5, 10). This *Order* is the source of that prophetic succession with which later Scriptures familiarize us, and is also the original idea of our Colleges and Universities. Dean Stanley says: 'Long before Plato gathered his disciples round him in the olive grove, or Zeno in the Portico, these institutions had sprung up under Samuel in Judaea'.

3 His intercessory ministry. Samuel's life was one of prayer. He was born, named, nurtured, housed, and trained in prayer. He considered intercession so much a part of his privilege and duty that to omit it would have been sin to him. In the beautiful picture which sanctifies the walls of some nurseries, Sir Joshua Reynolds has shown little Samuel kneeling in the Sacred Tent very late one night, and saying: 'Speak, LORD; for Thy servant heareth' (iii. 10).

At critical hours in the history of his people Samuel was on his knees (vii. 5, 8, 9; xii. 18, 19, 23; xv. 11, 35); and centuries after, and to our time, he was and is known as a man of prayer (Ps. xcix. 6; Jer. xv. 1; Eccles. xlvi. 16).

With such a man at the helm of affairs in Israel the Age of the Theocracy ended, and the Age of the Monarchy began. (Charts 27, 28). The relation to one another of the periods of Joshua and the Judges is summarized in Chart 46 (p. 201).

ACT I

SCENE 2

THE ISRAELITISH NATION

PERIOD B
THE AGE OF THE MONARCHY

The United Kingdom

SAUL

DAVID

SOLOMON

PERIOD B

THE AGE OF THE MONARCHY

FROM THE RISE OF SAUL TO THE CAPTIVITY OF ZEDEKIAH

1 Sam. viii.—2 Kings xxv.; 1 Chron. x.—2 Chron. xxxvi. 21
1095—586 B.C.   Over 500 years

IN the UNFOLDING DRAMA OF REDEMPTION, Scene 2 of Act I relates to THE ISRAELITISH NATION (Exod. i.—Ezra i.). This long story of more than eleven and a half centuries falls into three parts: the *Theocracy*; the *Monarchy*; and the *Dependency*. The first tells of the rule of *the Divine King*; the second, of the rule of *Native Kings*; and the third, of the rule of *Alien Kings*. The first reaches virtually from the Descent into Egypt (Gen. xlvi) to Saul; the second from Saul to Zedekiah; and the third, from Zedekiah to Zerubbabel. The first lasted for over 600 years; the second, for over 500 years; and the third, for 50 years (Chart 27).

It is of the utmost importance to keep these periods clearly in mind.

Having considered the first of them, *the Age of the Theocracy*, we now come to the second, *the Age of the Monarchy*, the record of which is in 1 Samuel viii.—2 Kings xxv.; 1 Chronicles x.—2 Chronicles xxxvi. 21; together with the literature of the period, poetic, philosophic, and prophetic.

The history of this Age is in three distinct parts; namely, the United, the Divided, and the Single Kingdoms. *The United Kingdom* lasted for 120 years; from Saul to Solomon. *The Divided Kingdom* lasted for 253 years; from Rehoboam to Hoshea. *The Single Kingdom* lasted for 136 years; from Hezekiah (6th year, 2 Kings xviii. 10) to Zedekiah—over five centuries in all.

These details may be more easily apprehended and remembered if seen in Chart form.

CHART 48

THE AGE OF THE MONARCHY

Over 500 Years. B.C. 1095–586

UNITED KINGDOM	DIVIDED KINGDOM	SINGLE KINGDOM
Saul to Solomon	Rehoboam to Hoshea	Hezekiah (6th) to Zedekiah
120 Years B.C. 1095–975	253 Years B.C. 975–722	136 Years B.C. 722–586
1 Samuel viii–1 Kings xi 1 Chronicles x–2 Chronicles ix	1 Kings xii–2 Kings xviii. 12 2 Chronicles x–xxviii	2 Kings xviii. 13–xxv. 21 2 Chronicles xxix–xxxvi. 21

The Literature of over five centuries: Poetry. Philosophy. Prophecy.

CHART 49

THE THREE DIVISIONS OF THE MONARCHY PERIOD

SAUL	DAVID	SOLOMON	ISRAEL	JUDAH
40	40	40		

THE KINGDOM

UNITED   DIVIDED   SINGLE

120 Years
B.C. 1095–975

253 Years
B.C. 975–722

136 Years
B.C. 722–586

ASSYRIAN CAPTIVITY
B.C. 722

BABYLONIAN CAPTIVITY
B.C. 586

FROM THEOCRACY TO MONARCHY

In Jeremiah xviii. 1-10 the incident is related of the prophet observing a potter at work on some clay; and he says: '*When the vessel that he made of the clay was marred in the hand of the potter, he made it again another vessel, as seemed good to the potter to make it*' (4). The reflections of Jeremiah on what he saw follow.

In this story the LORD is the Potter and Israel is the clay. Under the *Theocracy* the clay was marred in the hand of the Potter, so 'He made it again another vessel', *Monarchy*. A second time the clay defaulted, and the Potter made it yet again, and this time, a *Dependency* (Chart 27). The 'making again' was not a making *up*, but *down*; the two great changes in the history of Israel were changes for the worse, not for the better. The evidence of this is seen in the fact that whereas under the Theocracy Israel was delivered from Egyptian enslavement, under the Monarchy they went into Assyrian and into Babylonian captivity.

It is of vital importance to understand the significance of this change from Theocracy to Monarchy; and two things should be carefully considered: first, the long anticipation of a monarchy; and secondly, the Divine disapproval of it when it came.

1 *The long anticipation of a Monarchy*

The establishment of a kingly rule was in the Divine purpose, and was looked forward to in Deut. xvii. 14-20. Moses is called 'King of Jeshurun' (Deut. xxxiii. 5), but he was not followed in this by his sons. In the Book of Judges it is said four times: 'In those days there was no king in Israel' (xvii. 6; xviii. 1; xix. 1; xxi. 25).

After Gideon's victory the Israelites wanted to make him their king, and his sons after him; that is, they would have established a monarchy at that time; but Gideon firmly stood by the Theocracy (viii. 22, 23). Later, an illegitimate son of his, Abimelech (which means *king-father*, or father-king) usurped kingly authority, and reigned over Israel for three years (ix. 22). Thought had for long been moving towards a monarchy, and this form of government would seem to be a necessary part of the preparation for the Kingship and Kingdom of the Messiah (Ps. ii. 6; cx. 1, 2; Isa. ix. 7; xxxii. 1; Jer. xxiii. 5; Dan. vii. 14; Zech. ix. 9; Matt.

ii. 2; xxi. 5; xxv. 34; Luke i. 33; John i. 49; xviii. 37; 1 Tim.
vi. 15; Rev. xix. 16).

2 *The Divine disapproval of the proposed Monarchy*

In view of what has just been said, how is it that when the
elders of Israel asked Samuel to appoint a king 'the thing dis-
pleased Samuel', and the LORD said: 'They have not rejected
thee, but they have rejected Me, that I should not reign over
them' (1 Sam. viii. 1-9; xii. 12, 17, 19)?

The answer is, that Israel's sin was not in their desire for
a monarchical form of government, for the Judges had sadly
failed, but in their choice of a Monarchy *instead* of the Theocracy.
Had the kings been loyal to God the Monarchy would still have
been a Theocracy, God employing them as He had employed
the Judges; but Israel wanted to be 'like all the nations' (viii. 5),
though they had been chosen and called for a very different end
(Exod. xxxiii. 16; Lev. xx. 26; Num. xxiii. 9; Deut. vii. 6).

What God and Samuel condemned in Israel's seeking after
a king was, that they had shown themselves unworthy of having
God for their Ruler.

The time for the institution of a monarchical form of government was suitably chosen. The elders of Israel said: 'Behold
thou (Samuel) art old, and thy sons walk not in thy ways; now
make us a king to judge us like all the nations' (viii. 5).

And so the great change was made which was to bring to
power David and the Messiah; but that it was wrongly conceived
and entered upon, chapter viii of 1 Samuel makes quite plain.

And now we must consider the three great parts of the Monarchy
history (Charts 48, 49); the United, the Divided, and the Single
Kingdoms.

THE UNITED KINGDOM

SAUL TO SOLOMON

120 Years: B.C. 1095—975

1 Sam. viii.-1 Kings xi.:   1 Chron. x.-2 Chron. ix.

Charts 48, 49 provide a conspectus of this period. It is momentous not only for the fact that it makes a great change in Israel's

form of government, but for other reasons also. Of these, the two most important are the rise of a School of Prophets, and the commencement of Israel's era of Psalmody. There had been prophets before, and there had been some poetry before (Exod. xv.; 1 Sam. ii.), but there had been no *order* of prophets; nor before had music, vocal and instrumental, been taught and organized, nor national and devotional poetry written (1 Sam. x. 5; 1 Chron. xxv.; 2 Sam. xxiii. 1); but from David's time such poetry continued to be written for over nine centuries.

The product of the Prophetic Order is the Prophecies, oral and written, of the Old Testament; and the embodiment of the age of poetry and song is the Psalter. Both institutions had their genesis in Saul's time, and gave to his period of kingship its outstanding significance.

CHART 50

THE UNITED KINGDOM. SAUL TO SOLOMON. 120 YEARS

SAUL	DAVID	SOLOMON
1 Sam. viii-xxxi. 1 Chron. x.	1 Sam. xvi-1 Kings ii. 11. 1 Chron. xi-xxix	1 Kings i-xi. 2 Chron. i-ix
Years 40. B.C. 1095-1055	Years 40. B.C. 1055-1015	Years 40. B.C. 1015-975
His Election to the Throne. 1 Sam. viii-xii	His Testings. 1 Sam. xvi-xxxi. 1 Chr. xii. 1-22	His Friends and Foes. 1 Kings i-ii. 46. 2 Chron. i. 1
His Deflection from the Course. 1 Sam. xiii-xv	His Triumphs. 2 Sam. i-x. 1 Chron. xi. 1-9; xii. 23-40: xiii-xix	His Wisdom and Wealth. 1 Kings iii-iv. 34. 2 Chr. i. 2-13
His Rejection by the Lord. 1 Sam. xvi-xxxi. 1 Chron. x	His Troubles. 2 Sam. xi-xviii. 1 Chr. xx. 1-3	His Temple and Palace. 1 Kings v-ix. 9. 2 Chron. ii-vii
	His Testimonies. 2 Sam. xix-1 Kings ii. 11 1 Chr. xi. 10-47: xx. 4-xxix. 30	His Glory and Decline. 1 Kings ix. 10-xi. 43 2 Chron. i. 14-17: viii: ix
	LITERATURE	
PSALMS	PSALMS	PSALMS / THE SONG / PROVERBS / ECCLESIASTES

16

THE KINGDOM UNDER SAUL

1 Sam. viii.-xxxi. 1 Chron. x.

B.C. 1095—1055. 40 Years

SAUL is one of the most pathetic, most tragic, and most mysterious of Bible personalities.   Dr. Alexander Whyte says that 'God came upon Saul for outward and earthly acts, but never for an inward change of heart.'   'The anointed king of Israel had . . . neither part nor lot in the true kingdom of God'.   'As trials and temptations beset Saul, a hard and stony heart, a spirit of rebellion, and pride, and envy, and jealousy, and despair took possession of Saul, and held possession of Saul to his terrible end.'   This man had no deep-seated religious principle, no fear of God that influenced his life.   His day began in bright sunshine; by noon thick clouds began to gather; and night overtook him in a tempest of tragedy.   His bright rise passed through a decaying reign to ultimate ruin.

Saul's story is in three clearly marked parts.

1 HIS ELECTION TO THE THRONE (1 Sam. viii.-xii.)

Three times did Samuel charge the people with disloyalty to God in their insistence on a monarchy (viii. 10-22; x. 17-19; xii. 12); yet God sanctioned the change so that ultimately 'out of the eater might come forth meat'; that out of a human mistake might come the Divine Messiah.

The founding of the Monarchy and the establishment of Saul as the first king was in three stages.   First, *he was anointed at Ramah* (ix. 1-x. 16); then, *he was appointed at Mizpeh* (x. 17-27); and finally, *he was acclaimed at Gilgal* (xi.).

And now that the Monarchy is founded, Samuel concludes his ministry in a solemn address to the people (xii.).   This speech is of great historical and religious value.   Samuel retires in favour of Saul (1, 2); he asserts his integrity during his Judgeship (3-5); he reproves the people for their disobedience and ingratitude (6-12); he warns them with reference to the future (13-15); he announces his intention to ask the LORD to send thunder and rain, which intention he fulfils, and to which the LORD replies

(16-18); the people admit their sin in asking for a king, and entreat that Samuel would pray for them (19); he promises so to do, and adds further exhortations and warnings (20-25).

This part of the story is Saul's bright morning, now to become o'erclouded.

2 HIS DEFLECTION FROM THE COURSE (1 Sam. xiii.-xv.)

Each of these chapters shows that Saul's early promise was not going to be fulfilled. The three sins of which he was guilty are: *impatience* (xiii.); *wilfulness* (xiv.); and *rebellion* (xv.).

In the first test he was unfaithful to a fundamental principle of the theocratic kingdom, namely, implicit obedience to the revealed will of God. In the second test he displayed insensate waywardness in making two rash and foolish vows, namely, that his soldiers should not take necessary refreshment; and that, for unwittingly doing so, his son Jonathan should die (xiv. 24, 39, 44). And in the third test he definitely revolted against an explicit command, saving the spoil taken from the Amalekites, and Agag their king.

These were not moral lapses which later would be corrected, but disclose a state of mind and heart which was to go from bad to worse right on to the tragic end.

3 HIS REJECTION BY THE LORD (1 Sam. xvi.-xxxi.)

In asking for a king Israel had rejected the LORD (viii. 7), and now the king whom they chose is rejected by the LORD. This had been plainly intimated when by his impatience, wilfulness, and rebellion he revealed his attitude to God and His purpose (xiii. 14; xv. 23, 26, 28); and now the announcement is to become factual by the appointment of David to be king (xvi.). It is this fact that gives rise to all that follows; Saul's baseless suspicion, his bitter jealousy, his cruel vengeance, and his periodic madness. The Good Spirit left him, and an evil spirit took possession of him (xvi. 14), and at the end he was without help or hope. There was no Samuel to consult, no harp to soothe, no vision to illumine, no priest to advise, and no God to answer his prayer; and in his despair he resorted to a hag of a witch, and heard his doom pronounced once more in words than which none in the Bible are more poignant (xxviii. 15-19).

After this he met and fought the Philistines on the high places of Gilboa, but only to be slain with his three sons. The Philistines found his body, and did to him what David had done to their Goliath—they cut off his head, and 'fastened his body to the wall of Beth-shan' (xxxi).

Surely this is one of the saddest records in history! A man so near to being right, and yet becoming so wholly wrong! How unlike his namesake, Saul of Tarsus, who was wrong at the beginning, but wonderfully right at tl e end!

THE KINGDOM UNDER DAVID

1 Sam. xvi.-1 Kings ii. 11. Psalms.

1 Chron. ii.-iii.; xi.-xxix.

B.C. 1055—1015. 40 Years

Something must be said here about the source-materials for the whole history of the Monarchy from this point.

There were three great offices in Israel, the Prophet, the Priest, and the King, and to these must be added from now, the Poet, and each of them viewed Israel's history from its own standpoint. It is not surprising, therefore, that the records give us these four points of view.

In Samuel-Kings the record is *Executive*; in the Chronicles it is *Ecclesiastical*; in the Prophecies it is *Expository*; and in the Psalms it is *Emotional*.

It does not follow necessarily that these divers views are contradictory. All history can be written from various standpoints, and there is truth in each. In Samuel-Kings, the emphasis is on *politics*; in the Chronicles, it is on *worship*; in the Prophets, it is upon *religion*; and in the Psalms, it is upon *devotion*; and all four are needed for a complete view of Israel's story.

These differences of viewpoint largely account for the obvious distinction between the Samuel-Kings and the Chronicles records, for the omissions, additions, and differences in order.

Regarding for the moment the history of David only—when there was no written prophecy—and dividing the story into 52 sections, we find that 23 of them are in 2 Samuel-1 Kings ii only; 16 of them are parallel in 2 Samuel and 1 Chronicles; and 13 of them are in 1 Chronicles only; and to these, in places, Psalms must be added.   The following are the details.

2 SAMUEL and 1 CHRONICLES

A.   IN 2 SAMUEL ONLY

	REFERENCE	SUBJECT
1	i. 1-16	Account of Saul's death.
2	i. 17-27	David's Lamentation for Saul and Jonathan.
3	ii. 1-7	David made King of Judah.
4	ii. 8-32	Ishbosheth made King over Israel.
5	iii-iv	Decline and Overthrow of the House of Saul.
6	ix	David's Kindness to Mephibosheth.
7	xi. 2-26	David's Fall.
8	xi. 27-xii. 25	The Retributive Sentence on David, and his Penitence.
9	xiii. 1-22	Ammon's incest.
10	xiii. 23-38	Absalom's Revenge on Ammon, and his Exile.
11	xiii. 39-xiv. 33	Absalom's Recall and Restoration to Favour.
12	xv. 1-12	Absalom's Conspiracy and Rebellion at Hebron.
13	xv. 13-xvi. 14	David's Flight from Jerusalem.
14	xvi. 15-xvii. 23	Rival Counsellors in Jerusalem.
15	xvii. 24-xviii. 33	Absalom's Defeat and Death.
16	xix. 1-40	Reinstatement of David in his Kingdom.
17	xix. 41-xx. 26	Sheba's Rebellion, and its Suppression.
18	xxi. 1-14	Famine, and the Massacre of the Gibeonites.
19	xxii.	David's Thanksgiving for Deliverance from his Enemies.
20	xxiii. 1-7	David's Last Words.
21	1 Kings i. 1-4	David's Old Age.
22	1 Kings i. 5-53	The Succession to the Throne Challenged and Settled.
23	1 Kings ii. 1-11	David's Dying Charge to Solomon.

B.   PARALLELS IN 2 SAMUEL AND 1 CHRONICLES

	2 SAMUEL	1 CHRONICLES	SUBJECT
1	v. 1-5	xi. 1-3	David Anointed King over all Israel.
2	v. 6-10	xi. 4-9	Jerusalem Captured and made the National Capital.
3	v. 11-16	xiv. 1-7	David Established as King. His Family
4	v. 17-25	xiv. 8-17	Two Victories over the Philistines.
5	vi. 1-11	xiii	Removal of the Ark from Kirjath-Jearim.
6	vi. 12-23	xv-xvi. 3, 43	The Ark in Jerusalem. Removal Celebrations.
7	vii. 1-17	xvii. 1-15	David's Desire to Build a Temple, and God's Message to him through Nathan.
8	vii. 18-21	xvii. 16-27	David's Prayer and Thanksgiving.
9	viii	xviii	David's Wars and Victories.
10	x-xi. 1	xix-xx. 1	Defeat of the Ammonites and Syrians.
11	xii. 26-31	xx. 1b-3	Conclusion of the War with the Syrians.
12	xxi. 15-22	xx. 4-8	Exploits against Philistine Giants.
13	xxiii. 8-39	xi. 10-47	David's Heroes and their Exploits.
14	xxiv. 1-9	xxi. 1-6; xxvi. 23, 24	David's Offence in Numbering the People.
15	xxiv. 10-17	xxi. 7-17	Punishment of the Offence.
16	xxiv. 18-25	xxi. 18 –xxii. 1	Sacrifices, and the Cessation of the Plague.

C.   IN 1 CHRONICLES ONLY

	REFERENCE	SUBJECT
1	xii. 23-40	List of those who supported David on his Enthronement over all Israel (cf. xi. 1-3; 2 Sam. v. 1-5).
2	xiii. 1-4; xvi. 4-42	Appointment of Service and Song in Zion and Gibeah when the Ark was removed to Zion.
3	xxii. 2-19	David's Preparations for the Building of the Temple.
4	xxiii. 3-32	The Courses of the Levites.
5	xxiv. 1-20, 30, 31	The Courses of the Priests.
6	xxv	The Courses of the Singers.
7	xxvi. 1-19	The Courses of the Porters.
8	xxvi. 20-28	The Keepers of the Sacred Treasures.
9	xxvi. 29-32	The Officers and Judges.
10	xxvii. 1-15	The Captains of the Companies.
11	xxvii. 16-22	The Princes of the Tribes.
12	xxvii. 25-31	The King's Stewards.
13	xxviii-xxix. 25	David's Final Charges.

These details should considerably increase our interest in and understanding of this very important portion of Israel's history.

David was not only an individual, but also an institution. He was not only a sovereign, but also a symbol. His place in the historical unfolding of the redemptive purpose can hardly be exaggerated. There are some Bible characters we would not greatly miss, but if David's story were taken out of the Sacred Book, a gap would be made which nothing and no one could fill. He fe l lower than some men, but he also rose higher. His lapses should be to us a perpetual warning, and his virtues, a perpetual inspiration.

David is, in a real sense, the embodiment of all Israel's ideals; he compassed the gamut of all her varied life and institutions. He is a personification of the nation itself: shepherd, soldier, king, priest, prophet, musician, poet, diplomatist, administrator, hero, and saint; 'a man after God's own heart'; albeit a sinner, sadly sinning, but greatly repenting. In David Israel reached the zenith of the kingdom ideal, and so he is the type of the Messiah 'great David's greater Son'. The nation had a few other great kings, such as Hezekiah and Josiah, but David towers above them all; and in him was established the kingdom which shall have no end.

David's life can be divided into four periods, which may be spoken of as *Preparation, his Coming to the Throne*; *Subjugation, his Conquering from the Throne*; *Retribution, his Fleeing from the Throne*; and *Restoration, his Establishment on the Throne*.

Here, then, are his testings; his triumphs; his troubles; and his testimonies.

In each of these periods David wrote Psalms. Certain of these can be located with a degree of confidence; others may be placed conjecturally because of their suitability to the circumstances; and still others must remain unidentified as to their historical setting.

As David passed through two periods of great trouble, certain of his Psalms may be placed either in the time of his flight from Saul, or of his flight from Absalom; they are attached by title or internal evidence to one or other of these occasions.

In our allocations on page 253, those which are regarded as having a claim to the place which is given to them, are in heavy numbers; those which are located in more than one period are in light numbers in brackets; and those which are but con-jectural are in light unbracketed numbers.

I THE TESTINGS OF THE KING

The Preparation

COMING TO THE THRONE
(1 Sam. xvi.-xxxi. 1 Chron. xii. 1-22. Psalms)

It would appear that David was about fifteen years of age when he was anointed by Samuel (1 Sam. xvi. 11-13), and it would be about fourteen years after this before he came to the throne. This would mean that he was about twenty-nine years of age at the time of his coronation; and as he reigned for forty years, he would be sixty-nine or seventy at his death (1 Chron. xxix. 26-28).

The period, then, of his probation and preparation for his great task was protracted. On two occasions he could have precipitated it (1 Sam. xxiv., xxvi.), but he declined to do so on the ground that Saul, bad as he was as a man, was, as a king, 'the LORD's anointed' (1 Sam. xxiv. 6; xxvi. 9, 11, 16, 23). Four-teen years from the anointing to the crowning of David seems a long time, but great tasks demand much training. For Moses it was forty years; for Elijah, forty days; for Paul, three years; and for the greatest of them all, most sacred and most mysterious, it was thirty years at Nazareth. But David's training was not all rough. It was made bright by the counsel of Samuel, rich by the love of Jonathan, and full of inspiration by the devotion in various ways of Gad, Abishai, Michal, and Abigail.

Three phases mark this period of testing. David is introduced as a shepherd boy; then, as a courtier; and finally, for the major part of the time, he is a fugitive.

(i) DAVID THE SHEPHERD

(1 Sam. xvi., xvii. Psalms viii.; xix,; xxiii.; xxix.).

This part of the story is briefly but graphically told. The writer of the account chooses two incidents only, from much that might have been said, and these are of vital importance for all that follows. The first is the *selecting and anointing of David to be Israel's future king* (xvi.); and the second is *David's encounter with and defeat of Goliath the Philistine*. In the first is God's call to David; and in the second, David's answer to God.

> Latest born of Jesse's race,
> Wonder lights thy bashful face,
> While the Prophet's gifted oil
> Seals thee for a path of toil.

He wa his father's shepherd boy, and was about fifteen years of age. His poetic soul revelled in the beauty and glory of nature around and above him; and four Psalms reflect this period, whether or not they were written at this time.

The sweetest, best known and best loved of them all is *Psalm xxiii.*, which sees God to be the Shepherd of all shepherds, feeding and leading His flock. Then, many a night this boy must have gazed with awe upon the glory of the sky, where moon and stars told their divine story. This experience is celebrated in *Psalm viii.* (where, observe, there is no mention of the sun). But the day, and night, of the 23rd and 8th, are combined in *Psalm xix.*, where night passes into day with the rising of the sun. There, reflection leads on to that other light, the Law of the LORD, which obeyed will keep us from all sin. So the Sky, the Scripture, and the Soul unite in worship. But other experiences must have been David's when he was with his sheep in the open, and notably storms which would break forth in thunder, lightning, and torrential rain. Such a storm is depicted in *Psalm xxix.*, and is regarded by the poet as 'the voice of the LORD' (an expression which occurs seven times). Perhaps the reference to Him as King (ver. 10) is connected with this youth's anointing (1 Sam. xvi.); and it may be that this same anointing led the shepherd boy to write *Psalm cxxxi.* at this time, so expressive of humility and trust.

There is no need to assume a contradiction between ch. xvi. 19-23 and ch. xvii. 55-58, because it is clear that after David's first appearance before Saul he returned to his shepherding (xvii. 15); and, in any case, a man recovered from mental disaffection (xvi. 15-17) might well have forgotten much of what

happened at the time; and Abner's confessed ignorance (xvii. 55)
may not have been real, but only an evidence of his jealousy of
David. At any rate, we should give the record the benefit of the
doubt.

(ii) DAVID THE COURTIER

(1 Sam. xviii.—xix. 10. Psalms cxl., cxli.)

David's defeat of Goliath brought him to Saul's Court. 'Saul
took him that day, and would let him go no more home to his
father's house' (xviii. 7; implying that he had once gone back
home, xvii. 15).

This period, which must have been short, discloses the moral
phenomenon of love and hate converging on an individual.
David is the individual; the love was Jonathan's and Michal's
(xviii. 1, 20, 28); and the hate was Saul's (xviii. 7-11); the father
on one side, and the son and daughter on the other side. That
sets the scene, and introduces us to all that follows. Saul's hatred
of David, engendered by jealousy and fear, is the story of the rest
of this Book. Jonathan's love of David is seen in his covenants
with him; and Michal's love, in her deliverance of him from
death (xix. 11-17).

These experiences are reflected in Psalms cxl., cxli., where
David is seen to be in danger, and prays for protection and deliver-
ance. The men referred to in Ps. cxl. are, no doubt, Saul and
Doeg (1 Sam. xxii. 9). Both Saul and Jonathan discerned that
David was destined for the throne (xviii. 8; xxiii. 17), but their
reactions to their belief were totally different.

Three times it says that David 'behaved himself wisely' (xviii.
5, 15, 30), which carries the implication that he prospered,
and his prosperity was, at each stage, the measure of Saul's
animosity; and when a second time the king cast a javelin at the
youth (xviii. 11; xix. 10), he slipped out of his presence, and
fled (xix. 10).

(iii) DAVID THE FUGITIVE

(1 Sam. xix. 11—xxxi. 1 Chron. xii. 1-22. Psalms vii.,
xxxiv., lii., liv., lvi., lvii., lix., lxiv., cxlii.; and probably, xi.,
xiii., xvii., xxxi., xxxv.; and see also xxv., lviii., lxiii.).

PLACES NAMED IN DAVID'S OUTLAW LIFE

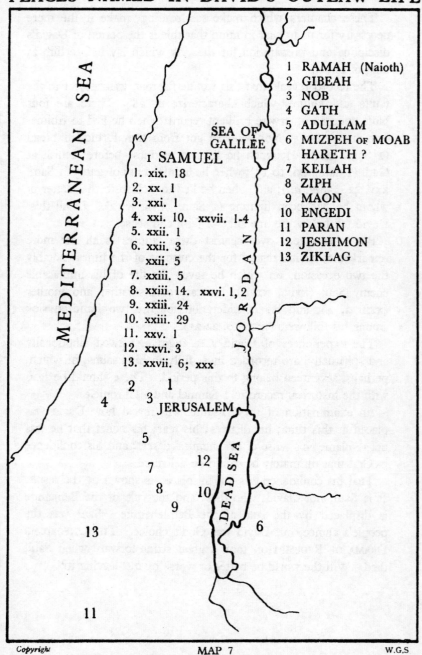

MEDITERRANEAN SEA

SEA OF GALILEE

JORDAN

DEAD SEA

JERUSALEM

1 RAMAH (Naioth)
2 GIBEAH
3 NOB
4 GATH
5 ADULLAM
6 MIZPEH OF MOAB HARETH ?
7 KEILAH
8 ZIPH
9 MAON
10 ENGEDI
11 PARAN
12 JESHIMON
13 ZIKLAG

I SAMUEL
1. xix. 18
2. xx. 1
3. xxi. 1
4. xxi. 10. xxvii. 1-4
5. xxii. 1
6. xxii. 3
   xxii. 5
7. xxiii. 5
8. xxiii. 14. xxvi. 1, 2
9. xxiii. 24
10. xxiii. 29
11. xxv. 1
12. xxvi. 3
13. xxvii. 6; xxx

These chapters which make sad reading, make it the more necessary for us to bear in mind that this is the period of David's discipline and preparation for the task which lay before him as king of Israel.

The record reveals that this wonderful man was subject to the faults and failures which characterize us all. There are four blots upon an otherwise brilliant record: when he lied to Abimelech the priest at Nob, and so got from him forbidden bread (1 Sam. xxi. 1-6); when he feigned madness before Achish at Gath (1 Sam. xxi. 10-15); when he indulged in polygamy (1 Sam. xxv. 42, 43, *et. al.*); and when he lied to Achish in the matter of whom he had been fighting (1 Sam. xxvii. 8-12). In all this. David fell below the line alike of faith and sense.

But what stands over against these failures is all the more remarkable, having regard for the customs of the times; notably the two occasions on which he saved the life of his implacable enemy Saul (xxiv., xxvi.); his care of his father and mother (xxii. 3, 4); and his consideration for the two hundred sick among his followers (xxx. 10, 22-25).

The experiences of David as a fugitive, viewed emotionally and spiritually, are recorded most fully in his Psalms, of which, perhaps, seventeen belong to this period. These should be read with the historical record in 1 Samuel and 1 Chronicles.

An examination of these Psalms will reveal how David was placed at this time; his distress; his fear; his belief that he was not to blame; his sense of his enemies' desert; and his confidence in God that ultimately he would be delivered.

That his confidence was not misplaced is shown by the result. It is Saul, not David, who dies; and the rule of the Benjamite is displaced by the rule of the Bethlehemite. Saul was the people's choice, but David was God's choice. THE UNFOLDING DRAMA OF REDEMPTION took a great stride forward when Saul. died. Will the world be better or worse by our leaving it?

PSALMS OF THE FUGITIVE PERIOD

PSALM	SETTING	OCCASION
lix Title	1 Sam. xix. 1, 2, 11-18	When Saul's agents watched David's house, waiting for the opportunity to kill him.
xi	1 Sam. xviii, xix	While David was at Court, before he fled.
xxxiv Title lvi Title	1 Sam. xxi. 10-15	When David feigned himself mad before Achish.
cxlii Title lvii Title (cxl., cxli, cxliii are in the same group).	1 Sam. xxii. 1, 2 1 Sam. xxiv. 1-3	The 'cave' may have been the one at Adullam, or the one at En-gedi.
lxiv	1 Sam. xxii. 6-8	Saul's determination to have David slain. David is confident he will not succeed.
lii Title	1 Sam. xxi. 7; xxii. 9	At the time of Doeg's treachery.
liv Title	1 Sam. xxiii. 19-23; xxvi. 1-3	When, on two occasions, David was the victim of Ziphite treachery.
xvi xvii, xxxi	1 Sam. xxiii. 24-26	When Saul hunted David in the wilderness of the Maon.
xxxv	1 Sam. xxiii-xxvi	Saul's continuous pursuit of David.
vii Title	1 Sam. xxiv. 9; xxvi. 19	Cush was one of Saul's followers who affirmed that David was seeking the king's life.
xiii	1 Sam. xxvii. 1	When David had long been hunted by Saul.

Among places mentioned in 1 Samuel, besides those shown on the Map, which are associated with David while he was a fugitive, are: Shiloh, Ebenezer, Aphek, Ashdod, Ekron, Beth-shemesh, Kirjath-jearim, Mizpeh of Benjamin, Bethel, Gilgal, Mt. Ephraim, Shalisha, Shalim, Zelzah, Michmash, Geba, Telaim, Havilah, Shur, Carmel, Bethlehem, Shochoh, Jerusalem, Gilboa, Endor, Jezreel, Jattir, Aroer, Siphmoth, Eshtemoa, Rachel, Hormah, Chorashan, Athach, Hebron, Bethshan, Jabesh.

These places constitute the stage on which the drama of this Book was enacted, and should be located on a map of Canaan.

2 THE TRIUMPHS OF THE KING

The Subjugation

CONQUERING FROM THE THRONE

(2 Samuel i.-x.   1 Chronicles xi. 1-9; xii. 23-40; xiii.-xix.   Psalms)

THE HOUSE OF DAVID (1 Chron. iii.)

This period in David's story is in two parts. The first relates to his rule over Judah at Hebron, which lasted for seven and a half years; and the second, to his rule over all Israel at Jerusalem, which lasted for thirty-three years. The first is recorded in 2 Sam. i.-iv.; and the second, in 2 Sam. v.-x., and in the parallel passages in 1 Chronicles (see Lists, pp. 245-246). The following Chart gives the details of the first of these parts.

CHART 51

DAVID KING OVER THE HOUSE OF JUDAH		
Capital: HEBRON.	*Duration*: 7½ Years.	*Record*: 2 SAMUEL i–iv
DAVID AND THE DEAD	TWO KINGS CROWNED	WAR BETWEEN JUDAH AND ISRAEL
Ch. i	Ch. ii. 1-11	Chs. ii. 12-iv. 12
A False Account of Saul's Death, and the Consequences. i. 1-16	David Crowned King at Hebron over the House of Judah. ii. 1-7	Joab, Abner, and Asahel. ii. 12-32
		David, Abner, and Ishbosheth. iii. 1-21
David's Lamentation for Saul and Jonathan. i. 17-27	Ishbosheth Crowned King at Mahanaim over All Israel. ii. 8-11	Joab, Abner, David and Abishai iii. 22-39
		The Murder of Ishbosheth and David's Execution of the Murderers. iv. 1-12

This analysis of 2 Samuel i.-iv. shows that the transfer of regal rule from Saul to David was not made immediately or peaceably. David had been anointed king by Samuel fourteen or fifteen years before. Saul and Jonathan his eldest son died, as did his other sons Abinadab and Melchi-shua; but one son remained, Esh-baal called Ishbosheth (1 Chron. viii. 33; ix. 39), and Israel, except Judah, wishing to maintain the line of Saul on the throne, crowned him king.

Here, then, is a sharp clash between the will of the people and the will of God, and, of course, the will of God prevailed. The House of David waxed stronger and stronger, and the House of Saul waxed weaker and weaker (iii. 1).

Probably Psalm xxvii. belongs to this period.

This delay of more than seven years in David's coming to the throne of Israel may well have been due to the fact that he had deserted his country and entered the service of the Philistines (1 Sam. xxvii.), an act which almost amounted to a renunciation of his anointing, and which all Israel, except Judah, so interpreted. The solemn fact is ever pressing itself upon our attention that our actions have consequences with which God does not interfere;

albeit often consequences which are overruled for our good by their disciplinary influence. To act out of the will of God always means a loss of precious time.

Now follows the second and major part of David's story.

DAVID KING OVER ALL ISRAEL

This embraces the remainder of the record in 2 Samuel, and 1 Chronicles to the time of David's death; but here, in the second part of the *Triumphs of the King* (p. 311) we have in view 2 Sam. v.-x., with the parallel passages, which present the essence of the subject. The King's *Troubles* and his *Testimonies* will be considered separately, though, of course, they fall in the period of his inclusive kingship.

CHART 52

DAVID KING OVER ALL ISRAEL	
Capital: JERUSALEM.	*Duration*: 33 Years
ESTABLISHMENT OF THE THRONE	EXTENSION OF THE KINGDOM
2 Sam. v-vii. 1 Chron. xi. 1-9; xii. 23-40; xiii-xvii. Psalms.	2 Sam. viii-x. 1 Chron. xviii-xix. Psalms.
The Anointing of David at Hebron. 2 Sam. v. 1-5. 1 Chron. xi. 1-3; xii. 23-40.	David's Wars and Victories. 2 Sam. viii. 1-14. 1 Chron. xviii. 1-13. Philistia, 2 Sam. viii. 1. 1 Chron. xviii. 1. Moab. 2 Sam. viii. 2. 1 Chr. xviii. 2.
The New Capital—Jerusalem. 2 Sam. v. 6-10. 1 Chr. xi. 4-9.	Syria. 2 Sam. viii. 3-8. 1 Chr. xviii. 3-8
The King's Family. 2 Sam. v. 11-16. 1 Chron. xiv. 1-7	Edom. 2 Sam. viii. 13, 14. 1 Chr. xviii. 12, 13 Submission of Hamath. 2 Sam. viii. 9-12. 1 Chron. xviii. 9-11
The First Conquests. 2 Sam. v. 17-25. 1 Chr. xiv. 8-17	David's Kindness to Mephibosheth. 2 Sam. ix
The Inauguration of Worship in Jerusalem. 2 Sam. vi. 1 Chr. xiii; xv; xvi	David's Conflict with the Ammonites and Syrians. The Occasion. 2 Sam. x. 1-5 1 Chron. xix. 1-5 1st Attack. 2 Sam. x. 6-14 1 Chron. xix. 6-15
The Covenant of God with David, and the King's Prayer. 2 Sam. vii. 1 Chron. xvii	2nd Attack. 2 Sam. x. 15-19 1 Chron. xix. 16-19 3rd Attack. 2 Sam. xi. 1

As our present object is not to go into expository detail, but to follow the main track of the UNFOLDING DRAMA OF REDEMPTION, we shall have regard only for the outstanding facts and features of the detailed analysis.

THE ESTABLISHMENT OF THE DAVIDIC THRONE

(2 Sam. v.-vii.   1 Chron. xi. 1-9; xii. 23-40; xiii.-xvii.)

The importance of these chapters cannot be exaggerated. Nearly a thousand years had passed since Abram was called to be the father and founder of the chosen race; and over five hundred and fifty years had passed since Moses had given to Israel laws and political unity; and now a great stride forward is taken, in the development of Israel as the Messianic Nation. We enter here on the history of the founding of Israel's Empire, an Empire which for the first time realized the Patriarchal description of the bounds of the chosen people (Gen. xv. 18-21).

David was anointed king three times: first, by Samuel (1 Sam. xv.); then, by 'the men of Judah' (2 Sam. ii. 4); and finally, by 'all the elders of Israel' (2 Sam. v. 3). 'In the fulness of time, at the right moment, in perfect vigour of mind and body, David grasped the supremacy which was offered to him, having passed through every outward stage of power and honour, and every inward test of heavy trial and varied strife' (Ewald).

Now king over all Israel, David declares the principles which shall regulate his private and public life. This he does in Psalm ci., in which is presented an excellent pattern for all who have the responsibility for the direction of others. In verses 1-4 David speaks of his Heart and Home, and in verses 5-8 of his Court and City.

In the establishment of the Davidic Throne, there were four dominating factors: the *City*; the *Ark*; the *Covenant*; and the *Victories*. By the first, a new and permanent Capital was secured; by the second, true worship was inaugurated in the new Capital; by the third, a revelation was vouchsafed of the everlasting Kingdom of the Son of God, the Messianic King; and by the fourth, the enemies of the Kingdom were encountered and defeated.

17

(i) **The City** (2 Sam. v. 6-10.   1 Chron. xi. 4-9).

The first thing that David did as king over all Israel was to secure a suitable Capital for his kingdom, for Hebron was too far away. This he did by capturing Jebus, the capital of the Jebusites, who, in the time of Joshua, Judah could not dispossess of their stronghold (Josh. xv. 63).

The first reference to it is in the time of Abram, when it was called Salem, which is the abbreviation of Jerusalem, and at that time Melchisedec was the king of it (Gen. xiv. 18). From the time of David's capture of the City, the latter name became generally used. It was also called Mount Zion, the City of David, and the Holy City (2 Sam. v. 7. Ps. lxxvi. 2. Isa. lii. 1).

What history centres in this City! It was the centre of David's rule, sin, suffering, repentance, re-establishment, and death; and the scene of the ministry, teaching, death, resurrection, and ascension of 'great David's greater Son.' The place of 'Zion' in the thought and life of Israel may be seen in the fact that, outside the historical Books, the name is found 38 times in Psalms, 47 times in Isaiah, 39 times in Jeremiah, and in 24 other poetic passages. For long centuries it has been a City of fortunes, sieges, dismantlements, and rebuildings; named *peace*, to this day it has been a scene of conflict. Jebusites, Hebrews, Greeks, Romans, Arabs, and Turks have all left their impress upon it, the great and sad story of which began when David captured it.

In part, David's Home Policy was centralization of worship. Hitherto there had been many centres of worship, but David saw that the hope of the future must depend upon a common worship, and a common centre of meeting. It was this which led him to attack and defeat the Jebusites whose stronghold was Jebus, that he might make it his great rallying centre for the Nation, and so it became known as the City of David.

(See 'Jerusalem', 2 vols, by George Adam Smith; and 'The City of Jerusalem', by C. R. Conder).

(ii) **The Ark** (2 Sam. vi. 1 Chron. xiii.; xv.; xvi.)

The history of the Ark began in the time of Moses, and instructions for the making and use of it are found in the Book of Exodus. During the Judgeship of Eli, in the conflict with the Philistines, the Israelites took it to the field of battle, and the Philistines captured it. Later it was returned to the Israelites, and was placed in the house of Abinadab in Kirjath-jearim, where it remained for twenty years (1 Sam. vii. 1, 2). When David captured Jerusalem and made it his capital he resolved that the Ark should be brought to the City. On the way from the house of Abinadab, Uzzah died for touching it, and it was taken to the house of Obed-edom, where it remained for three months (2 Sam. vi. 1-11). Then David brought it to Jerusalem, and placed it in a tent (2 Sam. vi. 17). Finally it came to rest in the Holy of Holies in the Temple of Solomon (1 Kings viii. 1-9); but from the destruction of Jerusalem by Nebuchadnezzar in B.C. 586 nothing has been heard of it. The last time it is mentioned is in Revelation xi. 19.

The Ark was a type of Christ, and the symbol of God's Presence, and when it was removed to Jerusalem its wanderings were over, and the City henceforth was dedicated to God. This event was a turning point in the history of the nation, and the day of it was the greatest in David's life. When the Ark was captured by the Philistines Eli's daughter-in-law bare a son whom she named *Ichabod*, 'the glory is departed'; but now the glory had returned. It is little wonder, therefore, that David celebrated such an event in Psalms (1 Chron. xiii. 8; xv. 16, 27).

> Who shall ascend into the hill of the LORD?
> Or who shall stand in His holy place?
> He that hath clean hands, and a pure heart.
>
> Lift up your heads, O ye gates;
> And be ye lift up, ye everlasting doors;
> And the King of glory shall come in.
> *Who is this King of glory?*
> The LORD strong and mighty,
> The LORD mighty in battle.
> The LORD of hosts;
> He is the King of glory. (Ps. xxiv. 3, 4, 7, 8, 10).

>   .   .   .

> LORD, who shall abide in Thy tabernacle?
> Who shall dwell in Thy holy hill?
> He that walketh uprightly,
> And worketh righteousness,
> And speaketh the truth in his heart. (Psalm xv. 1, 2).

> O worship the LORD in the beauty of holiness;
> Fear before Him, all the earth.
> Say among the heathen that the LORD reigneth;
> The world also shall be established
> That it shall not be moved;
> He shall judge the people righteously.   (Psalm xcvi. 9, 10)

Psalm xxxiii. may also be read in this connection.

David's Psalm of Thanksgiving when the Ark was brought to Jerusalem is recorded in 1 Chron. xvi., and it seems clear that it is made up of selections from other of David's Psalms, the 48th, 78th, 96th, 105th, 106th, 107th.   So deep was the impression made by this event that for centuries afterwards it was celebrated in the praises of Israel.

(iii) **The Covenant** (2 Sam. vii.   1 Chron. xvii.)

The passage 2 Sam. vii. 12-17, is one of the most important in the Old Testament, anticipating all others relative to Christ's universal and everlasting Kingdom.   It must be read with care because here the human and the divine, the local and the universal, the temporal and the eternal are merged.   It is quite clear that Solomon and his kingdom are referred to, who built the Temple (13), and who certainly committed iniquity (14); but it is not true that his house and kingdom were 'established for ever' (13, 16), for they have long since passed away.

The Israelitish Monarchy was, in respects, a promise and prophecy of the Messiah's Kingdom which is yet to be, and which is frequently spoken of in both Testaments (Pss. xlv. 6; lxxii; lxxxix. 36, 37; Isa. ix. 7; Dan. ii. 44; vii. 14; Luke i. 32, 33; Heb. i. 8; Rev. xi. 15).   This Messianic Covenant is placed between David's expressed desire to build a House for the LORD (1-11), and his prayer of thanksgiving (17-29).

(iv) **The Victories** (2 Sam. viii., x.: 1 Chron.   xviii, xix. Psalms)

The capture of Jerusalem, the removal of the Ark thither, and the Covenant which was made with David were not sufficient for the establishment of his kingdom, for he was surrounded by powerful enemies, and these would have to be conquered if Israel were to be secure.

How this was done is recorded in 2 Sam. viii., x.; and 1 Chron. xviii., xix. Here is a summary of the wars and victories whereby a struggling Race became a widespread Empire.

The conquered were the Philistines, the Moabites, the Zobahites, the Syrians, the Ammonites, the Amalekites, the Edomites, together with the voluntary capitulation of the King of Hamath (see Chart 52).

It should be kept ever in mind that these records are parts of the Unfolding Drama of Redemption, each part showing a little more clearly the Messianic Plan. It is this which makes the first ten chapters of 2 Samuel of such importance; for they show that the Messianic Kingdom (yet to come) will be united and not divided (v. 1-5); that it will have a Theocratic Centre (v. 6-10); that in that Centre the Presence of God will be specially manifested (vi.); that the Kingdom will be secure in perpetuity (vii. 12-16); and that all its enemies will be eliminated (viii., x.).

The Psalms, in which is found the spiritual interpretation of the historical events, are full of these ideas, as are also the Prophecies. There are many martial Psalms, as for example, ii., ix., x., xx., xxi., and xliv., but several relate specially to the Davidic conquests as anticipating the Messianic; xviii. (title); lx. (title); lxviii.; cx.; and these should be read in this context.

With this narrative the second part of David's history ends (see Chart 50).

3 THE TROUBLES OF THE KING

The Retribution

FLEEING FROM THE THRONE
(2 Sam. xi.—xviii.; 1 Chron. xx. 1-3; Psalms)

It should be observed that this period of David's life is not recorded by the Chronicler. He has not a word to say about what is told in 2 Samuel xi. 2—xii. 25; xiii.—xxi. 17; xxii.—xxiii. 7. The one author characteristically omits what the other with courageous eloquence narrates. The record of David's victories is summarized briefly, but the story of his downfall is given in circumstantial detail, because the emphasis of the

Bible is always on what is moral and spiritual. It should astonish us perhaps more than it does, that an Israelite should record this event in the life of the nation's greatest hero.

This third period of David's story may be considered along three connected lines: his Sin; his Sorrow; and his Sufferings.

DAVID'S SIN (xi)

Heights are giddy places. It takes a steady hand to carry a full cup. No degree of privilege or of eminence can, of themselves, be a safeguard against disaster. It was when David was at the zenith of his power and powers that he went crashing down to the nadir of murder and adultery.

> The gates of hell are open night and day;
> Smooth the descent, and easy is the way.

This sad story teaches us also that there is no such thing as a single sin. Sin is social, and must have company of its own kind.

> One sin another doth provoke;
> Murder's as near to lust, as flame to smoke.

The sordid details need not be recounted here, but they should be carefully pondered.

DAVID'S SORROW (xii)

The moral significance of this chapter cannot be over-estimated, as the reference to it in the Psalter makes evident. David's repentance was as deep as his sin was dastardly. 'No one buys a little passing pleasure in evil at so dear a rate, or keeps it for so short a time, as a good man' (Maclaren).

Out of David's tragic experience has come what, perhaps, is the most poignant utterance in universal literature, the fifty-first Psalm.

Mark the words that dominate this cry of a broken heart. 'My transgressions'; 'my iniquities'; 'my sin'; 'this evil'; 'blood-guiltiness'; 'Have mercy upon me'; 'wash me'; 'cleanse me'; 'purge me'; 'restore'; 'deliver'; 'cast me not away'.

Never was a sinner more prostrate at the feet of God. And what here David sought, in Psalm xxxii. he tells us he found, the blessedness of forgiveness.

'I acknowledged my sin unto Thee,
And mine iniquity have I not hid.
I said:
  "I will confess my transgressions unto the LORD";
And Thou forgavest the iniquity of my sin' (5)

It would seem that in the year between David's sin and his confession he fell seriously ill (2 Sam. xii. 13), and it is probable that during this period he wrote Psalm vi.

DAVID'S SUFFERINGS (xii.—xviii.)

The following is a summary of this period.

xiii. 1-20 -	- Amnon's Incest
xiii. 21-36	- Absalom's Revenge upon Amnon
xiii. 37-39	- Absalom's Flight and Exile
xiv. 1-33 -	- Absalom's Recall to Jerusalem
xv. 1-12 -	- Absalom's Conspiracy and Rebellion
xv. 13-xvi. 14	David's Flight across the Jordan
xvi. 15-xvii. 23	The Rival Counsellors in Jerusalem
xvii. 24-xviii. 8	The Course of the Rebellion
xviii. 9-33 -	- Absalom's Death, and David's Grief

We cannot study these chapters too carefully, for if the lessons they teach were learned sin would receive a devastating shock. The key verses are xii. 13, 14, 10.

'David said unto Nathan, "I have sinned against the LORD".
Nathan said unto David, "The LORD also hath put away thy sin; thou shalt not die. HOWBEIT".'
'The sword shall never depart from thine house'.

These seven chapters are written to show that repentance and forgiveness of our sin do not carry with them remission of penalty. Over a large area of experience pardon and retribution invariably go together. Our past is not done with us when we have repented of it, and have been forgiven.

Sorrow tracketh wrong
As echo follows song;
On, on, on, on.

'The sense of forgiveness differs from the sweetness of innocence'. Past sin carries with it inevitably deterioration of the present and future. The consequences of transgression remain long after the transgression is forgiven (Ps. xxxii. 1).

Follow in these chapters the consequences of David's great sin. (1) The child died. (2) Amnon, a son, is guilty of incest. (3) Absalom, another son, murders Amnon. (4) Absalom flees from home, and does not see his father for five years. (5) Absalom returns, rebels, and treacherously seizes the kingdom. (6) David takes to flight. (7) Ziba deceives David, and Shimei curses him. (8) Joab murders Absalom. (9) Sheba attempts to rend the kingdom. (10) David has caused the enemies of the Lord to blaspheme for 3,000 years.

> The wind is hushed and the storm is gone,
> Yet the waves of the ocean are rolling on,
> And, reckless of all they had done before,
> Madly they rush on the trembling shore,
> And whiten the beach with foaming spray,
> Like wreaths of snow on a winter's day.

The Nemesis of sin's normal consequences pursued David to the end.

The treachery of Absalom and of David's counsellors is much reflected in the Psalms. It should be borne in mind, however, that twice David was in flight, once from Saul, and once from Absalom, and certain Psalms may refer to either of these events. But reflecting this period of David's sufferings (2 Sam. xii.—xviii.) the following should be read: iii.; iv.; v.; xxv.; xxviii.; xxxviii.; xxxix.; xli.; xlii.; xliii.; lv.; lxi.; lxii.; lxiii.; cix.; cxliii.

4 THE TESTIMONIES OF THE KING

The Restoration

ESTABLISHED ON THE THRONE
(2 Sam. xix.—1 Kings ii. 11; 1 Chron. xx. 4—xxix. 30; Psalms)

Not much now remains of David's story, and soon his son will be on the throne. But what does remain may be summarized as the Final Discipline; the Final Songs; and the Final Charges.

THE FINAL DISCIPLINE
(2 Sam. xix.-xxi.; xxiii. 8-xxiv.; 1 Chron. xi. 10-47; xx. 4—xxi. 30).

After the death of Absalom a movement was set on foot to bring David back from exile, and this was done at the instigation

of Judah (xix. 1-14). At the crossing of the Jordan he was met
by men of Judah, and Shimei, and Ziba, with his sons and servants,
and by Mephibosheth, and Barzillai, and Chimham (xix. 15-40).

But the king's troubles were not at an end, for the people of
Israel were annoyed at Judah's share in the king's return, and
Sheba raised an insurrection (xix. 41-xx. 2).

David re-enters Jerusalem, and immediately takes steps to
quell the insurrection under Sheba (xx. 3-22).

What follows is in the nature of appendices, the items of which
are: three years of famine (xxi. 1-14); the exploits of David's
heroes (xxi. 15-22; xxiii. 8-39); David's offence in numbering
the people, and the consequences thereof (xxiv.).

The trail of woe which the king started by his great sin followed
him to the end of his life, and reappeared in his family after he
was dead. Our sin is not done with us when we are done with it.

THE FINAL SONGS

David was 'the sweet Psalmist of Israel' (xxiii. 1), and at
every stage of his varied life he wrote sacred songs.

In 2 Sam. xxii. is a wonderful Psalm of Thanksgiving for
Deliverances, which appears also in the Psalter (xviii.). It would
seem to have been written before David's fall, and its proper
place, in all likelihood, is at the close of chapter viii.

Here also is a short Psalm, which does not appear in the
Psalter, and which is spoken of as 'the last words of David'
(xxiii. 1):

> David the son of Jesse saith,
>   And the man who was raised on high saith,
> The anointed of the God of Jacob,
>   And the sweet psalmist of Israel:
>
> The Spirit of the LORD spake by me,
>   And His word was upon my tongue.
> The God of Israel said,
>   The Rock of Israel spake to me:
>
> *'One that ruleth over men righteously,*
>   *That ruleth in the fear of God,*
> *He shall be as the light of the morning,*
>   *When the sun riseth, a morning without clouds;*
>   *When the tender grass springeth out of the earth.*
>   *Through clear shining after rain'.*

> For is not my house so with God?
>   For he hath made me an everlasting Covenant,
>   Ordered in all things, and sure:
> For all my salvation, and all my desire,
>   Will He not make it to grow?
>
> But the ungodly shall be all of them
>   as thorns to be thrust away,
>   For they cannot be taken with the hand:
> But the man that toucheth them must be armed
>   with iron and the staff of a spear;
>   And they shall be utterly burned with fire in their place.

Of this impressive Psalm Dr. Payne Smith says:

'A long interval separates (it) from the preceding. The one was written when David had just reached the zenith of his power, and, when still unstained by foul crime, he could claim God's favour as due to his innocence. These last words were David's latest inspired utterance, written, probably, towards the end of the calm period which followed upon his restoration to his throne, and when time and the sense of God's renewed favour had healed the wounds of his soul'.

Obviously the Psalm is Messianic, and points to the day when 'the everlasting Covenant' (vii. 12-17) will be consummated, and the true 'Light of the Morning' will have shined forth, the LORD the Sun.

Other Psalms which probably belong to David's later life are: iii.; iv.; v.; xxii.; xxvii.; xxx.; xxxi.; xxxv.; xxxviii.; xxxix.; xli.; xlii.; xliii.; lv.; lxi.; lxii.; lxiii.; lxix.; cix.; cxliii. However, let it be said again, that the placing of many of the Davidic Psalms is conjectural, and that others may equally well be placed in one or other of similar circumstances, as for example, the flights from Saul and Absalom.

But not only did David write Psalms, he was also the father of all who cultivated Sacred Song in Israel. He organized twenty-four courses of Singers and Musicians under Asaph, Heman, and Jeduthun (1 Chron. xxv.), and this organization was indirectly the origin of all Christian sacred songs and choirs.

THE FINAL CHARGES

(1 Chron. xxii. 2-16; 17-19; xxviii.-xxix. 5; 1 Kings i. 28-35; ii. 1-9).

As the end of David's life drew consciously near he was guided to advise concerning the future. Of the charges which he delivered, three are recorded in 1 Chronicles only: (1) to the Officers

(xxii. 17-19; xxviii. 1-8); (2) to Solomon (xxii. 6-16; xxviii. 9-21); and (3) to the People (xxix. 1-5); and two are recorded in 1 Kings only (1) the charge concerning Solomon as David's successor (i. 28-35); and (2) the charge to Solomon himself, enjoining upon him true godliness (ii. 1-4); and advising him concerning certain persons in his kingdom (ii. 5-9). These were David's last words, and they are heavy with significance relative alike to the past and the future.

So ends the story of one of the greatest geniuses of the Biblical world, and one of the greatest humans of all time. More space is given in Scripture to him than to any other character, except 'great David's greater Son.' He is the only one of whom it is said that he was 'a man after God's own heart'; yet, more than any other Biblical saint did he fail, being guilty of lying, adultery, and murder. First of the theocratic kings, he was a great diplomatist, organizer, warrior, ruler, poet, and prophet. Versatile and vigorous, he dominated the drama of the monarchy for fifty-five years, and laid the foundation of its future ideal, alike that which is already history, and that which is still prophecy. His tragic fall teaches us that none should presume, and also, that none need despair. God must visit sin, 'yet doth He devise means by which His banished be not expelled from Him.'

The stage of this unfolding Drama is crowded with people: Ishbosheth, Abner, Joab, Asahel, Absalom, Adonijah, Michal, Nathan, Mephibosheth, Ziba, Uriah, Bathsheba, Solomon, Amnon, Tamar, Ahithophel, Hushai, Ittai, Zadok, Abiathar, Abishai, Amasa, Barzillai, Ahimaaz, Shimei, Sheba, Rizpah, Benaiah, Gad, Araunah, and David's 'mighty men'. These are the *dramatis personae* in the unfolding of the Divine purposes.

David was about fifteen years of age when he was anointed by Samuel; thirty when he was crowned king in Hebron; in his thirty-eighth year when he became king over all Israel; and in his seventy-first year when he died.

THE PROGRESS OF REVELATION IN DAVID'S TIME

In no period before the advent of Christ was such progress made in the revelation of His sovereign and redemptive purposes than in the time of David. The idea of the universal Messianic

Kingdom first took embodiment in the kingdom which David established; and he himself, his sins apart, was a luminous type of the Coming Messiah. In his recorded utterances also, in the histories and the Psalter, great advances are made in the revelation of the Person and purposes of God in Christ.

The Messianic references, warranted by the New Testament, and others to which the New Testament does not specifically refer, are numerous. These references tell of the Messiah's Manhood (viii. 4, 5: Heb. ii. 6-8); His Sonship (cx. 1: Matt. xxii. 42-45); His Priesthood (cx. 4: Heb. v. 6); His Conquests (cx. 5, 6: Rev. vi. 17); His Eternity (lxi. 6, 7: Heb. i. 10); His Universal Sovereignty (ciii. 19: Rev. xix. 16); His Obedience (xl. 6-8: Heb. x. 5-7); His Zeal (lxix. 9: John ii. 17); His Sufferings (lxix. 9: Rom. xv. 3); His Betrayal (xli. 9: Luke xxii. 48); His Death (xxii. 1-21: Gospels); His Resurrection (xvi. 10: Acts xiii. 33-36); His Ascension (lxviii. 18: Eph. iv. 8); and His Coming Again to Judge (xcvi.-xcviii.: 2 Thess. i. 7-9). References also in David's Prayer in 2 Sam. vii. 18-29, and in his two Songs in 2 Sam. xxii. and xxiii. 1-7, are unmistakably prophetic and Messianic.

Also in the histories and the Psalter there is clear revelation of Christ's Universal Kingdom, a Kingdom which will embrace all nations, and kindreds, and tongues. Such a Kingdom has not yet been established, but it will be.

'I will stablish the throne of his kingdom for ever.'
'Thine house and thy kingdom shall be established for ever before thee: thy throne shall be established for ever' (2 Sam. vii. 13, 16)
'I have set my king upon my holy hill of Zion.'
'I will give thee the uttermost parts of the earth for Thy possession' (Ps. ii. 6, 8)
'All the ends of the world shall remember and turn unto the LORD: and all the kindreds of the nations shall worship before Thee. For the Kingdom is the LORD'S: and He is the Governor among the nations' (Ps. xxii. 27, 28)
'He shall have dominion also from sea to sea, and from the river unto the ends of the earth.'
'All kings shall fall down before Him: all nations shall serve Him'.
'His name shall endure for ever: His name shall be continued as long as the sun: and men shall be blessed in Him: all nations shall call Him blessed' (Ps. lxxii. 8, 11, 17)
'Thy kingdom is an everlasting kingdom, and Thy dominion endureth throughout all generations' (Ps. cxlv. 13)

Before and beneath the Messianic and Kingdom references which are found plentifully in the writing Prophets are the revelations of both found in David. Saul sets forth the *idea* of the Monarchical Kingdom, but David unfolds the *nature*, *extent*, and *permanence* of it.

THE KINGDOM UNDER SOLOMON
1 Kings i.-xi. 2 Chronicles i.-ix.
Psalms. The Song. Proverbs. Ecclesiastes
B.C. 1015—975. 40 Years

The first period of the Monarchy, the United Kingdom, lasted for 120 years, during which three kings reigned, each for 40 years, Saul, David, and Solomon. Of these three Saul and Solomon were failures, and, his character apart, Saul was not of the royal tribe (Gen. xlix. 10; 1 Sam. ix. 1, 2). It is David, then, who gives importance and character to this period, and, indeed, to the whole kingdom concept and age, past and future. Solomon was in the right line, but he was not of the right quality, and because of him the unity of the kingdom was destroyed beyond recovery, until the true Messianic King fulfils all the prophecies in His universal and everlasting Kingdom, yet to come.

The Story of Saul occupies 25 chs. in 1 Samuel (including 2 Sam. i.), and 1 ch. in 1 Chronicles. The Story of David occupies 61 chs. in 1-2 Samuel, 1 Kings, and 1 Chronicles. The Story of Solomon occupies 20 chs. in 1 Kings and 2 Chronicles, and of these 10 relate to the building of the Temple, so that the personal history of this king is very scant.

It is important to observe what is recorded in 1 Kings i.-xi. only, and what is recorded in both Kings and Chronicles.

(1) SOLOMON'S STORY IN 1 KINGS ONLY

i. 1-4	David's old age.
i. 5-27	**Adonijah's Rebellion.**
i. 28-53	David Proclaims his Successor.
ii. 1-9	David's Charge to Solomon.
ii. 13-46	Offenders Judged.
iii. 1-3	Solomon Marries Pharaoh's Daughter.
iii. 16-28	Solomon's Wisdom Tested.
iv. 1-34	Solomon's Empire and Organization.
xi. 1-8	Solomon's Polygamy and Idolatry.
xi. 9-40	Gathering Trouble.

(2) SOLOMON'S STORY IN KINGS AND CHRONICLES

1 Kings	2 Chron.	
ii. 10-12	1 C. xxix. 23-30	Solomon's Accession.
ii. 46	i. 1	Solomon Established.
iii. 4-15	i. 2-13	Assembly at Gibeon. Solomon's Dream.
v.	ii.	Solomon and Hiram.
vi.	iii. 1-14; iv. 9	Building the Temple.
vii.	iii. 15-17; iv. 1-8; iv. 10-22; v. 1	Solomon's Other Buildings.
viii.	v. 2-vii. 10	Dedication of the Temple.
ix. 1-9	vii. 11-22	Solomon's Second Vision.
ix. 10-28	viii.	Solomon's Works and Trade
x. 1-13	ix. 1-12	The Queen of Sheba
x. 14-29	i. 14-17; ix. 13-28	Solomon's Wealth.
xi. 41-43	ix. 29-31	Solomon's Death.

From this it will be seen that the Chronicler omits what is derogatory to Solomon, as he does also in the case of David. But the authentic facts remain.

The Story of Solomon is in four parts, as follows (Chart 50);

THE FRIENDS AND FOES OF THE KING
    (1 Kings i.-ii. 46. 2 Chron. i. 1. Psalms ii., lxxii.)

THE WISDOM AND WEALTH OF THE KING
    (1 Kings iii.-iv. 34. 2 Chron. i. 2-13. Psalm xlv.)

THE TEMPLE AND PALACE OF THE KING
    (1 Kings v.-ix. 9. 2 Chron. ii.-vii. Psalm cxxvii.)

THE GLORY AND DECLINE OF THE KING
    (1 Kings ix. 10-xi. 43. 2 Chron. i. 14-17; viii., ix. The Song of Songs. Proverbs. Ecclesiastes).

Of the forty years of Solomon's reign we know of only four things to his credit: (1) his choice of wisdom at Gibeon; (2) his prayer at the dedication of the Temple, if Nathan did not write it; (3) his benediction after the dedication; and (4) the 72nd Psalm.

Over against this credit are: (1) his questionable severity in the executions by which he inaugurated his reign; (2) his unrestrained polygamy; (3) his multiplication of horses and chariots; (4) his vast accumulation of wealth; (5) his cruel employment of slave labour in the building of the Temple; (6) his condonation of idolatrous worship; (7) his proud display and gorgeous despotism; (8) his foreign alliances; and (9) his flagrant irreligion.

In respect of his wives, his stables, and his wealth, he spurned the Mosaic law (Deut. xvii. 14-17), and his tolerance of idolatry was wholly untheocratic and disastrous. During Solomon's reign the priesthood was quite subordinate, and there were no prophets. In his reign the idea of the theocratic king degenerated into that of the Oriental despot.

It is clear from the historian's record that the Temple was built by slave labour. Ten thousand Israelites were employed (1 Kings v. 13, 14), the conditions of whose service are evident from the complaint of Jeroboam and his followers (1 Kings xii. 4, 10, 11); and a hundred and fifty thousand heathen were employed (1 Kings. v. 15; 2 Chron. viii. 7-10), persons taken in war, or sold for debt, or home born. Seventy thousand were burden-bearers, and eighty thousand were quarry-men—150,000 in all—who 'laboured without reward, perished without pity, and suffered without redress.' The miserable posterity of these are referred to five hundred years later (Ezra ii. 55; cf. 1 Kings ix. 21). This is the slavery which the Israelites had endured in Egypt, under the Pharaoh, seven hundred years earlier (Exod. i.). No doubt it will shock many devout readers of Scripture to know that the most sacred building in all history was built under these conditions, but the fact is incontrovertible.

Solomon's immense harem is a blot on the history of his kingdom. In the matter of polygamy he went far beyond any other ruler of this people; yet, so far as we know, he had only one son and two daughters, and his son was a fool. Saul had only one wife, and one concubine, and David had seventeen wives; but Solomon's seraglio housed one thousand women, if the number in the text is correct (1 Kings xi. 1-3). That was bad enough in itself, but the idolatrous consequences of it affected the whole of his kingdom, and ran like a plague through the history of Israel for four hundred years.

The question whether Solomon was among the saved or the lost has been hotly discussed, and, says Dean Stanley, 'so equally balanced did it seem, that in the series of frescoes on the walls of the Campo Santo at Pisa, Solomon is represented in the resurrection of the last day as looking ambiguously to the right and to the left, not knowing on which side his lot would be cast'.

It is not for us to pronounce upon the subject, but it is a solemn fact that in the whole record there is no evidence of repentance in Solomon, and so no reference to forgiveness, as in the case of his father (2 Sam. xii.).

The three Writings which are associated with his name, The Song, Proverbs, and Ecclesiastes, represent three periods of his life: the first, his early life; the second, his mid-life; and the third, his late life. The first reflects his domestic weakness; the second, his ethical wisdom, which, however, he did not practise; and the third, his final disillusionment and disgust with everything 'under the sun'.

Solomon was a very gifted man, the father of Hebrew wisdom, and of Hebrew science. He was a naturalist, a botanist, a zoologist, a philosopher, a trader, a builder, a poet, and an administrator; yet, at the end, were darkness and disgrace. Of his 3,000 proverbs, less than one third are preserved in the Book of Proverbs; and of his 1,005 songs, only two are preserved in the Psalter, and there is The Song of Songs; and beyond these there is nothing but the eighteen apocryphal psalms which are attributed to him. Stanley says of him: 'That stately and melancholy figure—in some respects the grandest and saddest in the Sacred Volume—is in detail little more than a mighty "shadow". Yet in later Jewish records he is scarcely mentioned. Of all the characters in the sacred history he is the most purely secular; and merely secular magnificence was an excrescence, not a native growth of the Chosen People'.

The one outstanding thing he did—though he did it in so wrong a way—was to build the Temple, that strange structure which, with varying fortune, continued until Titus finally destroyed it in A.D. 70, nearly eleven hundred years later. This building, only 80 feet long, 40 feet broad, and 30 feet high, exactly double those of the Tabernacle, was meant for the symbolic habitation of God.

It was built on Mount Moriah, a site hallowed by the tradition of Abraham's sacrifice, and later, by David's vision of the Angel on the threshing-floor of Araunah, and now desecrated by the Mosque of Omar, the Dome of the Rock, and it took 180 thousand men $7\frac{1}{2}$ years to build it. It had been in David's heart to render this service, but he was prevented, and told that his son would build this House for God (2 Sam. vii.). This building of lavish costliness became 'the central point round which crystallized the entire history of the Chosen People'; and the building of it, together with the appointed worship, constituted the contribution of Solomon's age to the UNFOLDING DRAMA OF REDEMPTION

ACT I

SCENE 2

THE ISRAELITISH NATION

PERIOD B
THE AGE OF THE MONARCHY

The Divided Kingdom
SOUTHERN AND NORTHERN

KINGS AND PROPHETS

THE DIVIDED KINGDOM

Rehoboam to Hoshea

253 Years: B.C. 975—722.

1 Kings xi 26-40; xii.—2 Kings xvii. 2 Chron. x.-xxviii.
Joel. Jonah. Amos. Hosea. Isaiah (part). Micah. Psalms.

Charts 53, 54

THE GREAT DISRUPTION

For one hundred and twenty years (excepting the first seven of David's reign) the Monarchy of Israel had been a unity, but now that unity was about to be broken for ever. First of all the Kingdom was divided into two parts (Chart 52), and after the removal of the Northern part into captivity, the Southern part continued for one hundred and thirty-six years, and then it also went into captivity. The Northern Kingdom entirely disappeared, and the Southern Kingdom, after half a century of exile, became the Jewish Church, by the return from Babylon of large numbers of the exiled under Zerubbabel, Joshua, Ezra, and Nehemiah; and after the return the rulers of the Jews were priests until the time of Herod the Great (B.C. 37). It is of the utmost importance to distinguish these movements in the history of the Chosen People.

The actual disruption of the Kingdom is recorded in 1 Kings xii., but prediction of it is found in ch. xi., while Solomon was still reigning; and the cause of it has its roots in a distant past. The remote cause of the Disruption was Ephraim's jealousy of Judah's royal supremacy. Ephraim was proud and ambitious, and its history was one of great names and great achievements, and, in consequence, there was a disposition not to take for granted the Judaean succession, though hitherto no suitable occasion had arisen for action in the matter. Now, however, the time had come for Ephraim to make itself heard. This was due to the wild extravagance and cruel despotism of Solomon.

Jeroboam, a servant of Solomon's, a youth of vigour and ability, 'lifted up his hand against the king', and had to flee to Egypt. But the LORD had already told Solomon that He would rend the kingdom from him, and give it to his servant (1 Kings xi. 11, 12); and Ahijah the prophet had told Jeroboam that of the rent Kingdom ten tribes would be given to him, and that he would be 'king over Israel' (1 Kings xi. 29-39).

When Rehoboam, Solomon's son, came to the Throne, an influential deputation was sent to him, headed by Jeroboam, to ask that there might be some modification of the heavy exactions which his father had imposed. Rehoboam consulted two parties in his Court, 'the old men', who favoured changes, and 'the young men', who recommended an increase of the exactions. Rehoboam forsook the old men's counsel, and 'answered the people roughly', whereupon, on their behalf, Jeroboam replied:

> 'What portion have we in David? neither have we inheritance in the son of Jesse: to your tents, O Israel: now see to thine own house, David'.

'So Israel departed unto their tents' (1 Kings xii. 1-16); and from that time (B.C. 975) the Kingdom was irreparably divided.

THE COURSE OF THE KINGDOMS

In Chart 53 details of the two Kingdoms are given, from which it will be seen that their respective names were *Judah* and *Israel*; that in the South were 19 kings and 1 queen; and in the North, 19 kings; that the Southern capital was Jerusalem, and the Northern capital, Samaria; that in the South there was but one dynasty, but in the North, there were nine; that in the South were two Tribes, *Judah* and *Benjamin*, and members of the other Tribes who reverted to the South (2 Chron. xi. 16; Ezra vi. 17), and in the North, Ten Tribes, as predicted (1 Kings xi. 31; 2 Sam. xix. 43); that of the kings of the South five were good, three were unstable, and twelve were bad, whereas all the kings of the North were bad; that the conqueror of the South was Nebuchadnezzar, and of the North (136 years before), Shalman-eser; that the people of the South were deported to Babylonia, and the people of the North to Assyria; and that whereas there was a large return of the Southern captives, there was no retunr of the Northern exiles. The period represented by these details covers 253 years.

CHART 53

THE DIVIDED KINGDOM. B.C. 975-722: 253 Years

THE SOUTHERN KINGDOM		THE NORTHERN KINGDOM
Judah	**Name**	**Israel**
Nineteen and One Queen REHOBOAM-HEZEKIAH (6th)	KINGS	Nineteen JEROBOAM-HOSHEA
JERUSALEM	CAPITAL	SAMARIA
One	DYNASTIES	Nine
Two (mainly)	TRIBES	Ten
Good. Unstable. Bad. (5) (3) (12) (Chart 58)	CHARACTER of KINGS	All Bad
NEBUCHADNEZZAR	CONQUEROR	SHALMANESER. SARGON
BABYLONIA	PLACE of CAPTIVITY	ASSYRIA
A Large Return	AFTERWARDS	No Return

In Chart 54 is a comprehensive analysis of the Divided Kingdom period, presenting all the relevant details. The names of
the kings are given in the order in which they occur in the records.
Those belonging respectively to the South and the North are
indicated. The year in which each began to reign, and the
length of the reign of each are stated. The character of each
king is shown, and the end of each. It is indicated that in the
North were nine dynasties, and Chart 54 sets out the details.
This Chart also shows what prophets exercised ministry during
the Divided Kingdom period, and it shows also some of the
chief foreign events during this period.

Further, it should be observed that whereas the Books record
in summary the history of both kingdoms, the Chronicles record

that of the Southern Kingdom only. The reason for this is that the Chronicler's record is priestly and Messianic in character, and so presents the history of that division of the Kingdom which held the Capital, the Temple, the Levitical Priesthood, and the unbroken succession of David.

The Biblical record of the Kingdom-period is threefold, *Royal*, *Priestly*, and *Prophetic*. The first is in the books of the *Kings*, the second is in the *Chronicles*, and the third is in the *Prophetic Writings* which fall within the period (Chart 57).

Perhaps what makes this part of Bible history more difficult than other parts to read is the arrangement of the material. From Chart 54, columns one and two, it will be seen that the records of the two Kingdoms are intermixed—S. N. S. S., then six N.s, and an S., and so on. In some ways it would have been simpler to have had all the kings of Judah together, and all the kings of Israel; but this arrangement would not have shown the contemporaneousness of the kings. The difficulty which the average reader may feel in the 1-2 Kings record will largely be overcome if Chart 54 is followed.

CHART 54

COMPREHENSIVE ANALYSIS OF THE DIVIDED KINGDOM PERIOD

Time: B.C. 975-722: 253 Years

Name of King	North, South	Began to Reign, B.C.	Length of Reign	Character of King	End of King	Dynasty	Prophets	Principal Foreign Events	Comparative Record	
									Kings	Chronicles
REHOBOAM	S	975	17	Bad	Died		IDDO SHEMAIAH	SHISHAK of Egypt invaded Judah	I K. xii. 1-24; xiv. 21-31	2 C. x-xii
JEROBOAM	N	975	22	Bad	Stricken	1	IDDO AHIJAH		I K. xii. 25-xiv. 20	
ABIJAM	S	958	3	Bad	Died				I K. xv. 1-8	2 C. xii. 16-xiv. 1a
ASA	S	955	41	Good	Died		HANANI AZARIAH	Zerah the Ethiopian invaded Judah. Asa's alliance with Syria against BAASHA	I K. xv. 9-24	2 C. xiv. 1b-xvi
NADAB	N	954	2	Bad	Slain				I K. xv. 25-31	
BAASHA	N	953	24	Bad	Died	2	JEHU	Israel invaded by Syria	I K. xv. 32-xvi. 7	
ELAH	N	930	2	Bad	Murdered				I K. xvi. 8-10a	
ZIMRI	N	929	7 days	Bad	Suicide	3			I K. xvi. 10b-20	
OMRI	N	929	12	Bad	Died	4			I K. xvi. 21-28	

CHART 54—*Continued*

Name of King	North/South	Began to Reign. B.C.	Length of Reign	Character of King	End of King	Dynasty	Prophets	Principal Foreign Events	Comparative Record	
									Kings	Chronicles
AHAB	N	918	22	Bad	Slain		ELIJAH MICAIAH	Ahab married Jezebel of Zidon. Israel at war with Syria. Ahab's Treaty with Benhadad II. The war renewed, and Ahab slain	1 K. xvi. 29-xxii. 40	
JEHOSHAPHAT	S	914	25	Good	Died		Jehu Eliezer Jahaziel	Jehoshaphat's alliance with Ahab against Syria. He subdues Moab, Ammon, and the Philistines. 'The Moabite Stone'	1 K. xxii. 2-33, 41-50	2 C. xvii-xxi. 3
AHAZIAH	N	897	2	Bad	Accident				1 K. xxii. 51- 2 K. ii. 25	
JEHORAM	N	896	12	Bad	Murdered		ELISHA	Jehoram united with Jehoshaphat against Moab. Besieged in Samaria by Benhadad II, but was relieved.	2 K. iii-viii. 15	
JORAM	S	889	8	Bad	Smitten by God		OBADIAH (?)		2 K. viii. 16-24	2 C. xxi. 4-20
AHAZIAH	S	885	1	Bad	Killed				2 K. viii. 25-29	2 C. xxii. 1-9
JEHU	N	884	28	Bad	Died		ELISHA	Israel tributary to Assyria, Shalmaneser II. Hazael of Syria 'cut short' Israel east of Jordan	2 K. ix-x. 36	
ATHALIAH	S	884	6	Bad	Slain				2 K. xi.	2 C. xxii. 10-xxiii

CHART 54—Continued

Name of King	North, South	Began to Reign. B.C.	Length of Reign	Character of King	End of King	Dynasty	Prophets	Principal Foreign Events	Comparative Record Kings	Comparative Record Chronicles
JEHOASH	S	878	40	Unstable	Slain		JOEL (?)	HAZAEL of Syria came upon Jerusalem, but JEHOASH plundered the Temple to buy him off.	2 K. xii	2 C. xxiv
JEHOAHAZ	N	856	17	Bad	Died		ELISHA	Israel delivered into the hands of Syria.	2 K. xiii. 1-9	
JOASH	N	839	16	Bad	Died		ELISHA	JOASH conquered BENHADAD III.	2 K. xiii. 10-25	
AMAZIAH	S	839	29	Unstable	Slain			AMAZIAH defeated the Moabites.	2 K. xiv. 1-20	2 C. xxv.
JEROBOAM II	N	825	41	Bad	Died		JONAH AMOS HOSEA	SHALMANESER III of Assyria.	2 K. xiv. 23-29	
INTERREGNUM	N	784-773	11					Here are given the provisional B.C. dates.	2 K. xiv. 8- xv. 6	
AZARIAH (Uzziah)	S	810	52	Unstable	Leper		ZECHARIAH ISAIAH		2 K. xiv. 21, 22. xv. 1-7	2 C. xxvi.
ZACHARIAH	N	773	6 mths.	Bad	Murdered		HOSEA	TIGLATH-PILESER III of Assyria (Assyrian date, B.C. 745-727).	2 K. xv. 8-12	
SHALLUM	N	772	1 mth.	Bad	Murdered	6	HOSEA		2 K. xv. 13-16	

CHART 54—Continued

Name of King	North. South	Began to Reign. B.C.	Length of Reign	Charac- ter of King	End of King	Dynasty	Prophets	Principal Foreign Events	Comparative Record Kings	Comparative Record Chronicles
MENAHEM	N	772	10	Bad	Died	7	HOSEA	Israel tributary to PUL of Assyria.	2 K. xv. 17-22	
PEKAHIAH	N	761	2	Bad	Mur- dered		HOSEA		2 K. xv. 23- 26	
PEKAH	N	759	20	Bad	Mur- dered	8	HOSEA MICAH	PEKAH with REZIN of Syria attacked Judah. Israel subdued by TIGLATH- PILESER III of Assyria (PUL).	2 K. xv. 27-31	
INTERREGNUM	N	739- 730	9						2 K. xv. 27- xviii. I	
JOTHAM	S	758	16	Good	Died		ISAIAH MICAH		2 K. xv. 32-38	2 C. xxvii.
AHAZ	S	742	16	Bad	Died		ISAIAH MICAH	AHAZ delivered to Syria and Israel submits to Assyria.	2 K. xvi.	2 C. xxviii.
HOSHEA	N	730	9	Bad	Captive	9	HOSEA MICAH	HOSHEA, the vassal of Assyria, attempted to bring about an alliance with SO, king of Egypt, and was imprisoned. Samaria was besieged by SHALMANESER IV (727-722 B.C.) of Assyria. Later it was captured by SARGON (722-705 B.C.) who took the ten Tribes captive.	2 K. xvii. xviii. 9-12	
HEZEKIAH	S	727- 722	6th Year	Good			ISAIAH MICAH	MERODACH-BALADIN in Babylon (722-710 B.C.).	2 K. xviii. 1-8	2 C. xxix- xxxi.

CHART 55

DYNASTIES OF THE NORTHERN KINGDOM. B.C. 975–722.   253 Years

Dynasty			
I	B.C. 975–954	(22)	JEROBOAM
I	B.C. 954–953	(2)	NADAB
II	B.C. 953–930	(24)	• BAASHA
II	B.C. 930–929	(2)	ELAH
III	B.C. 929	(7 days)	ZIMRI
IV	B.C. 929–918	(12)	OMRI-TIBNI (6)
IV	B.C. 918–897	(22)	AHAB
IV	B.C. 897–896	(2)	AHAZIAH
IV	B.C. 896–884	(12)	JEHORAM
V	B.C. 884–856	(28)	JEHU
V	B.C. 856–839	(17)	JEHOAHAZ
V	B.C. 839–825	(16)	JOASH
V	B.C. 825–784	(41)	JEROBOAM II
V	B.C. 784–773	(11)	INTERREGNUM
V	B.C. 773	(6 months)	ZACHARIAH
VI	B.C. 772	(1 month)	SHALLUM
VII	B.C. 772–761	(10)	MENAHEM
VII	B.C. 761–759	(2)	PEKAHIAH
VIII	B.C. 759–739	(20)	PEKAH
VIII	B.C. 739–730	(9)	INTERREGNUM
IX	B.C. 730–722	(9)	HOSHEA

CHART 57

THE THREEFOLD ASPECT OF THE KINGDOM HISTORY

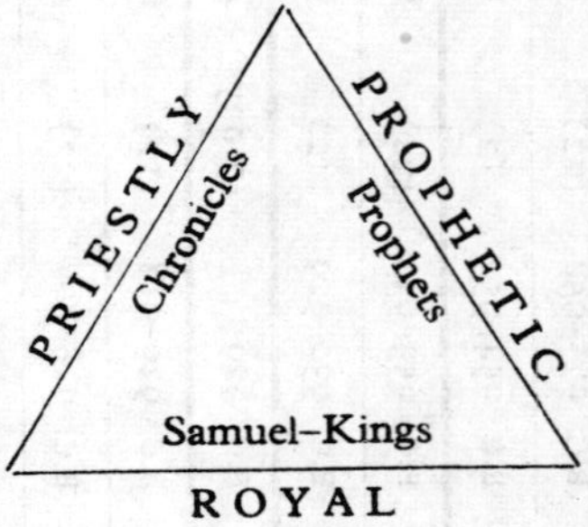

PROPHETIC — Prophets

PRIESTLY — Chronicles

ROYAL — Samuel-Kings

CHART 56

THE RELATION TO ONE ANOTHER OF THE HISTORICAL RECORDS. SAMUEL. KINGS. CHRONICLES

ADAM-SAUL	THE KINGDOM	CYRUS
First and Second Chronicles		
1 Chron. i-ix	1-2 Samuel / 1-2 Kings	2 Chron. xxxvi. / 22, 23
Anno Hominis (The Era of Man)		
Over 2,900 Years	Over 500 Years	B.C. 538-

It is scarcely to be wondered at that the kings in the North were all bad, for they had deliberately departed from the theocratic foundations; but it is grievous that of the twenty rulers in the South, twelve were bad, and three others were unstable.

CHART 58

CHARACTER OF THE KINGS OF JUDAH		
GOOD	UNSTABLE	BAD
Asa Jehoshaphat Jotham Hezekiah Josiah	Jehoash Amaziah Azariah	*In the Divided Kingdom Period* Rehoboam. Abijam. Jehoram. Ahaziah. Athaliah. Ahaz.
		In the Single Kingdom Period Manasseh. Amon. Jehoahaz. Jehoiakim. Jehoiachin. Zedekiah.
142 Years	121 Years	51 Years
		79½ Years

The only contribution to the Unfolding Drama of Redemption which the Northern Kingdom made was to show the need of it, excepting, of course, in the utterances or history of the prophets of the North, *Ahijah, Shemaiah, Elijah, Elisha, Jonah, Amos, Hosea,* and *Micah.* In their predictions, or in their persons, these men foreshadowed the coming and Kingdom of the Messiah in their opposition to the anti-Messiah attitude of the kings of the North.

But the Drama of Redemption was greatly unfolded in the Southern Kingdom by its institutions, its prophets, and some of its kings. In the tribe of Judah were focused those moral and spiritual elements which have given the Chosen People their abiding significance.

THE RELATION OF THE TWO KINGDOMS TO ONE ANOTHER

The Divided Kingdom period lasted for 253 years, and in respect of the relation to one another of the South and North it is divisible into three parts. First of all these kingdoms were antagonistic to one another; then, by a marriage, they became allies for a while; and finally, until the removal into captivity of the people of the North, they were again antagonistic. Study carefully the following Chart, from which it will be seen that in the first period of antagonism there reigned in the South three kings, and in the North, six; that during the period of alliance there were in the South four kings and a queen, and in the North five kings; and that in the period of final antagonism there were in the South five kings, and in the North, eight.

CHART 59

B.C. 975-722	THE DIVIDED KINGDOM	253 Years

THE RELATION OF THE SOUTH AND NORTH TO ONE ANOTHER

1. Period of the First Antagonism between South and North

SOUTH	NORTH
Rehoboam to Asa	Jeroboam to Omri
B.C. 975-914 = 61	B.C. 975-918 = 57

1 Kings xii-xvi. 28.   2 Chronicles x-xvi

2. Period of the Fateful Alliance between South and North
2 Chron. xx. 34-37; xxi. 6

SOUTH	NORTH
Jehoshaphat to Jehoash	Ahab to Jehoahaz
B.C. 914-839 = 75	B.C. 918-839 = 79

1 Kings xvi. 29-2 Kings xiii. 9.   2 Chronicles xvii–xxiv

3. Period of the Final Antagonism between South and North
2 Kings xiv. 8-14.   2 Chron. xxv. 17-25

SOUTH	NORTH
Amaziah to Hezekiah	Joash to Hoshea
B.C. 839-722 = 117	B.C. 839-722 = 117

2 Kings xiii. 10-xviii. 12   2 Chronicles xxv-xxix

61 + 75 + 117 = 253 Years	57 + 79 + 117 = 253 Years

THE KINGS OF JUDAH

In the Divided Kingdom Period

1 REHOBOAM

1 Kings xi. 43; xii. 1-18; xiv. 21-31. 2 Chron. ix. 31-xii. 16
B.C. 975—958 = 17 Years

Rehoboam was the only son of Solomon, so far as we know, and he rent the kingdom which his father began to tear.

He had the opportunity to pacify the spirit of discontent which had become evident in most of the Tribes, but, by following bad advice, he fomented it, and for want of 'tact, diplomacy, justice and good sense' he irreparably divided the kingdom. He would have gone to war with those who seceded, but was warned by the prophet *Shemaiah* not to do so. He fortified Judah against a possible invasion of the Egyptians, but in spite of this, in the fifth year of his reign *Shishak*, king of Egypt, invaded Judah and plundered the Temple, and would have subjugated the people, had not the king and the princes humbled themselves, in consequence of the remonstrance of *Shemaiah*.

2 ABIJAM

1 Kings xv. 1-8. 2 Chron. xiii.
B.C. 958—955 = 3 Years

Abijam was a son of Rehoboam, and followed his father in his polygamous ways. He went to war against Jeroboam, and defeated him, after having made a great speech from a mountain in the territory of Ephraim (2 Chron. xiii. 4-12). Study this speech. The design of it was to undo the damage which his father had done to the kingdom, but Jeroboam's resistance, and Abijam's own conduct (1 Kings xv. 3) made things still worse.

3 ASA

1 Kings xv. 9-24. 2 Chron. xiv.-xvi.
B.C. 955—914 = 41 Years

Asa, a son of Abijam, was one of the five best kings of Judah, yet he ended badly. The first ten years of his reign were peaceful.

He set himself against all idolatrous places and practices, and deposed his grandmother because she had made an image for an Asherah. Cities were fortified, and the army was strengthened. When Zerah, the Ethiopian, invaded Judah, Asa defeated him. Encouraged by *Oded* and *Azariah* the prophets, he prosecuted reforms, and renewed the Covenant with the LORD.

But in the 26th year of his reign (2 Chron. xvi. 1. The number 36 cannot be correct because by that time Baasha had been dead ten to twelve years), when Baasha king of Israel fortified Ramah, five miles north of Jerusalem, Asa sought the help of Benhadad I of Syria, and bribed him with treasure from the Temple and Palace. This course the prophet *Hanani* condemned, and was imprisoned for his pronouncement. The last fifteen years of Asa's reign were years of declension; and during the last two of them, being diseased in his feet, he resorted to the aid of foreign magicians who practised sorcery and incantations, and for this the Chronicler blames him.

It is worthy of notice that whereas good kings of Judah went from their goodness to badness, only one of them, Manasseh, turned from badness to goodness (2 Chron. xxxiii.).

With the reign of Asa ends the first period of antagonism between Judah and Israel (1 Kings xv. 16. See Chart 58).

The prophets of this period, in the South, were *Shemaiah*, *Oded*, *Azariah*, and *Hanani*.

4 JEHOSHAPHAT

1 Kings xxii. 2-33, 41-50.   2 Chron. xvii.-xxi. 3

B.C. 914—889=25 Years

Jehoshaphat was the second of Judah's five best kings, yet he also failed in his loyalty to the LORD in some respects. But he was a great and good king. He cleansed the land of idolatry; organized the religious education of the whole nation; fortified Judah, raised a great army; and appointed Judges on the Mosaic basis. Surrounding kingdoms feared and appeased him—the Edomites, Philistines, and Arabians—'and Jehoshaphat waxed great exceedingly' (2 Chron. xvii. 12).

But, alas, he failed in three important matters. (1) In the thirteenth year of his reign he allied himself with Ahab, king of Israel, by the marriage of his son *Jehoram* to *Athaliah* the daughter of Ahab and Jezebel, which proved fatal (2 Chron. xviii. 1). (2) With Ahab he marched against the Syrians, and nearly lost his life in the battle (2 Chron. xviii). (3) In a naval enterprise he allied Ahaziah, a wicked king of Israel, with himself, in consequence of which the enterprise failed (2 Chron. xx. 35-37).

For the first error he was rebuked by the prophet *Jehu*. In the second matter the prophet *Micaiah* was against him. The third mistake was condemned by the prophet *Eliezer* (2 Chron. xix. 1-4; xviii.; xx. 37). But when confronted by the forces of Ammon and Moab, *Jahaziel* the prophet encouraged Jehoshaphat to trust God, Who would give him the victory by singing, instead of by shooting (2 Chron. xx.).

These were the prophets of this reign.

5 JEHORAM
2 Kings viii. 16-24.   2 Chron. xxi. 1-20
B.C. 889—885 = 4 Years alone

Jehoram was the third of the twelve bad kings of Judah. He married Athaliah, the daughter of Ahab and Jezebel, and followed the evils of his wife and mother-in-law (2 Chron. xxi. 6). He established idolatry, and murdered all his younger brethren. In consequence of his sins a letter was sent to him, written, the Chronicler says, by *Elijah*, which predicted calamity for his people, and a horrible disease for himself (2 Chron. xxi. 12-15).

(It is very doubtful if *Elijah* of 2 Chron. xxi. 12, is the Tishbite, as it would appear from 2 Kings iii. 11 that he was dead; but it is not absolutely certain that *Elisha* is meant).

The prophecy was fulfilled when the Edomites, Libnahites, Philistines, and Arabian Ethiopians revolted against Jehoram, and when, after two years of great suffering, he died a terrible death.

'Though the mills of God grind slowly,
　　Yet they grind exceeding small;
Though with patience He stands waiting,
　　With exactness grinds He all'.

6 AHAZIAH

2 Kings viii. 25-ix. 29. 2 Chron. xxii. 1-9
B.C. 885 = 1 Year

Ahaziah was the fourth bad king of Judah. He continued the idolatry of his father, and also allied himself with Jehoram, king of Israel. When Jehu, who was to destroy the house of Ahab, went to Jezreel to kill Jehoram, Ahaziah was there with the wounded king, and Jehu slew them both, and also forty-two nephews and kinsmen of Ahaziah (2 Kings x. 12-14).

7 ATHALIAH

2 Kings xi. 2 Chron. xxii. 10-xxiii. 21
B.C. 884—878 = 6 Years

Athaliah was the daughter of Ahab and Jezebel, the wife of Jehoram of Judah, and the mother of Ahaziah. She and her mother are distinguished among the wicked women of history, among whom are Delilah, Zeresh, Herodias, and a host who have followed. She destroyed all the seed royal except Jehoash, who was rescued by his aunt Jehosheba and hidden in the Temple. She then usurped the throne and ruled tyrannously. After six years Jehoiada the priest, the husband of Jehosheba, crowned Jehoash king in the Temple; and hearing the shouting of the people, Athaliah went to the Temple and saw Jehoash standing there crowned as king. She cried 'Treason, treason', but was led out and slain.

8 JEHOASH

2 Kings xi., xii. 2 Chron. xxii. 10-xxiv. 27
B.C. 878-839 = 40 Years

Jehoash began well and ended badly. His career falls into three parts, which tell of (1) his promising start; (2) his swift apostasy; and (3) his tragic end. In the first part of his reign he 'did that which was right in the sight of the LORD'. He repaired the Temple which Athaliah 'had broken up', and collected the money to pay for it. But his rightness lasted only while Jehoiada the high priest lived; and when he died, Jehoash fell away to idolatry, and turned a deaf ear to the remonstrances of the prophets.

So basely ungrateful was Jehoash for all that Jehoiada had done for him that he slew Zechariah his son, who then was the high priest.

When Hazael, king of Syria, marched against Judah, Jehoash bribed him to depart by giving him treasures of the Temple; but later, the Syrians defeated the army of Judah, slew their princes, and sent all the spoil to Damascus.

But retribution overtook Jehoash, and he was murdered by his own servants in his bed while he was ill.

With this king the period of alliance between Judah and Israel ended (see Chart 59).

9 AMAZIAH

2 Kings xiv. 1-22. 2 Chron. xxv.

B.C. 839—810 = 29 Years

Amaziah, the son of the murdered Jehoash, began his reign by slaying his father's murderers, but, respecting the law of Deut. xxiv. 16, he spared their children. Designing to attack the Edomites he hired 100,000 Israelites to supplement his own army, but when a prophet remonstrated with him for doing this, he sent back the northern army, which, in anger, ravaged Judah as they returned. Amaziah did attack, and defeated the Edomites, and took Sela (Petra) at the southern extremity of the Dead Sea.

It was on his return from this expedition that he fell into the sins of idolatry and pride, which compassed his ruin. As to *idolatry*, he worshipped Edomite gods. A prophet rebuked him for this, but he heeded not. As to *pride*, elated by his victory over Edom, and incensed by the damage which the returning army of Israel had done, he challenged Joash, king of Israel, to battle, thereby ending the alliance between South and North, which had lasted nearly eighty years. Amaziah was warned not to do this, but persisted, and was utterly defeated. He survived Joash of Israel by fifteen years, and then was murdered by conspirators.

From the time of Amaziah's engagement with Joash, South and North were again antagonistic until the deportation of Israel to Assyria one hundred and seventeen years later (Chart 59).

10 AZARIAH

2 Kings xv. 1-7. 2 Chron. xxvi.

B.C. 810—758 = 52 Years

Azariah, as a king, was great rather than good, and in the latter part of his life he fell away badly. What we learn of him from the records relates rather to conflicts without and constructions within, than to matters moral and religious. In foreign affairs he subdued the Edomites, the Philistines, the Arabs, and the Ammonites; and in home affairs, he strengthened the walls of Jerusalem, built towers, invented powerful instruments of war, increased the army, and improved Jerusalem's irrigation system; and both near and far he made for himself a great reputation.

But all such things can be done without the doer of them being good; and in the case of Azariah, his want of true goodness is made evident at that point at which it might well have been displayed. 'The glorious reign had a ghastly conclusion'. For entering the Holy Place, which was the exclusive prerogative of the priests (Num. xviii. 7; Exod. xxx. 7), he was divinely smitten with leprosy, and for the rest of his life had to live in a house apart, and at last was not buried in the royal sepulchre.

During the lifetime of *Zechariah*, a prophet of whom we know nothing more, Azariah sought the LORD, but when the prophet died, the king's apparent godliness died also (cf. 2 Chron. xxiv. 17-19).

This man had two names: *Azariah*, which means *Jehovah hath helped*, and *Uzziah*, which means *Strength of Jehovah*. Probably both are alluded to in 2 Chron. xxvi. 7, 15.

It should be noted that in Azariah's time *Joel*, *Amos*, and *Hosea* were prophesying, and in the year of his death *Isaiah* began to minister (Amos i. 1; Hosea i. 1; Isaiah vi. 1).

11 JOTHAM

2 Kings xv. 32-38. 2 Chron. xxvii. Isa. vi.

B.C. 758—742 = 16 Years

Of this king little is recorded, all being compressed into as many verses as the years of his reign. It would seem that during almost the whole of his sixteen years reign he was judging on

behalf of his leprous father Azariah. Like his father he battled and
built, and it is expressly stated that he did not fall into his father's
folly (2 Chron. xxvii. 2). Wherein his father did right, so did
he; and wherein his father went wrong, he did not. The moral
and spiritual condition of the people at this time was very bad,
as *Isaiah* shows (chs. i., v.). There was a pretence of religion
without reality and scrupulous ceremonialism was made a cloak
for evil-doing. But, it would appear, Jotham was no party to this.
The records do not charge him with any form of sin, as is done
in the case of all the other kings of Judah. In his day *Amos*,
Hosea and *Isaiah* prophesied.

12 AHAZ

2 Kings xvi.   2 Chron. xxviii.   Isa. vii. 1-ix. 7; xiv. 28-32; xxxviii. 8

B.C. 742—726 = 16 Years

Ahaz was the wicked son of a good father. He was the worst
king of Judah, and is the typical apostate. 'He sinned against
light and knowledge; with every opportunity and incentive
to keep in the right path, he yet went astray'. Nothing but
evil is recorded of him, and at the age of thirty-six he died 'unwept, unhonoured, and unsung'. The phrase of the Chronicler,
'this is that Ahaz' (xxviii. 22), should be to all men, especially
to young men, a solemn warning.

A degenerate son, an apostate king, and an unsuccessful
warrior, his story is the blackest blot in the history of Judah.
He renounced the religion of Jehovah, and adopted the worship
of Baal and other false gods. He confirmed the use of idolatrous
altars in the land, and introduced new ones. He shut the doors
of the Temple, so that the only deity who was not worshipped
in Judah was Jehovah. His short life was full of iniquity, for
alike against the mercy of the LORD, and His repeated judgments,
Ahaz hardened his heart. He derided the true religion as worthless and unmeaning, and seemed to make God responsible for
his misfortunes.

Isaiah tells of the opportunities which were given him, and
makes evident the divine forbearance (chs. vii., viii.), but it was
all wasted on Ahaz who was an incorrigible sinner.

With the exception of the first six years of Hezekiah's reign, to which reference will be made in the Single Kingdom period, Ahaz's reign ends that part of the Divided Kingdom which relates to the South and we must now turn to the story of the North.

THE KINGS OF ISRAEL

We have seen that of these there were nineteen, that they were divided into nine dynasties, that they were all bad, and that the Kingdom lasted for 253 years (Charts 53, 55).

Before summarizing the records of these kings it will be well to get an approximate idea of the relation in time to one another of the kings of the South and the North. This will show what kings were contemporaries for a time.

CHART 60

CONTEMPORARY VIEW OF THE KINGS				
JUDAH		**ISRAEL**		
KING	REIGN	KING	REIGN	DYN.
Rehoboam	17	Jeroboam I	22	I
Abijam	3			
Asa	41			
		Nadab	2	
		Baasha	24	II
		Elah	2	
		Zimri	7 days	III
		Omri	12	IV
		(Tibni)	(5)	
		Ahab	22	
Jehoshaphat	25			
		Ahaziah	2	
		Joram	12	
Jehoram	8			
Ahaziah	1			
Athaliah	6	Jehu	28	V
Jehoash	40			
		Jehoahaz	17	
		Joash	16	
Amaziah	29			
		Jeroboam II	41	
Azariah	52			
(Uzziah)				
		(INTERREGNUM 11)		
		Zachariah	6 months	
		Shallum	1 month	VI
		Menahem	10	VII
		Pekahiah	2	
		Pekah	20	VIII
Jotham	16			
Ahaz	16			
		(INTERREGNUM 9)		
		Hoshea	9	IX
Hezekiah	to 6th year			

1 JEROBOAM I

1 Kings xi. 26-39; xii. 1-xiv. 20

B.C. 975—954=22 Years

The worst that can be said about any man is that he persistently sinned and made others to sin; a thing that is said twenty-five times of 'Jeroboam the son of Nebat'. No man ever had a finer opportunity, and never did any man so wickedly throw it away. He was told that if he would hearken to all that God would command him, and walk in His ways, and do what was right in His sight, and keep His statutes and commandments, God would be with him, and build him a sure house as He had done for David, and would give Israel unto him (1 Kings xi. 38). What more could a man want to have than that? Yet Jeroboam deliberately and persistently threw it all away by his sinning and making Israel to sin.

He instituted *new centres of worship* in Bethel and Dan (1 Kings xii. 29); *new objects of worship*, Egyptian gods (1 Kings xii. 28); *a new altar of sacrifice* (1 Kings xii. 33); *a new order of priests* (1 Kings xii. 31); and *a new annual feast* (1 Kings xii. 32, 33).

'A man of God', a prophet (so called 15 times: 1 Kings xiii.), remonstrated with the king, and predicted that disaster would overtake his false altar, and false priests, and the prophecy was literally fulfilled (cf. 1 Kings xiii. 2, and 2 Kings xxiii. 20).

When he was in trouble, Jeroboam sent to the prophet *Ahijah*, whom he hated, to ask what would be the fate of his sick son; and he was told that the child would die, and that the house of Jeroboam would be cut off, taken away like dung, and would not be buried (1 Kings xiv. 1-20; xv. 29).

'God's fiats are irrevocable, because with Him there is no changeableness, neither shadow of turning.'

> The moving finger writes, and having writ,
> Moves on; nor all thy piety nor wit
> Shall lure it back to cancel half a line,
> Nor all thy tears wash out a word of it'.

2 NADAB
1 Kings xv. 25-31
B.C. 954—953 = 2 Years

The record of the reign of this son of Jeroboam is given in seven verses, and no more are needed, for there were only two things to be said of him, namely, how he reigned, and how he died. He 'walked in the way of his father, and in his sin wherewith he made Israel to sin'; and 'Baasha conspired against him, and smote him'; and with his murder the first dynasty of the North ended, having lasted twenty-four years.

3 BAASHA
1 Kings xv. 16-22, 27-30, 32-xvi. 7.   2 Chron. xvi. 1-6
B.C. 953—930 = 24 Years

With Baasha began the second dynasty in the North. He was of the tribe of Issachar, and the only ruler of that slothful tribe (Gen. xlix. 14, 15), except the unknown Tola, the Judge (Judg. x. 1). Apparently he was a general in the army of Israel, and revolting, murdered the king, and proceeded at once to exterminate the whole house of Nebat. This ferocious act is said to be 'according unto the saying of the LORD, which He spake by His servant Ahijah the Shilonite; because of the sins of Jeroboam' (1 Kings xv. 29, 30; xiv. 7-16); yet it is condemned in 1 Kings xvi. 7. The mystery abides that often man is condemned for fulfilling God's will (2 Kings ix. 7, with Hos. i. 4. See Isa. x. 5-15; xlii. Acts iii. 18; iv. 28, xiii. 27).

When Baasha fortified Ramah, some six miles north of Jerusalem, for the purposes of protection and aggression, Asa, king of Judah, bribed Benhahad I of Syria to invade Israel, and Baasha was obliged to give up fortifying Ramah, and retired to Tirzah his capital.

Jehu, a prophet, told Baasha that his family would be exterminated; that what he had done to the family of Nebat would be done to his own; and this was fulfilled by Zimri two years after Baasha's death (1 Kings xvi. 8-13). Herbert Spencer said that 'motion once set up along any line becomes itself a cause of subsequent motion along that line'. The truth of this is abundantly illustrated by the whole history of the Northern Kingdom.

4 ELAH

1 Kings xvi. 6, 8-10

B.C. 930—929=2 Years

This man, the son of Baasha, was a befuddled fool, and while drinking himself drunk in the house of Arza his steward at Tirzah, Zimri, a captain in the army, murdered him; and with him the second dynasty ended.

5 ZIMRI

1 Kings xvi. 8-20

B.C. 929: 7 days

What Baasha had done to the house of Nebat, Zimri did to the house of Baasha; and though this was a shocking crime on Zimri's part, it was 'according to the will of the LORD' (1 Kings xvi. 12, 1-4, 20). When the people heard what had happened they made Omri, the captain of the army, king of Israel. Omri's first act was to deal with Zimri. This he did by besieging Tirzah the capital, and when Zimri saw that there was no escape, he set fire to the house in which he was and perished in the flames. This is all we know of one week of this man's life, except that he furnished a proverb of the terrible fate of rebels (2 Kings ix. 31).

6 OMRI

1 Kings xvi. 16-28

B.C. 929—918=12 Years

Omri's appointment to the throne was not acceptable to all Israel, and the dissentients chose as their king a man named *Tibni*, with the result that, for five or six years, Israel had two kings, but Tibni died, and Omri, for six or seven years, reigned alone. Like all his predecessors he was wicked. He 'wrought evil in the eyes of the LORD, and did worse than all that were before him'.

Several particulars relative to this king should be carefully noted.

1. He was the founder of the fourth dynasty, which lasted for 48 years; the influence of which was felt far beyond the territory of Israel, and long after Omri's time.

2. Omri chose Samaria to be the new capital, a place which became famous, and which Isaiah called 'the crown of pride' (xxviii. 1-4). For this place, which he did not find famous, but made it so, he paid between seven and eight hundred pounds.

3. Omri is the first Jewish king whose name is alluded to in Assyrian inscriptions. His name occurs twice on the *Moabite Stone*, to which reference must be made in the next reign.

4. That he was a brave soldier seems implied by the reference to 'his might' in 1 Kings xvi. 27. The *Moabite Stone* says:

'Omri, king of Israel, —— oppressed Moab for a long time . . .
And Omri took the whole land of Medeba, and occupied it all his days, and half of his son's days, forty years'.

5. With this king the period of Judah's and Israel's first antagonism ended (Chart 59).

7 AHAB

1 Kings xvi. 29-xxii. 40.   2 Chron. xviii.
B.C. 918—897=22 Years

More space is given to the period of Ahab's reign than to that of any other king of either Judah or Israel. This fact is due to Elijah and his ministry; to one of the greatest men of Old Testament story, and of all time. (See The Prophets).

As for Ahab, he is a moral mystery, combining in himself qualities both good and bad, but, alas, chiefly bad.

Outstanding facts of his life and reign are: his marriage to Jezebel, a heathen princess; his alliance with Jehoshaphat, the king of Judah, by the marriage of his daughter Athaliah to Jehoram the son of Jehoshaphat, by which union the two kingdoms were brought into peaceful relations with one another for nearly eighty years; his building enterprises (1 Kings xxii. 39); his prowess and success in warfare (1 Kings xx. 1-22, 23-33); his attitude in the matter of Naboth and his vineyard; and his contacts with Elijah. It would seem, also, that this king was the first polygamist of the kings of the North (1 Kings xx. 3).

Jezebel's character was uniformly and consistently wicked, but Ahab's was not. That he never abandoned the worship of Jehovah is seen in the names of some of his children: *Ahaziah*, 'Jehovah supports'; *Jehoram*, 'Jehovah is exalted'; *Athaliah*, 'Jehovah is strong'; and in the fact that his attendant, *Obadiah*, was, both by name ('worshipper of Jehovah'), and confession a servant of Jehovah. His sin was not that he forsook Jehovah for Baal, but that he tried to serve them both (1 Kings xviii. 21).

But, on the other hand, he sanctioned in Israel the worship of Baal, and of Ashtoreth, building an altar for Baal in Samaria, and there also erecting Asherim, upright wooden stocks of trees, for the worship of the Nature-goddess, Ashtoreth.

He did nothing to prevent the slaying of the prophets of Baal on Carmel, and nothing to prevent the slaying by Jezebel of the prophets of the LORD. He did not, and would not, slay Naboth in order to get his vineyard, but he readily availed himself of the opportunity which Jezebel's murder of Naboth presented. He broods over sinful wishes, and yet he hates Micaiah, and all who crossed him in any way. Like a shuttlecock he was bashed about between Jezebel and Elijah, between what was wrong and what was right. 'The land was ruled by Ahab: Ahab was ruled by Jezebel: Jezebel was under idolatry to Baal and Ashtoreth: and Baal and Ashtoreth were gods of blood and of uncleanness'.

JEZEBEL

Jezebel must be reckoned among the wickedest of women; in a class with Potiphar's wife, Athaliah, Herodias, Clytaemestra, Lady Macbeth, and with all who have used their femininity to seduce, and to oppose and persecute truth and those who proclaim it.

Jezebel was reckless, fierce, and licentious, fanatical and subtle; a proud heathen Canaanite, who, when she came into the stream of Israel's history, cursed it beyond recovery. Her arrogance, her thirst for power and her insensate cruelty, have given her a unique place in the history of devilry. Ahab did not sanction Baalism by endeavouring to exterminate Jehovahism, but Jezebel did. Her endeavour to wipe out the prophets of the LORD is not recorded in detail, but enough is said to show how merciless it was.   So thoroughgoing was her attempt at extirpation that Elijah thought he was the only one left (1 Kings xviii. 22; xix. 10, 14), and those who escaped death had to wander about in destitution, and to hide in dens and caves of the earth (1 Kings xviii. 4).   Jezebel first instituted religious persecution.   'She is the authentic authoress of priestly inquisitions'.

'Her character was strong, firm, unmalleable; a diamond heart, cold, passionless, cruel, and sharp as a dagger's edge'.   Ahab was no match for her, and virtually she ruled Israel, and her accursed influence was perpetuated in Judah through her daughter Athaliah; and more than a thousand years later God said: 'I have this against thee, that thou sufferest the woman Jezebel, who calleth herself a prophetess; and she teacheth and seduceth my servants to commit fornication, and to eat things sacrificed to idols' (Rev. ii. 20).

Her end will not allow us to forget that there is such a thing as retribution.   With shameless ignominy she was flung down from the palace tower into the street below, and her blood spurted upon the wall and on the horses of Jehu, who drove over her corpse, and entered the gate of her capital with his chariot wheels crimson with her blood.   'The wicked perisheth, and no man regardeth'.

8 AHAZIAH

1 Kings xxii. 51—2 Kings i. 18

B.C. 897—896 = 2 Years

The only thing for which this man is known is his sin, for he practised the evil both of Jeroboam and Jezebel.   He fell from an upper chamber window and was badly hurt; following which he sent to inquire, not of Jehovah, but of Baal-Zebub, a god of Ekron, as to his fate.   Baal-Zebub means *lord of flies*, with the significance of *fly-hatcher*, or *fly-catcher*.   Elijah confronted his messengers, and they returned to Samaria.   Then, in succession two troops of fifty men with a captain were sent to fetch the prophet, and on both he called down fire and consumed them.   A third troop was sent, and Elijah went with them to Samaria, and told Ahaziah that he would die, which he did, having reigned for about two years.

9 JORAM

2 Kings iii. 1-ix. 29. 2 Chron. xxii. 7-9

B.C. 896—884 = 12 Years

Joram was a son of Ahab, and a brother of Ahaziah. He followed the Baal but not the Phoenician idolatry. The Moabites had revolted against their submission to Israel, and Joram sought the help of Jehoshaphat, king of Israel, and of the king of Edom, in his intended attack upon Moab. This was done, and the three armies were successful, with the help of *Elisha* (2 Kings iii. 4-27). Benhadad II again besieged Sàmaria, but fled, being terrified by miraculous noises. A prophet anointed Jehu to be king of Israel, and he went to Jezreel, where Joram was, and shot him through the heart with an arrow, and cast his body into Naboth's field (cf. 1 Kings xxi. 17-24; 2 Kings ix. 24-26). Another failure.

10 JEHU

1 Kings xix. 15-18; 2 Kings ix., x.; xv. 12; 2 Chron. xxii. 7, 8: Hos. i. 4

B.C. 884—856 = 28 Years

Jehu was the founder of the fifth and longest dynasty in Israel. It lasted for 111 years and, in addition to an interregnum of 11 years, there were five kings: Jehu, Jehoahaz, Joash, Jeroboam II, and Zachariah. Jehu had followed Ahab (2 Kings ix. 25), and at this time was captain of the host of Israel (2 Kings ix. 5). *Elijah* had been told to anoint Jehu king over Israel, but he had not done so, and the task was left to *Elisha*, who was waiting for a suitable opportunity to accomplish it. That opportunity came when the kings of Judah and Israel, Ahaziah and Jehoram, were together in Jezreel, away from their capitals and armies.

How the commission given to Elijah was fulfilled is recorded in 2 Kings ix. 1-13; and the results are recorded in the narrative which follows.

This narrative brands Jehu as an arch-murderer. By a blood-bath he came to the throne, and in ferocity he exceeded all who had gone before him, and all who followed him. His murders were innumerable: 1. Jehoram. 2. Ahaziah. 3. Jezebel. 4.

20

Ahab's seventy sons. 5. Ahab's followers in Jezreel. 6. Forty-two of the brethren of Ahaziah. 7. Ahab's followers in Samaria. 8. The prophets, servants, and priests of Baal.

This ghastly and gory record must occasion the thoughtful reader much perplexity, because of the prophecy in 1 Kings xix. 16; xxi. 17-24; and the references in 2 Kings x. 10, 30. That the LORD determined the elimination of the house of Ahab, and that Jehu was chosen to accomplish it is clear; yet no one can believe that the atrocious cruelty of Jehu had Divine sanction. Two facts seem to emerge: first, that one may do a right thing in a wrong way; and secondly, that throughout all history there is evidence that the purposes of God have been accomplished by wicked men and women; but this fact never can justify the wicked means.

Jehu claimed Divine sanction for his diabolical work, but

> Crime was ne'er so black
> As ghostly cheer and pious thanks to lack.
> Satan is modest. At heaven's door he lays
> His evil offspring, and in Scriptural phrase
> And saintly posture gives to God the praise
> And honour of his monstrous progeny.
>
>   (J. G. Whittier)

When Jehu accomplished his last great crime he extirpated Baal-worship from Israel (2 Kings x. 19-28), but the symbolic worship of the golden calves remained (x. 29). 'Jehu took no heed to walk in the law of the LORD God of Israel with all his heart: for he departed not from the sins of Jeroboam, who made Israel to sin' (x. 31).

One wonders where *Elisha* was during all these happenings! After sending a young prophet, perhaps Jonah, to anoint Jehu king of Israel, he disappeared, and nothing more is heard of him for nearly half a century!

No man, however, gets away with his sin, and retribution overtook Jehu. His bloody deeds were condemned by *Amos* (i. 11; ii. 1) and *Hosea* (i. 4); and his degradation is depicted on the Black Obelisk of *Shalmaneser* II, now in the British Museum. There he is seen kneeling and grovelling at the feet of the Assyrian king, with his beard sweeping the ground.

11 JEHOAHAZ

2 Kings xiii. 1-9

B.C. 856—839 = 17 Years

Jehoahaz succeeded to a lamentable heritage, for *Hazael*, king of Syria, and after him, Benhadad III, destroyed Israel, 'and made them like the dust in threshing'. So reduced was the king that at one time he had but fifty horsemen, ten chariots, and ten thousand footmen.

When Jehoahaz 'besought the LORD', a temporary respite was granted to Israel, but the king turned not from the sins of the house of Jeroboam, and died after a fruitless seventeen years upon the throne. With his reign ended the period of fateful alliance between Judah and Israel (Chart 59).

12 JOASH

2 Kings xiii. 10-xiv. 16. 2 Chron. xxv. 17-25

B.C. 839—825 = 16 Years

Though this king, like all his predecessors, followed in the way of Jeroboam's sins, there are some things recorded which are to his credit. These are: his visit to the death-bed of Elisha, and his grief over the dying prophet; his three victories over the Syrians at Aphek, and recovery of all the cities which Hazael had taken from his father on the west of Jordan; and the mercy he showed to the very foolish king of Judah, Amaziah, who challenged him to fight, and who was thoroughly beaten. Joash had Amaziah in his power, but he did not slay him. and was outlived by him for fifteen years.

Of Joash's reply to the challenge of Amaziah, Farrar says it 'was one of the most crushingly contemptuous pieces of irony which history records, and yet it was eminently kindly and good-humoured'. It is the second of the only two fables in the Bible (2 Kings xiv. 9: cf. Judg. ix. 7-15).

Joash found Israel broken and dishonoured, and, after sixteen years, he left it largely recovered and prosperous. But, alas, he pursued a course of sin

13 JEROBOAM II

2 Kings xiv. 23-29

B.C. 825—784=41 Years

Edersheim says that 'Jeroboam II was certainly the most warlike king and the most successful administrator of all who occupied the throne of Israel'. And *Farrar*: 'He was by far the greatest and most powerful of all the kings of Israel, as he was also the longest-lived and had the longest reign.' And *Aglen*: 'About this the greatest of Samaria's kings, the history is the briefest'.

Politically this reign was great; distinguished by the complete defeat of Syria, and the recovery of all the territory which had been lost in previous reigns (2 Kings xiv. 25).

Religiously, it was deplorable. It is likely that Jeroboam's victories were gained in the early part of his reign, and the rest of the long period was spent in extravagant luxury and indulgence, and of deepest moral corruption. This information we get, not from the historian, but from the prophets of the period, *Amos* and *Hosea*. (See Hos. ii. 8; xii. 9; Am. iii. 15; vi. 4-6; and Hos. ii. 8, 13, 17; Am. iv. 4, 5; Hos. iv. 10, 11, 18; vi. 8-10; Am. ii. 6-8; iii. 10; v. 7, 11.)

But there is another angle from which this period must be viewed, namely, *prophetically*, and it is this which gives to it its chief distinctiveness. When, later, we consider the Prophets, more will be said about this, but it is important that we should see now that in Jeroboam's reign a new stage in prophecy began. Two things must be noted. Firstly, that from now prophetic *literature* began to make its appearance. There had already been great prophets, *Elijah* for instance, but their ministry was *oral*; but from now it began to be *literary*. *Jonah* spoke; but *Amos* and *Hosea* wrote, and they were followed by the others whose prophecies we have. And secondly, that henceforth the prophetic horizon enlarges, and the outlook of the prophets is more and more on the hope of the Messiah and His Kingdom.

Jeroboam can take no credit for this, for with him the hopes of the Northern Kingdom faded away, and the time had come for the birth of a new hope, the hope which was realized when *The Messiah* came.

With the death of Jeroboam the kingdom of Israel entered upon a dark and troublous period of eleven years, during which it had no king, and about which we know practically nothing; and in the forty years which followed, Israel swept swiftly to its doom, a doom from which it has not yet recovered.

14 ZACHARIAH

2 Kings xv. 8-12
B.C. 773: 6 Months

Jeroboam's son occupied the throne of Israel for six months, and then he was murdered. The only thing we know about him is that 'he did evil in the sight of the LORD'. Jehu had been promised a succession of four generations on the throne (2 Kings x. 30), and with Zachariah the period ended (2 Kings xv. 12). Possibly we have a picture of him and his circumstances in Hosea vii. 1-7.

'So did the dynasty of the mighty Jehu expire like a torch blown out in stench and smoke.'

15 SHALLUM

2 Kings xv. 13-15
B.C. 772: 1 Month

Shallum was a usurper, and introduced the sixth dynasty in Israel, which, however, lasted for one month only; at the end of which time he was murdered by Menahem.

16 MENAHEM

2 Kings xv. 16-22
B.C. 772—761 = 10 Years

Menahem slew Shallum, and introduced the seventh dynasty in Israel, which lasted for twelve years. We are told three things only of this man: firstly, that he was horribly cruel; secondly, that he followed in the way of Israel's past kings; and thirdly, that while he was king, *Pul*, or *Tiglath-Pileser* of Assyria invaded Israel, and Menahem paid him 'a thousand talents of silver' not to molest him; and Pul turned back. The anarchy of the time is depicted by *Hosea*. Menahem was the last king of Israel to die a natural death.

17 PEKAHIAH

2 Kings xv. 23-26
B.C. 761—759 = 2 Years

Of this son of Menahem we are told nothing, except that he followed the course of sin which all his predecessors had marked out; and that he was murdered by his chief cavalry officer.

18 PEKAH

2 Kings xv. 27-31; xvi. 2 Chron. xxviii. 5-15. Isaiah vii.-lx.
B.C. 759—739 = 20 Years

Pekah introduced the eighth dynasty in Israel, which lasted for the twenty years of his reign, and the nine years of interregnum which followed it. Like all who had gone before him, he worshipped the golden calves, and like so many of his predecessors he came to the throne by murder. The outstanding event of his reign was his alliance with Rezin, king of Syria, against Judah. The first invasion failed, but great damage was done to Judah on the second invasion; 120,000 men were slaughtered, and a multitude of captives were deported to Damascus. Also, Pekah carried 200,000 women and children to Samaria, but on the remonstrance of the prophet *Oded*, and the Elders of Israel, they were sent back (2 Chron. xxviii. 5-15). Ahaz, king of Judah, appealed to *Tiglath-Pileser*, king of Assyria, because of an invasion of Edomites and Philistines, and a threatened third invasion of Israel and Syria. With treasures from the Temple and Palace he bribed the Assyrian, who marched westward, defeated and slew Rezin; invaded Northern Israel; and carried away the two and a half tribes who were resident on the East of Jordan. So the first to be settled were the first to be deported. Isaiah vii.-viii. throws light on these events.

19 HOSHEA

2 Kings xv. 30; xvii.; xviii. 9-12. Ezek. xxiii. 5-10

B.C. 730—722 = 9 Years

Hoshea introduced into Israel the ninth and last dynasty, which terminated nine years later when he was deported to Assyria. This king also followed in evil ways, but, we are told, 'not as the kings of Israel that were before him'; by which is meant, perhaps, that he did not actively oppose the worship of Jehovah, nor put any hindrance in the way of Israelites who wished to attend the Passover at Jerusalem (2 Chron. xxx. 1-12). He reigned in subjection to Assyria, paying tribute to the king; but he foolishly turned to Egypt for help to throw off the Assyrian yoke. *Shalmaneser* got word of this, and came against Samaria. He took Hoshea captive, and laid siege to the capital. During this siege the Assyrian king died, and was succeeded by *Sargon*, who at the end of the third year of investment took Samaria and led into captivity, not all Israel (as is often supposed), but 27,280 of the chief inhabitants, including the priests (2 Kings xvii. 27), and thus, after 253 years (Chart 55) ended the Kingdom of Israel, B.C. 722.

THE TRAGIC NORTH

Scanning the history of the Kingdom of Israel throughout the 253 years of its existence, we must recognize that all the facts and features look in one direction, and that is *away from God*.

There were nineteen kings, and they were all bad. The succession from father to son was broken nine times. There were two periods—one of 11 years, and one of 9 years—during which there was no one on the throne. Only seven of the nineteen kings died a natural death. One was stricken by God; two died from battle wounds; one committed suicide; one fell from an upper room and was killed; six were murdered, and one was taken into captivity, and his fate is unknown. Twelve of the kings reigned for twelve years or less; one of them for six months; one, for a month; and one, for a week. Ten of them were involved in wars. Their records are not included in the account of the Chronicler.   Yet the Northern Kingdom had, up to this time, produced great and numerous prophets—*Ahijah, Elijah, Elisha, Iddo, Oded, Jehu, Micaiah, Obadiah* (?), *Jonah, Amos, Hosea*, and some unnamed prophets, but all to no purpose.

We are shown in these 'God-abandoned phantoms of guilty royalty' (Farrar), 'what ruins kingdoms and lays cities waste' (Milton).   The causes of Israel's overthrow are detailed in a striking passage in the account of it (2 Kings xvii. 7-23).

AFTER THE FALL OF THE NORTHERN KINGDOM

What at this point is relevant to our purpose can be briefly told.   *Sargon*, in keeping with the policy of Assyrian kings, deported from Israel to his own dominions the wealthy and educated population, and all the teachers of religion, and left behind only the poor and ignorant.   Then he deported from the East to Israel's territory a mongrel population (2 Kings xvii. 24. Cf. Ezra iv. 9, 10), speaking different languages, and following different religious customs.

The neglect of agriculture led to an increase of wild beasts in the land (2 Kings xvii. 25), which the Ephraimites regarded as a Divine judgment because the new settlers 'knew not the manner of the God of the land'.   A message was sent therefore to Sargon, explaining the situation, and asking that someone be sent who could teach this mixed throng 'how they should fear the LORD'. A deported priest was sent back from the East, but the effort was not effectual, for each nation followed its own god.   The result was that the whole mongrel population 'feared the LORD, and served their own gods.'

These conditions produced the Samaritans of whom we read later (Ezra, Nehemiah, the Gospels), and who now are the 'oldest and smallest sect in the world'.   The word occurs only once in the Old Testament (2 Kings xvii. 29), but John iv. 9 is explained by Ezra iv.

The so-called 'Ten Lost Tribes' cannot be lost, for their restoration in the future is clearly predicted; but where they are now chiefly located, and under what names, it were hazardous to say.

SYNCHRONISTIC SURVEY

In studying the 253 years of the Divided Kingdom, there are three things to which careful attention should be given, namely: the geographical relation of the Kingdoms to their neighbours, near and far; the rulers of the larger Powers who made contact with the Kingdoms, and who are introduced in the records; and the Prophets, oral and literary, who ministered during this more than two and a half centuries (Chart 61).

1 The Geographical Relation of the Kingdoms to their Neighbours

From Map 9 it will be seen that Palestine was bordered on the North, East, and South West by powerful nations, and the records tell us that it had contact with them all; how, and why, and with what result. Egypt and Assyria in particular were rivals, and Palestine lying between them was exposed to the armies of them both. Less powerful in some ways, but very formidable, was Syria in the North, with which each of the Kingdoms made a connection.

2 The Foreign Kings who Made Contact with Judah and Israel

In Chart 61 it will be seen when all these contacts were made by Judah and Israel, and who the kings were, Egyptian, Syrian, Assyrian, and Babylonian who came to their aid, or came against them. The Biblical references are given, but for some of the information we are dependent on the records of these foreign kings, as, for instance, in the reigns of Ahab and Jehu who are named in *Cuneiform Inscriptions*.

The following are the Assyrian Sovereigns of this period who were in contact with the Kingdoms in Palestine.

Shalmaneser II (III)	B.C. 911-876
Assyrian dates	B.C. 860-825
Tiglath-Pileser III (IV)	B.C. 745-727
Shalmaneser IV (V)	B.C. 727-722
Sargon II	B.C. 722-705

The following are the Syrian Sovereigns of the same period.

Benhadad I.	B.C. 950-920
Benhadad II.	B.C. 920-880
Hazael	B.C. 880-850
Benhadad III.	B.C. 850-840
Rezin	B.C. 740 (?)

3 THE PROPHETS OF THE DIVIDED KINGDOM PERIOD

It is interesting and important to observe that to the time of Azariah in Judah, and Jeroboam II in Israel, the prophecies were *oral*, and that from these reigns they began to be *written*. The prophecy of *Jonah* is not recorded, but we have *Amos, Hosea, Micah*, the early part of *Isaiah*, and almost certainly *Joel* in this period. In addition to the prophets named, there were one or two who are not named, but whose ministry was very important (See Chart 61).

The main literary period of prophecy was subsequent to the Captivity of the Northern Kingdom in B.C. 722.

CHART 61

SYNCHRONISTIC SURVEY OF THE DIVIDED KINGDOM PERIOD

JUDAH	PROPHETS	CONTEMPORARY KINGS			ISRAEL	PROPHETS
		EGYPT	SYRIA	ASSYRIA and BABYLONIA		
1. Rehoboam	Shemaiah 1 K. xii. 22-24; 2 C. xi. 1-4; xii. 5-8, 15. Iddo 2 C. ix. 29; xii. 15.	Shishak 1 K. xi. 40; xiv. 25, 26. 2 C. xii. 2-10	Rezon 1 K. xi. 23		1. Jeroboam	Ahijah 1 K. xi; xii. 15; xiv; xv. 29. 2 C. ix. 29; x. 15. 'A man of God' 1 K. xiii.
2. Abijah(m)	Iddo 2 C. xiii. 22				2. Nadab	
3. Asa	Oded 2 C. xv. 1, 8. Azariah 2 C. xv. 1-7 Hanani 2 C. xvi. 7-10.	Zerah (prob. Osarkon II) 2 C. xiv. 9-15; xvi. 8.	Benhadad I 1 K. xv. 16-21. 2 C. xvi. 1-5.		3. Baasha 4. Elah 5. Zimri 6. Omri (Tibni) 7. Ahab	Jehu 1 K. xvi. 1-4, 7 Elijah 1 K. xvii-xxii. 2 K. i-ii. Micaiah 1 K. xxii. 7-28. 'A certain man' 1 K. xx. 35

CHART 61—Continued

JUDAH	PROPHETS	Contemporary Kings — EGYPT	SYRIA	ASSYRIA and BABYLONIA	ISRAEL	PROPHETS
4. Jehoshaphat	Jehu 2 C. xix. 1-3; xx. 34; Eliezer 2 C. xx. 35-37		Benhadad II 1 K. xx. 2 K. vi. 24; viii. 7, 9.	Shalmaneser II (III) (Cuneiform Inscription).		
					8. Ahaziah	Elisha 2 K. ii-viii.
5. Jehoram			Benhadad II		9. Joram	Elisha 2 K. ix, x.
6. Ahaziah			Hazael 1 K. xix. 15, 17	Shalmaneser II (III) (Cuneiform Inscription)	10. Jehu	
7. Athaliah			Hazael 2 K. x. 32, 33			
8. Jehoash	Joel		Hazael 2 K. xii. 17,18; xiii. 3.		11. Jehoahaz	
			Benhadad III 2 K. xiii. 3-7			

CHART 61—Continued

JUDAH	PROPHETS	EGYPT	SYRIA	ASSYRIA and BABYLONIA	ISRAEL	PROPHETS
9. Amaziah			Hazael 2 K. xiii. 10-25; Benhadad III 2 K. xiii. 10-25		12. Joash	Elisha 2 K. xiii. 10-25
10. Azariah	Zechariah 2 C. xxvi. 5. Isaiah (vi. 1)		Benhadad III 2 K. xiv. 28		13. Jeroboam II	Jonah 2 K. xiv. 25. Arros (i. 1) Hosea (i. 1)
					14. Zachariah 15. Shallum	
				Pul (Tiglath-Pileser III (IV)) 2 K. xv. 19. 1 C. v. 6, 26.	16. Menahem	
					17. Pekahiah	
11. Jotham	Isaiah (i. 1) Micah (i. 1)		Rezin 2 K. xv. 37, 38. Isa. vii 1, 4, 8; viii. 6; ix. 11.	Tiglath-Pileser III (IV). 2 K. xv. 29; xvi. 7, 10. 1 C. v. 6, 26.	18. Pekah	Oded 2 C. xxviii. 9-15 (Isaiah vii-ix)

317

CHART 61—*Continued*

JUDAH	PROPHETS	CONTEMPORARY KINGS			ISRAEL	PROPHETS
		EGYPT	SYRIA	ASSYRIA and BABYLONIA		
12. Ahaz	Isaiah (i. 1) vii-xii. Micah (i. 1)		Rezin 2 K. xvi. 5, 6, 9 2 C. xxviii. 5	Tiglath-Pileser III (IV). 2 K. xvi. 7-18. Isa. vii-ix. 2 C. xxviii. 16, 20		
13. Hezekiah		So (Shabak) 2 K. xvii. 4		Shalmaneser IV (V). 2 K. xvii. 3-5; xviii. 9. Sargon 2 K. xvii. 6. Isa. xx. 1-6.	19. Hoshea	

318

(i) THE PROPHETS OF JUDAH

(a) THE ORAL PROPHETS

Shemaiah (1 Kings xii. 22-24. 2 Chron. xi. 1-4; xii. 5-8, 15)

A prophet in the reign of Rehoboam, called 'a man of God'. When the king prepared to fight the Israelites who had rebelled against him and formed another kingdom, Shemaiah was sent to warn him against such a course, and Rehoboam heeded the warning.

He also explained to Rehoboam that the invasion of Shishak, king of Egypt, was divinely intended, because of Judah's sins. This led to the king and princes of Judah humbling themselves, but Shishak took much treasure from Jerusalem.

Shemaiah also wrote a history of Rehoboam's reign.

Iddo (2 Chron. ix. 29; xii. 15; xiii. 22)

There is on record no prophetic utterance of this man, but certain writings of his are referred to. He wrote 'against Jeroboam the son of Nebat'; and made a register of David's genealogy; and left 'memoirs' of the reign of Abijah, king of Judah. Nothing is said of this prophet in the Books of Kings. These writings are lost, but they may have formed a part of the foundation of the Books of Chronicles.

Oded (2 Chron. xv. 1, 8)

Oded was the father of the prophet Azariah. If in verse 8 *Oded* is not a mistake for Azariah, he too was a prophet, though there is no record of what he said. The word 'and' would seem to distinguish him from his son. Another man of this name prophesied in the reign of Pekah, king of Israel, over 200 years later.

Azariah (2 Chron. xv. 1-8)

He was the son of Oded; and he encouraged Asa, king of Judah, in his religious reforms. His words should be rooted in our mind and conscience:

> 'The LORD is with you, while ye be with Him;
> and if ye seek Him, He will be found of you;
> but if ye forsake Him, He will forsake you' (2)

Hanani (2 Chron. xvi. 7-10)

It was because Asa did not continue to heed what Azariah had said to him, that Hanani condemned him. The king had asked Benhadad I of Syria to help him against Baasha, king of Israel, who was threatening Judah (1 Kings xv. 16-21), and Hanani told him he had done 'foolishly' in not trusting to the LORD only, and that henceforth he would have wars. For this rebuke and prophecy Asa was angry, and put the prophet in prison.

Jehu (2 Chron. xix. 1-3; xx. 34)

Jehoshaphat, king of Judah, united with Ahab, king of Israel, to attack Benhadad I, king of Syria. For doing this Jehu, the son of Hanani, condemned him. His words are memorable:

'Shouldest thou help the ungodly, and love them that hate the LORD?'

Jehu also denounced Baasha, king of Israel.

Eliezer (2 Chron. xx. 35-37)

Of this prophet, and the occasion which led him to prophesy, we know nothing beyond what these three verses tell us. Probably the ships were wrecked by a storm.

Zechariah (2 Chron. xxvi. 3-5)

It is recorded of this man that he 'had understanding in the visions of God'; and, it would seem, he encouraged Azariah (Uzziah) to seek the LORD, which the king did for a time.

(b) THE LITERARY PROPHETS

Joel (B.C. 837-800)

In the Hebrew Canon and in the Septuagint Version *Joel* is one of the first six of the Minor Prophets, though not in the same order in each case, being second in the Hebrew, and fourth in the Greek. Opinions differ widely as to the date of this Prophecy. but it is agreed that it must have been either very early, or very late, and opinions differ by five or six hundred years.

The words of Joel iii. 16 and Amos i. 2; and of Joel iii. 18 and Amos ix. 13, may have been quoted by either prophet from the other, and so do not decide which of the two was prior, though it is likely that Joel was. As no mention is made of Syria, or Assyrai, or Babylonia, it would seem that Joel prophesied either before or after these Powers impinged on the history of Judah and Israel.

The preponderance of the evidence places *Joel* early, as a prophet of Judah, about the time of Jehoash, and so in the pre-Assyrian period. 'The priestly interregnum that occurred during the minority of Je hoash furnishes the situation implied in Joel'.

Riehm says that 'the Book of Joel is amongst the most perfect prophetical Writings'; and Findlay, 'This is one of the choicest productions of Israelite literature'. The Book falls into two main parts. In the first, Joel speaks; and in the second, Jehovah speaks. The first part is historical, and the second prophetical. The first tells of desolation, and the second, of deliverance. The first is a summons to repentance; and the second is an assurance of mercy.

PART I. HISTORICAL—JOEL SPEAKS (i. 1-ii. 17)

DESOLATION

1 The Fact of Desolation (i. 1-20)
2 The Means of Desolation (ii. 1-17)

PART II. PROPHETICAL—JEHOVAH SPEAKS (ii. 18-iii. 21)

DELIVERANCE

1 The Promise of Present Blessing (ii. 18-27)
2 The Promise of Future Blessing (ii. 28-iii. 21)

'At the time when Israel was about to come in contact with the great powers of the ancient world, and fainting spirits might be tempted to tremble for the very existence of the people of God, Joel was inspired confidently to predict the final issue of the conflict between the people of God and the powers of the world. Be it never so long delayed, the day of Jehovah must come, when He will be finally triumphant over every enemy. Be

21

His own people never so obstinate, the goal must finally be reached, when the words shall be fulfilled: "*Jehovah dwelleth in Zion*'.' (Ps. ix. 11; Kirkpatrick, *The Doctrine of the Prophets* p. 79).

Isaiah (B.C. 758-698)

THE MAN

Of Isaiah's *ancestors* we know nothing beyond the fact that he was 'the son of Amoz' (i. 1), but it may be gathered from his circumstances that he belonged to the higher and wealthier classes.

His *name*, which was not uncommon, means 'the Salvation of Yahweh', and was singularly suitable to him as this was the subject which he was commissioned to set forth. We are told that he was *married*, and his wife was called 'the prophetess' (viii. 3). He had *two sons*, whose names, *Shear-jashub* and *Maher-shalal-hash-baz* are connected with his prophetical office, The former, his elder son (vii. 3), means 'A remnant shall return'; and the latter means 'Spoil swiftly, rob quickly'. The prophet was probably *a native of Jerusalem*, and in all likelihood his prophecies were delivered there.

The date of his prophetic call to the prophetic ministry is stated. It was in 'the year that king Uzziah died' (vi. 1), which was B.C. 758; and as he ministered certainly to the end of Hezekiah's reign in B.C. 698, the *duration of his ministry* was about sixty years. We do not know what his age was when he was called to his life-work, nor do we know how long he survived Hezekiah's death, but he must have lived to a ripe old age, to eighty or ninety years.

Isaiah's *call* is recorded in ch. vi. of his Book, but presumably it preceded the prophecies which form chs. i.-v. At the time when his thoughts were occupied with the death of a successful earthly sovereign, he was given a vision of the true Divine King of Israel, and was called to the discharge of a mission which was to absorb all his time and energies.

As to *his character*, Isaiah was undoubtedly the greatest of the Hebrew prophets, the foremost man in the nation in his time, and possibly, after David, the most conspicuous personage in the history of Israel; and, perhaps, more than any other prophet, he has powerfully influenced Jews and Christians for over twenty-seven hundred years. In a critical and eventful period of his nation's history he served the offices of prophet, statesman, reformer, teacher, writer, orator and poet.

The time and manner of his *death* are uncertain. It would seem that he died early in Manasseh's reign, and there is a tradition that he was sawn asunder with a wooden saw (cf. Heb. xi. 37).

THE HISTORICAL SITUATION

The historical circumstances at the time of the prophet's call are clear. When Uzziah came to the throne in Judah Jeroboam II had been reigning in Israel for fifteen years, and was to continue for another twenty-six years. In his reign the Northern Kingdom reached its highest level of prosperity. The Southern Kingdom also enjoyed a period of great prosperity under the rule of Uzziah, but in both countries prosperity engendered vices which, in the North were condemned by *Jonah*, *Amos* and *Hosea*; and in the South, by *Isaiah*, and *Micah*.

'In Judah the increase of wealth and of military strength had produced a proud sense of security; the inclination to idolatry was fostered by foreign trade, which led to the introduction of foreign superstitions; drunkenness was common; a spirit of scepticism and a confusion of moral distinctions penetrated society; and justice was corrupt'. This was the situation which confronted Isaiah, and it was his mission to denounce these evils, to announce judgment, and to tell of divine mercy.

That was the local situation, but there were wider circumstances which it is of the utmost importance to recognize. It was about the middle of the eighth century that *Assyria* began to make itself strongly felt in the regions of Western Asia, and in such a way as to determine for many years to come the history both of Judah and Israel. Before this time Assyria had been active westwards, but in Isaiah's time it, and later Babylonia, became dominating and formative factors in the history of the ancient world. Judah and Israel lay between the great Assyrian and Egyptian Powers, and could not but be affected by that fact.

In Judah, in Isaiah's time, one party looked to Assyria for help against the Syro-Ephraimitic war (2 Kings xvi. 7-9), and another party looked to Egypt (2 Kings xviii. 7), but Isaiah advised against both courses, and advocated reliance upon the Lord God (Isa. xxx. 1, 2). He did not, however, give Judah any encouragement to think they would escape subjection to Assyria, and when once it submitted to that Power the prophet counselled patient acceptance of the irksome political situation in which the people found themselves.

It was when Israel and Syria, under Pekah and Rezin, united against Assyria, and attempted to force Judah into the alliance, that the latter appealed to Assyria for help against this menace. The record of this is in 2 Kings xv. 37; xvi.; 2 Chron. xxviii.; Isa. vii.-x. 4; xvii. The price which Judah paid for her appeal to and reliance on Assyria largely constitutes the history of this people to the time of their Babylonian captivity.

THE BOOK

This treatise is not concerned, except incidentally, with critical questions, as its purpose is to unfold the Drama of Redemption, a truth which is not affected by literary criticism. What is called the *Book of Isaiah* is a collection of many prophecies, uttered or written at different times, and brought together in general chronological sequence.

> 'The entire Book presents the characteristics of a collection or compilation, an artificial gathering into one of prophecies uttered at various times and on various occasions, each of which was complete in itself, and originally intended to stand by itself, without proem or sequel'.

Yet, these many prophecies fall into three main parts, each with characteristics of its own. These parts are: chs. i.-xxxv; chs. xxxvi.-xxxix.; chs. xl.-lxvi.

Part I is Prophetical; Part II is Historical; Part III is Prophetical. In the first, the outlook is mainly Assyrian; in the third, it is mainly Babylonian; and in the second, both these powers are in view. Part I is chiefly Condemnatory; and Part III is chiefly Consolatory. In Part I the Messiah is presented as a Sovereign and Ruler; and in Part III as a Sufferer and Redeemer.

Between these two Parts is the historical narrative of certain events in the reign of Hezekiah.

CHART 62

ISAIAH			
"Concerning Judah and Jerusalem in the days of"			
UZZIAH	JOTHAM	AHAZ, HEZEKIAH	MANASSEH
PROPHETICAL i–xxxv	HISTORICAL xxxvi–xxxix		PROPHETICAL xl–lxvi
Condemnation	**Confiscation**		**Consolation**
ASSYRIAN	ASSYRIAN xxxvi– xxxvii	BABYLONIAN xxxviii– xxxix	BABYLONIAN
1. Chs. i–xii Prophecies concerning Judah and Jerusalem	2 K. xviii-xix 2 C. xxxii Invasion and De-struction of the Assyrian Army under Senna-cherib	2 K. xx Hezekiah's sickness and recovery	1. Chs. xl–xlviii The Deliverance
2. Chs. xiii–xxiii Predictions against Foreign Nations		Embassy of Merodach-Baladan	2. Chs. xlix–lvii The Deliverer
3. Chs. xxiv–xxxv Announcements of Judgments and Deliverances		Predic-tion of Judah's Conquest by Babylon	3. Chs. lviii–lxvi The Delivered

The part of Isaiah's prophecies which falls within the Divided Kingdom Period belongs to the reign of *Jotham* (i.-v.), and the reign of *Ahaz* (vii.-x. 4; xiv. 28-32). The former reflects the moral and spiritual condition of Judah at the time, and announces judgment. The latter relates to the Syro-Ephraimitic War, and announces deliverance.

Micah (B.C. 740-695)

Micah, which means *Who is like Yah?* was contemporary with *Isaiah*. The period of both of them was that of 'Jotham, Ahaz, and Hezekiah' (i. 1). Each faced the same situation, but they approached it in different ways, and this was due, in part at any rate, to the circumstances of their birth and upbringing. Isaiah was a high-bred man of the city; Micah was a homely man of the country. Isaiah was a statesman, with a world-outlook; Micah was occupied with his own land only, and the world immediately around him. Isaiah prophesied 'concerning Judah and Jerusalem'; Micah prophesied 'concerning Samaria and Jerusalem', that is, his prophecies related to both Kingdoms. Isaiah's themes were of wide range, both Jewish and Gentile; Micah's chief theme was the social corruption of the people, North and South, of his time. Yet, notwithstanding these differences of approach to the situation which confronted them, Micah and Isaiah were in fundamental agreement in their admonitions, and instructions for the then present, and in their hopes for the future.

The language of Micah is vigorous, graphic, and varied, and the power and effect of his ministry are illustrated by an important passage in Jeremiah xxvi. 16-19.

His collected utterances fall into three distinct parts, each beginning with the word 'Hear'. In the first part, *The People are Summoned to Attend* (chs. i.-ii.). In the second part, *The Leaders are Summoned to Attend* (chs. iii.-v.). In the third part, *The Mountains are Summoned to Attend* (chs. vi.-vii.).

The Messianic element in Micah is outstanding, and will be noticed later on. The notes of his ministry are, with varying emphasis, those of other Prophecies, namely, Transgression, Condemnation, Visitation, and Restoration.

(ii) THE PROPHETS OF ISRAEL

(a) THE ORAL PROPHETS

Ahijah (1 Kings xi. 29-39; xii. 15; xiv. 2-18; xv. 29; 2 Chron. ix. 29; x. 15)

This prophet, whose name means *Yah is Brother*, was a Shilonite. He dramatically announced to Jeroboam I, the division of Solomon's Kingdom into ten and two parts, by tearing into twelve parts a new garment which he was wearing, and giving ten of them to Jeroboam. The prophecy affirmed that if Jeroboam were obedient to the will of God his Kingdom would be established. This hope, we know, was not fulfilled, because Jeroboam from the beginning rebelled against God.

When Abijah, the son of Jeroboam fell sick, the king sent his wife, disguised, to enquire of Ahijah whether or not the boy would live. The LORD informed Ahijah of what was being done, and he bade her tell her husband that, on account of his sins, the boy would die, and that the family of Jeroboam would perish.

Both these prophecies were fulfilled. The Kingdom was divided; and 'the house of Jeroboam' was 'cut off'.

Jehu (1 Kings xvi. 1-4, 7 2 Chron. xix. 1-3; xx. 34)

Jehu was a prophet, and the son of a prophet—Hanani. He appears twice: first to announce to Baasha, king of Israel, the fate of his 'house' or dynasty; and later to rebuke Jehoshaphat for assisting the wicked king Ahab.

Elijah (1 Kings xvii.-xix.; xxi. 17-29; 2 Kings i.-ii. 14; ix. 36; x. 10, 17; 2 Chron. xxi. 12-15; Mal. iv. 5; Matt. xi. 14; xvi. 14; xvii. 3-12; Mk. vi. 15; ix. 4-13; Lu. i. 17; iv. 25, 26; ix. 8, 19, 28-31; John i. 20, 25; Rom. xi. 1-5; Jas. v. 17, 18)

Elijah whose name means *Yah is my El*, a name which is the embodiment of his creed and mission, is one of the greatest characters in Old Testament story, and, indeed, in religious history. No attempt can be made to do him justice in a few paragraphs, but the salient facts should be apprehended.

He was a prophet to the Northern Kingdom in the time of Ahab and Ahaziah; within the twenty-one years of B.C. 918-897. For the condition of things in Israel at this time see pp. 302-304.

Such a situation demanded a preacher of no ordinary strength and courage, and such an one was Elijah, a man rugged, stern, independent, aloof, and implacable. He had no attachments which could localize him, and so we find him swiftly moving over great distances; suddenly appearing, and suddenly disappearing. We see him now at Cherith in the Jordan Valley, and now in the forests of Carmel; now at Zarephath in Sidon, and now in the wilderness of Horeb; now at the entrance of Jezreel, and now in the wilderness of Damascus; now on the way to Ekron, and now in Beersheba; now at Gilgal, Bethel, Jericho, and the Jordan, and then he ascends to Heaven.

Without any introduction he crashes like a thunderbolt into the midst of Ahab's Court, denouncing idolatry and predicting judgment. Then, some years later, after the judgment of drought, he again appears suddenly and challenges Ahab to a contest on Carmel between Jehovah and Baal. The record of this is one of the greatest things in the Bible (1 Kings xviii.), and has found fitting modern expression in Mendelssohn's 'Elijah', with its haunting 'O Rest in the Lord', and 'He that shall endure to the end.'

Later again, he cuts across the path of Ahab and denounces him for securing, through murder, the vineyard of Naboth, and he predicted the king's tragic end, and that of his wicked wife Jezebel.

Yet his mood and action were not always on this level. After Carmel, when Jezebel threatened to kill him, he fled to Beersheba, taking with him a servant (who, Jewish tradition says, was probably the restored son of the Zarephath widow, *Jonah* the future prophet), and from there he went on to Horeb, made famous and sacred by the presence and experiences of Moses, over 670 years before. In that stern solitude he learned the greatest lessons of his life.

Physical exhaustion, mental reaction, forced inactivity, painful loneliness, and a sense of failure led Elijah to despair. He could well have said, and virtually did say:

> So much I feel my genial spirits droop,
> My hopes all flat, nature within me seems
> In all her functions weary of herself,
> My race of glory run, and race of shame,
> And I shall shortly be with them that rest.

But after he had been given sleep and food, those two physical essentials, he received a theophany, and after that, a new commission. Elijah had to learn that, in spite of Jezebel, all was not lost;

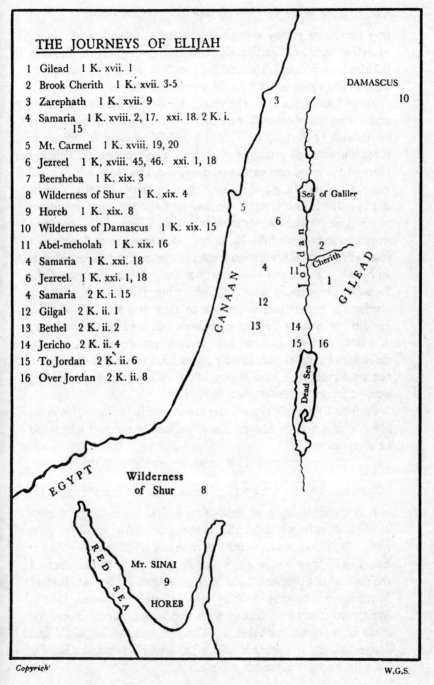

THE JOURNEYS OF ELIJAH

1 Gilead   1 K. xvii. 1
2 Brook Cherith   1 K. xvii. 3-5
3 Zarephath   1 K. xvii. 9
4 Samaria   1 K. xviii. 2, 17. xxi. 18. 2 K. i. 15
5 Mt. Carmel   1 K. xviii. 19, 20
6 Jezreel   1 K, xviii. 45, 46. xxi. 1, 18
7 Beersheba   1 K. xix. 3
8 Wilderness of Shur   1 K. xix. 4
9 Horeb   1 K. xix. 8
10 Wilderness of Damascus   1 K. xix. 15
11 Abel-meholah   1 K. xix. 16
4 Samaria   1 K. xxi. 18
6 Jezreel.   1 K. xxi. 1, 18
4 Samaria   2 K. i. 15
12 Gilgal   2 K. ii. 1
13 Bethel   2 K. ii. 2
14 Jericho   2 K. ii. 4
15 To Jordan   2 K. ii. 6
16 Over Jordan   2 K. ii. 8

DAMASCUS

Sea of Galilee

CANAAN

Jordan

GILEAD

Cherith

Dead Sea

EGYPT

Wilderness
of Shur   8

RED SEA

Mt. SINAI
9
HOREB

Copyright

W.G.S.

MAP 8

329

that there was mercy as well as judgment, 'a still small voice', as well as wind, and earthquake, and fire; that he was not the only faithful soul in Israel; and that his own task was not yet complete, that he had again to get into the current of things.

Some four years after the tragic meeting of Elijah and Ahab at the vineyard of Naboth, were his encounters with the messengers of Ahaziah (2 Kings i.). This is a painful story, and difficult to reconcile with any principle of justice. The prophet still believed more in the wind and earthquake and fire, than in the 'still small voice' (cf. Luke ix. 51-56); but it must be borne in mind that he did not live in the Gospel age, and that the religious conditions of his time required a sternness which in different circumstances would have been sinful. He is not represented in Scripture as a man without weaknesses and faults, but as 'a man of like passions with us'; yet without doubt he was one of the greatest of the Hebrew prophets, a man of unfaltering faithfulness, untiring obedience, unflinching adherence to duty and the call of God. He did not exhibit the power of love, but, rather, the authority of truth. He was not the bringer of a new revelation, but the defender of a revelation already given. He was not a theologian, but a reformer; the John Baptist of the Old Testament, heralding a new age, and a greater than himself.

Profoundly impressive was the manner of his going. 'He came like a whirlwind, he burned like a fire, and in fire and whirlwind he disappeared'.

(For reference to Elijah's miracles, see under ELISHA.)

Micaiah   (1 Kings xx. 35-43 (?); xxii. 8.-28; 2 Chron. xviii. 6-27)

It is the distinction of Imlah that he had a son of the quality of Micaiah, who was a prophet in the time of Ahab and Jehoshaphat. He stood squarely for the meaning of his name—*Who is like Yah*? In 1 Kings xx. 35-43 we read of 'a certain man of the sons of the prophets', and it is more than likely that this was Micaiah. Ahab, king of Israel, had defeated Benhadad, king of Syria, and instead of dealing with him as a defeated enemy 'he made a covenant with him'. This was highly impolitic and dangerous, and the prophet referred to severely rebuked Ahab for his folly, and predicted his downfall.

If this prophet was Micaiah it would account for what, a little later, Ahab said about him (xxii. 8), and also for the fact that he was under arrest (xxii. 9, 26) at the time he was sent for to advise Ahab about attacking the Syrians.

The story in 1 Kings xxii. is worthy to stand beside that of 1 Kings xviii. In both an individual is opposed to a crowd; in both the individual uses the device of irony; in both he faces a king; in both he is Jehovah's witness, but in one case the prophet triumphs, and in the other, he temporarily fails.

Elijah and Micaiah are made of the same stuff, and like Athanasius, and Luther, and John Knox, long centuries later, they dare to stand alone for God; *contra mundum.*

Four hundred false prophets urged Ahab to go up to Ramoth-Gilead against the Syrians, but Micaiah opposed this advice. For this faithfulness he was imprisoned, as was Jeremiah at a later date; but his prophecy was fulfilled; Ahab was slain; and probably the 400 false prophets were put to death by Jezebel. Truth is indestructible. There is neither argument nor sense in smacking the face of a witness (xxii. 24), and it is worse than ludicrous when it is done by a man whose name means *Justice of Yah*!

The part which Jehoshaphat played, or rather, failed to play in this crisis is a black stain in his story.

Elisha (1 Kings xix. 15-21; 2 Kings ii.-ix. 1; xiii. 15-21; Luke iv. 27)

Elisha, which means *My God is Salvation*, stood in relation to Elijah much as Joshua did to Moses, and as Timothy did to Paul; he was colleague and successor.

The comparisons and contrasts between the two men are interesting and instructive. Both were prophets to the Northern Kingdom; both held the office for a long time; both were associated with Schools of the Prophets; both faced kings; both multiplied temporal necessities; and both raised the dead to life.

But the contrasts are more than the comparisons. Elijah was a solitary man, but Elisha was social; the one lived in open spaces, the other, in cities; the dress of the one was peculiar, but of the other it was ordinary; the one was severe, but the other was tolerant; the one was the terror of the Court, but the other was the friend and counsellor of kings; the end of the one was miraculous, but of the other it was natural.

These, and other comparisons and contrasts lead us to think of the two men together. It may be safely said that Elijah was the greater of the two, but each accomplished the task assigned to him, and by circumstance, upbringing, and temperament was qualified to do so.

Elijah's ministry belonged to the reigns of Ahab and Ahaziah, and Elisha's, to the reigns of Joram, Jehu, Jehoahaz, and Joash. In both ministries there are gaps—in Elisha's case, about forty years—which leave us with no knowledge of where these men were, or of what they were doing.

What we are told of Elisha is in the form of a number of stories which are not in chronological sequence, and some of which present moral difficulties which we should not deny, or attempt to evade.

The period of Elijah and Elisha was one of miracles, and the reason for this should not be overlooked. Eleven belong to the period of Elijah, and eleven to that of Elisha.

Miracles of Elijah

1. The prevention of rain. 2. The supply of food by ravens. 3. The multiplication of meal and oil. 4. The raising from death of the son of a Zidonite. 5. The fire from heaven which consumed the sacrifice on Carmel. 6. The opening of the heavens in rain. 7. The cake and water provided for Elijah by an angel. 8. The fire from heaven which consumed fifty men. 9. Fire which consumed another fifty men. 10. Dividing of the waters of Jordan. 11. Translation of Elijah to heaven by a whirlwind.

Miracles of Elisha

1. Dividing of the waters of the Jordan. 2. The healing of the waters at Jericho. 3. The supply of oil to a widow. 4. The raising from death of a Shunamite's son. 5. The neutralizing of poison in a pot of food. 6. The multiplying of bread to feed a hundred men. 7. The cure of Naaman's leprosy. 8. The

smiting of Gehazi with leprosy.   9. The floating of the axe-head.
10. The blinding of the Syrians.   11. The raising of a man to
life by contact with Elisha's bones.

Three of Elijah's, and one of Elisha's miracles were of judgment,
and the remainder, eight, and ten, were of mercy, or providence.

Miracles were employed—always with a moral and spiritual
end—to reveal the sovereignty and power of God, and they were
particularly prominent in times of historical crisis.

A survey of the miracles of the Bible will show that there were
three such crises: (*a*) in the time of Moses, when the Israelites
were about to become a nation; (*b*) in the time of Christ, at the
junction of the ages of the Law and the Gospel; and (*c*) in the
time of Elijah and Elisha, as a protest against the prevailing
idolatry, and to call attention to the claims of Jehovah upon His
people.

In the main there are two ways of studying the miracles of
the periods of Elijah and Elisha.   That which is most
commonly pursued is to draw from them the lessons which
each may be considered to teach; and the other, too rarely followed,
is to discover, as far as may be possible, the reason for these
miracles in the time of these prophets, and the effect of them upon
Israel and Judah of that period.   The former method is *application*,
and the latter is *exposition*, and certainly, for an understanding
of the record, the latter is of primary importance.   This, of
course, is true of all miracles.

The chief value of the miracles of these two greatest of the
non-literary prophets is not in any lessons which any of them
may be said to teach, but in the witness of them to the activity
and action of Jehovah, alike in judgment and in mercy, among
and on behalf of His people.

Jonah   (B.C. 825-782   2 Kings xiv. 23-27)
The Book of Jonah.   Matt. xii. 40, 41

It should at once be recognized that the Book of Jonah is not
Jonah's prophecy referred to in 2 Kings xiv. 25, but the narrative
—historical, as I believe—of an experience which Jonah had; a
narrative of immense value because of the great lessons which
it teaches.

But our only interest in the Book in our present survey is for what it reveals to us of the character and ministry of the prophet himself.

Jonah's prophecy to Israel was in the reign of Jeroboam II, the most successful of all the kings of the North, and all that we are told is that Jeroboam's success in restoring to Israel her territory from Hamath on the middle Orontes, some eighty to ninety miles north of Baalbec, to 'the sea of the plain', the Dead Sea, was due to 'the word of the LORD God of Israel, which He spake by the hand of His servant Jonah, the son of Amittai, the prophet, which was of Gath-hepher' (xiv. 25). What in detail that prophecy was, we do not know; but from this statement, and the Book of Jonah, together with certain traditions, we must derive all that can be known about this man.

Jewish tradition has three things to say about him: firstly, that he was the son of the widow of Zarephath, whom Elijah raised from the dead (1 Kings xvii. 17-24); secondly, that he was the 'servant' who accompanied Elijah when he fled from Jezebel (1 Kings xix. 3); and thirdly, that he was the youth whom Elisha sent to Ramoth-Gilead to anoint Jehu King of Israel (2 Kings ix. 1-10). These legends are unsubstantial.

From 2 Kings xiv. 25 we learn that his father's name was Amittai; that his native town was Gath-hepher, a city of Zebulun, not far from Mount Tabor; that he lived in the time of Jeroboam II; that he was a prophet of the Northern Kingdom; and that his message was one, not of judgment, but of consolation.

From Hosea i. 1, and Amos i. 1, we learn that he was the contemporary of these prophets, though, probably, they ministered later than he did in the reign of Jeroboam.

From the Book which bears his name, we learn that he was commissioned to go to Nineveh with a message of hope; that, at first, he declined to do so; that later he went, but that he greatly disliked his mission.

These references, together with Matt. xii. 40, 41, are our only sources of information concerning Jonah, and from them we must form our opinion of his character. He would seem to have been very like Peter, a great patriot, strongly prejudiced, insular in thought and outlook, somewhat rash, and yet a very likeable person. And like Peter he was taught that

> '. . . the love of God is broader
> Than the measures of man's mind,
> And the heart of the Eternal
> Is most wonderfully kind'.

Heathen repented at his preaching, but his own people did not repent when God shewed them mercy, as is evident from Jonah's contemporaries Amos and Hosea.

Oded (2 Chron. xxviii. 1-15)

In the reign of Ahaz of Judah, Rezin of Syria and Pekah of Israel attacked and defeated the people of the South, killing 120,000 'valiant men' in one day, and taking a multitude captive. Of these, Israel took 200,000, chiefly women and children, to Samaria. Against this Oded protested, with the result that they were all sent back to Judaea. The words of Oded's protest are in 2 Chron. xxviii. 9-11.

(b) THE LITERARY PROPHETS

Amos (B.C. 810-785)

Amos was a prophet of the Northern Kingdom, and flourished in the reign of Jeroboam II. Most probably he was immediately preceded by Jonah (2 Kings xiv. 25), and was contemporary with Hosea, who would seem to have been his junior by a few years. He tells us that he was a herdsman from the region of Tekoa, that whilst pursuing his daily round of duties, he was, like Elisha, called to the high dignity of prophetic ministry. He was not of the Schools of the Prophets, that is, he had no professional training, nor was he in the line of the Prophets, yet his may be the earliest written Prophecy that we have. God thus shows that His instruments are determined by the law of His choice, and not by any law of succession or profession.

During the reign of Jeroboam II Israel reached its highest point of success and independence. This king restored to them by conquest the territory they had lost in conflict with the Syrians (2 Kings xiv. 25), and secured for them wide and continuous prosperity. The result of this success upon the character of the people was disastrous. So far from humbling themselves before God, and giving Him the praise, they congratulated themselves saying, 'Have we not taken to us horns by our own strength?' (Amos vi. 13), and they sank down into a life of luxury, cruelty, profligacy, and deceit. The voice of Amos rends this stifling air with his fiery denunciations and mournful annunciations. He obtains their ear by proclaiming judgment against seven other nations, knowing the readiness alas, of Israel, and of all of us I fear, to listen to the sins and sentences of and on others; but the storm that rapidly sweeps over these, gathers in, and concentrates upon Israel herself, and then in all its fury it bursts.

Jehovah had delivered them from Egypt, destroyed their enemies, and given them prophets, yet they were guilty of avarice, injustice, uncleanness, and profanity (ii. 6-12), and they even excused themselves on the ground that they were the Chosen People (iii. 2), and looked for the 'day of the LORD' (v. 18-20). But Amos taught them that their high privilege so far from being an excuse, aggravated the situation beyond all words; that responsibility is in the measure of privilege; 'you only have I known of all the families of the earth, *therefore* I will punish you for your iniquities'.

Confronting Israel's compromise and corruption, Amos proclaimed the sovereignty of God. The nation had to do with Him Who forms the mountains, creates the wind, makes the morning darkness, and knows the uttermost thoughts of men; Who makes the Pleiades and Orion, and calleth for the waters of the seas, and poureth them out upon the face of the earth; Who roars from Zion, and utters His voice from Jerusalem, causing the shepherds to mourn, and Carmel's top to wither (iv. 13; v. 8; i. 2). And the Lord still reigns; man's darkest day and deepest iniquities cannot serve to displace Him from His seat of authority.

Terrifying it should have been to such as Jeroboam to know that righteousness must rule, and judgment must fall upon all who forget God. Exile is predicted for Israel, and instead of silken couches there would be chains. The Assyrian (vi. 14) is seen on the horizon, who, about seventy years afterwards (according to the old chronology) took Israel captive in B.C. 722;

then were the predictions of Isaiah, Amos, Hosea, and Micah fulfilled.

The vision of the locusts (vii. 1-3) probably refers to the invasion of Pul, of 2 Kings xv. 19; the devouring fire, to Tiglath-pileser's assault spoken of in 2 Kings xv. 29; attacks that were not successful, because of Amos' prayers; and the third vision, that of the plumbline, no doubt has reference to the final overthrow under Shalmaneser, recorded in 2 Kings xvii. 3-6, from which there was no relief. So was the Word of God against Israel executed. As summer fruit (viii.) they were ripe for judgment, and for judgment were they plucked, for none could escape from the Divine presence or power (ix. 1-6). One appeal only is made in the Book, and but one promise given. The appeal (ch. v.) is to 'seek the LORD' and is five times repeated; and the promise, as in Joel, Isaiah, and Hosea, stands at the end of the Book, and tells of ultimate restoration for widely-scattered and sin-sick Israel.

The style of Amos is clear and energetic, and displays considerable literary skill. His imagery is based on the scenes amongst which he dwelt—wild beasts, the starry sky, flood, tempest and lightning; the waggon loaded with sheaves, the lion grovelling over his prey, the formidable bear, the snares set for birds, ploughing, cattle-driving, corn-winnowing, and the devouring locusts. Such imagery one would expect from a shepherd and husbandman.

The outline of this Book is compact, and its keynote is Judgment.

I   Eight Pronouncements of Coming Judgment   ..   i. 2-ii. 16.
II Five Discourses on Coming Judgment   ..   ..   .. iii.-vi.
       iii. iv. v. 1-17. v. 18-27. vi. 'Hear ye' (twice) 'Woe' (twice).
III Five Visions of Coming Judgment   ..   .. vii. 1-ix. 10.
       vii. 1-3. vii. 4-6. vii. 7-9. vii. 10-17. viii. 1-14. ix. 1-10.
IV One Prediction of Blessing Beyond Judgment   ..   ix. 11-15.

Hosea (B.C. 782-725)

The introduction says:

'The word of the LORD that came unto Hosea the son of Beeri, in the days of Uzziah, Jotham, Ahaz, and Hezekiah, kings of Judah, and in the days of Jeroboam the son of Joash, king of Israel'.

22

From this it would seem that Hosea's ministry extended over a period of from sixty to seventy years. It should be remembered that he was not a prophet to Judah, but to Israel, though Judah is referred to in his addresses; and, from internal evidence, it appears certain that his ministry continued for some time after the death of Jeroboam II and the fall of the house of Jehu, into the period of anarchy which followed in the reigns of Zachariah, Shallum, and Menahem.

Jonah and *Amos* were contemporaries of *Hosea* in Israel, and of *Isaiah* and *Micah*, in Judah; and, maybe, *Joel* was earlier than any of them.

The contrast between Hosea and Amos is impressive, and it has much to teach us. They both ministered in the reign of Jeroboam II, but they dealt with the situation in different ways. God chooses men to present different aspects of truth to the same people, and these varying emphases are not contradictory but complementary. Amos is a preacher of righteousness, but Hosea, of mercy. Amos embraces heathen nations in his survey, but Hosea never goes beyond Israel and Judah. What Amos has in width, Hosea has in depth. Amos sees the nation purified by judgment, but Hosea sees it surviving judgment by repentance. The emphasis of Amos is on the *justice* of God, but the emphasis of Hosea is on His *love*. Amos is very stern, but Hosea is very tender. Amos preaches God's sovereignty, but Hosea proclaims His salvation.

The style also of these two prophets is very different. Indeed, one wonders if it is right to speak of Hosea as having a style. The literary form of Amos is clear, but in Hosea one will look for such in vain; and this fact is due, in the main at any rate, to the circumstances and experiences of the prophet himself.

The extracts which we have in chs. iv.-xiv. of Hosea's messages are based on his tragic domestic experience, chs. i.-iii. The faithless wife and her faithful husband (i.-iii.) serve to illustrate the faithless nation and its faithful LORD (iv.-xiv.). In Part I is Personal Affliction; and in Part II, National Reflection.

It was through Hosea's domestic troubles that he reached the consciousness of his prophetic calling. The marrying of Gomer in all good faith, her subsequent unfaithfulness, her shameful degradation and enslavement, Hosea's steadfast love for her, and subsequent recovery of her for discipline and reinstatement, led him to see this tragedy on a much larger scale, whereon God is the faithful Lover, and Israel the unfaithful loved one.

Israel's apostasy was the counterpart of Gomer's adultery, and so the Prophecy is full of the language of uncleanness. Israel's drunkenness, robbery, dishonesty, oppression, and idolatry are spoken of as 'whoredom', and give great pain to Jehovah, as Gomer's conduct had given to Hosea. The Book is full of sobs and sighs, and in both the personal and national parts it throbs with emotion.

As in other Prophecies, its dominating notes are *transgression*, *visitation*, and *restoration*, and these are so intertwined in the Book as to make analysis almost impossible, but the following may serve as a guide.

THE FAITHLESS WIFE AND HER FAITHFUL HUSBAND (i.-iii.)

    The Children: Signs (i. 1-ii. 1)

    The Wife: Backsliding (ii. 2-23)

    The Husband: Deliverance (iii.)

THE FAITHLESS NATION AND THE FAITHFUL LORD (iv.-xiv.)

    The TRANSGRESSION of Israel is prominent (iv.-viii.)

    The VISITATION of Israel is prominent (ix.-xi. 11)

    The RESTORATION of Israel is prominent (xi. 12-xiv.)

CHART 63

The Prophets of Judah and Israel in the Divided Kingdom Period			
JUDAH		ISRAEL	
ORAL	LITERARY	ORAL	LITERARY
SHEMAIAH 1 Kings xii. 22-24		AHIJAH 1 Kings xi. 29-39	
	JOEL		AMOS
IDDO 2 Chron. ix. 29	B.C. 837-800	JEHU 1 Kings xvi. 1-4, 7	B.C. 810-785
ODED 2 Chron. xv. 1, 8		ELIJAH 1 Kings xvii.-xix.	
AZARIAH 2 Chron. xv. 1-8	ISAIAH	MICAIAH 1 Kings xx. 35-43	HOSEA
	B.C. 758-698		B.C. 782-725
HANANI 2 Chron. xvi. 1-10		ELISHA 1 Kings xix.- 2 Kings xiii.	
JEHU 2 Chron. xix. 1-3	MICAH	JONAH 2 Kings xiv. 23-27	
ELIEZER 2 Chron. xx. 35-37	B.C. 740-695	ODED 2 Chron. xxviii.- 1-15	
ZECHARIAH 2 Chron. xxvi. 3-5			

ACT I

SCENE 2

THE ISRAELITISH NATION

PERIOD B
THE AGE OF THE MONARCHY

The Single Kingdom
FIRST AND SECOND REFORMATIONS
KINGS AND PROPHETS

THE SINGLE KINGDOM

Hezekiah to Zedekiah

B.C. 722-586: 136 Years

2 Kings xviii.-xxv. 26. 2 Chron. xxix.-xxxvi. 21

Isaiah. Micah. Zephaniah. Jeremiah. Nahum.
Habakkuk. Daniel. Ezekiel. Obadiah. Psalms.

THE Hebrew Monarchy had three distinct stages. For 120 years it was *United*, under Saul, David, and Solomon. Then, for 253 years it was *Div ded* into two Kingdoms, from Jeroboam I to Hoshea in the North, and from Rehoboam to Hezekiah in the South. And finally, for 136 years, the Southern Kingdom continued after the Northern Kingdom had ceased to exist (Chart 64). This is the *Single* Kingdom of which we now speak; and it extends from Hezekiah to Zedekiah. In duration, then, the Monarchy was nearly equal to the period from the birth of Moses to the death of Samuel.

The Divided Kingdom record has been of engaging interest and importance historically, spiritually, psychologically, and prophetically, and now we are to follow the last phase of the Monarchy's history with its belying hopes, and its tragic issues.

It falls into two main parts, each of which begins with a reformation movement; first, under Hezekiah; and then, under Josiah. Following each of these was rapid decline, which eventually brought the Monarchy to an end (Chart 64).

CHART 64

THE SINGLE KINGDOM. B.C. 722-586. 136 Years

FIRST PERIOD. B.C. 722-641: 81 Years	SECOND PERIOD. B.C. 641-586: 55 Years
JUDAH'S FIRST REFORMATION AND FOLLOWING DECLINE	JUDAH'S LAST REFORMATION AND FINAL DECLINE
HEZEKIAH (6th Year) B.C. 722-698 .. .. = 23 Years	JOSIAH B.C. 641-610 .. .. = 31 Years
MANASSEH B.C. 698-643 .. .. = 55 Years	JEHOAHAZ B.C. 610 .. .. = 3 Months
AMON B.C. 643-641 .. .. = 2 Years	JEHOIAKIM B.C. 609-598 .. .. = 11 Years
	JEHOIACHIN B.C. 598 .. .. = 3 Months
	ZEDEKIAH B.C. 597-586 .. .. = 11 Years

CHART 65

COMPREHENSIVE ANALYSIS OF THE SINGLE KINGDOM PERIOD

TIME: B.C. 722-586: 136 YEARS

Name of King	Began to Reign	Length of Reign	Character of King	End of King	Prophets	Home Events	Foreign Events	Comparative Record	
								KINGS	CHRONICLES
HEZEKIAH	(726) 6th Year 722	29	Good	Died	ISAIAH MICAH	Religious Reforms Revival of the Passover. Growth of Hebrew Literature.	Assyrian invasion of Judah bought off. Embassy of MERODACH-BALADAN. Assyrians attack Jerusalem. Their defeat.	2 K. xviii-xx	2 C. xxix-xxxii
MANASSEH	698	55	Bad	Died	ISAIAH MICAH	Idolatry reintroduced, and later eradicated.	Assyrians under ESAR-HADDON invaded Judah	2 K. xxi. 1-18	2 C. xxxiii. 1-20
AMON	643	2	Bad	Slain	ISAIAH MICAH			2 K. xxi. 19-26	2 C. xxxiii. 21-25
JOSIAH	641	31	Good	Killed in battle	ZEPHANIAH JEREMIAH HULDAH NAHUM HABAKKUK	Religious Revival. A Law Scroll Discovered. Great Passover.	Invasion of Judah by Pharaoh NECHO.	2 K. xxii-xxiii	2 C. xxxiv-xxxv

CHART 65—Continued

COMPREHENSIVE ANALYSIS OF THE SINGLE KINGDOM PERIOD

TIME: B.C. 722-586: 136 YEARS

Name of King	Began to Reign	Length of Reign	Character of King	End of King	Prophets	Home Events	Foreign Events	Comparative Record	
								KINGS	CHRONICLES
JEHOAHAZ (Shallum)	610	3 months	Bad	Deported to Egypt	JEREMIAH		Invasion of Judah by Pharaoh Necho.	2 K. xxiii. 31-33	2 C. xxxvi. 1-4
JEHOIAKIM (Eliakim)	609	11	Bad	Slain	JEREMIAH DANIEL URIJAH	*1st Stage of the Exile.* Daniel and the three Hebrews taken to Babylon.	Fall of Assyrian Empire. Rise of Chaldean and Medo-Persian Powers. Necho defeated by NEBUCHADNEZZAR, who takes Jerusalem.	2 K. xxiii. 34-xxiv. 7	2 C. xxxvi. 5-8
JEHOIACHIN (Coniah)	598	3 months	Bad	Deported to Babylon	JEREMIAH EZEKIEL	*2nd Stage of the Exile.* 10,000 taken to Babylon, including *Ezekiel* and Kish.	Jerusalem besieged by NEBUCHADNEZZAR.	2 K. xxiv. 8-16. xxv. 27-30	2 C. xxxvi. 9, 10
ZEDEKIAH (Mattaniah)	597	11	Bad	Deported to Babylon	JEREMIAH EZEKIEL DANIEL OBADIAH(?)	*3rd Stage of the Exile.* The nation deported to Babylon.	League with Egypt. Nebuchadnezzar invests and takes Jerusalem.	2 K. xxiv. 17-xxv. 26	2 C. xxxvi. 11-21

It will be seen from Chart 65 that of the eight kings of the Single Kingdom period, only two were good, Hezekiah and Josiah, and that the reigns of these two covered 54 of the 136 years of the period, leaving 82 years to evil rulers. It should be remembered that the reckoning is from the *sixth* year of Hezekiah's reign, as his previous years fell in the Divided Kingdom period, contemporaneously with Hoshea of the Northern Kingdom.

It is 373 years since Saul was crowned by Samuel, and the kingdom has had a chequered history. At the point we have now reached, the tribes which seceded after Solomon's death have been taken into Assyrian captivity, and the tribes of the South are to continue for another 136 years before being taken into Babylonian captivity. This period, though comparatively short, was singularly full, and witnessed the ministry of the greatest of the prophets, *Isaiah, Jeremiah* and *Ezekiel,* besides *Micah, Zephaniah, Nahum, Habakkuk, Obadiah* and *Daniel.*

Up to this point Judah had had three good, three unstable, and six bad kings (Chart 58), and was to have two more good kings, Hezekiah and Josiah, and six bad ones.

The two Revivals of this period, which, at the time, seemed to be effective, proved to be only temporary, and the nation hastened to its doom.

Let us now consider the eight kings of the Single Kingdom period.

HEZEKIAH (B.C. 726-698)

2 Kings xvi. 20; xviii.-xx.; xxi. 3.   2 Chron. xxviii. 27-xxxii.; xxxiii. 3. Isaiah xiii.-xxxv.; xxxvi.-xxxix.   Proverbs xxv. 1.   Jeremiah xxvi. 16-19.   Psalms cxx.-cxxxiv.; xlvi., xlvii., xlviii., lxv.-lxvii., lxxv., lxxvi.

THE HISTORICAL SITUATION

CHART 66

RELATION OF HEZEKIAH TO THE DIVIDED AND SINGLE KINGDOM PERIODS				
H O S H E A				
B.C. 730-722				
1st	3rd	7th	9th	End of Northern Kingdom
730	727	724	722	
	H E Z E K I A H			
		B.C.	7 2 7 -	6 9 8
	1st	- 4th	6th	29th
2 K. xvii. 1	2 K. xviii. 1	2 K. xviii. 9	2 K. xviii. 10	
D I V I D E D K I N G D O M				Single Kingdom

Hezekiah's position in the history of the Southern Kingdom indicates the difficulty of his task, and the degree of his success. His reign fell between two which were morally and spiritually barren, that of his father Ahaz, and that of his son Manasseh. These two men were the worst kings of Judah, and we cannot but be left wondering how Hezekiah could be so good with a father so bad, and why a father so good should have a son so bad. The fact proves at least that heredity and environment do not necessarily determine anyone's character. Between the sixteen years of the reign of Ahaz, and the fifty-five of Manasseh, were the twenty-nine of Hezekiah.

The reign of Ahaz was one unbroken course of sin, and his son inherited the consequences. That he did so with such zeal for the highest traditions of his nation, was due very largely to the influence of Isaiah and Micah.

THE REFORMATION

According to the record (2 Chron. xxix. 3) Hezekiah at once set about correcting his father's abuses, and he did so with a sureness and swiftness which are astonishing. He first attacked idolatry, removing high places, breaking obelisks, cutting down Asherah, and destroying Moses' brazen serpent (2 Kings xviii. 1-8). He opened the doors of the Temple, which had been closed, and had this place of worship cleansed and sanctified; solemn sacrifices were reinstituted, and once again 'the song of the LORD began', and, we are told, 'the thing was done suddenly' (2 Chron. xxix. 36).

Hezekiah then called for a celebration of the Passover, of which there is no record since the time of Joshua, about 725 years before. This celebration is unique in that not only Judah, but all the tribes from Dan to Beersheba were invited to participate, and some of them came to it (2 Chron. xxx., xxxi.). This fact shows that the celebration was before the captivity of Israel, probably in the third or fourth year of Hoshea.

These activities of Hezekiah show that his work, like Jeremiah's, was twofold: to root out, and to plant; to pull down, and to build up; and this must always be the course of true reformation and revival

THE KING'S SICKNESS

'In these days' (2 Kings xx. 1; 2 Chron. xxxii. 24), is a vague expression, but it seems clear that Hezekiah's sickness occurred *before* the invasion of Sennacherib, because after that event the anxiety expressed in 2 Kings xx. 6 would not have been felt, nor could Hezekiah have shown to Merodach-Baladan treasures which Sennacherib had obtained (2 Kings xviii. 14-16).

The record of the sickness is very detailed, and is full of instruction (2 Kings xx.; 2 Chron. xxxii. 24-31; Isaiah xxxviii., xxxix.); and its cause, course, and cure should be carefully considered.

MERODACH-BALADAN

Taking advantage of the trouble in Assyria at the time of Shalmaneser's death and Sargon's usurpation, Merodach-Baladan, about B.C. 722, shook off the Assyrian yoke, and made himself king of Babylon, over which he reigned for twelve years. In the fourteenth year of Hezekiah's reign he fell very ill, nigh unto death, but he was healed, and fifteen years were added to his life. As he was twenty-five years old when he began to reign, his illness occurred when he was thirty-nine years of age, and his death when he was fifty-four. Merodach-Baladan had heard of this illness and restoration, and being anxious to secure allies against the likely attack upon him of Assyria, he sent 'letters and a present to Hezekiah', by way of congratulating him on his good fortune, but evidently with a view to making an alliance with him against Assyria. This visit pleased Hezekiah, and he showed the embassy from Babylon 'the house of his precious things'; 'there was nothing in his house, nor in all his dominion, that Hezekiah showed them not'.

The prophet Isaiah severely condemned Hezekiah for this, and predicted that the Babylon in which he had confided would one day destroy his kingdom and take his people captive. This happened about 128 years later.

Shortly after this visit of Merodach-Baladan, Sennacherib attacked Judah.

The Assyrian Invasion

Sargon, who took Israel of the Northern Kingdom into captivity, was succeeded as king of Assyria by his son Sennacherib, who reigned for twenty-four years, and then was murdered by his sons (2 Kings xix. 37). Sennacherib's expedition against Judaea is given, not only in the Biblical account, but also in Assyrian records. The Assyrian king, with his army, was at Lachish, and Hezekiah fearing him sought to make peace with him, and offered to buy him off an attack upon Jerusalem (2 Kings xviii. 14-16). Later, however, Sennacherib sent 'a great host' against the capital (2 Kings xviii. 17-xix. 5), and openly insulted the Jews and blasphemed God (xix. 9-34), but Isaiah predicted his overthrow, which was complete, though the Assyrian monuments say nothing about it (xix. 6-8, 35-37. 2 Chron. xxxii. Isaiah xxxvi, xxxvii.).

Rab-shakeh's boastful reproach, Hezekiah's humble prayer,

and Isaiah's firm prediction of Assyria's overthrow should be carefully pondered (xix.); and read again Byron's poem beginning,

'The Assyrian came down like the wolf on the fold'.

Here also should be read Psalm xlvi., the *Te Deum* of this deliverance, which the Septuagint calls 'An Ode to the Assyrian', and Psalms xlvii., xlviii., lxv.-lxvii., lxxv., lxxvi. Of all the attempted explanations of *The Songs of the Degrees*, the most satisfactory is that which relates them to the Assyrian invasion and repulse, and which regards Hezekiah to be the author of ten of them (see my *Psalms*, Vol. 3, pp. 189-302).

ISAIAH AND MICAH

From the first verse in each of these Prophecies we see that they were contemporary, and that both ministered during the reigns of Jotham, Ahaz, and Hezekiah in the South, while Pekah and Hoshea were reigning in the North. The influence of these prophets is reflected in the character and work of Hezekiah. In different ways this king's reformation was the culminating point of their ministries; and, perhaps, it is not too much to say that but for them the Hezekiah chapter would never have been written.

It may be said that Isaiah i.-vi. belongs to Jotham's reign; chs. vii.-x. 4; xiv. 28-32, to the reign of Ahaz; and chs. x. 5-xxxix., to the reign of Hezekiah (See *Isaiah*, p. 325).

In Micah, chs. i.-v. may be said to belong to the time just previous to Hezekiah's reforms, and chs. vi.-vii. to the time of the reforms (see *Micah*, p. 326).

MANASSEH (B.C. 698-643)

2 Kings xx. 21; xxi. 1-18, 20; xxiii. 12, 26; xxiv. 3. 2 Chron. xxxii. 33; xxxiii. 1-20, 22, 23. Jer. xv. 4. The Prayer of Manasses (Apocrypha). Psalms xlix., lxxiii., lxxvii., cxl., cxli.

The bad Ahaz was followed by the good Hezekiah, and the good Hezekiah was followed by the bad Manasseh. The explanation of this is hidden from us, but, of course, the strength of the current of influence has something to do with it. So far as we know there was no Isaiah, and no Micah, in the life of Manasseh;

but the influence of his father and mother, Hezekiah and Heph-zibah, should have been strong enough to keep him from the course, which, alas, he chose to pursue, so that moral and religious inclination, as well as influence, has much to do with a man's character and career.

This man was well named Manasseh, *one who forgets*, and although he was young when he became king, he speedily forgot all that he should have remembered, and remembered all that he should have forgotten.

Hezekiah reversed almost all the evil which his father had done, and Manasseh reversed all the good which his father had done. The record of Manasseh's wicked reign is given briefly, although he was on the throne longer than any other king of either kingdom—fifty-five years.

His story falls into two parts, the second of which is given by the Chronicler only. Part one tells of his wicked life and rule; and part two, of his captivity, repentance, return to his kingdom, and his belated reforms.

Religious apostasy and moral degeneracy characterize the first part of his story. He cultivated, to the point of fanaticism, a fatal and incongruous religious syncretism, introducing all kinds of idolatrous systems, and excluding only the true worship of Yah-weh. He substituted ritual and asceticism for truth and reality; consecrated immoral impulses and passions; introduced human sacrifices; cultivated Assyrian, Phoenician, Canaanite, and Babylonian elements of idolatry; and promoted the worship of the stars. Side by side with this was the persecution of all who opposed him, until he filled Jerusalem from end to end with innocent blood (2 Kings xxi. 16). This persecution is reflected in Psalms xlix., lxxiii., cxl., and cxli.

The priests and the people were willing parties to all this, and the faithful prophets of the time were soon disposed of.

And now follows the second part of Manasseh's story, recorded only by the Chronicler (ch. xxxiii.).

Suspecting the loyalty of Manasseh, who was virtually subject to Assyria, Assurbanipal, the Sardanapalus of classical writers, sent captains to Judaea and took Manasseh captive to Babylon, where he was kept in degradation and misery. While there he came to see the sinfulness of his ways, repented, and sought mercy of the LORD. Assurbanipal supposing perhaps, that Manasseh would be of more use to him in Jerusalem than in Babylon, sent him back to his kingdom. Manasseh, now repentant, attempted to undo the evil of his reign before captivity. He removed the strange gods, and the idolatrous altars which he had built, 'and the idol out of the house of the LORD'; and he rebuilt the altar of the LORD, and offered true sacrifices thereon; and though altars in the high places were allowed to remain, only sacrifices to the LORD God were allowed to be offered thereon.

Frequent reference is made to a prayer he offered (2 Chron. xxxiii. 13, 18, 19), but the text of it is not given. There is, however, in the Apocrypha, a *Prayer of Manasses* which, though of late date, purports to represent the substance of the prayer of this penitent; and as a prayer composed by Greek-speaking Egyptian Jews it is worth studying for what it reveals of religious thought at the time it was written.

Manasseh's reformation came too late to save his land, or to obliterate the memory of the past. His very name continued to be abhorred by all the faithful. He is one of the kings whom the Rabbis-hold to have no part in the life to come—the others being Jeroboam and Ahab—though Rabbi Johanan did say, 'Whoso saith, "Manasseh hath no part in the world to come", discourageth the penitent'.

Yet the solemn statements of 2 Kings xxiii. 26, xxiv. 3, 4, and Jer. xv. 4 stand. Sins, repented of, will be forgiven, but the consequences of them cannot be stayed (cf. pp. 263, 264).

CHART 67

REFORMATION and APOSTASY DURING THE SINGLE KINGDOM PERIOD		
B.C. 727-586 = 140 Years		
REFORMATION		REFORMATION
HEZEKIAH B.C. 727-698 29 Years		JOSIAH B.C. 641-610 31 Years
	APOSTASY	APOSTASY
	MANASSEH-AMON B.C. 698-641 57 Years	JEHOAHAZ-ZEDEKIAH B.C. 609-586 23 Years
REFORMATION: 60 Years. APOSTASY: 80 Years		

AMON (B.C. 643-641).

2 Kings xxi. 18-26.   2 Chron. xxxiii. 20-25.

Little is said of this king, and that little is not to his credit. 'His brief reign', says Farrar, 'is only a sort of unimportant and miserable annex to that of his father'.   The latter part of Manasseh's life, as recorded by the Chronicler, made no impression on his son, though he must have witnessed his father's repentance and reforming zeal.   On the contrary, he not only followed the wicked part of his father's reign, but 'multiplied trespass'.

He is the only Jewish king who bears the name of a foreign—an Egyptian—deity.   Mercifully he reigned for two years only, and his wretched career ended wretchedly.

It would appear that from the time of Micah, for about 85 years, there was no prophet in Judah of whom we know anything. God's displeasure has often been manifested by His silence.

JOSIAH (B.C. 641-610).

2 Kings xxi. 24, 26; xxii.-xxiii. 30. 2 Chron. xxxiii. 25; xxxiv.-xxxv.
1 Kings xiii. 2. Nahum. Zephaniah. Jeremiah i.-vi.; xi., xii.
Psalms xxxvii.; lix.

Josiah, which means *Yah healeth*, had a bad father, Amon,
and a good mother, Jedidah, which means *Beloved of Yah*. He
began to reign when he was eight years of age, and he reigned
for thirty-one years. When he was sixteen he began the work
for which his reign is distinguished, and when he was twenty it
was well on its way (2 Chron. xxxiv. 3). After 57 years of apostasy
(Chart 67) the tide set again to revival, and although it was
externally thoroughgoing the nation had gone too far from God to
wish for that change of heart which alone could save it from
dissolution. It was on a steep gradient, and the brake of reformation could now only slow down for a while the rush downward
and the disaster at the bottom. As soon as Josiah died the
people 'turned again to folly', and committed all the old idolatries
except the worship of Moloch.

Josiah was fortunate in the influences which he allowed to
direct him—his mother, Jeremiah, Zephaniah, Huldah, Shallum,
Hilkiah, Shaphan, Ahikam, Achbor, and Asahiah—men and
women who were the salt in Judah which preserved it for a while
from utter corruption. Supported by them the king set about
his reforming work.

The things he dealt with were: all idols, the Asherah in the
Temple, the Baal vessels, graven and molten images of all kinds,
sun images, horses and chariots of the sun, high places, Tophet,
houses of Sodomites, altars of Ahaz on housetops, and altars of
Manasseh in the courts of the house of the LORD. Also he attacked
the false priests, and burned some of them in fulfilment of a
prophecy which had been uttered about 350 years earlier (1 Kings
xiii. 2, 2 Kings xxiii. 16).

But his work was constructive as well as destructive. He
repaired the Temple which had fallen into a state of sinful
neglect, and he reinstituted the celebration of the Passover. It
was while the Temple was being repaired and cleaned that a
scroll was found which proved to be a copy of 'the Book of the
Torah of Yahweh, by the hand of Moses'. The Rabbinical

tradition is, that 'the Book' was found beneath a heap of stones, under which it had been hidden when Ahaz was engaged in his work of destruction; or, may be, it had lain hid in the Ark itself, which Manasseh had thrown aside into some of the many cells, or chambers, round the Temple, where it might easily have remained unnoticed till the searching eagerness of the commission discovered it (Geikie).

What we can be sure about is, that the finding of the scroll was not a fraud on the part of Hilkiah, and that the scroll itself was not a forgery. As to how much it contained we cannot be so sure. The minimum would be the Book of Deuteronomy, but in all likelihood there were also other portions of the Law.

At any rate, the finding of this scroll created a great stir. Josiah himself read the document to the assembled throng, and avowed that he would fully keep the covenant of the LORD. The elders declared that they also would do so, and all the people said, Amen.

The relation at this time of Assyria to Egypt, and of Judah to them both, and also the threatened invasion of Judah by a Northern foe—the Scythians and Cimmerians—(Jer. iv. 7-27; v. 15-17; vi. 1, 22-24) supply the political background of the Judaean Kingdom in Josiah's time.

Ths might of Assyria was declining, and that of Egypt was in the ascendant, and this fact introduces the final scene in this reign.

Pharaoh Necho of Egypt resolved to attack Nabopolassar, the king of Babylon, called 'the king of Assyria' (2 Kings xxiii. 29) because at this time he was virtually that. Josiah decided to cut across the path of Necho, though urged by the Egyptian king not to do so. However, he persisted, and was fatally wounded, and so, at the age of thirty-nine, the last good king of Judah died. Undoubtedly Josiah was wrong in attacking Necho, and with his decease ended the reformation of Judah, and the nation's hope of independent survival. Twenty-four years after this the Monarchy came to an end, when Nebuchadnezzar deported the Jews to Babylon.

The two blots on Josiah's otherwise godly life and reign were his ferocity in the matter of the false prophets (2 Kings xxiii. 20), and his interference with Necho. But we should ponder his career. The years of his age, eight, sixteen, twenty, and twenty-six mark the stages of his developing character and ministry, and it is little wonder that his death was so deeply mourned (2 Chron. xxxv. 24, 25). It is written in Ecclesiasticus:

'The remembrance of Josias is like the composition of the perfume that is made by the art of the apothecary: it is sweet as honey in all mouths, and as musick at a banquet of wine.

'He behaved himself uprightly in the conversion of the people, and took away the abominations of iniquity. He directed his heart unto the Lord, and in the time of the ungodly he established the worship of God. All except David and Ezekias and Josias were defective: for they forsook the law of the most High, even the kings of Juda failed' (xlix. 1-4).

JEHOAHAZ (B.C. 610).

2 Kings xxiii. 30-34. 2 Chron. xxxvi. 1-4. Jeremiah xxii. 10-12. Ezekiel xix. 1-4.

The story of Jehoahaz—which means *The LORD's possession*, or *The LORD holds*—is short and sad. He was not the natural heir to the throne, not being Josiah's eldest son, and so, when chosen by the people, he had to be anointed. We do not know the reason for this irregularity in the succession, but the result was doubly grievous. It was grievous because this young man, twenty-three years of age, chose to follow in the ways of Manasseh and Amon instead of in the ways of Hezekiah and Josiah; and it was grievous because he was almost immediately taken as a captive to Egypt, and died there, the first king of Judah to die in exile.

That Jehoahaz was never to see his native land again is the burden of Jeremiah's lament (who calls him Shallum); and his prowess is emphasized in Ezekiel's lament:

'He learned to catch the prey,
Mankind he devoured'.

Probably Jehoahaz was opposed to Egypt, which would account for the action of Pharaoh Necho in deporting him.

JEHOIAKIM (B.C. 609-598).

2 Kings xxiii. 34-xxiv. 7. 2 Chron. xxxvi. 4-8. Jeremiah xxii. 13-19; xxvi. 20-23; xxxvi. 20-32; lii. 2. Jeremiah vii.-x.; xiii.-xx.; xxii., xxiii.; xxv., xxvi.; xxxv., xxxvi.; xlv.-xlix. Habakkuk. Daniel i.-ii.

It would appear that Josiah had four sons (1 Chron. iii. 15). Of the first, Johanan, we know nothing. The other three, in order of age, were Jehoiakim, called Eliakim; Jehoahaz, called Shallum; and Zedekiah, called Mattaniah.   From this it will be seen that, for some unknown reason, the firstborn did not come to the throne (perhaps he was dead); and that for some reason, which may be gathered from Ezek. xix. 1-4, the second son, Jehoiakim, was passed over, and the people put the third, Jehoahaz, on the throne.   After his removal to Egypt, Jehoiakim was made king by Necho.   He was followed by *his son*, Jehoiachin, and after three months, by *his brother*, Josiah's fourth son, Zedekiah. This irregularity in the succession reflects the confused state of the kingdom after Josiah's death.

For about four years from the time of Jehoiakim's accession (B.C. 609-605) the people of Judah were left unmolested, save by the prophets, whose voices could not be silenced from denunciation and entreaty.

Jehoiakim did try to get rid of this source of annoyance to himself in the case of Urijah, who at this time prophesied against Judah and Jerusalem (Jer. xxvi. 20, 21).   His words were so keen that the king, the princes, and the mighty men were stirred to indignation, and attempted his life.   Urijah fled into Egypt, from whence, however, he was sought out, brought back to Jerusalem, slain with the sword, and his body was thrown into the cemetery of the common people.

Such methods, however, did not serve their purpose, and the voice of Jeremiah rang out louder and louder against the corruptions of the times.

Meanwhile the king lived in luxury, and by forced labour built a palace for himself.   He said, 'I will build me a wide house, and large chambers, and cut me out windows, and ceil it with cedar, and paint it with vermilion' (Jer. xxii. 13-19); and Jeremiah replied: 'Shalt thou reign because thou closest thyself in cedar?'

But mighty changes were at this time taking place.   The great Assyrian Empire—the first dynasty of which reaches back to about B.C. 1450, that is, nearly eight and a half centuries before the time we are now considering—began to disintegrate before the Babylonians and Medes about B.C. 615; and about B.C. 607-6 Nineveh fell.   Almost at once thereafter, Nebuchadnezzar marched against the Egyptians under Pharaoh Necho, and utterly defeated him in battle at Carchemish, an ancient fortress commanding the passage of the Euphrates, the battle which decided the fate of Western Asia, in B.C. 606-5. On this battle Jeremiah wrote an Ode of Triumph (xlvi. 1-12).

'Nebuchadnezzar's host poured like a torrent over mountain and plain, from Carchemish to Aleppo, from Aleppo down the broad Coele-Syrian valley, across the roots of Lebanon, over Galilee, Samaria, Judaea, Philistia, and Edom into Egypt. No one thought of resistance any more'. Jehoiakim submitted at once to the conqueror, and became his vassal for three years. It was in this same year (606-5) that Jeremiah made Baruch write in a Book his prophetic denunciations of judgment, which, when they were read to Jehoiakim, were cut in pieces by him and thrown on the fire (Jer. xxxvi.).

Nebuchadnezzar's projects against Egypt were suddenly interrupted by the death of Nabopolassar his father. In order to avoid a disputed succession the young prince hastened back to Babylon. 'He broke up his camp, entrusted the bulk of his forces, together with his prisoners—among them Daniel, and the three Hebrews—and booty to some of his generals, with orders to return to Babylon by the usual circuitous route, through Coele-Syria, and then to Aleppo and Carchemish to the Euphrates Valley, while he himself, with a few light troops, crossed the desert and hastened to the capital by way of Tadmor or Palmyra'.

After three years' subjection to Nebuchadnezzar Jehoiakim revolted (B.C. 602). The Babylonian king was busily occupied with his interests at home at the time, and so did not go himself to quell the insurrection, but sent against Jehoiakim bands of the Chaldees, Syrians, Moabites, and Ammonites (2 Kings xxiv. 1, 2). This policy did not prove altogether effective, and when, four years later, in B.C. 598, the king of Tyre rebelled also, Nebuchadnezzar felt it was necessary that he himself should go and deal with the rebels. This he did, and in that same year Jehoiakim, who had fallen into his hands, was executed, and he received 'the burial of an ass', as Jeremiah had predicted (xxii. 19; xxxvi. 30); though, it appears, his remains were afterwards collected and interred in the sepulchre of Manasseh; but he was 'unwept, unhonoured, and unsung'.

CHART 68

JEHOIAKIM		
Vassalage to EGYPT	Vassalage to BABYLON	Unsettled Independence
609-605	605-602	602-598
4 Years	3 Years	4 Years
B.C. 609-598 = 11 Years		

JEHOIACHIN (B.C. 598).

 2 Kings xxiv. 6, 8-16; xxv. 27-30. 2 Chron. xxxvi. 8-10. Jeremiah xxii. 20-30; xiii. 18; xxix. 1, 2; xxxvii. 1; lii. 31-34. Ezekiel i. 1, 2; xvii. 4, 12; xix. 5-9; xl. 1. Esther ii. 5, 6. Baruch i. 1-14.

The story of Jehoiachin is a strange one. His name means *Yah will establish*, or *Yahweh makes steadfast*. He is also called Jeconiah, Jeconias, and Coniah. What is said of him in 2 Chron. must be corrected by what is said in 2 Kings. He was *eighteen* years of age when he ascended the throne, not *eight*, as he was married, and had some family (2 Kings xxiv. 15); and he was not the *brother*, but the nephew of Zedekiah. He was the son of the previous king, Jehoiakim, and his mother's name was Nehushta which means *Brass* (cf. 2 Kings xviii. 4). Her father was Elnathan one of the chief nobles in Jerusalem, and the envoy who dragged back from Egypt the martyr-prophet Urijah (Jer. xxvi. 22). Nehushta was the Queen-mother, and, evidently, a person of some distinction and influence.

For some reason not recorded Jehoiachin reigned for one hundred days only (2 Chron.), and then Nebuchadnezzar, in the eighth year of his reign, came against Jerusalem and took it; and all the important people, over 10,000 of them, were deported to Babylon, including the king, his mother, his wives, his eunuchs, and 'the mighty of the land; also craftsmen, smiths, and men who were able to fight'. It was at this time that Ezekiel was taken to Babylon (Ezek. i. 1, 2), and also ancestors of Mordecai (Esth. ii. 5).

The year in which Jehoiachin, aged eighteen, was deported to Babylon was B.C. 598-7, and thirty-seven years later, at the age of fifty-five, he is still in Babylon, but his status there is changed. Evil-Merodach, the son and successor of Nebuchadnezzar, showed him favour, restored him to rank, and admitted him to the royal table. This continued till his death, the date of which is not recorded.

ZEDEKIAH (B.C. 597-586).

2 Kings xxiv. 17-xxv. 21. 2 Chron. xxxvi. 10-21. Jeremiah xxi. 1-10; xxiv.; xxvii.; xxviii.; xxix. 1-23; xxxii. 1-5; xxxiv. 1-22; xxxvii.-xxxix. 10; li. 59-64; lii. 1-30. Lamentations. Ezekiel iv.-v.; vii.; xii. 1-16; 21-28; xvii. 5, 6, 13-21; xxi. 1-27; xxiv. Psalms lxxix.; lxxx.

Zedekiah's is a very sad story. His previous name, Mattaniah, means *Gift of Yah*, and his changed name means *Righteousness of Yah*, and he was neither the one nor the other to Judah which still awaits Him whom Jeremiah predicted (xxiii. 5, 6).

Zedekiah was the third son of Josiah to come to the throne, and like his two brothers, Jehoahaz and Jehoiakim, 'he did that which was evil in the sight of the LORD'. It is grievous to contemplate that all Josiah's sons, of whom we know anything, were bad men. Was this due to any defect in their upbringing, or is it just another illustration of the fact that moral qualities, good or bad, are not necessarily hereditary (cf. Ahaz and Hezekiah; Hezekiah and Manasseh; Amon and Josiah)?

Zedekiah inherited an appalling situation. One brother had been deported to Egypt, and another was executed and received 'the burial of an ass', and his nephew who immediately preceded him was taken captive to Babylon. The condition of things in Jerusalem at this time is set forth in Ezekiel viii. and xxii. The flower of the nation had been deported to Babylon (2 Kings xxiv. 12-16), and, except for a few individuals, only the social and moral dregs were left.

This was the kingdom which Zedekiah inherited, yet, at first, he showed signs of an intention to obey the Law of Moses, and in his foreign policy to follow the counsels of Jeremiah. He persuaded those who had slaves to set them free (Jer. xxxiv. 8-10); and he sent a peaceable embassy to Babylon with advice to the Jewish exiles there to be loyal subjects to the king, and 'seek the peace of the city whither they had been carried away captive, and to pray unto the LORD for it' (Jer. xxix. 4-7).

Also, he went himself to Babylon in his fourth year, B.C. 594-3, probably to renew his fealty, and to disabuse Nebuchadnezzar's mind of any suspicions that he was entertaining respecting him (Jer. li. 59). The oath of allegiance which he had taken at Jerusalem on his appointment to be king (Ezek. xvii. 13, 14) was most likely repeated on this occasion, and Zedekiah returned to his capital more than ever pledged to be a faithful vassal of the Babylonian crown.

At this time Jeremiah was exhorting the people to remain subject to the Chaldean Power as the only way of averting a worse fate, and this he proclaimed as 'the word of the LORD' (xxvii.); but his advice was regarded as that of a traitor, or a madman, and severely did the prophet suffer for it.

Necho was succeeded in Egypt by Psammetichus II, who again was followed by Hophra. The petty kings whose territories bordered on Judaea sent ambassadors to Jerusalem to induce Zedekiah to join them in open rebellion against Nebuchadnezzar (Jer. xxvii. 3). Zedekiah entertained these suggestions, and sent to Egypt offering his allegiance, and asking for assistance (Ezek. xvii. 15). A secret treaty was made, and about B.C. 589, in the ninth year of his reign, the Jewish king took the fatal step, and, despite the warnings of Jeremiah, broke his fealty to Babylon, and openly raised the standard of rebellion against his suzerain (2 Kings xxiv. 20).

And now we enter upon the closing terrible scene. Nebuchadnezzar and all his host came up against Judah, and settled themselves against Jerusalem in the year B.C. 589-8. After a while, when the condition of the inhabitants was becoming desperate, it was made known that Hophra of Egypt was on his way to aid the beleaguered city (Jer. xxxvii. 5-7). This raised the hopes of the people, hopes which seemed to be realized when Nebuchadnezzar raised the siege and went to meet Hophra.

Precisely what happened we do not know. Whether, as we might infer from Jeremiah, the Egyptian king returned home without engaging in battle with Nebuchadnezzar, or whether, according to Josephus, he was defeated in battle, we cannot say; but the Babylonian king returned to Jerusalem, as Jeremiah had predicted he would (xxxvii. 8-10).

And now the state of the city and of the people became altogether desperate, as we gather from the Book of Lamentations. Dean Stanley has described it thus:

'Famine and its accompanying visitation of pestilence ravaged the crowded population within the walls. It was only by a special favour of the king that a daily supply of bread was sent to Jeremiah, in his prison, from the bakers' quarters, and at last even this failed. The nobles, who had prided themselves on their beautiful complexions, purer than snow, whiter than milk, ruddy as rubies, polished as sapphires (Lam. iv. 7), had become ghastly and black with starvation. Their wasted skeleton forms could hardly be recognized in the streets. The ladies of Jerusalem, in their magnificent crimson robes, might be seen sitting in despair on the dunghills. From these foul heaps were gathered morsels to eke out the failing supply of food (Lam. iv. 5). There was something specially piteous in the sight of the little children, with their parched tongues, fainting in the streets, asking for bread, crying to their mothers for corn and wine (Lam. ii. 11, 12, 19). There was something still more terrible in the hardening feeling with which the parents turned away from them. The Hebrew mothers seemed to have lost even the instincts of the brute creation, to have sunk to the level of the unnatural ostriches that leave their nests in the wilderness (Lam. iv. 3). Fathers devoured the flesh of their own sons and their own daughters (Ezek. v. 10; Baruch ii. 3). The hands even of compassionate mothers have sodden their own children, the mere infants just born (Lam. ii. 20; iv. 10).'

At last, Nebuchadnezzar, after a siege of eighteen months, broke into the city, and the end had come. From scattered references in Kings, Chronicles, Jeremiah, Lamentations, and Ezekiel we learn what took place during these days.

Zedekiah, together with his wives, children, a number of princes, and a part of the military, made good their escape from the city during the night, and went by way of Jericho to the Jordan. They were, however, pursued by the Chaldeans on information having been given by Jewish deserters (Josephus), and the king, with his family, were taken to Nebuchadnezzar at Riblah. There Zedekiah's sons were slain before him, and afterwards his eyes were put out, and he was taken in chains to Babylon, where he was kept in prison until the day of his death (Jer. lii. 7-11).

The Temple was burnt, the walls of Jerusalem were broken down, and the palaces were devoured with fire. Jeremiah, however, was spared and shown great consideration by Nebuchadnezzar.

Thus ended the Monarchy of the People of Israel which had lasted for over 500 years (Charts 27, 48, 49, 53, 64).

THE LAST FIFTY YEARS OF THE JUDAEAN MONARCHY

The last fifty years of the Monarchy is of interest and importance because it was the last fifty, and for other reasons also.

Josiah's reign was important because of the character of the king, and of what he accomplished. His reformation was the last before the dissolution of the Monarchy, and although it was vigorous, it turned out to be superficial. What would have happened if Josiah had not so foolishly encountered the Egyptian Pharaoh Necho, it is not possible to say, but with his death the last hope of Judah faded away.

Twenty-three years now remained before the Monarchy terminated, and this period may be called *The Dependency*, distinguishable from *The Theocracy*, and *The Monarchy* (see Chart 27).

In the *Theocracy* the Chosen People were under the Rule of God; in the *Monarchy* they were under kings of their own; and in the *Dependency* they were under alien kings.

In the period we are now considering this last statement must be safeguarded, because the last three kings of Judah were Jews —Jehoiakim, Jehoiachin, and Zedekiah—who, though not *free* kings, held their position by the will, first of Egypt, and then, of Babylon.

CHART 69

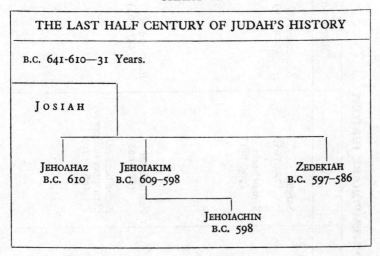

THE LAST HALF CENTURY OF JUDAH'S HISTORY

B.C. 641-610—31 Years.

JOSIAH

JEHOAHAZ
B.C. 610

JEHOIAKIM
B.C. 609-598

ZEDEKIAH
B.C. 597-586

JEHOIACHIN
B.C. 598

The Single Kingdom. Contemporary History

IT should be borne in mind that the foreign nations whose history is touched upon in the Scriptures are brought to notice because of their relation to the Chosen People, and not for the reason that they were great and occupy the place they do in secular history. The Bible does not give history for history's sake, but only as the unfolding of a Divine redemptive purpose. Everything is viewed from the Divine standpoint, and this will explain both the selections and omissions in the story. The principal Powers which affected, more or less, the course of Israel and Judah were three in number, *Egypt, Assyria*, and *Babylonia*. The chronological sequence is not always clear, and the dates on the Monuments are not always in agreement with the Bible dates, but in the main there is a wonderful harmony, and we may confidently look for further light as the work of excavation proceeds in the East.

CHART 70

THE SINGLE KINGDOM PERIOD—CONTEMPORARY HISTORY

B.C.	JUDAH	EGYPT	ASSYRIA	BABYLONIA
722	Hezekiah. 6th Year (2 K. xviii. 9, 10)		Sargon (722–705)	Merodach-Baladan (722–710)
713	Hezekiah's illness (14th year)		Sennacherib (705–681)	
701	First attack by Sennacherib (2 K. xviii. 13-16)	Tirhakah (701–667)		
699	Second attack by Sennacherib (2 K. xviii. 17-xix. 36)			
698	Manasseh (2 K. xxi. 1)			Esarhaddon (681–668)
			Esarhaddon (681–668)	
			Assur-bani-pal (Asnapper of Ezra iv) (668–626)	
643	Amon (2 K. xxi. 19)	Psammetichus I (650?–610)		
641	Josiah (2 K. xxii. 1)			

CHART 70—*Continued*

THE SINGLE KINGDOM PERIOD—CONTEMPORARY HISTORY

B.C.	JUDAH	EGYPT	ASSYRIA	BABYLONIA
623–2	Josiah's Great Passover (2 K. xxiii. 21-25)			Nabopolassar (625–604)
610	Battle of Megiddo. Josiah killed (2 K. xxiii. 29, 30)	Necho (610–595)		
610	Jehoahaz (2 K. xxiii. 30, 31)			
609	Jehoiakim (2 K. xxiii. 34)			
606			Assyrian Empire ends	
605	Jehoiakim submits to Nebuchadnezzar. Daniel and the three Hebrews taken to Babylon.		Battle of Carchemish (606–605)	Nebuchadnezzar (605–562)
602	Jehoiakim rebels against Nebuchadnezzar (2 K. xxiv. 1)			
598	Jehoiakim slain (Jer. xxii. 19)			

CHART 70—*Continued*

THE SINGLE KINGDOM PERIOD—CONTEMPORARY HISTORY

B.C.	JUDAH	EGYPT	ASSYRIA	BABYLONIA
598	Jehoiachin (2 K. xxiv. 8). Taken to Babylon with Ezekiel and over 10,000 captives.			
597	Zedekiah (2 K. xxiv. 18)	Psammetichus II (595–590)		
		Hophra (Apries) (590–571)		
588	Nebuchadnezzar lays siege to Jerusalem (2 K. xxv. 1)			
586	Jerusalem falls. Zedekiah and 'the rest of the people' taken to Babylon (2 K. xxv)			
562	Jehoiachin favoured in Babylon (2 K. xxv. 27–30)			Evil-Merodach (562–560)

Jeremiah twice speaks, in connection with Babylon, of a period of *seventy years* (xxv. 11; xxix. 10). Sir Robert Anderson, Dr. Bullinger, and others distinguish three periods, each of seventy years, the *servitude*, the *captivity*, and the *desolations*. This is done by assuming that the two references in Jeremiah relate to two distinct, though partly concurrent, periods. But it is simpler to regard both the references as pointing to the period B.C. 606-536, from the beginning of Nebuchadnezzar's subjection of Judah, to the return of the people, with the permission of Cyrus, in B.C. 536, though the Persian Power overthrew the Babylonian Power two years earlier than this date.

What should be noticed is that the *servitude* and the *captivity* run parallel, for the latter was in three stages: in B.C. 606-605, when Daniel and the three Hebrews were taken to Babylon (Dan. i. 1); in B.C. 598, when Jehoiachin, his family, and over 10,000 of the chiefs of Jerusalem were deported (2 Kings xxiv. 11-16); and in B.C. 586, when Zedekiah and the remainder of the people (except a poor remnant) were taken to Babylon. This last date, B.C. 586-536, is only fifty years, so that Jeremiah's 'seventy' must go back to B.C. 606-605.

CHART 71

RELATION OF JUDAH'S LAST FOUR KINGS TO EGYPT AND BABYLON	
Under EGYPT	Under BABYLON
JEHOIAKIM B.C. 609-605—4 Years.	JEHOIAKIM B.C. 605-598—7 Years. JEHOIACHIN B.C. 598—3 Months. ZEDEKIAH B.C. 597-586—11 Years.

CHART 72

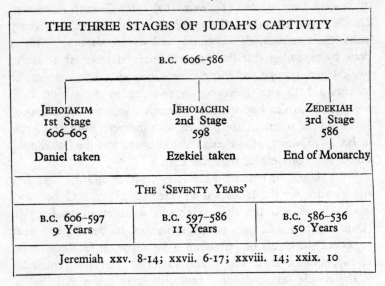

THE THREE STAGES OF JUDAH'S CAPTIVITY

B.C. 606–586

JEHOIAKIM	JEHOIACHIN	ZEDEKIAH
1st Stage	2nd Stage	3rd Stage
606–605	598	586
Daniel taken	Ezekiel taken	End of Monarchy

THE 'SEVENTY YEARS'

B.C. 606–597	B.C. 597–586	B.C. 586–536
9 Years	11 Years	50 Years

Jeremiah xxv. 8-14; xxvii. 6-17; xxviii. 14; xxix. 10

It may be useful to those who wish to follow the course of each of the great Powers, Egypt, Assyria, and Babylon, and the contacts of the Hebrew People with them, if these are briefly outlined as follows.

Egypt

EGYPT is a very old civilization. Flinders Petrie claims that its first age goes as far back as 8000 B.C.; but though details of its history are relatively clear, the dates are uncertain, and can only be approximate.

The Old Testament references to the contacts between the Chosen Nation and Egypt are considerably more than those of Assyria or Babylon. They go back to the time when Abram went down into Egypt (Gen. xii. 5, 10). Then follow: the selling of Joseph into Egypt (Gen. xxxvii.), and his experiences there (Gen. xxxvii.-xlv.); the descent into Egypt of Jacob and his family (Gen. xlvi.-l); the oppression of the Israelites in Egypt (Exod. i.); the birth and eighty years of Moses' life (Exod. ii.-iv.); the conflict between Moses and Pharaoh (Exod. iv.-xii.); the Exodus (Exod. xii.).

Solomon married an Egyptian princess, and became brother-in-law to *Shishak*, a king of Egypt, who attacked Jerusalem in the time of Rehoboam, Solomon's son (1 Kings xiv. 25. 2 Chron. xii. 2-4). Later, in the time of Asa, *Zerah*, another Egyptian king, an Ethiopian, invaded Jerusalem unsuccessfully (2 Chron. xiv. 9; xvi. 8). Two and a quarter centuries later, in the time of Hoshea of Israel, a viceroy of Egypt, *Shabak* or *So*, made an alliance with the Northern king, who withheld the tribute to Assyria (2 Kings xvii. 4). Then, in the time of Hezekiah, *Tirhakah*, the last and greatest of the Ethiopian kings of Egypt, came to Hezekiah's help against Assyria (2 Kings xix. 9). Next, in the time of Josiah of Judah, *Necho II* marched to Carchemish against Assyria. Josiah intercepted him at Megiddo and was mortally wounded (2 Kings xxiii. 29, 30. 2 Chron. xxxv. 20-24).

Hophra, or *Apries*, assisted Zedekiah against Nebuchadnezzar, and his overthrow was predicted by Jeremiah, a prediction which was fulfilled when Nebuchadnezzar invaded Egypt in 586 B.C. (2 Chron. xxxvi. 13. Ezek. xvii. Jer. xliv. 30; xxxvii. 5).

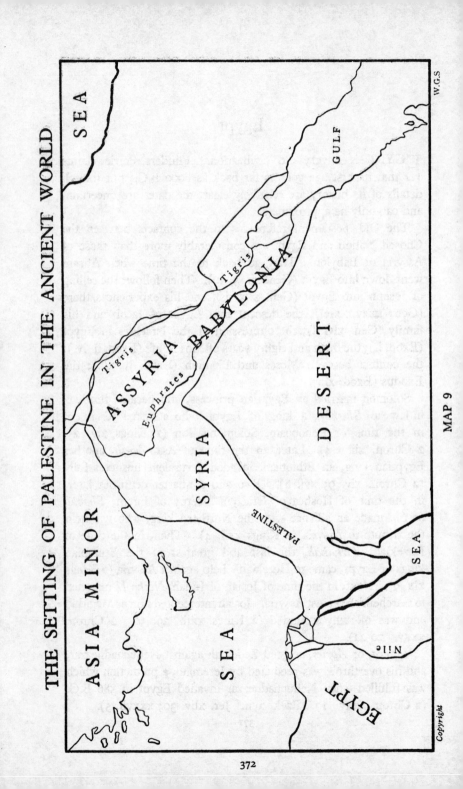

THE SETTING OF PALESTINE IN THE ANCIENT WORLD

SEA

SEA

ASIA MINOR

SYRIA

PALESTINE

DESERT

ASSYRIA BABYLONIA

Tigris

Tigris

Euphrates

GULF

EGYPT

Nile

W.G.S

Copyright

MAP 9

Assyria

THE histories of Babylon and Assyria are interwoven from the very earliest times, and it is sometimes difficult to disentangle them. The first reference goes back to Gen. x. 11. There appear to have been five dynasties, as follows:

CHART 73

ASSYRIAN DYNASTIES: B.C. (about) 1450-615 = 835 Years				
First	*Second*	*Third*	*Fourth*	*Fifth*
1450–1220 230 Years	1220–1090 130 Years	930–745 185 Years	745–722 23 Years	722–615 107 Years
10 Kings	6 Kings	10 Kings	2 Kings	5 Kings
		Bible Contacts (Chart 74)		

The Bible contacts begin with Shalmaneser II (III) of the Third Dynasty, and include both kings of the Fourth Dynasty, and four of the five kings of the Fifth Dynasty (Chart 74).

The Assyrian Empire began to fall about B.C. 625, and fell in B.C. 606-5. About B.C. 635 Nahum predicted the fall of that city which 180 years earlier, B.C. 815 (?) repented at the preaching of Jonah. 'The Assyrian Empire vanishes from the earth so suddenly and so noiselessly, that its fall is only known to us through the reduced grandeur of the palaces of its latest king, and through the cry of exultation raised over its destruction by the Israelitish Prophet', Nahum. (Stanley).

CHART 74

ASSYRIAN RULERS CONNECTED WITH BIBLE HISTORY = 234 or 285 Years

Name	Date B.C.	Years	Reference	Event	Record
SHALMANESER II (III)	911–876 (Assyrian date 860-825)	35	I K. xx. 34; xxii. 1-3. I K. xix. 15-17; 2 K. viii. 7-15; 2 K. ix. 1-6.	In B.C. 905 Benhadad and Ahab fought Shalmaneser and were defeated. Shalmaneser received tribute from Jehu during the latter's expedition against Hazael.	A monolith in the British Museum. The 'Black Obelisk' in the British Museum
TIGLATH-PILESER III (IV) (his Assyrian name). PUL (his Babylonian name). For 2 years he was also king of Babylon (see Chart 76).	745–727 (Uncertain) 729–727	18	2 K. xv. 19, 28, 29; xvi. 10-16. I C. v. 6, 26; 2 C. xxviii. 19-21. Isaiah viii. 1-ix. I. Amos vii. 1-3.	Much relating to Tiglath-Pileser is conjectural, because of the 'deplorable state' of his annals. Menahem paid him tribute. Ahaz bribed him for help.	Five kings of Judah and Israel are mentioned by this Sovereign in Assyrian Inscriptions: Azariah; Menahem; Rezin and Pekah; Ahaz; and Hoshea.
SHALMANESER IV (V)	727–722	5	2 K. xvii. 3.	Besieged Samaria, but did not capture it.	
SARGON II First king of Assyria to come into actual conflict with Egypt.	722–705	17	2 K. xvii. 4-6, 24; xviii. 9, 10. Isaiah xx. 1-6. Nahum iii. 8 (Thebes).	Captured Samaria, and ended the kingdom of Israel. Conquered So, king of Egypt, in the battle of Raphia. Warrior and builder.	Cuneiform Inscriptions. Assyrian Eponym Canon. Monuments at the Louvre.

CHART 74—Continued

ASSYRIAN RULERS CONNECTED WITH BIBLE HISTORY=234 or 285 Years

Name	Date B.C.	Years	Reference	Event	Record
SENNACHERIB Son of Sargon II. Father of Esar-Haddon. First Assyrian monarch to make Nineveh the seat of Government.	705–681	24	2 K. xviii. 13-16.	First attack upon Hezekiah; unsuccessful.	Inscriptions on clay cylinders, marble slabs, terra cotta bowls, bas-reliefs, bricks and plates, and carvings in rocks. (See under Babylon: Chart 76).
ESAR-HADDON 'Most potent of the kings of Assyria.' He ruled over Assyria and Babylon for 13 years. (See Chart 76).	681–668	13	2 K. xix..37; xxi. 13, 14 2 C. xxxiii. 11. Ezra iv., 2, 9.	Manasseh paid tribute to him. He conquered Palestine, and carried Manasseh into captivity, later releasing him. Those who opposed the building of the Second Temple were planted in Samaria by this king.	Inscriptions, cylinders, slabs, tablets, and rock engravings. Warrior and builder.
ASSUR-BANI-PAL The last great king of Assyria, which fell, most probably in B.C. 606. He may be the Asnapper of Ezra iv. 2, 9, 10. The Greek Sardanapalus.	668–626	22	2 K. xxi. 2. 2 C. xxxiii. (Nahum). Ezra iv. 2, 9, 10.	He says that Manasseh was one of 22 kings who became tributary to him, and kissed his feet. He destroyed Thebes in 664. Between Esar-Haddon and Assur-bani-pal was another King, Shamashshum-ukin, 668–647 = 21 years.	Cylinder C. Two petty kings followed Assur-bani-pal from B.C. 626-606. It appears that he was the virtual ruler in Babylon for about 42 years.

Babylon

THERE were ten Babylonian Dynasties reaching from about B.C. 2230 to B.C. 538, some 1692 years. But there were Babylonian kings as early at least as B.C. 2500.

CHART 75

| BABYLONIAN DYNASTIES: B.C. 2500-538 (about) = 1962 Years |||||
First	Second	Third	Fourth	Fifth
2230–1936 294 Years	1936–1568 368 Years	1568–1075 493 Years	1075–1003 72 Years	1003–982 21 Years
11 Kings	11 Kings	36 Kings	11 Kings	3 Kings
Sixth	Seventh	Eighth	Ninth	Tenth
982–961 21 Years	961–955 6 Years	955–732 223 Years	732–625 107 Years	625–538 87 Years
3 Kings	? Elamite	18 Kings	16 Kings	7 Kings

This period is not certain, and the names of many of the kings are not known, but the dates and names of the last two Dynasties, which are related to the Bible records, may be taken as correct. It will be seen from Charts 74 and 76 that some Assyrian kings ruled over Babylon also, but for many centuries the two Powers were in conflict with one another. The Babylonian Power was God's instrument for the chastisement of Judah, but the Prophets predicted its overthrow (Isa. xlvii. cf. x. 5-19; Jer. xxv. 12; l.-li.; Dan. v.), which took place B.C. 538; and if to this date two years are allowed for the beginning of the separate reign of Cyrus, B.C. 536, the period of 70 years, B.C. 606-536, will be seen to be the fulfilment of Jeremiah's prophecy (xxix. 10).

CHART 76

BABYLONIAN RULERS CONNECTED WITH BIBLE HISTORY

THE NINTH BABYLONIAN DYNASTY: B.C. 732-625: 107 Years

Name	Date B.C.	Years	Reference	Event	Record
PUL The Babylonian name of TIGLATH-PILESER III of Assyria (745-727).	729-727	2	2 K. xv. 19, 20, 29; xvi. 10-16. 1 C. v. 6, 26; xxviii. 19-21. Amos vii. 1-3.	Menahem paid tribute to him. Ahaz bribed him for help.	Two years king of Babylon. (See under Assyria, Chart 74.)
MERODACH-BALADAN	722-710	12	Isaiah xxxix. 2 K. xx. 12-21. 2 C. xxxii. 31.	He sent Princes to Jerusalem to congratulate Hezekiah on his recovery to health, and gave him presents; his real intention being to secure Hezekiah as an ally against Assyria. Hezekiah showed them all his treasures; for which Isaiah condemned him, and predicted Judah's overthrow.	When Sargon seized the throne of Assyria, the Babylonians revolted and made Merodach-Baladan king of Babylon. In 710 he was forced to submit to Sargon, but returned to the throne for 9 months in 703-2, at the end of which he was driven out by Sennacherib.
	703-702	9 months			
SARGON II (See under Assyria, Chart 74). King of Assyria and Babylon.	710-705	5	2 K. xvii. 4-6; 24; xviii. 9, 10. Isaiah x. 5-11, 28-32; xx. 1.	He completed the siege of Samaria which Shalmaneser IV commenced, and in 9th year of Hoshea, captured the city, and deported the people to Assyria. So ended the Northern Kingdom, B.C. 722-1.	Tablets from the Royal Library at Nineveh, now in the British Museum. Cylinders, Bricks, Jars, Vases, Bowls; also in the British Museum.

CHART 76—Continued

Name	Date B.C.	Years	Reference	Event	Record
SENNACHERIB (See under Assyria, Chart 74).	705-703 688-681	2 7	2 C. xxxii. 9. Isaiah xxxvi. 1, 2. 2 K. xviii. 13-16. Isaiah xxxvii. 33-37 (Nahum iii. 3, 15). Ps. cxxiv. 7, 8. 2 K. xviii. 17-xix.	Attacked Lachish. Hezekiah paid him tribute. 2nd attack on Hezekiah.	'The Taylor Cylinder' in the British Museum. Tablets. The 'Eponym Canon.' Bowls. Bricks. Other Cylinders.
ESAR-HADDON I. Son of Sennacherib. (See Chart 74).	681-668	13	2 K. xix. 37. 2 C. xxxiii. 11. Ezra iv. 2, 9.	He put Manasseh under tribute, and later took him captive, but soon released him.	Tablets. Cylinders. Bricks. Inscription.
ASSUR-BANI-PAL, Virtual ruler in Babylon for over 40 years. (See Chart 74).	668-626	42		He conquered and restored Babylon; and placed Assyrian governors in Egypt.	

THE TENTH BABYLONIAN DYNASTY: B.C. 625-538 = 87 Years

| NABOPOLASSAR The father of Nebuchadnezzar. Founder of the new Babylonian Empire. First king of the 10th Babylonian Dynasty. | 625-604 | 21 | | It was in the year of this king's accession that Assyria began to fall. | |

378

CHART 76—Continued

Name	Date B.C.	Years	Reference	Event	Record
NEBUCHADNEZZAR Most famous of the Babylonian kings. Statesman, Warrior, Builder. The 'Head of Gold' of Daniel ii.	604-561	43	2 K. xxiv-xxv. 26. 1 C. vi. 15. 2 C. xxxvi. 1-21. Prophecies of Jeremiah from the 4th year of Jehoiakim. Habakkuk. Ezekiel. Daniel.	Defeated the Egyptians at Carchemish. Subjected the last three kings of Judah. Conquered Judah and deported the nation to Babylon. This ended the Hebrew Monarchy.	Inscriptions. Annals.
EVIL-MERODACH Son of Nebuchadnezzar.	561-559	2	2 K. xxv. 27-30. Jeremiah lii. 31-34.	Known for his kindness to Jehoiachin in the 37th year of his captivity.	Tablets 157-162 in the Babylonian and Assyrian Room of the British Museum.
NERIGLISSAR Brother-in-law and murderer of Merodach. (Nergalsharezer).	559-556	3-4	Jeremiah xxxix. 11-14.	One of those who took care of Jeremiah.	Cuneiform inscriptions.
LABOROSOARCHOD Son of Neriglissar.	555	9 months.		Murdered by conspirators.	
NABONIDUS Father of Belshazzar.	555-538	17		Built the Temple of the Moon-god in Ur. Taken captive by Cyrus.	Annals and Inscriptions. Cylinders.
BELSHAZZAR	538	4 months.	Daniel v. Jeremiah xxv. 12. Jer. l.-li. Isaiah xlvii.	Babylon taken by Cyrus. Belshazzar slain. Medo-Persian Empire displaces the Babylonian.	

The Literary Prophets of the Single Kingdom Period

THE Single Kingdom lasted for 136 years—B.C. 722-586, and during this period seven prophets spoke or wrote, or did both; five of them at home, and two of them abroad. As the dates cannot be fixed with exactness, they must be regarded as approximate.

CHART 77

Prophet	King	Date (app.)	Reading
NAHUM	Manasseh-Josiah 697—610 2 K. xxi-xxii. 2 C. xxxiii-iv.	640—630	His Book. Habakkuk. Zephaniah ii. 13–15. Jeremiah l-li. Isaiah x; xiv; xxx; xxxvi-xxxvii.
ZEPHANIAH	Josiah. 641—610. 2 K. xxii. 2 C. xxxiv.	640—610	His Book. Jer. i-vi; xxv; xlvi-li. Ezek. xxv-xxxii.
JEREMIAH	Josiah. 641—610. 2 K. xxii. 2 C. xxxiv.	627—586 (and later)	His Book. Zephaniah. Habakkuk. Daniel i-iv. Ezekiel.
HABAKKUK	Jehoiakim. 609—598. 2 K. xxiii; xxiv. 2 C. xxxvi.	609—598	His Book. Jer. vii-x; xiv-xx; xxxv; xxxvi; xlv; xxv; xlvi-xlix; xiii; xxii; xxiii. Nahum. Zephaniah. Daniel ii.
DANIEL i–iv	Jehoiakim. Jehoiachin. Zedekiah. 605—586 (and after)	606—586 (and (after)	
EZEKIEL	Zedekiah. 597—586	592—572	2 K. xxiv. 17 - xxv. 27. 2 C. xxxvi. 11-21. Daniel iv.
OBADIAH	Zedekiah. 588—586 (and after)	586—583	

380

This summary indicates what voices were heard during these momentous years; and of great importance are their respective standpoints and themes.

NAHUM (B.C. 640-630)

The Book of Nahum is not dated, but it appeared at some time *after* the fall of No-Amon, that is Thebes, in B.C. 664 (iii. 8), and *before* the fall of Nineveh in B.C. 606. This gives a period of 58 years within which this extraordinary Book was written. Attempts have been made to limit Nahum's period more narrowly, and perhaps he wrote at about B.C. 640-630; towards the end of Manasseh's reign, and the beginning of Josiah's.

Where he resided cannot be determined. Four different localities have been claimed, but proof is wanting. *Capernaum* means 'the village of Nahum', and he may have resided there, but it is quite possible that he lived, wrote, and died abroad.

His name means *Consoler*, or *Comforter*, which he was to Judah, but not to Nineveh.

His Book is the complement and the counterpart of the Book of Jonah. Both are about Nineveh; but in *Jonah* the subject is the *mercy* of God, and in this Book it is His *justice*. Davidson says: 'Jonah and Nahum form connected parts of one moral history, the remission of God's judgment being illustrated in the one, the execution of it in the other; the clemency and the just severity of the Divine government being contained in the mixed delineation of the two books'. Jonah prophesied and wrote in the time of Jeroboam II (2 Kings xiv. 25: 825-782), so that he and Nahum may have been separated in time by a century to a century and a half, in which time the rulers in Assyria were Tiglath-Pileser, Shalmaneser IV, Sargon II, Sennacherib, Esar-Haddon I, and Assur-bani-pal. During this period Nineveh had fallen back into the violence of which it had repented.

CHART 78

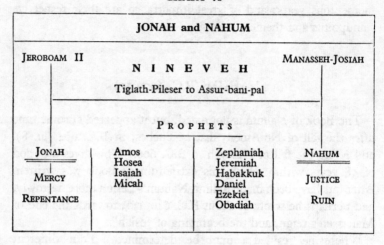

JONAH and NAHUM			
JEROBOAM II			MANASSEH-JOSIAH
	N I N E V E H		
	Tiglath-Pileser to Assur-bani-pal		
	P R O P H E T S		
JONAH	Amos	Zephaniah	NAHUM
	Hosea	Jeremiah	
MERCY	Isaiah	Habakkuk	JUSTICE
	Micah	Daniel	
REPENTANCE		Ezekiel	RUIN
		Obadiah	

As the theme of this prophet is *Nineveh,* and the ruin of it, it will be well to get the background which accounts for and justifies the destruction which is here described.

NINEVEH

THE CITY

Nineveh lay on the eastern side of the Tigris, and was one of the greatest—if not the greatest—of the cities of antiquity. It had 1,200 towers, each 200 feet high, and its wall was 100 feet high, and of such breadth that three chariots could drive on it abreast. It was 60 miles in circumference, and could, within its walls, grow corn enough for its population of 600,000. Xenophon says the basement of its wall was of polished stone, and its width 50 feet. In the city was a magnificent palace, with courts and walls covering more than 100 acres. The roofs were supported by beams of cedar, resting on columns of cypress, inlaid and strengthened by bands of sculptured silver and iron; its gates were guarded by huge lions and bulls sculptured in stone; its doors were of ebony and cypress encrusted with iron, silver, and ivory, and panelling the rooms were sculptured slabs of alabaster, and cylinders and bricks with cuneiform inscriptions. Hanging gardens were filled with rich plants and rare animals, and served with other temples and palaces, libraries and arsenals, to adorn and enrich the city; and all was built by the labour of foreign slaves.

CRUELTY OF THE ASSYRIANS

These people ruled with hideous tyranny and violence from the Caucasus and the Caspian to the Persian Gulf, and from beyond the Tigris to Asia Minor and Egypt. The Assyrian kings literally tormented the world. They flung away the bodies of soldiers like so much clay; they made pyramids of human heads; they sacrificed holocausts of the sons and daughters of their enemies; they burned cities; they filled populous lands with death and devastation; they reddened broad deserts with carnage of warriors; they scattered whole countries with the corpses of their defenders as with chaff; they impaled 'heaps of men' on stakes, and strewed the mountains and choked the rivers with dead bones; they cut off the hands of kings, and nailed them on the walls, and left their bodies to rot with bears and dogs on the entrance gates of cities; they cut down warriors like weeds, or smote them like wild beasts in the forests, and covered pillars with the flayed skins of rival monarchs (Farrar): and these things they did without sentiment or compunction.

From these details we see that the city appeared impregnable, and the people unconquerable, after having exercised power for some six to eight hundred years.

THE FATE OF CITY AND PEOPLE

Read the Book of Nahum in the light of the foregoing facts, and surely it will be felt that this utterance is not one of insensate vengeance, but of retributive justice. Just because God is God this had to be. The destruction of Nineveh, the defeat of the Assyrians, and the overthrow of the Empire were sudden and complete. Within half a century of the prophecy (in all likelihood) so completely did Nineveh perish that no trace was left of where it once was. Alexander the Great marched over its site, and did not know that a world-empire was buried under his feet, and nearer our own time (18th cent.) Niebuhr, the traveller, rode through Nineveh unknowingly. This was the first instance in the history of mankind of a Power so great perishing so instantly, and for ever.

Before this event, and since, cities have remained while empires have passed away, as witness, Rome, Athens, Istanbul, Damascus, Alexandria, Venice, and other cities, but never before or since, has a city suddenly disappeared as Nineveh did.

'The fiery empire of conquerors sank like a tropic sun. Its wrath had burned, unassuaged, "from", (in their own words) "the rising to the setting sun". No gathering cloud had tempered its heat or allayed its violence. Just ere it set in those last hours of its course, it seemed as if in its meridian. Its blood-stained disc cast its last glowing rays on that field of carnage in Susiana; then, without a twilight, it sank beneath those stormy waves, so strangely raised, at once and for ever. All, at once, was night. It knew no morrow'.

(Pusey)

Added to human conflict—which could not have had such an issue—were the elements of water and fire.

'The gates of the rivers are opened,
And the palace melts away' (ii. 6).

In B.C. 625 the Tigris had overflowed, and despairing of the safety of the city, Assur-bani-pal 'made an exceeding great pile in the palace, heaped up there all the gold and silver, and the royal apparel, and having shut up his concubines and eunuchs in the house formed in the midst of the pile, consumed himself and all the royalties with them all' (Pusey). Nahum predicted that again fire would assail Nineveh, which it did twenty years later, in B.C. 606.

'Fire will devour your barriers.
Fire shall devour you;
It shall devour you as the locust does'
(iii. 13, 15).

Rawlinson says that 'recent excavations have shown that fire was a great instrument in the destruction of the Nineveh palaces. Calcined alabaster, masses of charred wood and charcoal, colossal statues split through with the heat, are met with in parts of the Ninevite mounds, and attest the veracity of the prophecy.'

THE GREAT LESSON OF THE BOOK

Nahum has but one theme, and this is that kingdoms built on the foundation of force and fraud shall certainly be destroyed; and that the Kingdom of God, reared on the foundation of truth and righteousness, is bound to triumph. Nineveh represented worldly power in antagonism to Yahweh, and so it had to perish. This is the theme which Nahum insists on with concentrated passion. 'He strikes but one chord in the harmony of prophetic song, (and) he strikes it with splendid decision and energy' (Findlay). He scarcely refers to Judah, and when he does, it is not to her sins and future punishment (i. 12-15; ii. 2), but she is viewed ideally, not actually.

Nahum is the prophet of *Nemesis*; of certain retribution for all evil, whether individual or national. The most recent illustration of this truth is the defeat of Germany and Italy in the last Great War (1939-1945), and it would be well if all intending aggressors and transgressors were to ponder it.

THE BOOK AS LITERATURE

Findlay says: 'This little Book ranks amongst the finest things in Hebrew literature. In poetic fire and sublimity it approaches the best work of Isaiah'; and he instances its unity of conception, its artistic handling of its theme, its wealth of metaphor and brilliance of description, its firm swift movement, and vehemence of passion; and this is the verdict of those best able to judge.

OUTLINE

The Prophecy is in three main parts:

  I Judgment on Nineveh Declared (i)

  II Judgment on Nineveh Described (ii)

 III Judgment on Nineveh Defended (iii)

ZEPHANIAH (B.C. 640-610)

This Prophet, whose name means *he whom Yah hath hidden* (ii. 3), appears to have been the great-great-grandson of King Hezekiah (i. 1). He prophesied in the reign of Josiah (B.C. 640-610), and, it is commonly agreed, in the early part of his reign, before his reformation began, probably about 630-626.

His contemporaries were Nahum and Jeremiah. He vividly portrays the state of Judah and Jerusalem in his time. Dark had been the days of Manasseh and Amon, and in consequence,

25

Judah was characterized by irreligion and immorality (iii. 3, 4), in which the priests, princes and prophets were alike involved.

Zephaniah was confronted with men who did not believe in God's moral purpose, and who, accordingly, were free to swear both by Him and by Milcom (i. 5). Seven classes of offences are cited which reflect, as in a mirror, the character of the times (i. 4-6), and which later brought down upon the heads of the guilty people a full and fitting judgment (14-18).

The framework of most of the prophecies is followed here also, for Zephaniah *denounces* the people's sin, *pronounces* judgment consequent upon it, and *announces* a day of revival and restoration through the goodness of God.

It is practically certain that the menace which he indefinitely announced was the irruption of the Scythian hordes who a little later poured down over Western Asia (630-621). This judgment would fall upon the nations in every direction, West and East, South and North; from Ekron to Ammon, and from Ethiopia to Nineveh; none would be excluded from the just visitation, the consequence of sin (ii.).

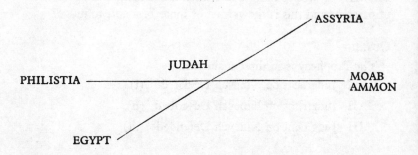

This Divine judgment is called THE DAY OF THE LORD, a DAY which is referred to twenty times in this Book. It is the *Dies Irae* of Thomas of Celano, which has become the hymn of the Last Judgment for all Christendom. Joel and Zephaniah are chiefly the Prophets of this Day, though it is spoken of by most of the other Prophets; but Zephaniah predicted a judgment both wider and more complete in destructiveness than that which was foretold by the earlier prophets. His is the vision of a world-wide catastrophe, which has not yet been fulfilled to the letter. Kirkpatrick rightly says:

'In part Zephaniah's words still await fulfilment, and we do him no injustice if we say that he could not anticipate how distant their fulfilment would be. It was given to those ancient prophets to soar above the earth-born mists which becloud human vision, and see God's purposes rising majestically against the clear firmament of His righteous sovereignty, like sunlit Alpine peaks against the azure sky; but it was not given them to see all at once how many an obstacle must be surmounted, how many a disappointment endured, ere the longed-for goal could be attained'.

The fulfilment of Nahum's prophecy concentrated on Nineveh, but that of Zephaniah concentrated on Jerusalem (i. 4-6, 8-12. iii. 3, 4). Nahum views judgment as an end in itself, but Zephaniah views it as the appointed means for the purification of Israel and the conversion of the nations. But these prophets are one in the conviction that righteousness must and will triumph over iniquity; and in a sublime passage (iii. 14-20) Zephaniah says that where there is repentance there is hope.

'The LORD your Elohim is in the midst of you
A victorious warrior.
He will rejoice over you with gladness,
He will renew you in His love.
He will exult over you with a shout,
As in the days of a festival'.

What Micah and Isaiah had been to Hezekiah, Zephaniah and Jeremiah were to Josiah, and the latter prepared the way for the final—but, alas, ineffective—reformation.

The Prophecy is in three main parts:

I   A Declaration of Retribution (ch. i.).

II An Exhortation to Repentance (chs. ii. 1–iii. 8a).

III A Promise of Redemption (ch. iii. 8b–20).

JEREMIAH (B.C. 627-586)

Because of the unique and vital place which Jeremiah occupied for over 40 years in the history of Judah, we must go into more detail relative to his person and work than it is necessary to do in the case of any other prophet of this period; and by considering his times, and person, and ministry, we are following divisions suggested by the composition of his Book, which is at once historical, biographical, and prophetical.

I THE TIMES OF JEREMIAH

1 PREDECESSORS AND CONTEMPORARIES

To a right understanding of this, or any other character or work, we must be conversant with its setting. *Isaiah* had been dead over 70 years; and the good king Hezekiah was followed by his wicked and worthless son Manasseh, during 40 years of whose reign no prophetic voice was raised; then *Nahum* arose, and prophesied between the end of Manasseh's reign, and the beginning of Josiah's reign. It was just about the time when his ministry ceased that *Zephaniah* and *Jeremiah* commenced theirs, to be followed about 20 years later by *Habakkuk*, a couple of years later again by *Daniel*, and about 20 later still by *Ezekiel*; in other words, Jeremiah prophesied for over 40 years; during the reigns of Josiah, Jehoahaz, Jehoiakim, Jehoiachin, and Zedekiah (i. 2, 3). The prophets contemporary with him, were *Zephaniah*, *Habakkuk*, *Daniel*, and *Ezekiel*, and probably *Obadiah*. He was to Josiah, what Isaiah had been to Hezekiah.

2 THE SITUATION

Manasseh had left Josiah a frightful heritage of iniquity, but in the strength of God he faced it, and his reign was conspicuous as one of Reformation. Five or six years after Jeremiah's call, the Book of the Law was found in the Temple, the reading of which resulted in widespread confession of sin and wholesale destruction of both idols and idolatrous priests. Judah rose to the occasion with Josiah, but at the height of his prospects, he went uncommissioned against Necho, king of Egypt, and was mortally wounded at the battle of Megiddo. With his death Judah's hope died. He was followed by Jehoahaz who reigned but three months; then Jehoiakim came to the throne, and with him the days of folly and idolatry, of injustice and cruelty were revived. The reformation of Josiah had come too late, 'it did not reach the deeply-seated, widespread corruption which tainted rich and poor alike'; the work was superficial and therefore only temporary; sin was like a cancer, eating away at the very heart of the nation; it was 'written with a pen of iron, and with the point of a diamond; graven upon the table of their hearts, and upon the horns of their altars' (xvii. 1). They said 'there is no hope, we will walk after our own devices, and we will everyone do the imagination of his evil heart' (xviii. 12). Deceit, idolatry, and injustice were rampant, a wonderful and horrible thing was committed in the land, the prophets prophesied falsely, the priests bore rule by these means, and the people loved to have it so.

But this notwithstanding, they persevered with all the outward symbols of piety, and when challenged with their sins, retorted, 'The LORD liveth. The temple of the LORD, the temple of the LORD, the temple of the LORD are these. We are wise, and the law of the LORD is with us. What is our iniquity or what is our sin that we have committed against the LORD our God?' (v. 2; vii. 4; viii. 9; xvi. 10). But, said the LORD, 'Run ye to and fro through the streets of Jerusalem, and see now and know, and seek in the broad places of the way, if ye can find a man, if there be any that executeth judgment, that seeketh the truth, and I will pardon it'; but the offer was in vain.

3 THE DRIFT OF THE NATION

The past should have sufficed to teach them the folly of forgetting or forsaking their God, but they failed to learn, and so multiplied to themselves the iniquity of their fathers that nothing but doom could await them. The nation was rushing headlong to destruction; the attempt to arrest it, or turn it back, was of no avail; it would plunge over the precipice into the wide weltering ruin. And Jeremiah was raised up for such a time as this, and stared these issues in the face; it is when we have in some measure realized what that meant, that we shall be prepared to understand him and his message.

II THE PERSON OF JEREMIAH

1 HIS COUNSELLORS

The first time the prophet's name occurs is in connection with Josiah's death, and then, with the whole nation, he is bewailing his loss, and probably he wrote an ode in commemoration of it (2 Chron. xxxv. 25). But we can gather from other passages what in all probability was the trend of his early days. During the reign of Josiah there was a group of people who were the very salt of the decaying Nation, and who, without any doubt, restrained the speedy downfall. They are referred to in 2 Kings xxii. 14, 'Hilkiah the priest, Ahikam, Achbor, Shaphan, Asahiah, and Huldah the prophetess'. To these names two must be added, Josiah the king, and Jeremiah the prophet, the youngest of that illustrious band, but destined to become the most illustrious of them all. It was in this society, no doubt, that his passion for reform was born and fostered, and from thence it broke out as a restless wave, both in word and work.

All great movements are so begotten and nourished, and too close attention can never be paid to one's innermost circle of friends. To be ever in company with our inferiors will be sure to beget in us a spirit of pride, if it does not become positively wearisome; and to be only in the company of our equals, is almost sure to hinder rapid progress; but to make choice of our superiors for company can never fail to beget within us, and to draw out from us, the best of which we are capable. This is especially true in the Christian Society; and when, as often, one is not so placed as to have the privilege of personal friendship with those who are deeply taught in the things of God, and in whose hearts burn the revivals of coming days, there is always open to such the company of their best books.

2 HIS CHARACTER

To mark the differences between the characters of those whom God employs for the accomplishment of His purposes, is in itself an excellent study. Elijah was as a mighty hammer that mercilessly fell upon the rocky heart of Ahab; he was a stern man, almost fierce, a force to be reckoned with; Moses was meek, but very firm; Ezekiel was rugged and rough; but Jeremiah was timid, sensitive, and intensely sympathetic, 'No single one of all the Old Testament prophets comes so near to us in a human way as Jeremiah. He has all the powerful utterance of Hosea, and at times can deal blows as heavy as Isaiah's, but at the same

time his heart is overflowing with a human feeling for the misery
of his people, and he weeps hot tears over the piteous fall of his
fatherland.   Yet duty to his God calls him and compels him to
blame, when he would willingly have consoled.   With a bleeding
heart he enters on a terrible struggle with himself; and though no
better patriot ever lived, he bears the stigma of a traitor to his
country for the sake of Jehovah and truth'.

Plaintive and retiring, he reveals his soul in the first words
that escape his lips, 'Ah, Lord God! behold, I cannot speak,
for I am a child' (i. 6).   It is this child-like tenderness which
adds force to the severity of his denunciations, and to the
bitterness of his grief, as it is 'the wrath of the little Lamb',
in the 'Revelation', that will strike terror to the heart of men
in the Judgment Day.   It is the man who in obedience to his
commission pronounces the doom of his people (xxiv. 9, 10),
who cries, 'Oh that my head were waters, and mine eyes a fountain
of tears, that I might weep day and night for the slain of the
daughters of my people' (ix. 1).   In all this, as in many other
respects, he is a true type of Him in whom severity and
sympathy met for the first and last time in perfect proportion
and blend.

3 His Call

The record of this is found in ch. i. 4-9, and is full of instruction.
First of all there is the announcement of Jeremiah's fore-ordination
to the office and work of a prophet (5); then the youth's remonstrance on the ground of his age and inexperience (6); and lastly
his Divine equipment for the task that lay before him, and
encouragement for dark days to come (7-9).   He said, 'I cannot',
but the Lord said, 'thou shalt', and then He made the task possible
by putting words into the prophet's mouth, and giving him the
promise of His constant companionship.

Jeremiah's remonstrance is wholly commendable, for we
cannot have too great a sense of our own complete unworthiness
and inability to take any share in the outworking of the Divine
Will; satisfaction with one's own qualities for such a task would
be the greatest proof of one's unfitness.   Solomon cried, 'I am
but a little child, I know not how to go out or come in'; Paul

said, 'Who is sufficient for these things?' and even the Lord Himself, in speaking of the mission on which He had been sent, said, 'I am straitened until it be accomplished'. The service of Christ is a solemn thing, it is not a series of spiritual picnics, but often will involve great sacrifices of time, of means, of strength, and of human pleasures. But the gains are infinitely greater than the losses; the recompenses, than the renunciations. We go not to work and war at our own charges, but our Divine Leader finds the will, the strength, the occasion, the reward, and is Himself with us all the while; 'Lo, I with you Am, unto the ages'.

We are in the embrace of the Divine I AM (Gr). When He calls you, rise; whither He sends you, go; what He commands you, speak; what He permits you, suffer; and throughout all let it be your sufficient recompense to be well-pleasing in His sight. One might have thought that for such a task as this, a strong hard hearted, brazen-faced man would have been more suitable, but God's thoughts are not ours, and for it He chose a sensitive youth; He put the treasure in a fragile vessel of clay, that the power might the more conspicuously be of God. (2 Cor. iv. 7. Rotherham). And so we are not the best judges of what service we are fitted for, and it is never safe for us to choose; let Him do all, and then He bears all responsibility.

III THE WORK OF JEREMIAH

1 THE TASK

What lay before this newly-ordained young prophet is clearly set before him at the beginning (i. 10-19), as it had been for Isaiah (ch. vi.). He was to root out, to pull down, to destroy, to throw down, to build up, and to plant (10); he was to address a people who had forsaken God, burned incense to other gods, and worshipped the work of their own hands (16). They would scowl at him, and scoff, and threaten vengeance, but the LORD was pledged to make him as a defenced city, as an iron pillar, and as brazen walls against the whole land. The whole community would be against him, princes, priests, and people, but they would not prevail against Jeremiah plus Jehovah, for these two were more than a match for any nation, and for all the nations.

This prophet was, as Dean Stanley has pointed out, 'one of those rare instances in Jewish history, in which priest and prophet were combined, and by a singularly tragical fate he lived precisely at that age in which both of those great institutions seemed to have reached the utmost point of degradation and corruption; both, after the trials and vicissitudes of centuries, in the last extremity of the nation of which they were the chief supporters, broke down and failed. Between the Priesthood and the Prophets there had hitherto been more or less of a conflict, but now that conflict was exchanged for a fatal union, and he who by each of his callings was naturally led to sympathize with each, was the doomed antagonist of both, a victim of one of the strongest of human passions, the hatred of Priests against a Priest who attacks his own order, the hatred of Prophets against a Prophet who ventures to have a voice and will of his own'. He had to proclaim unwelcome, unpalatable truth, and he had his full share of the consequences that have always followed upon such a task.

2 HIS MESSAGE

This passes through certain well-defined stages. First of all there is the note of—

(i) DENUNCIATION

And first, denunciation of Judah on account of her sins, which is set forth in language at once forceful and convincing. They had walked after vanity, and had become vain; they had forsaken Jehovah the fountain of living waters, and had hewed them out cisterns, broken cisterns that could hold no water. God had gloriously delivered them from Egyptian bondage, had brought them through the wilderness and into the land, but they had defiled it, and made His heritage an abomination; the prophets prophesied by Baal, and walked after things that did not profit; they spoke visions of their own hearts and not according to the mouth of the LORD; indeed, He had not called them, nor sent them; they were false prophets whose hands were full of iniquity; the priests were just as bad, and the people followed their lead (chs. ii., xxiii.). What hope was there for such a nation? Could the Ethiopian change his skin, or the leopard his spots? As well

might these people be expected to do good. Following hard upon
this was the prediction of—

(ii) *VISITATION*

Sin must be punished; indeed, it carries its own punishment
with it. Jehovah had pleaded with His people, but they were
hardened in sin, and now the end was fast approaching. 'Behold
I will cause to cease out of this place in your eyes, and in your
days, the voice of mirth, and the voice of gladness, the voice
of the bridegroom, and the voice of the bride. I will cast you out
of this land into a land that you know not, and there shall ye serve
other gods day and night; where I will not show you favour'
(xvi. 9, 13). 'And this whole land shall be a desolation, and an
astonishment; and these nations shall serve the king of Babylon
seventy years' (xxv. 11). But still Jehovah was more than un-
willing that this disaster should befall 'the dearly beloved of
His soul' (xii. 7), and so another note is struck, the note of—

(iii) *INVITATION*

A note of pleading and of counsel. 'Thus saith the LORD of
Hosts, the God of Israel, Amend your ways and your doings,
and I will cause you to dwell in this place' (vii. 3). No situation
is from the first hopeless, and up to the last there were conditions
which, if met, would bring a reversal of the penalties pronounced.
'At what instant I shall speak concerning a nation, and concerning
a kingdom, to pluck up, and to pull down, and to destroy it;
if that nation, against whom I have pronounced, turn from their
evil, I will repent of the evil that I thought to do unto them.'
And the reverse was equally true: 'at what instant I shall speak
concerning a nation, and concerning a kingdom, to build and to
plant it; if it do evil in my sight, that it obey not my voice, then
I will repent of the good wherewith I said I would benefit them'
(xviii. 7-10).

Thus Jeremiah urged upon Judah not to resist the manifest
will of God. He had raised up Nebuchadnezzar to execute
His purposes, and the people's only hope lay in quiet submission
to that Eastern Power, but if they resented and rebelled against

it, then they would drink the cup of retribution to the dregs
(xxi. 8-10; xxxviii. 2, 17, 18). And this they chose to do, and
the judgment predicted fell fully and fatally upon that generation.
But, throughout all Israelitish Prophecy, a wide horizon sweeps
around which glows with the promise of a distant day.

And Jeremiah, like Isaiah, has his Book of—

(iv) CONSOLATION

In this, restoration is promised to Israel, and the advent and
rule of the Messiah is predicted (xxx.-xxxiii.). These prophecies,
of course, had a partial fulfilment when the Jews returned from
Babylonian captivity, and a yet further fulfilment at the first advent
of Christ; but their complete fulfilment is still in the future, when
the LORD will return to rule, not only over restored Israel and
Judah, but also over all the nations of the earth. So out of the storm
and gloom Jeremiah saw the dawning of a better day, and by his
prophetic insight he discerned a nobler city arising out of the
ruins of the old, and the new covenant taking the place of that
which seemed to have been so decidedly annulled.

Jeremiah's commission concerned not Israel only, but 'the
nations'; he was the exponent of God's world-plan in that age
of convulsion and upheaval; his mission was primarily to pluck
up and to break down, though ultimately, to build and to plant;
in other words, he announced the removal of the existing order
of things, to make room for a new one (xxv. 12-38; xlvi.-li.).

And the method infrequently adopted in the execution of this
enormous and hazardous task, was both striking and suggestive.
He went to the Euphrates, and there hid his girdle in a hole
of the rock, and after many days dug it out, and held it up before
Judah as the symbol of how Jehovah will carry them away thither
and mar them (xiii.). Again, he took a party of elders to the valley
of Hinnom, and dashed an earthen pitcher into a thousand
fragments before them, to indicate what God was about to do
with His rebellious people (xix.). And again, when the Chaldeans
had already invested Jerusalem, he bought some property in
his native Anathoth, in token and proof that 'houses and fields
and vineyards should again be possessed in that land' by the
chosen people (xxxii.).

3 THE RESULTS

So far as the Prophet himself was concerned, his mission brought to him perpetual martyrdom. The inhabitants of his native place plotted against his life (xi. 18-20), and even his relatives and friends dealt treacherously with him (xii. 6). He was prohibited to marry (xvi. 2), and spent his life in isolation and solitude, save when he was delivering his messages. He was constantly watched, that revenge might be taken on him (xx. 10), and on one occasion his life was saved only by the firm pleading of a friendly prince (xxvi.). For bearing his faithful witness he was put in the stocks (xx.), in the court of the prison (xxxvii.), and at last into a miry pit, where, but for the intervention of a heathen friend, he would have been starved to death (xxxvii.). He was ultimately carried away to Egypt, and tradition says he was stoned at Daphnae by the Jews, who became impatient and angry at his repeated denunciations of their idolatries. With him it was *per crucem ad lucem* in very truth.

And let it be remembered that this persecution was not at the hands of heathen nations, but of the elect people. Would to God it had ended there, but, alas, it has been repeated many times in our own age, beginning with Him Who could not do many mighty works in His own country because of the people's unbelief; and for centuries the prophets of the Church have been subjected to petty persecution, and actual martyrdom, at the hands of those who have professed to be followers of Jesus Christ. This story then is full of interest and pathos for us. And so far as the results to the Nation were concerned, as predicted, national sin brought national ruin; the chosen people in Jeremiah's own day, and beneath his very eyes, were taken away captive to Babylon, their city wrecked, their Temple burned, and those of them who were left behind, fled to Egypt. God's mills grind exceeding small.

IV THE BOOK OF JEREMIAH

This, the longest Book in the Bible, is the loosest in its structure, and it is difficult—if indeed possible—to discern its scheme. Yet attempt should be made, as far as this may be possible, to arrange its parts chronologically.

Between the *Call of the Prophet* in ch. i., and the *Historical Postscript* in ch. lii., there appear to be *four Books*, as follows:

CHART 79

THE BOOK OF JEREMIAH, No. 1		
I	II	III
The Call of the Prophet	THE FOUR BOOKS	The Historical Postscript
Ch. i	Chs. ii–li	Ch. lii
B.C. 627 The Prophet's Origin and Period (1–3) The Divine Commission (4–10) The Prophet's Visions (11–16) The Enduement for Service (17-19)	The Great Book of Doom ii–xxix　　B.C. 627–605 The Little Book of Consolation xxx–xxxiii.　　B.C. 587 The Book of Personal Memoirs xxxiv–xlv.　　B.C. 605–586 The Book of Foreign Oracles xlvi–li　　B.C. 608–586	B.C. 586 The Fall of Jerusalem (1–30). (2 Kings xxiv. 18-xxv. 26) The Restoration of Jehoiachin (31–34) (2 Kings xxv. 27-30)

That the Prophecies were collected and written at intervals is clear from ch. xxxvi. 2, 32, to which Roll others were added later.

CHART 80

THE BOOK OF JEREMIAH, No. 2. 627–586 B.C. (and after). Chronologically Arranged

Ch. i	PROPHECIES BEFORE THE FALL OF JERUSALEM		PROPHECIES AFTER THE FALL OF JERUSALEM	Ch. lii
				CONCLUSION. Ch. lii. A Historical Supplement (2 K. xxv. 1–26)
	IN THE REIGN OF JOSIAH 627–610 B.C. 18 Years. Chs. ii–vi, xi–xii, xiii? Jeremiah's Message before Josiah's Reformation.		586–?	
	IN THE REIGN OF JEHOIAKIM 609–598 B.C. 11 Years. Probable Order of Prophecies. vii–x. xlvi–xlix. 33. xxv. xxxvi. 1–8. xlv. xxxvi. 9–32. xiv–xv. xvi. xvii. xviii–xix. 13. xix. 14–xx. xxxv. xxii–xxiii. 8. xxiii. 9–40. xiii ?		THE REMNANT IN JUDAH xl–xliii. 3	
	IN THE REIGN OF ZEDEKIAH 597–586 B.C. 11 Years. Probable Order of Prophecies. xxiv. xxvii. xxviii–xxix. xlix. 34–li. xxi. xxxiv. xxxvii–xxxviii. xxxix. 15–18. xxxii. xxxiii. xxx. xxxi. xxxix. 1–14.		THE REMNANT IN EGYPT xliii. 4–xliv	
INTRODUCTION. Ch. i. The Prophet's Call and Commission				

Perhaps it will help, if at this point is shown the connection between the first two great Prophets, *Isaiah* and *Jeremiah*; for this view will give a conspectus of about 170 years—from the beginning of Jotham's reign to the end of the Monarchy.

CHART 81

ISAIAH AND JEREMIAH
TWO REFORMATIONS AND THREE FALLS

JOTHAM TO HEZEKIAH	MANASSEH-AMON	JOSIAH TO ZEDEKIAH
758–698	698–641	641–586
60 Years	57 Years	55 Years
Hezekiah's Reformation		Josiah's Reformation
ISAIAH 757–627 = 130 Years		JEREMIAH
Micah, Hosea	No Prophets	Nahum, Zephaniah, Habakkuk, Obadiah
FALL OF SAMARIA 722		FALL OF NINEVEH 606; FALL OF JERUSALEM 586

HABAKKUK (B.C. 609-598)

It is practically certain that Habakkuk delivered his message in the reign of Jehoiakim (B.C. 609-598). Nahum's Prophecy related to the fall of the Assyrian Empire, and Habakkuk's relates to the rise of the Chaldean power. Yahweh had destroyed one instrument He had used for the chastisement of His people, but He at once lays hold of another.

Iniquity, violence, strife, and injustice were widespread in Judah, and Habakkuk cries out against it all (i. 2-4), but he cannot understand why God should use for punishment so cruel and wicked a people as the Chaldeans (i. 5-17), and he virtually challenges God to justify His action (ii. 1).

For reply Yahweh bids the Prophet write a message on tablets, and put it in a public place, so that people on the run may be able to read it; and this is the message:

> *'Behold, his soul is lifted up, It is not upright in him;*
> *But the righteous shall live in his faithfulness'* (ii. 4).

This statement crystallizes the principles on which death and life depend in nations and individuals. The unrighteous shall perish, and the righteous shall endure. The first line of the Oracle refers to the Chaldeans, and the second, to Israel, regarded ideally and represented by the godly and faithful in all her history. The Chaldeans would perish, not because they were Chaldeans, but because they were not upright; and Israel would survive, not because they were Israel, but because at the heart of their history was the principle of faith.

The Apostle Paul takes up this truth, and uses its three dominating words in three of his Epistles.

'The just', Romans i. 17; 'by faith', Galatians iii. 11; 'shall live', Hebrews x. 38.

The remainder of this Prophecy is a development of the two clauses of the Oracle: ch. ii. 5-20, relating to Chaldea; and ch. iii., relating to the true Israel. For the Chosen People recollection of the past is the ground of hope for the future.

> 'Thou art come forth for the salvation of Thy people,
> For the salvation of Thine anointed' (iii. 13).

This was a solemn and gladsome message for Judah as the relentless Chaldeans were approaching them to overthrow them; solemn, because they were to be severely punished by this cruel race; and gladsome, because it was revealed to them that this punishment was not for their extinction, but for their purification. And so it eventuated, for seventy years later the Chaldean Empire fell, and the Judaean captives were given leave to return to Palestine.

The tragedy is that Jehoiakim paid little or no attention to the message, but hurried on to his doom.

DANIEL AND EZEKIEL

As these two men are pre-eminently Prophets of the Exile, both being captives in Babylon, we shall consider their ministries in the Exile period (pp. 419-436).

ACT I

SCENE 2

THE ISRAELITISH NATION

PERIOD C
THE AGE OF THE DEPENDENCY

The Remnant in the West
JEREMIAH   OBADIAH

The Exiles in the East
DANIEL   EZEKIEL

C

PERIOD OF THE DEPENDENCY

The Rule of Aliens

From the Fall of the Monarchy to the Return from Captivity

2 Kings xxv. 22-30. Obadiah

Jeremiah xl.–xliv.; lii. Lamentations

Ezekiel xxxiii.-xlviii. Daniel iii.-ix. Isaiah xl.-lxvi. Psalms
xlii.-xliv.; lxxiv.; lxxvii.; lxxix.; lxxx.; lxxxix.; xciv.; cii.;
cxxx.; cxxxvii.

B.C. 586-536. 50 Years.

IN the UNFOLDING DRAMA OF REDEMPTION, Scene 2 of ACT 1 is
the history of the ISRAELITISH NATION, and this is in three main
periods: *The Theocracy,* or Rule of God; *The Monarchy,* or
Rule of Native Kings; and *The Dependency,* or Rule of Aliens.

With the fall of Jerusalem and the deportation to Babylon
of the Judaeans in B.C. 586, the period of the *Monarchy* ended,
and the period of the *Dependency* became absolute. This last
statement must be explained.

The period of the *Dependency* did not *begin* in B.C. 586,
but twenty years earlier, in B.C. 606, with the fall of the Assyrian
Empire, and the rise of Babylon to world power. When Nebuchadnezzar marched against Jerusalem, Jehoiakim was made
subject to him, as were also the two following kings of Judah,
Jehoiachin and Zedekiah. So Judah was subject to Chaldea from
B.C. 606-586, though Jewish kings were reigning, and it was,
therefore, under the rule of Aliens.

This period of twenty years must be added to the fifty years
of Exile, from B.C. 586-536, to make the seventy years of Captivity, referred to by Jeremiah. This Captivity began with the
first contingent of captives that went to Babylon in B.C. 606,
in the reign of Jehoiakim; it was added to in B.C. 598, in the
reign of Jehoiachin; and it was completed in B.C. 586, with the
removal of Zedekiah and all except a small and uninfluential
remnant, as Charts 71, 72 show.

The complete Exile was from B.C. 586-536, a period of fifty years, during which the nation was entirely under aliens. The distinction, therefore, between the twenty years, and the fifty, may be described as the *Subjection*, and the *Servitude* (Chart 82).

CHART 82

THE DEPENDENCY OF JUDAH	
THE SUBJECTION	THE SERVITUDE
B.C. 606–586	B.C. 586–536
20 Years	50 Years
The 70 Years of Jeremiah (xxv. 11–13; xxix. 10, 11)	
2 Kings xxiv-xxv. 21 2 Chron. xxxvi. 1-21	2 Kings xxv. 22-30

The remnant which was left in the land, on the removal to Babylon of Zedekiah and the nation as a whole, was left there by the will and under the authority of Nebuchadnezzar (2 Kings xxv. 22-26); and, of course, all who were deported were Babylon's captives. After Zedekiah, there was no national king in the Davidic line until Christ came, David's rightful heir, but He was rejected and crucified, and so the Chosen People have had no king for over 2,500 years (Hos. iii. 4), though there were some in the Interlude Period who were called kings.

From this it will be seen that, strictly speaking, the *Dependency Period* virtually began in B.C. 606, but absolutely it began in B.C. 586; so that the first twenty years of the *Dependency* were also the last twenty years of the *Monarchy*.

We have more literature than history of the Servitude period of fifty years, but the literature throws much light on what took place at the time of the fall of the Monarchy, and afterwards.

In the Dependency Period the people of Judah must be seen in two directions: the Remnant in the West, and the Exiles in the East.

CHART 83

COMPREHENSIVE ANALYSIS OF THE DEPENDENCY PERIOD
606-536 B.C.—70 Years

Stages of the Period				Prophets	Home Events	Foreign Events
1: SUBJECTION. 606-586 B.C. 20 Years						BABYLON
Name of King	Began to Reign	Length of Reign	Character			
JEHOIAKIM	609	8	Bad	JEREMIAH	JEHOIAKIM reigned 8 years in this Period, from 606-598 B.C. and 3 years in the Single Kingdom Period, 609-606 B.C. NEBUCHADNEZZAR plundered Jerusalem.	Ninevah falls before Babylonian and Median armies. Pharaoh NECHO defeated by NEBUCHADNEZZAR at the battle of Carchemish, 606 B.C.
					FIRST STAGE OF THE EXILE	
				DANIEL	DANIEL and the three Hebrews taken to Babylon.	
JEHOIACHIN	598	3 Mths.	Bad	JEREMIAH	Jerusalem taken by NEBUCHADNEZZAR.	
					SECOND STAGE OF THE EXILE	
					EZEKIEL taken to Babylonia. JEHOIACHIN taken to Babylon.	

407

CHART 83—Continued

COMPREHENSIVE ANALYSIS OF THE DEPENDENCY PERIOD
606-536 B.C.—70 Years

Stages of the Period				Prophets	Home Events	Foreign Events
ZEDEKIAH	597	11	Bad	EZEKIEL	ZEDEKIAH plays fast and loose with Babylon and Egypt. Jerusalem besieged by NEBUCHADNEZZAR. After two years' siege, Jerusalem is captured and laid waste, and Judah is taken to Babylonia. THIRD STAGE OF THE EXILE ZEDEKIAH taken to Babylon. Israelitish Monarchy dead for over 2,500 years.	
2. SERVITUDE. 586-536 B.C. 50 Years No Kings				JEREMIAH OBADIAH EZEKIEL DANIEL	JEREMIAH remained in Palestine GEDALIAH made governor of the remnant that was left in the Land. The Governor Slain. JOHANAN carried JEREMIAH and the remnant to Egypt.	BABYLON The Southern Tribes in Exile. JEREMIAH in Egypt. DANIEL a high official in Babylon Death of NEBUCHADNEZZAR. Accession of EVIL-MERODACH. Release of JEHOIACHIN. 2 K. xxv. 27-30. CYRUS. 538-529 B.C. CYRUS conquers Media. CYRUS captures Babylon. 538-536 B.C. CYRUS emancipates the Jews.

THE CAPTIVITIES OF ISRAEL AND JUDAH

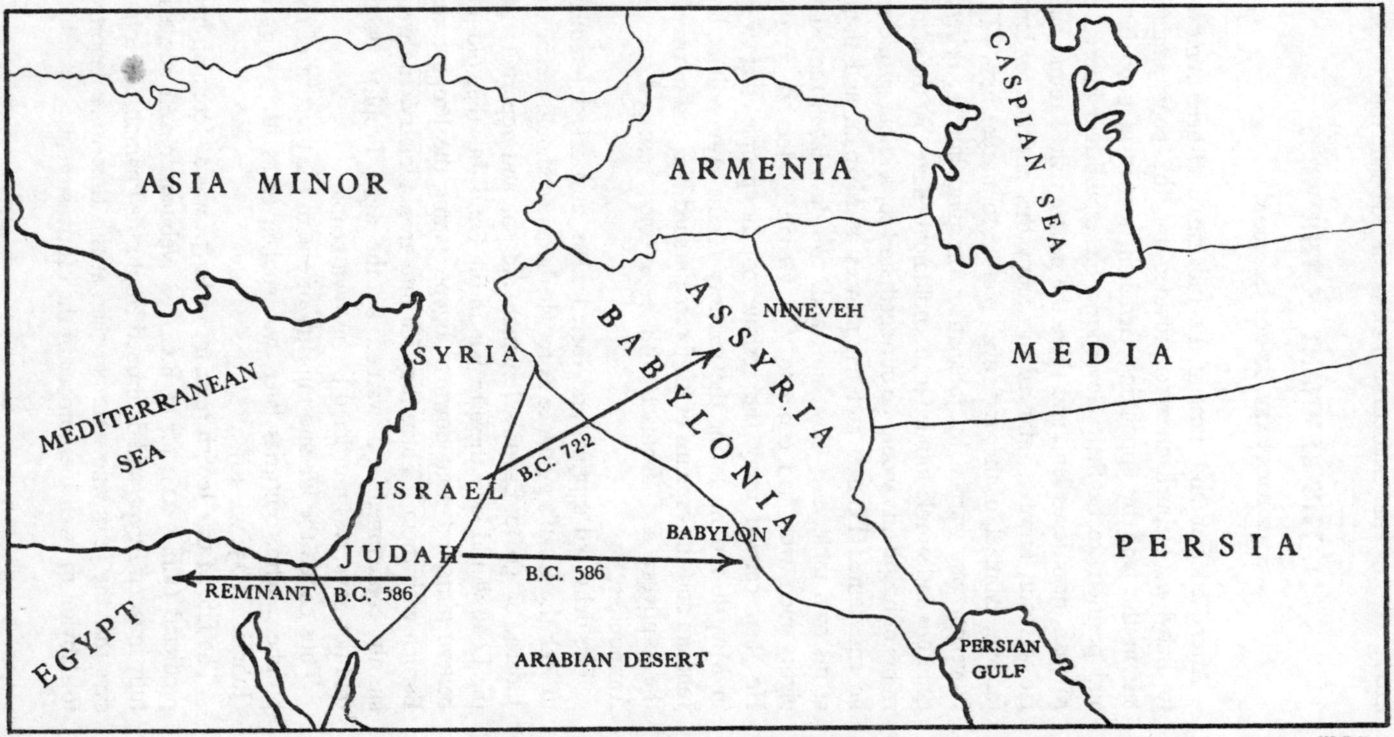

CASPIAN SEA

MEDIA

PERSIA

PERSIAN GULF

ARMENIA

NINEVEH

ASSYRIA

BABYLONIA

BABYLON

ARABIAN DESERT

ASIA MINOR

SYRIA

ISRAEL B.C. 722

JUDAH

B.C. 586

REMNANT B.C. 586

MEDITERRANEAN SEA

EGYPT

W.G.S.

Copyright

MAP 10

I. THE REMNANT IN THE WEST

(2 Kings xxv. 22-26; Jer. xl.-xliv.)

After Zedekiah and most of the Judaeans had been removed to Babylon, Nebuchadnezzar provided for the poor remnant left in the land by appointing Gedaliah, a man of good birth and position, to be their Governor. He established himself at Mizpah, near Jerusalem, and there the people rallied round him. He was not, however, allowed to occupy this position for long, for one, Ishmael, of the seed royal, plotted to murder him. The Governor was warned by Johanan of the plot, but he, being a generous and simple-minded man, could not believe that the sacred rights of hospitality would be outraged, and so, without suspicion, he entertained Ishmael and ten princes at Mizpah, and there, at his own table, they slew him; and, two days later, they slew eighty men who had come to visit Gedaliah (Jer. xl. 13-16). He then carried away the residue of the people that were in Mizpah and made for the territory of the Ammonites; but Johanan and the captains of his forces pursued him and recovered the captives; and Ishmael with eight men, escaped to the Ammonites.

The delivered captives and their leaders now asked Jeremiah to seek the LORD's guidance as to whether they should remain in Judaea, or go to Egypt. Jeremiah did so, and reported that the LORD would have them remain in the Land; but they did not believe him, and went down to Egypt, taking the Prophet and Baruch with them. There they fell into gross idolatry, and were sternly condemned and warned by the aged Prophet, who, tradition says, was murdered by his own people.

Thus ended the life and ministry of one of the greatest of the prophets, who, centuries later, was spoken of as 'the prophet' (John i. 21, 25; vii. 40).

The fate of this Jewish remnant in Egypt was as Jeremiah had predicted (xlii. 7-22); for in B.C. 568 Nebuchadnezzar successfully invaded Egypt, and dethroned Hophri its Pharaoh. Josephus says that the Jews who were not slain at this time were deported to Babylon to swell the number of the captives there.

The Literature of the Period

Consider now the Writings, produced in the West, which belong to the period of the final overthrow of the Monarchy.

The Lamentations

Five Elegies constitute this Book, Elegies relating to the overthrow of Jerusalem in B.C. 586. They are called *the Lamentations of Jeremiah*, though this prophet's name does not occur in them. To this Book the Septuagint prefixes these words:

'And it came to pass after Israel was led into captivity, and Jerusalem laid waste, that Jeremiah sat weeping, and lamented with this lamentation over Jerusalem, and said:'

This statement presents a very early tradition, and it is found also in the Vulgate, with the addition:

'and in bitterness of heart sighing and crying.'

The Targum and Peshito also assign the Book to Jeremiah.

These lamentations have nothing to do with those referred to in 2 Chron. xxxv. 25; but that passage shows that Jeremiah wrote dirges. As the author (some think there was more than one) of Lamentations was a witness of the things he relates, it is natural to suppose that they are the work of Jeremiah.

Elegy 1 is a wail of distress for Jerusalem. *Elegy* 2 says that the judgment on Zion is of God, because of the sins of the people. *Elegy* 3 is personal, and describes the suffering of the writer; but perhaps the sufferer thinks of himself as personifying the nation. *Elegy* 4 depicts the sufferings of various classes, and describes the malignant joy of the Edomites. *Elegy* 5 enumerates the insults heaped upon the Jews by their enemies, and a prayer is offered to the LORD not to forsake His people altogether.

In all likelihood these poems were written by Jeremiah between Jerusalem's overthrow and his enforced transport to Egypt. The literary form is acrostic (except in the fifth). In 1, 2, 4, 5 the verses answer to the Hebrew alphabet, and in the 3rd, three verses are given to each letter.

Here, however, we are concerned, not with literary details, but with the contribution of Lamentations to the Unfolding Drama of Redemption.   There is a striking similarity between these lamentations over fallen Jerusalem, and the lament of Christ over the oncoming fall of the same city:

'O Jerusalem, Jerusalem, thou that killest the prophets, and stonest them that are sent unto thee, how often would I have gathered thy children together, even as a hen gathereth her chickens under her wings, and ye would not!   Behold, your house is left unto you desolate'.

Both laments stand at corresponding epochs in history, a witness to the sins of the Jews, and to herald their hopes.

These Lamentations call attention to the fact that catastrophe awaits any community, however highly favoured, which forgets that public and private righteousness alone secures permanent prosperity.

Obadiah (B.C. 586-583)

In the Old Testament there are eleven persons of this name—which means, Worshipper of Yahweh—but of the man who wrote this Vision nothing whatever is known, except that he was a Judaean.

The Writing itself is the shortest in the Old Testament, and is characterized by vividness of detail, and conciseness of statement.   Also it is vigorous, terse, poetic, and rapid; a truly original pronouncement.

The date of the Vision continues to be a matter of controversy, and the periods which have been assigned to the writer have a range of 600 years, a period longer than from William the Conqueror to Oliver Cromwell.

The subject is the part which Edom played at the time of Jerusalem's overthrow.   But in the Old Testament we read of four occasions on which Jerusalem was taken.

1 By Shishak, in the reign of Rehoboam.
       (1 Kings xiv. 25; 2 Chron. xii. 2)

2 By Philistines and Arabians, in the reign of Jehoram.
       (2 Kings viii. 20-22, and 2 Chron. xxi. 16, 17)

3 By Joash, king of Israel, in the reign of Amaziah, king of Judah.
(2 Kings xiv. 10. 2 Chron. xxv. 19)

4 By Nebuchadnezzar, in the reign of Zedekiah.
(2 Kings xxv. 2 Chron. xxxvi. 11-21)

Of these, only the second and fourth could supply for Odadiah an occasion for writing as he has done; and of these two it is practically certain to have been the fourth, for his language better suits the total overthrow of the City, than it does what happened in the time of Jehoram.

The fact that verses 1-9 of Obadiah are found in Jeremiah xlix. 7-22, presents a difficulty if Obadiah wrote after B.C. 586, because Jeremiah wrote his Oracle against Edom probably about B.C. 605, but both may have drawn upon a lost source.

The value of 'Obadiah' is both historical and ethical. Historically it has a place in the long grievous story of Edom's hatred of Judah. These two peoples sprang from the brothers Esau and Jacob; but the Edomites could not forget that Jacob robbed Esau their ancestor of his birthright, and they would not forgive it. So when the Chaldeans laid siege to Jerusalem and finally destroyed it, the Edomites helped them, and gloated over Judah's overthrow.

Ethically the Writing is a solemn indictment of family feuds, of the quarrels of brethren, of which there are many illustrations; for example, Cain and Abel, Joseph and his brethren, Absalom and Amnon; but of them all, the age-long feud between Esau and Judah is the worst; and the former's attitude in the day of the latter's distress was base beyond words.

'In the day that thou stoodest on the other side, in the day that strangers carried away captive his forces, and foreigners entered into his gates, and cast lots upon Jerusalem, even thou wast as one of them.''

The Prophet enumerates the things that Edom did, and should not have done when Jerusalem was overthrown (12-14), and he predicts that what they had done would be done to them (15, 16). This prediction was progressively and finally fulfilled, so that, in his time Origen could say that their name and language had wholly perished.

Of Edom's attitude to Judah, Dean Stanley has eloquently said:

'Deepest of all was the indignation roused by the sight of the nearest of kin, the race of Edom, often allied to Judah, often independent, now bound by the closest union with the power that was truly the common enemy of both. There was an intoxication of delight in the wild Edomite chiefs, as at each successive stroke against the venerable wall, they shouted

"Down with it, down with it,
even to the ground" (Psalm cxxxvii. 7)

'They stood in the passes to intercept the escape of those who would have fled down to the Jordan valley; they betrayed the fugitives; they indulged their barbarous revels on the temple hill.

'Long and loud has been the wail of execration which has gone up from the Jewish nation against Edom. It is the one imprecation which breaks forth from the Lamentations of Jeremiah (iv. 21, 22); it is the culmination of the fierce threats of Ezekiel (xxv. 12-14; xxxv.); it is the sole purpose of the short, sharp cry of Obadiah; it is the bitterest drop in the sad recollections of the Israelitish captives by the waters of Babylon (Ps. cxxxvii. 7); and the one warlike strain of the Evangelical Prophet is inspired by the hope that the Divine Conqueror should come knee-deep in Idumean blood (Isa. lxiii. 1-4).'

This throbbing pronouncement is in two main parts:

I THE DOOM OF EDOM (1-16)

II THE DELIVERANCE OF JUDAH (17-21)

Under the first are: The *certainty* of the overthrow (1-9); the *reason* for it (10-14); and the *nature* of it (15, 16). And under the second are: The *triumph* of Judah (17, 18); its *possessions* (19, 20); and its *establishment* (21).

It is not unlikely that Obadiah wrote this Prophecy while a captive in Babylon.

Solomon said: 'A brother offended is harder to be won than a strong city; and their contentions are like the bars of a castle'.

And Jesus said: 'With what measure ye mete, it shall be measured unto you again'.

The Babylon of the Captivity

We look now eastward, to the land to which the Jews were taken captive, and it will be well to get just a glimpse of the magnificence and might of the Capital of the Chaldean Empire. Now only a few weird and desolate mounds remain of the staggering splendour of ancient Babylon, where, for a generation, the fortunes of Judah and the religious hopes of the world were imprisoned. Within a century of the Jewish captivity thither-ward, Herodotus visited the City and the impression left by his description has been abundantly confirmed by the examination of the site made by more recent travellers.

The City was a vast square, intersected by the Euphrates, as London is by the Thames, each side having a length of fifteen miles, enclosed by walls more than 370 feet high, and so broad that between the buildings that lined them on both sides there was room for a four-horse chariot to turn. The magnificence of the City, says Herodotus, exceeded that of any other city in the world. A hundred brazen gates gave entrance to the huge enclosure, where parks and gardens were intermingled with the houses, so as to present the appearance of the suburbs of a great metropolis rather than the metropolis itself. The streets all ran in straight lines, not only those parallel to the river, but also to the cross streets leading to the water side, and at the river end of these were low gates, also of brass, in the fence skirting the stream.

City walls towering high were no novel sight to Jews accustomed to the appearance of Jerusalem from the valley of the Kidron, but the prodigious scale on which the public buildings of Babylon were planned, and the wealth of ornament lavished upon them, offered a spectacle for which even Solomon's Temple had not prepared them.

The great Palace of the Kings was itself a city within a city. It had a circuit of seven miles. Its gardens rose one above another to the height of more than seventy feet. Its walls within and without were gorgeous with painting and sculpture.

But the most wonderful of all was the Temple of Bel-Merodach. It stood in a square enclosure with a side of 440 yards. In the middle rose a tower of solid masonry, built like a pyramid, square on square, the lowest having a side of 220 yards, the Temple proper, a silver shrine, shining out over the vast level plains that surrounded it at a height of 600 feet.

Though the materials of its architecture, as of that of all the City, were only brick and bitumen, these were made to yield effects as bright and as varied as those produced by porcelain or metal. The several stages of the Temple were black, orange, crimson, gold, deep yellow, brilliant blue, and silver white.

Life in this magnificent City corresponded to its magnificence. Scattered here and there amid the contemporary Hebrew Writings and floating down, no doubt with some exaggeration, in the traditions preserved by later writers, we come upon records of the impressions produced on the captive Jews by the scenes that met their eyes.

We, too, can almost behold them. The chariots and horses, the captains, all of them princes to look at, with their brilliant blue and crimson uniforms, their variegated sashes, their elaborate armour; the magicians, and the astrologers, and the sorcerers, and the celebrated wise Chaldeans (Dan. ii. 2; iv. 6, 7), the satraps, deputies, governors, judges, treasurers, counsellors, sheriffs, all the rulers of the provinces (Dan. iii. 3) present even to us a gorgeous display of military and official splendour. The traffic on the rivers, that is, the many streams or canals leading to and from the Euphrates, and on the wide lake or sea into which it opened immediately below the City, reaches our ears, unless it is drowned by the music of the bands in whose concerts the Babylonians delighted, and in which all the instruments known to the ancient world were represented (Dan. iii. 7).

This is the Babylon which Nebuchadnezzar boasted he had created (Dan. iv. 30), and in the magnificence of which Daniel and his companions passed their days.

The Babylonian Kings

At this point it will be well briefly to state who were the kings of Babylon during the sixty-eight years, B.C. 606-538.

NABOPOLASSAR	625-604	21 years
NEBUCHADNEZZAR	604-561	43 years
EVIL-MERODACH	561-559	2 years
NERGAL-SHAREZER	559-555	4 years
LABOROSOARCHOD	555	9 months
NABONADIUS	555-538	17 years
BELSHAZZAR	538	4 months

(co-regent with his father Nabonadius)

Nebuchadnezzar created the mighty Empire over which he ruled, and it may be said to have died with him, for twenty-three years after his death Babylon, without a blow, yielded to Cyrus the Persian, in fulfilment of prophecy (Isa. xlv. 1-3).

Evil-Merodach his son succeeded him, and after two years he was murdered. All we know of him is that he released from prison Jehoiachin of Judah, who had languished there for thirty-seven years (2 Kings xxv. 27-30. Jer. lii. 31-34). Jehoiachin was about eighteen years of age when he was taken captive and imprisoned, and so he was about fifty-five when he was released.

Nergal-Sharezer, or NERIGLISSAR, Merodach's brother-in-law, who probably held a command in Nebuchadnezzar's army (Jer. xxxix. 3), murdered Merodach, and reigned for four years. He had married a daughter of Nebuchadnezzar. The only palace which has been discovered on the right bank of the Euphrates was built by him.

Laborosoarchod, who was just a boy, succeeded his father, and was murdered after a reign of about nine months.

Nabonadius now came to the throne and ruled for seventeen years. Latterly his son BELSHAZZAR shared the throne with him, and it is he who was slain when Cyrus captured Babylon in B.C. 538 (Dan. v.). Nabonadius, therefore, was the last king of Babylon.

This summary will help us to see the place which Daniel occupied in the captivity period (p. 419).

2. THE EXILES IN THE EAST

What may be known of the circumstances of the Jews who were taken captive to Babylon by Nebuchadnezzar between B.C. 606 and 586, must be learned almost entirely from the literature, poetical and prophetical, which relates to the seventy years predicted by Jeremiah (xxiv. 11; xxix. 10); that is, from Isaiah, Jeremiah, Daniel, Ezekiel, Obadiah, Lamentations, and some Psalms. From scattered references in these Writings a fairly detailed picture can be drawn of the conditions under which the captives lived, and of their sins, fears and hopes.

We have seen (Chart 72) that the Captivity was effected in three stages over a period of twenty years, beginning in the fourth year of Jehoiakim, and ending in the eleventh year of Zedekiah; to which must be added, it would appear, a contingent

27

of 745 persons in the year B.C. 583 (Jer. lii. 30), three years after the Monarchy ended.

Doubtless many of the captives died on the way to Babylon, but those who arrived seem to have been settled in colonies here and there in the land, working at all forms of bond-service, but chiefly at agriculture. The extreme harshness of their lot is reflected in Isaiah xiv. 3; xlii. 22; xlvii. 6; li. 13; liv. 11; Jer. l. 17, and elsewhere; yet it was not as bad as the lot of their ancestors in Egypt over eleven hundred years before.

That their circumstances were not intolerable is seen in the fact that so many did not accept the opportunity which Cyrus gave them to go back to Judah. Probably the majority of these had been born in captivity, and so had never known the home-land.

Jeremiah had told them to build houses, and plant gardens, and make comfortable homes for themselves (Jer. xxix. 5-7), and this, no doubt, they were allowed to do.

They learned the language of their captors, and some of them assumed Chaldean names, as, for example, Zerubbabel, and Mordecai, which is either Babylonian or Persian. It will also be remembered that parts of the Books of Daniel and Ezra are in Aramaic or Chaldee.

Alas, the Jews fell into idolatry in Babylon, and were charged with it by Isaiah (lxv. 3-11; lxvi. 17), and by Ezekiel (xiv. 1-5), but after the Captivity they were no longer guilty of this sin. We read also of false prophets among the people, who stirred false hopes, and against whom the word of the LORD was sent by Jeremiah (xxix. 8, 9).

But there were some, perhaps many, of the captives who were true to their best traditions, and loyal to their ancient faith. Notable among these were Ezekiel by the Chebar, and Daniel, Hananiah, Mishael, Azariah, and others, no doubt, in Babylon. These were as preserving salt in the midst of much corruption, and were a moral and spiritual rallying centre, at any rate for the older generation of captives.

The Literature of the Period

This consists of all DANIEL except the first two chapters, half of EZEKIEL, the latter part of ISAIAH, (p. 437), and some PSALMS.

DANIEL (B.C. 606-534)

THE MAN

We do not take the view that the Book of this name was a product of the 2nd century B.C.; but that it belongs to the time of the Daniel to whom Ezekiel refers (xiv. 14, 20). Our survey, therefore, will be from this standpoint.

Daniel was born during the reign of Josiah, probably about the time when this king began his great work of reformation in B.C. 623-622, so that his childhood and early youth were spent in a time of religious revival, and under influences which definitely moulded his character. He was contemporary with Jeremiah, and may have been acquainted with Habakkuk.

When he was about seventeen years of age, in B.C. 606-605, he was deported to Babylon, with other Jews, by Nebuchadnezzar, and the first chapter of his Book bears this date, a great date in Jewish history, because then commenced the 70 years of captivity which Jeremiah had predicted (xxix. 10).

In the middle of verse 1 of 2 Kings xxiv. there is a break of three years, B.C. 605-602, during which Jehoiakim was subject to Nebuchadnezzar, and it is in this period that the events of Daniel i.-ii. fall, events which are momentous.

Daniel lived through the whole period of the Empire of Babylon, that is, from B.C. 606-538, and through the first four or five years of the Persian period, B.C. 538-534. His Book, therefore, covers a period of 72 years, and probably he was about 92 years old at the time of his death, of which about 73 years had been spent in Babylon.

THE BOOK

Daniel never claimed to be a prophet, and nowhere in the Old Testament is he spoken of as such. Nor is he placed in the Hebrew Bible among the prophets, but is included in the group of the *Hagiographa*, a group of miscellaneous Writings which contains thirteen of the Old Testament Books.

Yet part of this Book is prophetical, and marks a new stage in the history of prophecy, being apocalyptic in character. Daniel, more definitely than any other writer of Holy Scripture, presents a *Philosophy of History*, and shows the relation of the kingdoms of this world to the Kingdom of God, a Kingdom which is sovereign and eternal; which is immanent in history, and which characterizes it. In a wonderful way it unfolds the Drama of Redemption, and reveals the progressive and final triumph of the Messiah.

The major part of Daniel's Book belongs to that period of the Dependency which follows the Fall of the Monarchy, that is, to the time of the Exile, from the deportation of Zedekiah and the people of Judah, to the return under Zerubbabel fifty years later, which the following Chart shows.

CHART 84

THE BOOK OF DANIEL											
MAINLY HISTORICAL: i–vi						MAINLY PROPHETICAL: vii-xii					
i	ii	iii	iv	v	vi	vii	viii	ix	x	xi	xii
Hebrews at a Heathen Court	A Dream of Destiny	Faithfulness Tested by Fire	The Tragedy of a Tree	The Feast and the Fingers	The Lion-hearted and the Lions	Godless Kingdoms and the Kingdom of God	The Ram and the He-Goat	A Prophet at Prayer	The Mystery of a Man	A Struggle for Sovereignty	A Vision of Victory
CHRONOLOGICAL ORDER OF THE CHAPTERS											
i	ii	iii	iv	vii	viii	v	ix	vi	x	xi	xii
606	603	Undated		541	538	538	538	537	533	533	533
NEBUCHADNEZZAR				NABONADIUS BELSHAZZAR			DARIUS		CYRUS		
606–534 = 72 Years											

The Book of Daniel is not a history of this long period, for between ch. ii. and ch. vii., is a period of 62 years, of which nothing is said, except what is related in the two undated chapters iii., iv., which, however, fall in the time of Nebuchadnezzar.

No reference is made to the two years of Evil-Merodach, nor to the four years of Nergal-Sharezer, nor to fifteen years of the reign of Nabonadius (see p. 416). After the death of Nebuchadnezzar in B.C. 561, Daniel's next pronouncement is in the last two years of Nabonadius, when Belshazzar was co-regent with him (chs. vii., viii., v.), over twenty years after Nebuchadnezzar's death.

THE JEWS AND THE GENTILES

In the chapters which belong to the time of Nebuchadnezzar (i.-iv.), the advancing purpose of God is indicated in two ways which run parallel: (a) by the loyal witness of the Jews to YAHWEH, at the very heart of the heathen Empire; shown in their declining to eat food which had been dedicated to idols (ch. i.); and then, by their refusal to worship the image of a heathen god (ch. iii.); and (b) by the revelation in a dream to Nebuchadnezzar of the fall of Gentile civilization by the precipitation of the Messianic Kingdom (ch. ii.); and then, by compelling Nebuchadnezzar to acknowledge that God has omnipotent control in the earth, that the heavens do rule, that the Almighty abases the mightiest for his pride, that the Most High ruleth in the kingdom of men, and giveth it to whomsoever He will (ch. iv.).

THE COLOSSUS AND THE BEASTS

The importance of Nebuchadnezzar's dream (ch. ii.), together with Daniel's Visions (chs. vii., viii.) cannot be exaggerated; and though the Visions are separated from the Dream by 62 and 65 years, they should be looked at together because they both represent the long period of Gentile dominion which began with Nebuchadnezzar. What from earth's standpoint appears as a Colossal Man, all-powerful and unconquerable, is seen to be, from heaven's standpoint, a beastly thing; and what both the Dream and the Visions predicted has, so far, been literally fulfilled, though the end is not yet.

There is no more encouraging prophecy in all the Bible than this, for it shows that beyond 'Man's Day' will be the 'Day of the LORD', and a Kingdom which shall never pass away.

CHART 85

"THE TIMES OF THE GENTILES": Luke xxi. 24			
NEBUCHADNEZZAR'S DREAM—A COLOSSAL MAN			
Gold	Silver	Brass	Iron and Clay
Head	Breast and Arms	Belly and Thigh	Legs and Feet
DANIEL'S VISIONS—FOUR BEASTS			
Lion	Bear	Leopard	Fourth
INTERPRETATION			
BABYLONIA	MEDO-PERSIA	GREECE	ROME
606–538	538–333	333–63	63–? A.D.

From this it is clear that a new era in world-history was inaugurated with the rise of Nebuchadnezzar, an era which is still progressing, and which will last until Christ returns, Whose Kingdom is represented by the Stone which fell upon the feet of the Image and brought it down in ruins. This era, which has existed already for over 2,550 years, is called 'the times of the Gentiles' (Luke xxi. 24), and by its termination will be introduced Messiah's universal and abiding Kingdom (Dan. ii. 35, 44; vii. 13, 14, 27).

DANIEL'S VISIONS OF THE BEASTS

Though the Vision of ch. viii. is more than two years after that of ch. vii., the two are vitally connected.

The Bear of ch. vii., is a Ram in ch. viii.; and the Leopard of ch. vii., is a He-goat in ch. viii.; and in both Visions the Bear-Ram is Medo-Persia, and the Leopard-Goat is Greece. The details are as follows.

CHART 86

DANIEL'S EMPIRE VISIONS			
Chapter ii	Chapter vii	Chapter viii	Key
Gold	Lion		Babylon
Silver	Bear	Ram	Medo-Persia
Brass	Leopard	He-goat	Greece
Iron	Non-descript		Rome

CHART 87

THE BEAR AND THE RAM		
Chapter vii	Chapter viii	Key
Bear	Ram	Medo-Persia
Two Sides	Two Horns	Media and Persia
Raised on one side	One horn higher than the other	Persia more prominent than Media
	Higher horn came up last	Persia the younger of the two Kingdoms
Three ribs between the teeth	Pushed West, North, South	Countries Conquered

CHART 88

THE LEOPARD AND THE GOAT		
Chapter vii	Chapter viii	Key
Leopard	He-goat	Greece
	"Came from the West"	
"Dominion was given to it"	"Over the face of the whole earth"	Extent of Conquest
Four wings of a bird	Touched not the ground	Celerity of Progress
	A notable horn between its eyes	Alexander the Great
Four Heads	Four Notable Horns	Alexander's Generals
	The 'little horn' out of one of them	Antiochus Antichrist

It should be borne in mind that the Visions of chs. vii., viii., were vouchsafed in the time of Belshazzar, that is, in the Babylonian period, so that they were predictive, and began to be fulfilled in about two years from the time they were received (ch. v.).

But what is said of the He-Goat in ch. viii. goes far beyond Daniel's time, for verses 5-8 refer to Alexander the Great, and to his Generals, who flourished between B.C. 333-63; and while what follows was partly fulfilled in the time of Antiochus Epiphanes some of it still remains to be fulfilled, for the Vision was for 'the time of the end' (17, 19).

THE FALL OF BABYLON

Ch. v. follows chs. vii.-viii. in time, and tells us how the seemingly unconquerable Babylon came crashing down in a single night without a blow being struck. This was in B.C. 538, a date to be remembered (Chart 84).

THE TIME OF DARIUS THE MEDE

So far, the chapters in chronological order have been i.-iv., under Nebuchadnezzar; and vii., viii., v., under Nabonadius and Belshazzar.

The next two are ix. and vi., under Darius the Mede; and the years are B.C. 538, and 537 (Chart 84).

Chapter ix. is of tremendous import, and indicates that Daniel, who had been studying Scriptures at his disposal, was aware that a crisis had been reached in the history of the Jews (2).

In *prayer* he seeks light (1-19), and in *prophecy* Gabriel gives it to him (20-27). The great revelation vouchsafed is in verses 24-27, as follows.

THE SEVENTY SEVENS

24 'Seventy Sevens have been severed off upon thy people, and upon thy Holy City, to shut up the transgression, and to seal up sins, and to cover iniquity, and to bring in everlasting righteousness, and to seal up vision and prophet, and to anoint a Holy of Holies.

25 Know, therefore, and understand; From the going forth of a commandment to restore and to build Jerusalem unto an Anointed One, a Prince, there shall be Seven Sevens, and Sixty and Two Sevens: it shall be built again with street and moated wall, even under pressure of the times.

26 And after the Sixty and Two Sevens an Anointed One shall be cut off, and there shall be nothing for Him.
And the City and the Sanctuary shall the people destroy of a Prince that shall come; and his end shall be in the flood; and, until the end, there shall be war, a decree of desolations.

27 And he shall confirm a covenant with the many for One Seven: and during half of the Seven he shall cause sacrifice and offering to cease, and upon a wing of abominations he shall come desolating, even until the consumption, and that that is determined, which shall be poured upon the desolated' (PEMBER).

A detailed exposition of this astonishing revelation would take us beyond the scope of the present work, but what is clear is that a period of 490 years is predicted, which is so divided as to cover a very long period of time, a period the end of which is not yet.

Undoubtedly the *Sevens* are years, and not weeks; and the divisions are:

Seven Sevens,	i.e.	49 years:
Sixty-Two Sevens,	i.e.	434 years:
One Seven,	i.e.	7 years: Total 490 years.

These Sevens begin 'from the going forth of a commandment to restore and to build Jerusalem' (25), and this command was given by Artaxerxes in B.C. 445 (Neh. ii.). If from this date we reckon 483 prophetic years of 360 days a year—the first two periods of the Seventy Sevens—we are brought to the week in which Jesus was crucified. This is what Gabriel revealed; 'After the Sixty and Two Sevens, an Anointed One shall be cut off, and there shall be nothing for Him' (26).

About this, Pember quite reasonably says: 'Both starting-point and goal are so clearly indicated in Scripture that, as believers, we have no need to trouble ourselves with the uncertainties of human computation, but may at once assume that the Interval was exactly Four Hundred and Eighty-three Years'.

In 1 Cor. x. 32 Paul speaks of 'the Jews, the Gentiles, (and) the Church of God'. The New Testament Church of God does not appear in the Old Testament, but the Jews and Gentiles do. In Daniel ii., vii., viii., the prophecies relate to the Gentiles; but here (ix. 24-27) 'thy people,' and 'thy holy city' relate to the Jews, and the time covered is 490 years. But what is said in verses 26b, 27 has not yet been fulfilled, though more than 2390 years have passed since the prophecy began to be fulfilled (B.C. 445). The explanation is simple when we realize that the prophecy is exclusively Jewish, and that between the Four Hundred and Eighty-Three Sevens, and the Seven Sevens, there is a great gap; nothing less than the whole period of the Christian Dispensation. This interpretation is borne out by other Prophecies, and by the Book of the Revelation; and in the light of it we see in Chart 89 the place of the Seventy Sevens in world-history.

It is only right, however, to say that there are other computations of the Seventy Sevens and of the final events which do not call into question the integrity of this chapter, or of the Book as a whole.

CHART 89

THE SETTING OF THE 'SEVENTY SEVENS' IN THE PLAN OF HISTORY. Daniel ix. 24-27

Its Relation:— 1. To the Jewish State.
2. To the 'Times of the Gentiles.'
3. To the Christian Dispensation.
4. To the Millennial Age.

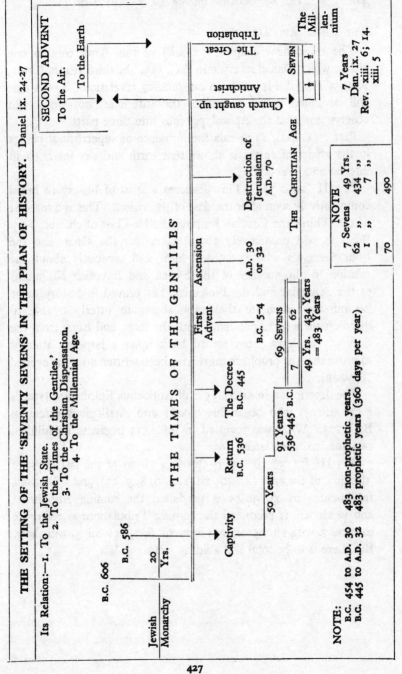

NOTE:
B.C. 454 to A.D. 30 — 483 non-prophetic years.
B.C. 445 to A.D. 32 — 483 prophetic years (360 days per year)

427

THE FINAL APOCALYPSE

The three final chapters (x.-xii.) of this Book contain one vision, which Daniel received in B.C. 533, 'the third year of Cyrus, King of Persia'. It is also an outstanding revelation. The details will be noted in the period of the Interlude; but we should observe now that the Apocalypse falls into three parts.

Part I (x. 4-xi. 1) reveals the influence of supernatural beings in the affairs of earth; it shows that earth and sky interlock in interest and in action.

Part II (xi. 2-35). This discloses a span of history to begin comparatively soon after the date of the vision. This is a forecast of the Third, the Grecian Empire, the He-Goat of ch. viii. 5-25. What is said predictively about Alexander the Great and the Four Generals who succeeded him, and especially about the relation to one another of the Syrian and Egyptian Kingdoms of the Selucidae and the Ptolemies, has proved in history to be 'so minutely accurate that rationalists are utterly unable to discredit their correspondence with the facts, and have, from the days of Porphyry, been forced back upon a hopeless attempt to prove that the prophecy must have been written after the events' (PEMBER).

The description in xi. 21-35 is of Antiochus Epiphanes, Israel's great enemy, who began his bloody and sacrilegious career in B.C. 175. What was revealed in B.C. 533 began to be fulfilled two hundred years later.

Part III (xi. 36-xii. 13) is clearly a vision of the last days, of 'the time of the end' (xi. 40; xii. 1, 4, 6, 8, 9, 13), and still awaits fulfilment. In xi. 36-45 is predicted the coming Antichrist; and in ch. xii. is predicted the coming Tribulation, as reference to verse 7, with vii. 25; ix. 27; Rev. xii. 6, 7, 14; xiii. 5, will show. But there is to be total and abiding victory at last.

EZEKIEL (B.C. 592-572)

Ezekiel was the last of the Major Prophets, and was contemporary in part with Jeremiah and Daniel. Because of his importance in prophecy let us consider his person, mission, message, method, and book.

CHART 90

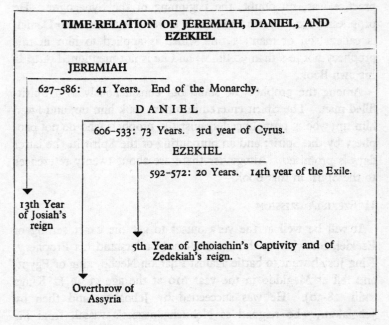

TIME-RELATION OF JEREMIAH, DANIEL, AND
EZEKIEL

JEREMIAH

627-586: 41 Years. End of the Monarchy.

D A N I E L

606-533: 73 Years. 3rd year of Cyrus.

EZEKIEL

592-572: 20 Years. 14th year of the Exile.

13th Year
of Josiah's
reign

5th Year of Jehoiachin's Captivity and of
Zedekiah's reign.

Overthrow of
Assyria

I Ezekiel himself

Jeremiah's Prophecy is conspicuous for the many personal details that enter into it, but Ezekiel's, for the omission of such; what we know of the man himself can be put into brief compass. His name, which means *God is strong*, is fully indicative of his mission, and also, to a large extent, of his character as a prophet, stern and strong, although he was not lacking in tenderness. He was the son of Buzi, and was of priestly descent. If the 'thirtieth year' of ch. i. 1 refers to his age, he was born at about the time the Book of the Law was found in the temple by Hilkiah, 622 B.C. The influence upon Ezekiel of such a setting in the history of his nation cannot be over estimated; his childhood was spent in days of revival, and his training was in accord with them.

He is introduced to us in exile; unlike Jeremiah (xvi. 2) he had a wife, who died in the ninth year of his exile (xxiv.), and he lived in a house of his own, to which the captives came from time to time to seek counsel from him (viii. 1; xiv. 1; xx. 1). This practice was, no doubt, the beginning of the Synagogue. He prophesied for 22 years and died in exile. He alone, with Daniel, is called 'son of man', a title which is applied to him in this prophecy not less than 90 times; and he is not mentioned outside his own Book.

Among the prophets he stand out conspicuously as a Spirit-filled man. The Spirit entered into him, took him up, and lifted him up; woe is pronounced against the prophets who do not prophesy by the Spirit; and an outpouring of the Spirit in the latter days is promised. Altogether there are about twenty references to the Spirit in this Book.

II EZEKIEL'S MISSION

It will be well at the very outset to get the exact setting of Ezekiel, for without this we shall not understand his Prophecy. King Josiah went to battle against Pharaoh Necho, king of Egypt, and fell at Megiddo in the year 610 at the age of 39 (2 Kings xxiii. 28-30). He was succeeded by Jehoahaz, and then by Jehoiakim, who reigned as Nebuchadnezzar's vassal, from his 4th year (B.C. 605) but rebelled against him in B.C. 602. After the battle of Carchemish in 606-5, Daniel, the three Hebrews, and other Jews were deported to Babylon (2 Kings xxiv. 1; Dan. i. 1). This was the first of three stages of the captivity of Judah (Chart 72).

Jehoiachin succeeded Jehoiakim, but after reigning for three months he was, with 10,000 captives, taken by Nebuchadnezzar to Babylon in the year 598 B.C. With this contingent of captives was Ezekiel, a youth 25 years of age (2 Kings xxiv. 8-16; Ezek. i. 1, 2). He was silent in exile for five years, and then his ministry began, and lasted, as we have said, for over twenty years (i. 1, 2; xxix. 17). He was stationed at Tel-Abib, by the banks of the

Chebar (iii. 15), a place it is supposed, about 200 miles north
of Babylon; and while he was prophesying there, Jeremiah was
prophesying at Jerusalem, and Daniel at Babylon. More than a
century before, Isaiah had blown the silver trumpet of evangelism;
Jeremiah was now playing the mournful flute over Judah's sin;
and Ezekiel was to strike the iron harp of Divine justice consequent upon that sin.

The contrast is greater than the comparison between Jeremiah
and Ezekiel, the one being distinguished for his tearful sympathy
with the people, and the other, more for his zeal for God; the
one being characterized by feeling and action, and the other,
more by reason and reflection, although of course these characteristics were not mutually exclusive. "Each of the two prophets,
without communicating with the other, is the echo of the other's
sorrow. Deep answers to deep across the Assyrian desert;
the depth of woe in him who, from the walls of Zion, saw the
storm approaching, is equalled, if not surpassed, by the depth
of woe in him who lived, as it were, in the skirts of the storm
itself, 'the whirlwind, the great cloud, the fire unfolding itself
from the North', gathering round the whole horizon before it
reached the frontiers of Palestine" (Stanley). Such then was
Ezekiel's setting in the history.

III EZEKIEL'S MESSAGE

We do not find in this Prophecy the sustained flight of Isaiah,
or the mother-tenderness of Jeremiah, both flight and tenderness
being subject to directness and definiteness of address such as
are common only to stern, strong natures.

The framework of Isaiah, Jeremiah, and Ezekiel is substantially
the same, namely, (1) Denunciation of Israel's sin; (2) Declaration
of impending doom; (3) Indictments and Judgments against
Foreign Nations; and (4) Promises of Restoration for Israel.
But the manner in which the prophets handle these subjects
widely differs.

Ezekiel, like our Lord, began his ministry by a river, when he
was thirty years of age, and there he saw a complex and mysterious
vision symbolizing the Divine omnipotence, omniscience, and
omnipresence. There were four living creatures, and each had

four faces, a lion's, king of beasts; an ox's, king of cattle; an eagle's, king of birds; and a man's, crown of all creation. This is a revelation of God's *omnipotence*, and though here, no doubt, the vision has reference to the attributes of God, yet these attributes are centred and summed up in the Person of Christ, who is presented to us in Matthew as the Lion of the Tribe of Judah; in Mark as the obedient Servant, Ox-like; in Luke as the true Man; and in John as the Divine Son, the soaring Eagle.

Then Ezekiel saw with these living creatures wheels full of eyes round about them, which is a revelation of God's *omniscience*, Who sees the end from the beginning; and these wheels, with the living creatures, moved rapidly between earth and heaven, which is a revelation of God's *omnipresence*. Strength, Intelligence, and Activity are revealed in the Cherubim (cf. ch. x.), who act on behalf of the Son of God who sits on His Throne above the firmament.

Before this sight Ezekiel fell on his face, and after the vision, came the Voice bidding him stand upon his feet, and receive his commission. His message may be summed up as 'through repentance to salvation', and its constituent parts are (*a*) SIN. Judah had been led and cared for by God, but had fallen into the basest idolatry, and seemed happy and comfortable in it; they had sadly and for long backslidden from Him in Whom was their only hope, and consequently there was nothing for it but (*b*) PUNISHMENT. God could not be Love, if He were not also just, and so His sinful people must suffer in consequence of their apostasy in Babylonian captivity. But the prophet had a message also of (*c*) REPENTANCE for them. 'The wicked shall not fall in the day that he turneth from his wickedness', 'As I live, saith the Lord God, I have no pleasure in the death of the wicked; but that the wicked turn from his way and live; turn ye, turn ye, from your evil ways; for why will ye die, O house of Israel?' (xxxiii. 11, 12). All the prophets had called the people to repentance, but they seemed only to harden in their sins, and yet if only they would turn, what prospects of (*d*) BLESSING were held out to them. The Land of Canaan lay before those wanderers in the wilderness, and they were bidden enter in, but most of them died in the desert. It is possible to be on the very margin of full blessing and yet never to step over into it. God would and will bless existing Israel, but the Israel of that day missed it. Sin, Punishment, Repentance, and Blessing, were the notes of this strong man's ministry, and on what ears they fell a reading of the Book fully discloses. To destroy false hopes and to awaken true ones was the burden of his soul, and he discharged his ministry most faithfully.

IV EZEKIEL'S METHOD

This was very varied, and includes 1. *Visions*, such as his journey through the chambers of imagery in the temple at Jerusalem (viii.); the journey through the streets of Jerusalem of the scribe with the inkhorn, marking the foreheads of the faithful (ix.); and the vision of the caldron and the flesh (xi.). 2. *Symbolic Action*. Taking a tile, he draws a picture of Jerusalem upon it; he then surrounds the tile with mounds, and thus mimics before the people the siege of the city by Nebuchadnezzar (iv. 1-3); also, he eats filthy food to indicate to what straits the inhabitants would be reduced during the siege (iv. 14-17); and he cuts off the locks of his hair, weighs and divides them; a third part he burns, to indicate the destruction of the city; another third part he smites about with a knife, to indicate how large numbers of the people would be slain with the sword; and the other third part he throws to the wind, to indicate how many would be scattered before the enemy (v. 1-4). Also he speaks by 3. *Similitudes*, such as the Vine, which is Judah, about to be burned; and the Adulteress in ch. xvi. The prophet also speaks by 4. *Parables*, as in ch. xvii, where an eagle (Babylon) is represented as perching on the topmost branch of a cedar (the Royal House of Judah), and breaking off one of the topmost young twigs carries it (Jehoiachin) to Babylon. The eagle also planted a vine-seed in the Land (Nebuchadnezzar putting Zedekiah on the throne), but another eagle came (Egypt), and the roots of the vine turned to it (Zedekiah turning to Egypt for help). 5. *Poems* (xix), 6. *Proverbs* (xii. 22, 23; xviii. 2), 7. *Allegories* (xvi., xxiii.), and 8. *Prophecies* (vi., xx., xl.-xlviii.) are also among the methods which this great man used to bring home to the people a sense of their sin, and of the Divine righteousness and grace.

28

No artist has given us pictures so inspiring, so mysterious, so charming, and so terrifying as these. Some are given in a stroke or two, but others are given in minutest detail, and stand forth from the canvas of history with convincing reality. 'Through the piercing eyes of Ezekiel, we see the Queen of ancient commerce in all her glory, under the figure of one of her own stately vessels, sailing proudly over her subject seas, with the fine linen of Egypt for her white sails, with the purple from the isles of Greece for the drapery of her seats, with merchant princes for her pilots and mariners. We see her suddenly overtaken by the storm from the East, and foundering in her final shipwreck, amidst a wail of despair and anguish from all the coasts of the Mediterranean (xxvii.).

Or take again, the Vision of Dry Bones. It is the graveyard of the Jewish nation that the Prophet sees, the helpless, dismembered, denationalized people, whose return and restoration to the favour of God and to national unity are as resurrection from the dead (xxxvii.)'.

Throughout his prophecies Ezekiel lays emphasis on the greatness, goodness, and glory of God, and on the importance of his own message as from God. 'Thus saith the LORD' occurs about 120 times; the title 'LORD God' about 200 times; and 'They shall know that I am the LORD', also many times. Then the arraignment of the nations reveals God to be the God of history, as we have seen Him to be in Isaiah and Jeremiah, and elsewhere. His whole message is full of majesty. The terrible character of sin, and its inevitable consequences are set forth, and the responsibility of the individual is emphasised more fully here than anywhere else (xviii., xxxiii.). Ezekiel should be regarded strictly as the Seer; his ministry began beneath the opened heavens by a river (i. 1), and ended beneath the opened heavens upon a high mountain (xl. 2).

It was because of such visions that he was possessed of such passions, and engaged in such missions. His vision was of great range. No doubt in part it was fulfilled when the Jews returned from Babylon in the reign of Cyrus, but it stretched far beyond that, to the time yet future, when the scattered flock shall be gathered again, and the Shepherd-King shall lead them (xxxiv.); when there will be on the part of the chosen people repossession of the inheritance, redistribution of the land, rehabitation of the City of Zion, and reconsecration of themselves to their God. The Seer of Patmos and the Prophet by the Chebar both worked towards the same centre, for in the Revelation, as here, we see the City, the Temple, The Throne, and the glorified Man upon it, and the Rainbow round about it; Gog and Magog are overthrown, and the glory of God enfolds all things. Surely it is witness sufficient to the inspired character and divine authority of the Scriptures, that men separated by over 660 years should see visions so closely corresponding.

V Ezekiel's prophecies

The prophecies of Ezekiel are in three distinct groups, corresponding to the three periods of his ministry. No doubt they were first of all spoken to the elders of the nation (viii. 1; xiv. 1; xx. 1; xxxiii. 30); but it is clear that they were carefully prepared for publication, in marked contrast to the prophecies of Jeremiah.

It should be observed that so long as Jerusalem was standing, and the Monarchy was in existence, Ezekiel's messages were a Denunciation of Judah (i.-xxiv.); but when once he heard that the end had come, he turned, first to pronounce Judgment on Foreign Nations (xxv.-xxxii.), and then, to predict the Restoration of Israel (xxxiii.-xlviii.). As his prophecies are carefully dated we are able to follow the trend of his thought throughout the twenty years of his ministry.

CHART 91

THE PROPHECIES OF EZEKIEL: B.C. 592-572=20 Years

BEFORE THE SIEGE OF JERUSALEM	DURING THE SIEGE OF JERUSALEM	AFTER THE SIEGE OF JERUSALEM
B.C. 592-588=4 Years	B.C. 588-586=2 Years	B.C. 586-572=14 Years
Denunciation of Judah Chs. i-xxiv	**Visitation of Nations** Chs. xxv-xxxii	**Restoration of Israel** Chs. xxxiii-xlviii
The Prophet's Call and Commission (i-iii) FIFTH YEAR	Ammon. xxv. 1-7 NINTH YEAR	Predictions of New Life to be Bestowed. xxxiii-xxxix TWELFTH YEAR
Prophecies of Approaching Judgment (iv-vii) FIFTH YEAR	Moab. xxv. 8-11 NINTH YEAR	
The Moral Necessity for Judgment (viii-xi) SIXTH YEAR	Edom. xxv. 12-14 NINTH YEAR	
The Absolute Certainty of Judgment (xii-xix) SIXTH YEAR	Philistia. xxv. 15-17 NINTH YEAR	Descriptions of the New Order to be Established. xl-xlviii TWENTY-FIFTH YEAR.
The Character of Judah the Cause of Judgment (xx-xxiv)	Tyre. xxvi-xxviii. 19 ELEVENTH YEAR	
SEVENTH YEAR. xx-xxiii	Sidon. xxviii. 20-26 ELEVENTH YEAR	
NINTH YEAR. xxiv	Egypt. xxix-xxxii	
	(1) xxix. 1-16 TENTH YEAR	
	(2) xxix. 17-21 TWENTY-SEVENTH YEAR	
	(3) xxx. 1-19 TWENTY-SEVENTH YEAR	
	(4) xxx. 20-26. ELEVENTH YEAR	
	(5) xxxi. 1-18. ELEVENTH YEAR	
	(6) xxxii. 1-16. TWELFTH YEAR	
	(7) xxxii. 17-32. TWELFTH YEAR	

The Chronological references are from the year of Jehoiachin's captivity in B.C. 598

ISAIAH xl.-lxvi.

The consideration of Isaiah xl.-lxvi. at this point does not imply that these chapters were written on the eve of the Jews' deliverance from Babylonian captivity, nor that the author of them was not Isaiah. If it is granted that they are predictive, it is as easy to believe that the predictions were a century and a half before the fulfilment, as that they were one year before. The critical questions which arise are outside the scope of this work; but placing these chapters here simply means that the subject of them, whenever written, is the coming deliverance of the people of God in B.C. 536, and far beyond that date. The value of this magnificent Book of Consolation is not determined by the time it was written, nor by who wrote it, but by its contents, forecasting the second great Exodus of the captive people of God.

There is no reason why the divisions which this Book provides should not be accepted. At the end of ch. xlviii. it is said: 'There is no peace, saith the LORD, unto the wicked'. This is repeated at the end of ch. lvii.: 'There is no peace, saith my God, to the wicked'; and this is reiterated in substance, though not in words, at the end of the Book (lxvi. 24), where the doom of the rebels against the LORD is described.

The divisions we may regard therefore as follows:

I THE DELIVERANCE (xl.-xlviii.)
   GOD and the gods: Israel and the heathen compared.

II THE DELIVERER (xlix.-lvii.)
    The Sufferings and the Glory of Jehovah's Servant compared.

III THE DELIVERED (lviii.-lxvi.)
     The faithful and the unfaithful compared, and their respective ends.

That this great Prophecy was written in the light of the Babylonian captivity is everywhere evident. References to the sad condition of the exiles is found in xlii. 22-25; xlviii. 10; xlix. 21; l. 1; lxiv. 10, 11; to the ruined state of Jerusalem, in lxiv. 10, 11; to the place of captivity, in xliii. 14; xlviii. 14. 20; and ch. xlvii.; to the weariness of the exiles, in xl. 27; xlix. 14; to the coming redemption, in xl.; xli. 27; xliii. 1; xliv. 21-28; xlix. 16 ff; lii. 7-12; lvii. 18; lxv.; to the doom of Babylon and

of the oppressing Chaldeans, in xliii. 14; xlviii. 14; xliii. 14-21;
lx. 14; and it is predicted that Cyrus will be the instrumental
deliverer, xliv. 28; xlv. 1, 13.

This Prophecy of Redemption was fulfilled, so far as Israel
was concerned, in B.C. 536, and the following history.

Perhaps, without exaggeration, it may be said that this *Rhapsody
of Zion Redeemed* is the most eloquent portion of Holy Scripture,
and contains more memorable sayings than any other Book.

PSALMS

Certain Psalms, which in all probability were written during
the Exile, must be regarded as part of the literature of the period;
and certain others which reflect the experiences of the Exile,
even though they may not have been written in that period,
may well be read in this connection. These Psalms are characterized by experience of suffering, the fear that God has forgotten
the sufferers, longing for home, and hope of deliverance.

Psalms xlii.-xliv. contain sentiments which answer to the
Babylonian Exile as well as to any other similar situation.

> 'Thou hast given us like sheep appointed for meat;
> And hast scattered us among the heathen.
> Thou makest us a reproach to our neighbours,
> A scorn and a derision to them that are round about us.
> Thou makest us a byword among the heathen.
> Arise, cast us not off for ever.
> Wherefore hidest Thou Thy face,
> And forgettest our affliction?
> Arise for our help,
> And redeem us for Thy mercys' sake'.

In Psalms lxxiv. and lxxix. there appear to be references to
the destruction of Jerusalem in B.C. 586; to the continued
desolation of the city, and the humiliation of Israel; and also
to the mockery of the neighbouring peoples. The Psalm has
parallels with Jeremiah, Lamentations, and Ezekiel.

In Psalm lxxvii. Israel is in exile, and is greatly distressed,
but from the past she derives hope for the future. He who delivered from Egypt, can deliver from Babylon.

'Will the Lord cast off for ever?
And will He be favourable no more?
Is His mercy clean gone for ever?
Doth His promise fail for evermore?
Hath God forgotten to be gracious?
Hath He in anger shut up His tender mercies?

I will remember the years of the right hand
    of the Most High.
I will remember the works of the LORD:
Surely I will remember Thy wonders of old'.

In Psalm lxxx. the homeland is overrun by enemies, and
the national existence seems to be at an end (12-16), yet the
exiles pray for deliverance (3, 7, 19).

'Turn us again, O God,
And cause Thy face to shine,
And we shall be saved'.

Two emotions meet in Psalm lxxxix. 'On the one hand,
the assured lovingkindness and faithfulness of God, and His
explicit promise of an eternal dominion to the house of David
(1-18); and on the other hand (19-51), the sight of the representative of that house a discrowned exile (Jehoiachin), and his
kingdom plundered and desolate. How could the contradiction
be reconciled?' (Kirkpatrick).

Almost certainly Psalm cii. belongs to the closing years of
the Babylonian Exile. Zion is in ruins, but the Psalmist looks
for the fulfilment of the prophecies of Jeremiah and of Isaiah
xl.-lxvi.

About Psalm cxxxvii. there can be no doubt whether it was
written during or after the Exile.

'By the rivers of Babylon, there we sat down,
Yea, we wept, when we remembered Zion.
We hanged our harps upon the willows in the midst thereof.
For there they that carried us away captive
Required of us a song; and they that wasted us
Required of us mirth, saying:

    "Sing us one of the songs of Zion".

How shall we sing the Lord's song
In a strange land?
If I forget Thee, O Jerusalem,
Let my right hand forget her cunning.
If I do not remember thee,
Let my tongue cleave to the roof of my mouth;
If I prefer not Jerusalem above my chief joy'.

It would have been strange indeed if the experiences of the exile had not drawn from the captives the songs that 'tell of saddest thought'.

In Act I of the UNFOLDING DRAMA OF REDEMPTION we have already considered two of the three Scenes which constitute it: *The Hebrew Family*, and *The Israelitish Nation*; and we are now to consider *The Jewish Church*; but it will be well here to get a conspectus of the various relations of the Prophets—to One Another, to the Surrounding Empires, and to the Babylonian Captivity; and this will introduce the three Prophecies which belong to *The Jewish Church* period—Haggai, Zechariah, and Malachi.

CHART 92

THE RELATIONS OF THE PROPHETS	
1. TO ONE ANOTHER	
NORTH	Jonah. Amos. Hosea. Micah.
SOUTH	Joel. ISAIAH. Micah. Nahum. Zephaniah. JEREMIAH. Habakkuk. Daniel. Obadiah. EZEKIEL. Haggai. Zechariah. Malachi.
2. TO THE EMPIRES	
PRE-ASSYRIAN	Joel.
ASSYRIAN	Jonah. Amos. Hosea. ISAIAH. Micah. Nahum. Zephaniah.
ASSYRIAN and BABYLONIAN	JEREMIAH.
BABYLONIAN	Habakkuk. Obadiah. EZEKIEL.
BABYLONIAN and MEDO-PERSIAN	Daniel.
MEDO-PERSIAN	Haggai. Zechariah. Malachi.
3. TO THE CAPTIVITY	
BEFORE B.C. 850–606	NORTH. Jonah. Amos. Hosea. Micah. SOUTH. Joel. ISAIAH. Micah. Nahum. Zephaniah. JEREMIAH. Habakkuk.
DURING B.C. 606–536	Daniel. Obadiah. EZEKIEL.
AFTER B.C. 536–425(?)	Haggai. Zechariah. Malachi.

ACT I

SCENE 3

THE JEWISH CHURCH

The First Return

THE MEDO-PERSIAN EMPIRE

CYRUS

ZERUBBABEL AND JOSHUA

HAGGAI.   ZECHARIAH I-VIII

SCENE 3

THE JEWISH CHURCH

The Post-Captivity Period

2 Chron. xxxvi. 22, 23. Ezra i.-iii.: iv.-vi. Haggai. Zechariah. Esther. Ezra vii.-x. Nehemiah. Malachi. Psalms lxxxv., lxxxvii., cv., cvi., cvii., cxv., cxviii., cxxvi. 1 Esdras v..-ix.

IN Act I of the UNFOLDING DRAMA OF REDEMPTION *The Hebrew Family* expanded into *The Israelitish Nation* and then contracted into *The Jewish Church.*

CHART 93

ACT I		
Scene 1	**Scene 2**	**Scene 3**
THE HEBREW FAMILY	THE ISRAELITISH NATION	THE JEWISH CHURCH
Abram to Joseph	Joseph to Zerubbabel	Zerubbabel to Nehemiah
360 Years	1100 Years	110 Years (app.)
Abram Isaac Jacob Joseph	Theocracy Monarchy Dependency	Return Reconstruction Revival Relapse

During the more than 1200 years of the Nation's history—from the descent into Egypt to the time of Nehemiah—there were three captivities which should be viewed in relation to one another as follows:

CHART 94

THE THREE CAPTIVITIES OF THE ISRAELITES		
EGYPTIAN	ASSYRIAN	BABYLONIAN
B.C. 1706-1491	B.C. 722-	B.C. 606-536
215 years		70 years
Deliverer M O S E S		Deliverer C Y R U S
Eight hundred and eighty-five years between the end of the first captivity and the beginning of the last		
THEOCRACY	MONARCHY	DEPENDENCY
Slaves of the Pagan Kingdom of Egypt	Subjects of the Northern Kingdom of Israel	Subjects of the Southern Kingdom of Judah
Total Deliverance	No Deliverance	Partial Deliverance
Preceded by the HEBREW FAMILY		Followed by the JEWISH CHURCH

The period of the Jewish Church lasted from the first return of captives from Babylon under Zerubbabel, to the Jews' rejection of the Messiah in A.D. 30 (or 32), that is, about 560 years, but the major part of this period lies outside the scope of the Bible records, and belongs to what, in our present scheme, we call the *Interlude*, that is, from the time of Nehemiah and Malachi to the Birth of the Messiah, the inter-testament period.

We cannot state with exactness the length of time from the First Return under Zerubbabel to the conclusion of the Old Testament in Nehemiah and Malachi, but we can be sure it was over one hundred years, and it may have been considerably longer.

This new period reverts to the first period in the history of The Israelitish Nation, in that it is again a Theocracy. The Jews have never had a king in the Davidic line since Zedekiah was dethroned in B.C. 586, and the native rulers in the period of the Jewish Church were chiefly not kings, but priests. The sacerdotal tribe of Levi took the place of the royal tribe of Judah.

This fact, which is prominent in the *Interlude*, becomes evident in the persons of Joshua and Ezra, both priests, in this last period of Old Testament history.

The deportation to Babylon had been in three stages (Chart 72), and the return was also in three stages.

CHART 95

THE RETURN FROM BABYLON		
First Stage	*Second Stage*	*Third Stage*
Under ZERUBBABEL	Under EZRA	Under NEHEMIAH
B.C. 536	B.C. 458	B.C. 445

This century and more in the history of the Jews was of great importance for their future, because it meant for them rehabilitation and re-establishment as a people in their own land. This result was effected mainly by three men, Zerubbabel, Ezra, and Nehemiah, together with the support of three prophets, Haggai, Zechariah, and Malachi.

The course of events may be summarized in four words: *Return, Reconstruction, Revival,* and *Relapse*; and the order of events is indicated in Chart 98.

Because of the varied contents of the Book of Ezra, it will be worth-while looking at its main details, to get a conspectus of the whole as in the following Charts.

The Book is in two distinct parts, with a long interval between.

CHART 96

THE BOOK OF EZRA (1)		
PART I		PART II
Chapters i–vi	INTERVAL	Chapters vii–x
B.C. 536–516	B.C. 516–458	B.C. 458–457
Twenty Years	Fifty-Eight Years	One Year
A Compilation	The Story of ESTHER	An Original Work
By Ezra (?)		By Ezra
Written before B.C. 445	B.C. 490 Battle of Marathon	Written before B.C. 445
Rebuilding of the Temple	B.C. 484 Birth of Herodotus	Reformation of the People
The Material Church	B.C. 480 Battles of Salamis and Thermopylae	The Spiritual Church
First Return under Zerubbabel and Joshua		Second Return under Ezra
Written in Aramaic iv. 8-vi. 18	B.C. 479 Return of Xerxes from Greece after his disasters	Written in Aramaic vii. 12-26
	B.C. 478 Confucius died	First Person Section vii. 27-ix. 15 Third Person Section vii. 1-26; x
	B.C. 477 Buddha died	

CHART 97

THE BOOK OF EZRA (2)

Chs. i-vi. B.C. 536-516. 20 Years	Chs. vii-x. B.C. 458. 1 Year
THE RETURN FROM CAPTIVITY UNDER ZERUBBABEL	**THE RETURN FROM CAPTIVITY UNDER EZRA**
EMANCIPATION OF THE JEWS. (i-ii) Restoration. (i) Registration. (ii)	PROCLAMATION OF ARTAXERXES. (vii)
INCEPTION OF THE WORK. (iii-iv) Reconstruction. (iii) Opposition. (iv)	LIBERATION OF THE JEWS. (viii)
DEDICATION OF THE TEMPLE. (v-vi) Investigation. (v) HAGGAI ZECHARIAH Consummation. (vi)	INTERCESSION OF THE PRIEST-SCRIBE. (ix)
	REFORMATION OF THE PEOPLE (x)

CHART 98

A CENTURY OF JEWISH HISTORY

ORDER OF READING

Ezra i-iv	Ezra v, vi	Esther	Ezra vii-x	Interval	Nehemiah
Daniel x-xii	Haggai Zechariah	(Interval of 58 Years)			Malachi
536–520	520–516	483–465	458–7	457–445	445–433
16 Years	4 Years	18 Years	1 Year	12 Years	12 Years
Cyrus Ahasuerus Artaxerxes Darius	Darius	Xerxes	Artaxerxes Longimanus		

CHART 99

EZRA: A COMPILATION (1)

1. Narrative (109)*	i. 1		i. 5-11		i. 1 -iv. 10	iv 17			iv. 23 -v. 6		vi. 1, 2			vi. 13-22	vii. 1-11		vii. 27, 28		viii. 15-ix. 5		x. 1-17	
2. Registers (111)*				ii. 1-70			iv. 1-16											viii. 1-14				x. 18-44
3. Letters (44)*								iv. 17-22		v. 7-17		vi. 2-12				vii. 12-26						
4. Proclamation (3)*		i. 2-4																				
5. Excerpt (3)*													vi. 3-5									
6. Prayer (10)*																				ix. 6-15		

* The figures are the number of verses.

CHART 100

EZRA: A COMPILATION (2)

Narrative: 109 verses

Registers: 111 verses

Letters: 44 verses

A Proclamation: 3 verses

An Excerpt: 3 verses

A Prayer: 10 verses

Total: 280 verses

2 *Registers*: Three

A. Of the Exiles returning with Zerubbabel (ch. ii.).

B. Of the Exiles returning with Ezra (ch. viii. 1-14).

C. Of offenders in the matter of foreign marriages (ch. x. 18-44).

3 *Letters*: Five

A. Of Rehum to Artaxerxes charging the Jews with rebuilding the *walls* of Jerusalem (iv. 11b-16).

B. Of Artaxerxes in reply, authorizing that the work of rebuilding be stopped (iv. 17b-22).

C. Of Tatnai to Darius, telling him that the *Temple* in Jerusalem was being rebuilt; and asking what the king's pleasure was in the matter (v. 7-17).

D. Of Darius in reply, commanding that the work should proceed, and that the Jews be given every help (vi. 2-12).

E. Of Artaxerxes (Longimanus) to Ezra, giving permission to the Jews still in captivity to return to Jerusalem; and specially commissioning Ezra (vii. 12-26).

CHART 101

THE FOUR DECREES				
DE-CREE	KING	DATE	OBJECT	REFERENCE
1	CYRUS	536	Rebuilding of the Temple	Ezra i.
2	DARIUS I (Hystaspes)	520	Completion of the Temple	Ezra iv. 24; vi. 1-15.
3	ARTAXERXES (Longimanus)	458	Beautifying of the Temple, and Restoration of Worship	Ezra vii. 27
4	ARTAXERXES (Longimanus)	445	Rebuilding of the City	Dan. ix. 25 Neh. ii. 5

THE FIRST RETURN FROM BABYLON

(Ezra i.-ii.; Neh. vii.)   B.C. 536

In the history of Israel there were two *Exodus* movements: one from Egypt, in the South West, to Canaan; and the other from Babylon, in the far East, to Canaan; and the one was separated from the other by more than 950 years; both taking place in the same month. The first Exodus marked the beginning of the first Theocracy, and the other marked the beginning of the second Theocracy. Had there been no return from Babylon Judah would have shared the fate of Israel, and have blended with the East; the Hebrew Scriptures would have been lost; many of them now possessed would never have been written; and it is difficult to see how Christianity could ever have been.

But this return had been predicted, and the Exile had prepared a remnant to hazard a long and dangerous journey to fulfil the divine design to keep the nation alive for the coming of the Messiah. Minute details are given of the company that set out on this four months' migration across the pitiless desert. Of the entire host of Jewish captives only 42,360 returned, besides 7,337 slaves, 200 of them being trained singers; 4,000 priests, representing only four of the twenty-four priestly 'courses'; and, strange to say, only 74 Levites; and these were accompanied by an escort of 1,000 cavalry. That there should have been only 8,136 beasts of carriage for 50,000 people shows that all but a few marched on foot.

Of treasure carried by these Pilgrim Fathers, and that by the order of Cyrus, were the sacred vessels of silver and gold which had been carried off by Nebuchadnezzar at the destruction of Jerusalem: 5,400 salvers, cups, tankards, spoons, and basins (Ezra i. 7; 2 Chron. xxxvi. 10-13; Jer. xxvii. 16-22; xxviii. 2, 3; Dan. v. 3, 4).

Well may these returning pilgrims have sung:

> 'When the LORD turned again the captivity of Zion,
> We were like them that dream.
> Then was our mouth filled with laughter,
> And our tongue with singing.
> Then said they among the heathen,
> "The LORD hath done great things for them".
> The LORD hath done great things for us,
> Whereof we are glad'   (Ps. cxxvi. 1-3)

The richer Jews and many who had been born in captivity were quite content with their lot, and remained where they were, eventually becoming absorbed in the East, as were the Lost Tribes so-called. The Book of Esther is evidence of this.

The leaders of this new beginning were *Zerubbabel*, the civil head, and *Joshua*, the priestly head, assisted by ten others (Neh. vii. 7), perhaps in touching allusion to the original number of the Tribes.

Zerubbabel was the only person of royal blood who returned at this time. He was a grandson of Jehoiachin, and his name seems to indicate that he was born in Babylonia—*Zerua Babel, begotten in Babylon*; or *Ziri-Babil, seed of Babel*.

He, as civil head, and those associated with him, had to face the difficulties, disappointments, and dangers of the return to the land, troubles which were considerably reduced by the time Ezra returned 78 years later.

There was no Temple; Jerusalem was in ruins; the Edomites possessed much of the land, and the centre of it was in the hands of the descendants of the mixed races which were placed there after the destruction of Samaria, races with whom Israelites had intermarried, and who together are known as the Samaritans. The situation was depressing and discouraging, like that which confronted the Pilgrim Fathers in 1620. But these pilgrims returned, not to re-establish the kingdom, but to inaugurate a Church.

THE SECOND TEMPLE (Ezra iii-vi.)

The Return was not a political but a religious movement. The pilgrims, profoundly penitent for past backslidings, and forever cured of idolatry, were now set on restoring the ancient faith, and so they gave their attention first of all, not to the setting up of the walls of Jerusalem, but to the rebuilding of the Temple, which again was to be the centre and symbol of their faith; and for this, gifts poured in (Ezra ii. 68, 69; iii. 7).

Provision was made, first of all, for all that was most essential in the ritual of religion. The people did not begin by building the Temple, but by erecting the Altar, offering the Sacrifices, and observing the Feast of Tabernacles (iii. 1-7). They began at the centre, and not at the circumference. The essential thing in true religion is not its accompaniments, but the Cross, without which all else would be in vain. If we would worship God aright we must begin at Calvary.

Then, 'in the second year', in B.C. 535, the foundation of the Temple was laid amid the restored musical services of David, and shouts of joy mingled with the wailing of the older Jews (iii. 8-13).

Perhaps it was on this occasion that Psalm cxv. was sung, with its contempt of idols, and its trust in God.

> 'The LORD hath been mindful of us: He will bless us.
> We will bless the LORD
> From this time forth and for evermore'.

To this time in all likelihood belong Psalms lxxxv., lxxxvii., cv., cvi., cvii., cxviii., cxxvi., and cxxxvi.

PSALMS

Psalms lxxxv. and lxxxvii. appear to refer to the early days of the Return from Babylon, and were written to cheer the drooping spirits of those who were disheartened by the contrast between the weakness and insignificance of their circumstances, and the grandeur and magnificence of the prophetic promises of Zion's future glory and greatness (Isa. xl.-lxvi.).

> "Wilt Thou not revive us again,
> That Thy people may rejoice in Thee?
> Shew us Thy mercy, O LORD,
> And grant us Thy salvation."

> "The LORD loveth the gates of Zion
> More than all the dwellings of Jacob."

Psalm cv. is one of thanksgiving and cvi is one of confession as the returned captives remember God's goodness to them.

> "Talk ye of all His wondrous works;
> Glory ye in His holy name."

> "He remembered for them His covenant,
> He made them also to be pitied
> Of all those that carried them captives."

Psalm cvii. is closely related to the two former Psalms, and is a call to thanksgiving for restoration from exile.

> "O, give thanks unto the LORD, for He is good,
> For His mercy endureth for ever.
> Let the redeemed of the LORD say so,
> Whom He hath redeemed from the hand of the enemy,
> And gathered them out of the lands,
> From the East, and from the West,
> From the North and from the South."

Whenever Psalm cxxvi. was written, and by whomsoever, the first part of it (1-4) perfectly reflects the jubilation which restoration from captivity produced.

> "When the LORD turned again the captivity of Zion,
> We were like them that dream.
> Then was our mouth filled with laughter,
> And our tongue with singing."

It may be that Psalm cxxxvi. reflects the occasion when the foundation stone of the Second Temple was laid, because in

Ezra iii. 11 it is said: "They sang together by course in praising and giving thanks unto the LORD, because He is good, for His mercy endureth for ever toward Israel. And all the people shouted with a great shout when they praised the LORD, because the foundation of the house of the LORD was laid."

OPPOSITION AND DELAY

But no good work is allowed to proceed unchallenged; and such challenge may come in one or other of two ways, by *opposition* or by *patronage*. In the present instance it came by patronage. The Samaritans, a race of mingled Jews and heathen (2 Kings xvii. 24; Ezra iv. 9, 10) offered to help the Jews rebuild the Temple, and their offer was absolutely declined (Ezra iv. 1-3), for a very good reason. To have accepted would have been to identify themselves with heathen customs, and also with idolatry, and this would have been fatal to the entire purpose for which the pilgrims had returned home.

Not infrequently, for the Church and for the individual occasions arise for the making of definite choices and decisions, and at such times compromise is nothing less than treason.

The refusal of Zerubbabel and Joshua to accept help was bitterly resented, and immediately wily patronage turned to open opposition, with the result that for fifteen years the rebuilding of the Temple was stopped (Ezra iv. 4, 5, 34; v. 1, 2); B.C. 535-520. In these long and weary years the moral tone and spiritual zeal of the Jewish colony must have suffered much.

HAGGAI AND ZECHARIAH

But God does not allow the consciences of His people to disintegrate. When we are in danger of fatal coma He rouses us by some challenging voice, and starts us once more in the path of duty.

After fifteen years of enervating delay in rebuilding the Temple, two prophets arose to stir the Jews once more to action. One was an old man, and the other was young (Hag. ii. 3; Zech. ii. 4); and they so spake that work was vigorously recommenced, and ceased not until it was completed (Hag. i. 14, 15).

The Temple was the outward symbol of the dwelling of God in the midst of Israel, and not to have rebuilt it would have meant the extinction of the national religion, and would have been a practical denial of the truth which alone gave meaning to the return from exile; and as the Jews were rapidly reconciling themselves to an existence without a Temple, the ministries of Haggai and Zechariah were of the utmost importance for the future of the nation and the Messianic hope.

The important dates for the twenty years from the Return are as follows:

CHART 102

THE RETURN AND THE TEMPLE: B.C. 536–516				
536	535	535–520	520–518	516
Return from Captivity.	Altar erected Foundation of Temple laid.	No work on the Rebuilding of the Temple.	Ministries of HAGGAI and ZECHARIAH	The Temple finished, twenty years after the Return.

The relation in time to one another of the ministries of Haggai and Zechariah is as follows:

CHART 103

THE MINISTRIES OF HAGGAI AND ZECHARIAH						
B.C. 520–518						
B.C. 520					B.C. 519	B.C. 518
MONTHS					Silence	MONTH
6th	7th	8th	9th	11th		9th
			I 2			
Haggai	Haggai	Zechariah	Haggai	Zechariah		Zechariah
i. 2–11	ii. 1–9	i. 1–6	ii. 10–19 ii. 20–23	i 7– vi. 15		vii–viii

HAGGAI (B.C. 520)

Haggai, who is five times called 'the prophet', and once 'the LORD's messenger', and who is otherwise unknown, prophesied in the year 520 B.C. No doubt He was born in captivity, and returned with Zerubbabel. The foundation of the Temple was laid, but the work had been at a standstill for some time, because of opposition. The people were getting accustomed to being without a Temple, and had this disposition prevailed, as the Chosen People they must have ceased to be. But for such a crisis as this, Haggai was raised up. His ministry lasted for about four months, during which time he delivered four messages.

1 HIS FIRST MESSAGE. Sixth month. First day. i. 2-11

A Word of Reproof

Therein he remonstrates with the people for their negligence in not building the Temple. No doubt it satisfied them to say, 'the time is not come that the LORD's House should be built' (2), but that was a vain excuse, for their own houses were built, and they were comfortably settled in them (4). The Prophet calls upon them to 'consider their ways', a call that is repeated five times in this Book; and he further points out, that the troubles that have befallen them, drought and poverty, are the fruit of their sinful indifference to the claims of God (9). This pointed message had its desired effect, for the work of rebuilding was commenced twenty-four days later (12-15).

2 HIS SECOND MESSAGE. Seventh month. Twenty-first day. ii. 1-9

A Word of Support

It was not long before the first enthusiasm passed away, and depression began to settle down upon the people. Haggai meets this with a word of encouragement which gathers up the whole history of the Temple under the term 'this House' (9). He speaks of the magnificence of Solomon's Temple (3a), of the necessity for Zerubbabel's Temple (3b-5), and of the excelling glory of Messiah's Millennial Temple (6-9); and thus he encourages the people and their leaders to 'Be strong . . . and work' for the LORD is with them.

**3 HIS THIRD MESSAGE.   Ninth month.   Twenty-fourth day.
ii. 10-19**
A Word of Blessing

By two questions addressed to the priests, and two answers obtained from them, he shows that sin, not holiness, is diffusive and contagious (11-13), and applies this truth to the people, pointing out that as long as the LORD's House remains incomplete and their worship and service is half-hearted, everything is tainted and unclean (14-17). He follows this up by a gracious promise of blessing to date from that day (17-19).

**4 HIS FOURTH MESSAGE.   Ninth month.   Twenty-fourth day.
ii. 20-23**
A Word of Promise

This is a personal message to Zerubbabel who was the civil head of the restored community and the representative of David's line. The sentence pronounced upon Jehoiachin his grandfather (Jer. xxii. 24), is now revoked, and the word of promise is given that when the thrones of all kingdoms are overthrown, Zerubbabel shall abide in the secret of the LORD. That the son of Shealtiel had some experience of this promise, we cannot doubt, but the terms of it carry us forward to the time when, under the Messiah, all rebellion will be put down, and the Christ will administer the Kingdom of His Father.

The main lesson of this Book for us is, do the duty that lies to your hand with unwavering faith and steady perseverance, in spite of opposition. 'Be strong . . . and work', not regarding opposition as evidence that God's time has not yet come; for indeed, if we wait until the devil is agreeable to spiritual progress, we shall make none at all. Our foundation is laid (1 Cor. iii. 11; Eph. ii. 19-22), but it remains for us to build upon it, being 'steadfast, unmovable, always abounding in the work of the Lord, forasmuch as we know that our labour is not in vain in the Lord' (1 Cor. xv. 58).

ZECHARIAH (B.C. 520-518)
(For Chart outlines of 'Zechariah' see Nos. 105, 106, 107)

Zechariah, which means 'One whom Jehovah remembers', was contemporary with Haggai, and his junior in years (ii. 4).

The same circumstances which called the one into public life, drew forward the other. Some years before this date, under the supervision of Zerubbabel and Joshua, the foundation of the Temple had been laid (Ezra iii.); but the work had been at a standstill, partly on account of the indulgence of the Jews, and partly because of opposition which was offered them by the Samaritans and others (Ezra iv.). 'Then the prophets, Haggai the prophet, and Zechariah the son of Iddo, prophesied unto the Jews that were in Judah and Jerusalem in the name of the God of Israel, even unto them.'

Haggai had prophesied in the sixth, seventh, and ninth months of the second year of Darius; Zechariah began in the eighth month of the same year (i. 1), and continued in the fourth year of Darius (vii. 1).

Zechariah begins by warning the Jews against displeasing God as their fathers had done, assuring them that the Divine word can never pass away, and that punishment must overtake sin. He then tells them of a succession of visions which he had one night, visions designed to reveal God's will and purpose for the Jews, both at that time, and far up the future's broadening way.

1 THE ANGELIC HORSEMEN i. 7-17

These are Jehovah's messengers who walk to and fro through the earth, and see all the nations at rest, while Judah is distressed and Jerusalem is in heaps; but in answer to the Angel's cry 'How long?' Jehovah promises that the Temple will be rebuilt, and that He will return to Judah.

2 THE FOUR HORNS AND THE FOUR SMITHS i. 18-21

These horns are the Empires that have harassed and scattered the Chosen People, but they are to be overthrown by agents, represented as 'smiths', whom the LORD will raise up to bring these enemies to judgment.

3 THE MAN WITH THE MEASURING LINE ii.

In prospect of the City being rebuilt, a man goes forth to lay it out and measure it, but he is instructed that his labour will be in vain, for the New Jerusalem will need no walls, its boundary will be undefined, it will spread abroad, and the LORD Himself will be the protection round about, and the glory in the midst. On the ground of this promise, an appeal is made to the captives still in Babylon to return. The LORD further reveals that 'in that day' many nations shall be joined to the LORD, and shall be His people.

4 JOSHUA THE HIGH PRIEST iii.

In this chapter Joshua is made to represent the Jewish people. He stands before the Angel of the LORD, and Satan is there also, to charge him with uncleanness. But the LORD who had plucked His servant from Babylon, as a brand might be plucked from the burning, was not going to forsake him now, so he is cleansed, clothed, and crowned, and made to stand before the LORD, and a time of felicity is promised to Israel under the dominion of their Messiah the Branch.

5 THE CANDLESTICK AND THE OLIVE TREES iv.

This Candlestick represents restored Israel; and the Olive Trees represent the two great elements in their national life, the Royal and the Priestly, as reflected respectively in Zerubbabel and Joshua; and the Oil symbolizes the Holy Spirit, through Whom alone the task of reconstruction could be accomplished and maintained.

6 THE FLYING ROLL v. 1-4

The design of this is to show that a curse will fall upon the people if they continue in sin, and two representative sins are named: *theft*, or sin against one another; and *swearing*, or sin against the name of God.

7 THE EPHAH AND THE WOMAN v. 5-11

This woman is the personification of Wickedness, which was hidden in the common affairs of the people, as she was hidden in the ephah; but this wickedness was not to remain with them, therefore it is transported to Babylon, the place typical of un-righteousness and unholiness, and probably the source of Israel's corruption, and there it is to remain.

8 THE FOUR CHARIOTS AND HORSES vi. 1-8

These are the powers which the LORD will raise up to deal with the nations, particularly Babylon, which have dealt cruelly with His People; they are the instruments of Divine Judgment.

Here the Visions end, and there follows immediately a symbolic act (vi. 9-15), the crowning of Joshua the Priest—designed to show that the promised Branch will exercise, as did Melchisedec, the double office of Priest-King, when He returns to the earth to set up His Millennial Kingdom.

In the fourth year of the reign of Darius, a deputation was sent to Jerusalem to inquire whether certain Fasts were to be continued, which had been instituted to commemorate the sad overthrow of the Jews, and which they had observed during the seventy years of captivity (Jer. vii. 1-3; xxxix. 2; lii. 6, 7, 12-14; xli. 1-3).

To this inquiry a fourfold answer was given by the Prophet.

(a) They should discover their motive in fasting, and remember the former years. vii. 4-7.

(b) The LORD requires inward righteousness rather than outward forms. vii. 8-14.

(c) The LORD will restore to His people what they had lost. viii. 1-17.

(d) Their Fasts will be turned into Feasts, bringing joy and gladness. viii. 18-23.

Apart from the question as to whether or not chapters ix.-xiv. were written by Zechariah, they are not included at this point of our survey, not being concerned with the rebuilding of the Second Temple.

Stimulated by the warnings and encouragements of Haggai and Zechariah the rebuilding of the Temple was carried to a successful conclusion. 'This House was finished on the third day of the month Adar, which was in the sixth year of the reign of Darius the King'; that is in B.C. 516.

At the dedication of the Building sacrifices were offered 'for all Israel' (Ezra vi. 17; 2 Chron. xi. 16); and thereafter the

Passover and the Feast of Unleavened Bread were observed with much joy (Ezra vi. 19-22).

This joy must have been expressed in song, and there are some Psalms which, in all likelihood, belong to this celebration, such as cv.; xcv.-c.; and cxliv.-cxlviii. The Septuagint title of Psalm xcvi. is 'When the House was built after the Captivity'; and in the titles of Psalms cxlvi.-cxlviii. are the names of Haggai and Zechariah.

CHART 104

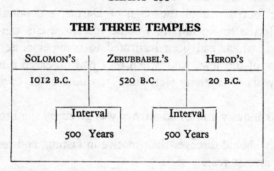

THE THREE TEMPLES		
SOLOMON'S	ZERUBBABEL'S	HEROD'S
1012 B.C.	520 B.C.	20 B.C.
Interval		Interval
500 Years		500 Years

THE FIFTY-EIGHT YEARS, B.C. 516-458

It is very important to recognize that between chs. vi. and vii. of 'Ezra' there is a period of Fifty-Eight Years. Have we any records of these years? Yes; in the Bible certainly one, and possibly two; and outside the Bible, much in pagan history and literature.

Pagan History and Literature

Here is a great illustration of the fact that Biblical history is selective; that its object is not to record world events of importance but to make plain the progress of God's redeeming purpose by means of, or in spite of, men and nations. In pursuance of this object pagan peoples and world events are introduced only as they have a bearing on this Unfolding Drama of Redemption. The Bible does not give us histories of Egypt, Assyria, Babylonia, and Persia, but refers to these, and others, only as they became connected with the people of Israel whom God had chosen to be the medium of His redemptive design.

During this period of Fifty-Eight Years, in China *Confucius* lived and died; in India *Buddha* lived and died; and Greece reached her Golden Age.

Herodotus, the first great literary historian, and *Thucydides*, the first great philosophical historian flourished at this time. *Socrates* and *Anaxagoras* were propounding their philosophies. *Aeschylus*, *Euripides*, and *Sophocles* were writing their Tragedies. *Pindar* was penning his Lyrics, and *Aristophanes*, his Comedies. *Pericles*, *Themistocles*, and *Aristides*, were swaying public judgment by their Oratory.

In this period great battles were fought on land and at sea: *Marathon*, *Thermopylae*, *Salamis*, *Plataea*, and *Mycale*, battles which decided the issue between Asiatic barbarism and Eastern civilization, achieving the victory of freedom for all after ages in the Western Continent.

But in the Bible all this is passed over in silence. Heaven's standard of values is not the same as earth's.

Zechariah ix.-xiv. (B.C. 516-458)

Any reader of 'Zechariah' will recognize that it is in two distinct parts: chs. i.-viii., and ix.-xiv.; which plainly differ both in content and character. Most critics take the view that the latter part is not the work of Zechariah; some holding that it is pre-exilic, and some, that it is post-exilic. But a change of time and circumstance would naturally lead a writer to a change of subject; and as in chs. ix.-xiv. there is nothing to indicate the time they were written, and nothing to prove that Zechariah did not write them, we take the view that this prophet did write these chapters, and did so in the period of the Fifty-Eight Years.

What were the circumstances? Prophecies of return from captivity, especially in 'Isaiah' and 'Jeremiah', held out to the captives a great and glorious prospect, and over seventy years after the Return these predictions had not been realized. Very many of the captives declined to cross the desert; the building of the Temple had been delayed for fifteen years; the walls of Jerusalem still lay in ruins; the people were still under the authority of Persia; the community was poor, and taxation was heavy; Zerubbabel was of Davidic descent, but he had been only

30

a Governor, not a King, and with his death the long honoured royal line sank out of sight; and all the ancient enemies of Judah seemed to prosper. The outlook of the colony was far from hopeful, and, no doubt, an atmosphere of discontent and depression prevailed. What above all things the people needed was a bright outlook, some assurance that the future would be better than the past.

This assurance is given them in Zech. ix.-xiv., but they would have to learn that these predictions, like those of Isaiah and Jeremiah, already referred to, could not be immediately realized, but looked far down the centuries to the coming of the Messiah, and to the ultimate establishment of His Kingdom. Zechariah i.-viii. deal with an immediate issue, the rebuilding of the Temple; but chs. ix.-xiv. deal with ultimate issues at both the first and second advents of the Messiah.

If Zechariah wrote these predictions shortly before Ezra returned to Palestine, he would be an old man, perhaps forty years older than when he wrote chs. i.-viii., and to place him at such a time, and in such circumstances, is quite as probable as any other suggestion.

The contents of the whole Prophecy, then, are as follows:

CHART 105

THE MINISTRY OF ZECHARIAH	
B.C. 520-518	B.C. 516-458
Chapters i-viii	Chapters ix-xiv
THE CHOSEN PEOPLE AND THE TEMPLE	THE MESSIANIC KING AND THE KINGDOM
1. The Visions of the Seer i-vi (i) A Word of Warning. i. 1-6 (ii) A Series of Visions. i. 7-vi. 8 (iii) A Symbolic Act. vi. 9-15	First Burden 1. The Final Restoration of Judah and Israel. ix-xi (i) The Destruction of the Enemy. ix. 1-8 (ii) The Restoration of the People. ix. 9-x (iii) The Good and the Evil Shepherds. xi
2. The Fasts and the Feasts. vii-viii (i) An Urgent Inquiry concerning Fasts. vii. 1-3 (ii) A Fourfold Answer Introducing Feasts. vii. 4-viii	Second Burden 2. The World - Drama of Judgment and Redemption. xii-xiv (i) The Messianic Forecast. xii-xiii. 6 (ii) The Messianic Method. xiii. 7-xiv. 15 (iii) The Messianic Triumph. xiv. 16-21

These prophecies belong to four distinct periods.

CHART 106

THE PERIOD OF ZECHARIAH'S PROPHECIES			
i-viii	ix-x	xi	xii-xiv
MEDO-PERSIAN	GRECIAN	ROMAN	THE 'END' TIME

'In that Day', which occurs seventeen times in chs. xii.-xiv. points to the prophetic 'Day of the LORD' beyond this Christian Dispensation.

To those who believe that prediction is age-long, and detailed, the following Chart may help to an understanding of this fascinating Book.

CHART 107

ZECHARIAH vii-xiv

1	2	3	4	5	6	7
PAST HISTORY	CAPTIVITY	RETURN	MESSIAH	PRESENT AGE	DANIEL'S 7oth WEEK	MILLENNIUM
vii. 11, 12	vii. 1-7 vii. 13-14	vii. 1-3 vii. 8-10 viii. 9-17 ix. 1-8	ix. 9 xi. 7-14 xiii. 7a	Between ix. 9, 10 xi. 14, 15 xiii. 7a, 7b	(ix. 1-8) ix. 11-15 x. 1-5 xi. 1-6 xi. 15-17 xii. 1-9 xiii. 7b-9 xiv. 1-5a xiv. 12-15	viii. 1-8 (viii. 9-17) viii. 19-23 ix. 10, 16, 17 x. 6-12 xii. 10-14 xiii. 1-6 xiv. 5b-11 xiv. 16-21
			Chs. ix.-xi.			Chs. xiii.-xiv.

THE FIRST BURDEN

The Prophet speaks of the restoration of Judah and Israel, and rapidly indicates the course of events. The rebellious nations are to be overthrown, and the land thus prepared for Israel (ix. 1-8); the Messiah will enter the Royal City in triumph (9-10); the people will be victorious over all their foes (11-17); these blessings are to be sought of the Lord, and not of idols (x. 1, 2); evil rulers are to be deposed (3, 4); the scattered People are to be gathered, and united Israel is to dwell in her own land protected and blessed by Jehovah (5-12).

But before all this can take place the hand of God will rest heavily on His people for their sins. The Prophet personifies the Good Shepherd who will feed His flock, but Who, in return, will be deposed, and paid off at the price of a common slave. He then breaks his two staves, to indicate in the one case, that the people are cut off from God, and in the other case to indicate the dissolution of Israel and Judah. The Prophet is then commanded to act as a cruel shepherd, in token that the Lord would raise up such, to destroy the people who had refused Him (xi).

THE SECOND BURDEN — Chs. xii.-xiv.

This last section of the Book outlines the same great period presented in chapters ix-xi, but from a somewhat different standpoint, and with some additional details. The nations which will gather against Jerusalem are to be utterly overthrown (xii. 1-9). The people of God will look upon Him whom they pierced, and in solitary separation will make confession (10-14), which will be followed by national cleansing (xiii. 1-6). But it is revealed here, as in the former 'burden,' that before all this can take place, Israel is to pass through dark days. In consequence of their rejection of Messiah (7) great tribulation will come upon them (8-xiv. 2); but the Lord will not forget them, speedily will He come and deliver them (3-11). Their enemies will be visited in judgment (12-15) and those who are left of the nations will be brought into subjection (16-19), and united Israel will enter upon a period of unbroken national felicity, characterized throughout by 'HOLINESS UNTO THE LORD.'

That these predictions have reference, to the end of the Gentile Age, that is, to 'the Day of the LORD,' there can be little doubt, and for a full and proper understanding of their details, the whole prophetic chart as presented in all preceding prophecy, must be carefully studied. Meanwhile, this remarkable Book is not without profound and far-reaching spiritual truth.

The Book of Esther (B.C. 484-465)

Some doubt may attach to the idea that Zechariah ix.-xiv. belongs to the period between Ezra vi. and vii., but the story told in the Book of Esther certainly falls within these years.

Only about 50,000 Jews acted upon the Decree of Cyrus in B.C. 536, and returned to Palestine. All the others deported to Babylon, or born in captivity, elected to remain where they were. Many of them must have been owners of property, and many must have been engaged in commercial enterprises which were profitable, and those who had never seen Palestine had less motive for running the risks of months in the dreaded desert for a land unknown to them. We cannot say how many Jews remained in Babylon, but there must have been very many, and these occasioned the Book of Esther.

The scene of the narrative is Susa, the Persian capital, and the time was in the reign of Xerxes, the son of Darius, called Ahasuerus in this Book (B.C. 486-465). 'Esther' is unique among the Books of the Bible. In character it is more Persian than Jewish. Minute details are given concerning the Persian Empire and Court, and from it we may learn much concerning Persian etiquette. The Persian King is referred to not fewer than 190 times, and many Persian customs and phrases are explained. There can be little doubt that the record is based substantially on archives of the Persian Kingdom (ii. 23; vi. 1).

This would account for many things in the Book, as, for example, that the Jews are mentioned only in the third person; that Esther is called 'the Queen', and Mordecai, 'the Jew'; and that no mention is made of Palestine, Jerusalem, the Temple, or the Law.

It is commonly affirmed that the name of God does not occur in this Book, and *directly* it does not; but some time ago Dr. E. W. Bullinger pointed out that the name *Yahweh*, Y H V H, the sacred tetragrammaton, occurs four times in the Book in acrostic form, and these occurrences are at the pivotal points in the narrative. In two instances the Name is spelt *backwards*, and in two, *forwards*; two form the Name by *initial* letters, and two by *final*. It is impossible that this is a mere coincidence, for the details are too intricate and exact.

The tetragrammaton is, Y H V H (Hebrew is read from right to left), translated in the R.V., *Jehovah*, and in the A.V., LORD. Taking the latter translation, Dr. Bullinger shows where and how these letters appear acrostically in 'Esther'.

First (i. 20)

'*All the wives shall give*': '*D*ue *R*espect *O*ur *L*adies shall give to their husbands'. Here the letters are *initial* and *backward*.

Second (v. 4)

'*Let come the King and Haman this day*': '*L*et *O*ur *R*oyal *D*inner this day be graced by the King and Haman'. Here the letters are *initial* and *forward*.

Third (v. 13)

'*This availeth to me nothing*': 'sa*D*; fo*R* n*O* avai*L* is all this to me'. Here the letters are *final* and *backward*.

Fourth (vii. 7)

'*That evil was determined against him*': 'evi*L* t*O* fea*R* determine*D*'. Here the letters are *final* and *forward*. Dr. A. T. Pierson has put this in four couplets thus:

> '*D*ue *R*espect *O*ur *L*adies, all
> Shall give husbands, great and small.
> *L*et *O*ur *R*oyal *D*inner bring
> Haman, feasting with the king.
> Gran*D* fo*R* n*O* avai*L* my state,
> While this Jew sits at the gate.
> Il*L* t*O* fea*R* decree*D*, I find,
> Toward me in the monarch's mind'.

It will at once be evident that this is not coincidence, but design, and that the presentation of God in 'Esther' is *hidden* but *active*, that is, God is here as Providence. This truth is clearly stated in Lowell's words:

> 'Careless seems the great avenger: History's pages but record
> One death grapple in the darkness, twixt old systems and the Word.
> Truth forever on the scaffold; wrong forever on the throne:
> But that scaffold sways the future; and behind the dim unknown
> Standeth God, within the shadow, keeping watch above His own'.

Behind every line of this story is God, watching, protecting, and planning for His Chosen People. The great end in view is their deliverance, and the realization of this is built upon three series of events, each complete in itself, and each necessary to the upholding of the Divine design.

Series 1

The king holds a feast. Intoxicated, he makes a base request. This request is refused by the Queen. This refusal leads to counsel, by which Vashti is deposed. Her deposition results in the search for another Queen, and Esther is chosen because of her beauty. In consequence of this choice, two of the chamberlains determine a conspiracy against the king. Mordecai discovers this, and reports it.

Series 2

A man called Haman is made chief vizier. Mordecai the Jew will not bow to him. Haman issues a cruel decree against the Jews. Mordecai sits in sackcloth and mourns. Esther's maids notice this, and report it to her. She sends to her uncle, and a correspondence results. Arising out of this, Esther goes before the king and finds favour.

Series 3

Haman plots to hang Mordecai. One night the king is troubled with sleeplessness. The chronicles are read to him, and in consequence of past service Mordecai is exalted. Esther tells of Haman's cruelty, and makes request; the king is angry with Haman. Haman is hanged. His decree is nullified. The Jews slaughter their enemies.

The Book teaches two great lessons, which are closely related to one another, namely: the inscrutable providence of God (iv. 14), and the certain retribution of the wicked (vii. 10).

The chief characters introduced in the narrative are: Xerxes, Vashti, Esther, Haman, and Mordecai. In Xerxes, we have a man of uncertain judgment, of wild passion, of weak mind, and of a cruel disposition. In Vashti, we find a woman of excellent modesty, of chaste dignity, and of strong determination. In Esther, is presented a young, beautiful and patriotic Jewess, who risked everything for the sake of her oppressed people. Haman, 'was a man of utmost vanity, blindest prejudices, and capable of the deadliest enmity; a time-serving, selfish, implacable, swaggering bully, a man whose mind was covered over at the top, so as to shut out all lofty aspirations; and closed in at the sides, so as to shut out all kindness; and open only at the bottom, for the incoming of base passions, pride, haughtiness, and hate'. But Mordecai is the chief actor in this story, a true Jew, who clung tenaciously to his kindred, who refused to render to any man the honour and worship due only to God, and in whose character is no trace of vanity or worldly ambition, but who faithfully played his part in the midst of the varied and trying circumstances in which he was placed.

The influence of Jews in heathendom is a factor of significant importance, and in the Old Testament there are five outstanding illustrations: *Joseph* in Egypt; *Daniel* in Babylon; *Ezekiel* by the Chebar; *Mordecai* and *Esther* at Susa; and *Nehemiah* at Shushan.

If these people had not been where they were, and had not done what they did, the whole course of history would have been of a different pattern. In the present Dispensation are *Jesus Christ*, and *Karl Marx*, and the Christianity of the One will conquer the Communism of the other.

ACT I

SCENE 3

THE JEWISH CHURCH

The Second Return

PAGAN HISTORY AND LITERATURE

ZECHARIAH IX-XIV

QUEEN ESTHER

EZRA AND REVIVAL

THE SECOND RETURN FROM BABYLON
(Ezra vii.-x.). B.C. 458. (Chart 95)

These chapters represent the events of one year. For the composition of the record see Chart 96.

It is now 78 years since Zerubbabel and Joshua led a host of captives back to Judaea, and 58 years since the Temple was rebuilt, but the situation seemed to be somewhat at a standstill. In some ways more progress seems to have been made among those who still remained in captivity. Idolatry was abandoned (as indeed it was in Judaea) in every Jewish home on the Euphrates; marriage was permitted only within their own race; in its ritual details the faith of their fathers became their rule of life; and the cause of this seems to have been a new and intense study of the Law, a movement which produced the Order of the Scribes.

At the head of this movement stood Ezra, who was both a scribe and a priest, and was famous for his knowledge of the Law. God put it into the heart of this man to visit his brethren in the West, and in B.C. 458 he set out with a caravan which, with women and children, may have numbered 5,000 souls.

He received great encouragement and assistance from the Persian King Artaxerxes, the son of the murdered Xerxes. The details of this event are given in chs. vii. 1-viii. 31. The journey from the Euphrates to Jerusalem took over four months, and was made without untoward incident, for, says Ezra, 'the hand of our God was upon us'.

On arrival Ezra became the head of the community, as the events which followed show.

The first thing to engage his attention was the matter of mixed marriages, and he dealt with it with relentless severity. The adult males in Judaea numbered probably about 40,000, and of these only 113 had married foreign wives. No doubt these wives were Jewish proselytes, and their male children were, almost certainly, circumcised. These women had not introduced idolatry to the community, and one cannot but feel that to divorce them all and send them back to their own people, was wanting in humaneness. Ch. ix. 1 should read: 'The people of Israel . . . have not separated themselves from the people of the lands *in respect of* their abominations.' This does not mean that these women had introduced idolatry, or that the Jews had fallen into it, though purity of religion may, in some way, have been threatened.

But it must be admitted that the presence of these women in a community so recently released from captivity, and with a hard struggle before them, was a danger. And then, there was the Law: Thou 'shalt not make marriages with (foreigners); thy daughter thou shalt not give unto his son, nor his daughter shalt thou take unto thy son. For they will turn away thy son from following me, that they may serve other gods; so will the anger of the LORD be kindled against you, and destroy thee suddenly' (Deut. vii. 3, 4).

The fact that Moses, and Boaz, and David, and Solomon, had broken this law, did not abrogate it, and Ezra took his stand squarely on it, though with some degree of harshness.

But another part of Ezra's story is yet to come, and in the light of the whole record, it must be admitted that his action was regrettably necessary, and safeguarded a dangerous situation.

ACT I

SCENE 3

THE JEWISH CHURCH

The Third Return

NEHEMIAH

FIRST VISIT

SECOND VISIT

MALACHI

NEHEMIAH

Between 'Ezra' and 'Nehemiah' (B.C. 457-445)

'Megabyzos the Satrap of Syria had successfully defied the king (Persian), and forced him to agree to his own terms of peace, thus giving the first open sign of the internal decay of the Empire. It is possible that the disaffection of the Satrap may account for the silence in Scripture as to the events which followed Ezra's reform. Deprived of the royal support, he would no longer be able to maintain himself as Governor in face of the opposition he was certain to experience from the Samaritans. It would also account for the condition in which we find the Jews when the Book of Nehemiah opens. The walls of the City are still unbuilt, Ezra has ceased to be Governor, the people are in great affliction and reproach, the Arabs are encamping close to Jerusalem, Sanballat and his allies are all-powerful, and priests and laity alike have gone back to their heathen and foreign wives'.

(SAYCE)

THE THIRD RETURN FROM BABYLON

B.C. 445 'NEHEMIAH' (Chart 95)

Perhaps this can scarcely be called a return, as Nehemiah did not bring with him a contingent of Jews; yet this man was a host in himself, and the consequences of his return were as considerable as those of Zerubbabel, and scarcely less so than those of Ezra (Chart 108).

The period covered by this Book is not known, because it cannot be said with certainty what is meant by 'after certain days', or 'after some time', or 'at the end of days', in ch. xiii. 6. Some have thought it means a year, and others, anything up to twelve years. What is affirmed is that the first period of Nehemiah's governorship was twelve years (v. 14): B.C. 445·433.

If after this period Nehemiah was in Babylon for several years which would give time for the abuses named in ch. xiii. to develop—we may reasonably suppose that the second period of his governorship lasted from about B.C. 428-425.

The message or messages of 'Malachi' almost certainly were delivered within the period B.C. 432-425.

The contents of the Book of Nehemiah are shown in Chart 108.

CHART 108

THE BOOK OF NEHEMIAH

1	2	3	4
Chs. i-vii	Chs. viii-x	Chs. xi. 1-xii. 26	Chs. xii. 27-xiii. 31
REBUILDING OF THE WALL OF JERUSALEM	SPIRITUAL REVIVAL OF THE PEOPLE	SUNDRY CATALOGUES OF IMPORTANCE	THE SECOND PERIOD OF NEHEMIAH'S GOVERNORSHIP
(a) Preparation for the Effort (i-ii)	(a) CONVOCATION for Instruction (viii)	(a) Dwellers in Jerusalem, and their Chief Officers (xi. 1-24)	(a) Dedication of the Wall of Jerusalem (xii. 27-43)
(b) Reconstruction of the Wall (iii)	(b) CONFESSION of the People (ix)	(b) Country Towns occupied by the returned Israelites (xi. 25-36)	(b) Arrangements for the Temple Service (xii. 44-47)
(c) Opposition to the Project (iv-vi. 14)	(c) COVENANT with the LORD (x)	(c) Priestly and Levitical families that returned under Zerubbabel (xii. 1-9)	(c) Rectification of various Abuses (xiii)
(d) Completion of the Task (vi. 15-vii. 3)	PSALM cxix	(d) High Priests from Joshua to Jaddua (xii. 10, 11)	MALACHI
(e) Registration of the People (vii. 4-73)		(e) Heads of the Priestly families in the time of Joiakim (xii. 12-21)	
		(f) Chief families of Levites and Porters (xii. 22-26)	
NEHEMIAH	EZRA	Archives	NEHEMIAH
	B.C. 445 - 433		B.C. 432 (?)—425 (?)

31

Divisions 1 and 4 tell of Nehemiah's work, and division 2, of Ezra's. Outside of division 2 Ezra is mentioned only in Catalogue (*f*) (xii. 26), and in connection with the dedication of the wall of Jerusalem (xii. 36); but we do not know when this dedication took place, as the account of it is separated from the account of the completion of the wall (vi. 15).

The material, social, and religious condition of the Jews when Nehemiah arrived in Jerusalem, and the way in which he dealt with the situation are made evident in chs. ii.-vii. We cannot say where Ezra was during the twelve years previous to Nehemiah's arrival, but he did not reappear until after the wall of Jerusalem was rebuilt, and then he came suddenly on the scene, and as suddenly disappeared. But during his few months of ministry he brought about a considerable revival of religion (viii.-x.). A holy convocation was followed by widespread confession, and issued in the making of a covenant with the LORD.

In B.C. 433 Nehemiah returned to Babylon to report to the king, which he had promised to do (ii. 6; v. 14) but, no doubt, and perhaps more than once, he had been granted an extension of time. When he returned again to Judaea, he found that the abuses which he and Ezra had dealt with years before had again become prevalent, and, supported by Malachi, he at once proceeded to right the wrong (xiii.).

There were four abuses which he attacked: (*a*) the desecration of the Temple (4-9); (*b*) the non-payment of the tithes to the Levites (10-13); (*c*) the profanation of the Sabbath (15-22); and (*d*) mixed marriages (23-28). These evils Nehemiah handled with great promptitude and firmness; and the Book ends with one of his many prayers for remembrance (v. 19; xiii. 14, 22, 29, 31). Flagrant evils require stern treatment, and even the Lord adopted the method of physical resistance (John ii. 13-17); but Christian action is regulated by another principle (2 Cor. x. 3-5).

MALACHI (B.C. 433-425?)

What Haggai and Zechariah had been to Zerubbabel and Joshua, Malachi was to Nehemiah. It is most probable that he exercised his ministry during the period of Nehemiah's absence from Jerusalem between B.C. 433 and the unknown date of his return. During this period the abuses referred to in ch. xiii. would have had time to arise, and it is these that Malachi attacks. Had Ezra been in Jerusalem at the time, it is not likely that these evils would have arisen.

His indictment was against the *religious declension* (i.-ii. 9), the *social debasement* (ii. 10-16), and the *moral defection* (ii. 17-iv. 6) of the people.

Malachi's is the last of the Old Testament prophecies. Nothing is known of the writer, whose name means 'My messenger', but we may gather from its contents of what spirit he was. The times demanded a strong and courageous man, and such was found in Malachi.

There had been a great religious awakening in Judah, and the people had entered into a solemn covenant to separate themselves from several prevailing abuses which are specified (Neh. x. 28-39). Better times seemed in store for the people, had not their goodness proved to be as the morning cloud. But they became discouraged. True they were back in their own land and city, but their expectations had not been realized. The restoration from Babylon had brought with it none of the ideal glories predicted by Isaiah; and this led many among the people to doubt the Divine justice. The result was religious indifference and moral laxity, for which Malachi severely rebuked them. Happy indeed was the state of things at Jerusalem when Nehemiah left to return to the Persian Court, but when he came back he saw 'the dog had returned to its vomit again, and the sow that was washed to her wallowing in the mire'. The very things which the people had covenanted to forsake they were now embracing, and both Malachi and Nehemiah plunged into the midst of them with fearless hands (Neh. xiii. 4-31), and burning words, but the attitude of the people is exhibited in the sevenfold 'Wherein' (i. 2, 6, 7, ii. 17, iii. 7, 8, 13). The charge brought against them by Malachi was fourfold in its character.

I RELIGIOUS

The people were all astray through the degeneracy of the priests. Hosea had said, 'like people like priest' (iv. 9), but the order is here inverted to the utter shame of the Tribe of Levi. They called God their Father, but they did not honour Him; they said He was their Master, but they did not fear Him; on the contrary they went to the furthest extremes of profanity and sacrilege in their vaunted worship of Him. Polluted bread, blind, lame, and sick sacrifices, and grudging, greedy service, were what they brought Him. The prophet incisively says: 'You would not dare to treat those who are over you in civil affairs as you are presuming to treat Jehovah your God; the very Gentiles, whom you despise, will be accepted before you'. It is not enough that we worship, we must yield spiritual worship, for 'God is a Spirit, and they that worship Him must worship Him in spirit and in truth.'

II MORAL

Sorcery, adultery, perjury, fraud, and oppression (iii. 5) were rife at this time, and against these the LORD'S face is set; but the people had said, 'Everyone that doeth evil is good in the sight of the LORD, and he delighteth in them', and, 'where is the God of judgment?' The Prophet then tells them plainly that the God of judgment will come and cast them all into the refining pot, and make the fire to burn fiercely until the dross is separated; a process of intense pain, but it must so be. Religion is spiritual, but it is also intensely ethical, a fact too often disbelieved or neglected in our own day. God has regard to all our social and civic relations, and injustice, bribery, and oppression will most surely receive their fitting recompense.

III SOCIAL

One of the greatest sources of sin and corruption in the history of Israel had been their connection and compromises with the strangers around them. They had been separated from the nations and placed in the midst of them in order to be a witness to Jehovah the One God, in contradistinction to prevailing polytheism; and in order to remain pure it was necessary that they married only within their own nation, for the introduction of strange wives often meant the introduction of false worship (cf. 1 Kings xi. 1-13). Ezra and Nehemiah both had spoken and acted very

severely in regard to this, but the people fell back again into
this sin and Malachi lifted up his voice in pointed denunciation.
They were divorcing their Hebrew wives and marrying foreigners,
and the tears of the divorced covered the altar, so that the LORD
would have no further regard for the offerings of these cruel
husbands. How could the seed be holy if the stock was unholy;
and how could family blessing and prosperity be expected so
long as a man dealt treacherously with the wife of his youth?
With these charges and challenges the prophet made the people
face their sin.

IV MATERIAL

The offerings which went to the maintenance of the Levites
had been stopped, and the tithes were not brought into the
storehouse to the LORD, and poverty ensued. No doubt in many
instances there was a literal observance of the precepts respecting
the 'tenth', but the observance was perfunctory and grudging.
The consequence was that, as in material things they dishonoured
God, in material things they were made to suffer (ii.). When we
become Christ's our money becomes His also, and while we may
yield a part to- Him consistently, it is only to indicate that the
whole is His, and at His disposal. The value of a gift to the
Lord is determined by the spirit of the giver, and He values our
offerings according to what it costs us to bring them.

Malachi's indictment of the people was fourfold, Religious,
Moral, Social, and Material, covering the whole life; and the
judgment was in the ratio of the neglect.

There was, however, as there always will be, a faithful remnant
who thought about God, and had fellowship with one another,
and to them rich promises were made.

Then the Prophet concludes by referring back to Moses,
exhorting to obedience of the law, and forward to Elijah (John
the Baptist), by regarding whose message they would be spared
the threatened curse.

The message of Malachi to his day is pre-eminently suited
to our own, for each of the above abuses has its counterpart
in the modern Church. How prevalent is 'a form of godliness'

the power being denied; how weak are multitudes of Christians in respect to great moral questions; how frequent is the alliance in marriage of saved with unsaved; and how shamefully lax are the people of God in regard to the consecration of all that they are, and have. To all such the message of Malachi should come as a solemn warning.

At the end of the first Book of the Old Testament, we read of a 'coffin', and at the end of the last Book, of a 'curse', indicating that, as yet, all was failure; but the Second Man, the Lord from Glory having come, the New Testament ends in better terms, and its last note tells of wondrous 'grace'.

EZRA: The Scribe and Priest

Ezra, who has been called the 'Second Founder of the Jewish State', united in himself many qualities, and, if tradition can be trusted, accomplished many important works. He was student, statesman, reformer, antiquary, historian, preacher, teacher, governor, priest, scribe, and saint. Few indeed have possessed and employed so many qualities, and it is little wonder that he made so profound an impression upon the Jews of his time, and one still greater beyond his time.

When he arrived in Jerusalem from Babylon, he at once became the head of the Jewish community, and ruthlessly enforced the law which prohibited mixed marriages (Ezra ix., x.). During the twelve or thirteen years of silence between the end of 'Ezra' and the beginning of 'Nehemiah', we may assume that he was occupied with the literary work which has given to us 1-2 Chronicles, and the Book which bears his name. This involved him in wide and careful research, as his references to sources indicate (1 Chron. xxix. 29; 2 Chron. ix. 29; xii. 15; xiii. 22; xx. 34; xxiv. 27; xxvi. 22; xxxii. 32; xxxiii. 19). In addition to this, he is credited with a general settling of the Canon of the Old Testament; but whether this is so or not, most critics admit that the idea of collecting together the sacred Hebrew literature belongs to Ezra's time, and no one but Ezra could have done it. Maybe he began his work while still in Babylon (Ezra vii. 6, 10, 14).

Jewish tradition assigns also to Ezra the origination of certain institutions which had for their object the systematic instruction of the people in religious knowledge. Perhaps chief among such was the fellowship out of which emerged at a later stage the 'Great Synagogue', and later still, the 'Sanhedrin'. Canon Rawlinson says that 'to Ezra probably belongs the introduction into Judaea itself of local synagogues—places of worship distinct from the Temple—spread widely over the land, and thus multiplying almost indefinitely the centres of religious influence, whence instruction flowed to the people.'

Later Judaism derived from Ezra all that was best in it—zeal, patriotism, and passionate attachment to the Law; but he must not be credited with the extravagances and rigidity of the Judaism of our Lord's time.

Ezra was the father of the Order of the Scribes. Under the Monarchy the Scribe was a state secretary, but from Ezra's time it meant much more than this; it meant a diligent student of the Law. Ezra was 'a ready scribe in the law of Moses', and 'set his heart to *seek* the LORD, and to *do* it, and to *teach* in Israel statutes and judgments' (vii. 10).

From the day that this man conducted a three-hour's service in public in Jerusaelm (Neh. viii.), the Bible took on a new significance, and was given a new place in the life of the people. 'The Bible,' says Stanley, 'and the reading of the Bible as an instrument of instruction, may be said to have been begun on the sunrise of that day when Ezra the scribe unrolled the parchment scroll of the Law'; and Dr. Whyte says that Ezra was 'the father of all our expository and experimental preachers —the first Scriptural preacher'.

His faith in God is shown in his favourite phrase, 'the hand of the LORD my God' (vii. 6, 9, 28; viii. 18, 22, 31). So completely did he bank on God that he declined a military escort across the dangerous desert (viii. 22); and his great prayer (ix. 5-15) shows how profound was his piety, and how humble his spirit. Notwithstanding a degree of emotionalism in ıus temperament he was severe and exacting; his zeal was uncompromising, and his actions decisive. Truly he came to the kingdom for such a time as that!

NEHEMIAH: The Governor

Nehemiah, which means *Consolation of Yah*, stands out quite distinctly from all other Bible characters. His significance as an individual, and in the history of the Jews from the middle of the fifth century B.C., can be apprehended and appreciated only by the reading of his Book at a sitting, and the frequent reading of it in this way. For the practical Christian idealist there is no more inspiring Book in the Bible. Elsewhere is found hard work, and elsewhere religious devotion, but here they are combined. The movements of the Book are swift, because the inspirer of them is swift. The reading of chs. i.-vii., and xii. 27-xiii. 31, omitting what lies between, will reveal the scope and intenseness of this man's labours.

His virtues are many, and his faults are few, and his example is a model for all who would be successful servants of Jesus Christ. The first thing which his story exhibits is his *patriotism*. The news of the condition of his brethren in Judaea produced in him sorrowful consternation. 'When I heard these words, I sat down and wept, and mourned certain days, and fasted, and prayed before the God of heaven' (i. 4), and at the end of four months Artaxerxes observes the sadness of his countenance (ii. 2). This is the more remarkable seeing that he was born in captivity, and, therefore, had never been in Palestine. But patriotism is not in one's location, but in one's blood.

This patriotism of Nehemiah was wedded to true *piety*. His record begins with a prayer, and ends with a prayer (i. 4; xiii. 29-31), and prayers are all the way between (ii. 4; iv. 4, 9; vi. 9, 14; xiii. 14, 22, 29, 31). The first of these prayers is lengthy (i. 4–11), but most of them are ejaculatory, short, sharp cries to God, as occasions demanded. It may be thought that in some of these Nehemiah is too self-complacent, earnestly desiring to be remembered (xiii. 14, 22, 29, 31), but what he specifies was worth remembering, and was remembered.

Another evidence of his piety was *his conception of God*, and with this goes his sense of what he and his people owed to God. To Nehemiah, as to Ezra, the Deity was 'the God of heaven' (i. 4, 5; ii. 4, 20; Ezra i. 2; v. 11, 12; vi. 9, 10; vii. 12, 21,

23); and 'the great and terrible God' (i. 5; iv. 14; ix. 32); a God to be feared, obeyed, and worshipped. Hence the need to know Him (viii.), to confess Him (ix.), to covenant with Him (ix.-x.), to keep separate from surrounding heathen (xiii. 23-28; Ezra x.), and to observe fasts, feasts, the Sabbatic and Levitical Laws (i. 4; ix. 1; viii. 13-18; xii. 43, 44-47).

Nehemiah believed that God was interested in his life, that He would guide him, and give him success (i. 11; ii. 8, 12, 20; v. 15; vii. 5; iv. 15).

Great was Nehemiah's *courage*, both physical and moral. Bravely he faced the four month's journey through the desert, and in Jerusalem he places himself in the line of danger while the work of rebuilding proceeds (ch. iv.). His attitude to opposition is admirable, and the answers he gave to his enemies reveal his moral strength (ii. 20; iv. 9, 14, 20-23; vi. 3, 4, 8, 11). His courage is exhibited also in the way he dealt with internal abuses (v.; xiii. 3, 7, 8, 17-22, 25-28). Espousing the cause of the poor and enslaved he attacked the ruling classes, and wrought reforms; and departure from observance of the Law he handled with *promptitude* and *vigour*.

Also *sagacity* and *prudence* characterized Nehemiah. Before he began to rebuild the walls, he went over the ground to survey the situation and see what had to be done (ii. 11-16). He did not take any needless risk, but took every precaution against attack (iv. 9). The way in which he got everyone to work and allocated their work exhibits great wisdom (iii.).

His *energy* never abated, as is seen in his early start of the work, and swift completion of it (ii. 11, vi. 15). Not only did he organize the rebuilding of the walls, but he worked at it (iv. 23). After twelve years he returned to Shushan to report, as he had promised to do (ii. 6), and when he heard that the people had sadly backslidden in his absence, he returned and vigorously wrought a second reformation (xiii).

This man's *integrity*, deep *earnestness* of purpose, *fearlessness*, *unselfishness*, and *generosity*, are everywhere evident, and but for him it is difficult to see, notwithstanding Ezra's work, how the Jewish State could have survived.

EZRA AND NEHEMIAH

God often sets men in pairs: Moses and Joshua; David and Jonathan; Jeremiah and Baruch; Paul and Timothy; and here, Ezra and Nehemiah. But these pairs are never duplicates of one another. Generally one is old, and the other young, and they are the complements of one another.

Scarcely anything is more interesting and important in history than the meeting of men who have left their impress on their own and following generations. Of such meetings may be named those of Alexander the Great and Diogenes the Cynic; of Petrarch and Charles IV; of Martin Luther and Charles V.; of Milton and Galileo; of Frederick the Great and Voltaire; of Garibaldi and King Victor Emmanuel; of Livingstone and Stanley; and of Wellington and Blücher. But in its nature, significance, and results, the meeting of Ezra and Nehemiah, in the Old Testament, and of Peter and Cornelius in the New, are as great as any of them.

How long Ezra and Nehemiah were associated we do not know. What we do know is that Ezra went to Palestine twelve or thirteen years before Nehemiah did, and that they were associated, probably in B.C. 444, in sweeping reforms in Judah (Neh. viii.-x.; xii. 27-43). Their ability, training, and provinces were quite different, but all coalesced most perfectly in the fulfilment of God's plan for His people at that time.

Ezra was a religious reformer, and Nehemiah was a political leader. Ezra was a spiritual teacher and guide, and Nehemiah was a warrior and statesman. Ezra was occupied chiefly with internal difficulties, those of the heart, and Nehemiah, chiefly with external difficulties, those of the city. Ezra was the Ecclesiastical Chief, and Nehemiah was the Civil Governor. While Ezra's attention was given mainly to spiritual advancement, Nehemiah's was devoted chiefly to material prosperity. The Pastor and the Ruler worked together in most perfect harmony. The Theologian and the Architect supplemented one another. One was a student, and the other was a soldier. Their combined work constituted a movement which marked a turning-point of deep interest in Jewish history. Both were glorified in the traditions of their country; and both have left imperishable records of their work.

It would have been well for the Christian Church, and for all of us, if we had learned the lessons of such a colleagueship. What mountains of misunderstanding would have been avoided, and what a vast amount of work, now undone, would have been accomplished.

THE JEWISH CHURCH

This, then, is the history of the Jewish Church, which was instituted when in B.C. 536 a host of captives returned from Babylon to Palestine, and re-formed the Jewish State. The Biblical Records—Ezra, Haggai, Zechariah, (Esther), Nehemiah, and Malachi—cover a period of about 110 years (536-425?), and the founders of this Church were Zerubbabel, Joshua, Ezra, and Nehemiah. The King was exchanged for the Governor, and the Priest superseded the Prophet. A new era was inaugurated, which found expression, as we shall see, in new institutions, offices, and activities, until Christianity displaced Judaism.

CHART 109

FOUNDERS OF THE JEWISH CHURCH				
B.C. 536–516		'ESTHER'. B.C. 484–465	B.C. 458–444	B.C. 445–425
ZERUBBABEL	JOSHUA		EZRA	NEHEMIAH
Prince-Governor	Priest		Scribe and Priest	Lay-Governor
Rebuilding of the Temple			Religious Reform	Rebuilding of Jerusalem's Walls
Ezra i–vi			Ezra vii–x. Neh. viii–x	Neh. i–xiii
HAGGAI	ZECHARIAH			MALACHI

CHART 110

SIX PERSIAN KINGS				
Name	Date	Years	References	Note
CYRUS	558-529	29	Ezra i (B.C. 536)	Thought by some to be
CAMBYSES (Ahasuerus)	529-522	7	Ezra iv. 6 Dan. xi. 2	XERXES
GOMATES (Artaxerxes Pseudo Smerdis)	522-521	8 months	Ezra iv. 7 Dan. xi. 2	ARTAXERXES (Longimanus) This would make Ezra iv. 6-23 a parenthesis, belonging to a period after ch. vi.
DARIAS HYSTASPES	521-486	35	Ezra iv. 5, 24; v-vi Dan. xi. 2	
XERXES (Ahasuerus)	485-465	21	Book of Esther Dan. xi. 2	
ARTAXERXES (Longimanus)	465-425	40	Ezra vii- Neh. xiii	

CHART 111

THE HEBREW PROPHETS			
ORDER	THE PROPHET	HISTORICAL SETTING	DATE B.C.*
1	JOEL	2 Kings xi–xv. 7	837–800
2	JONAH	2 Kings xiii–xiv	825–782
3	AMOS	2 Kings xiv. 23–xv. 7	810–785
4	HOSEA	2 Kings xv–xviii	782–725
5	ISAIAH	2 Kings xv–xx. 2 Chron. xxvi–xxxii	758–698
6	MICAH	2 Kings xv. 8–xx. Isaiah vii–viii Jer. xxvi. 17-19. 2 Chron. xxvii–xxxii.	740–695
7	NAHUM	(Jonah. Isaiah x. Zeph. ii. 13–15)	640–630
8	ZEPHANIAH	2 Kings xxii–xxiii. 34. 2 Chron. xxxiv–xxxvi. 4.	640–610
9	JEREMIAH	2 Kings xxii–xxv. 2 Chron. xxxiv–xxxvi. 21.	627–586
10	HABAKKUK	2 Kings xxiii. 51–xxiv. 2 Chron. xxxvi. 1–10.	609–598
11	DANIEL	2 Kings xxiii. 35–xxv. 2 Chron. xxxvi. 5–23.	606–534
12	EZEKIEL	2 Kings xxiv. 17–xxv. 2 Chron. xxxvi. 11–21.	592–572
13	OBADIAH	2 Kings xxv. 2 Chron. xxxvi. 11–21	586–583
14	HAGGAI	Ezra v–vi.	520
15	ZECHARIAH	Ezra v–vi.	520–518
16	MALACHI	Nehemiah xiii.	433–425

*These dates cannot be fixed with certainty, and the margin here given is that *within* which the prophet is likely to have ministered, and does not represent the *duration* of his ministry.

MESSIANIC PROPHECY

What must be plain to every student—and I would say, to every reader also of Holy Scripture—is that Christ is the sum and substance of its revelations, their object and their end. 'In the volume of the book it is written of me' (Ps. xl. 7; Heb. x. 7; Luke xxiv. 27, 44; John v. 39). That which constitutes the UNFOLDING DRAMA OF REDEMPTION is the fact that throughout the History, Prophecy, Wisdom, Poetry, and Apocalypse of the Old Testament, Christ is being revealed, and His coming is being prepared for. 'Prepare ye the way of the LORD, make straight in the desert a highway for our God' (Isa. xl. 3); and throughout the New Testament, Christ is the fulfilment of the prophecies, and is much more than their fulfilment—the Christ of history, of experience, and of universal dominion.

It is comparatively easy to find texts in the Old Testament which have their fulfilment in the New, but the subject of *Messianic Prophecy* is not quite as simple as that. The endeavour to apprehend the scope of the term will lead us to the conclusion that it has a wider, and a narrower sense. The *narrower* sense relates to the ideal Theocratic King of the House of David, the personal Messiah; and the *wider* sense embraces—as RIEHM has shown in his 'Messianic Prophecy'—the *Covenant* which God made with Abram and Israel, the idea of the *Kingdom*, as it is unfolded in the Old Testament, the Divinely ordained *Institutions* of Israel, and, indeed, the whole *History of Israel* ideally conceived. This wider sense could have no being apart from the personal Messiah; and the personal Messiah could not function except through the media of the foregoing.

For a right view of Messianic Prophecy certain things should be apprehended.

1. That such prophecy is *partial*.

Nowhere can we get a complete picture of the grand design. Only fulfilment could present such a view.

2. That such prophecy is *progressive*.

The purposes of God were more clearly made known as time progressed, and as the people were better able to understand their unique relation to God.

3. That such prophecy was often presented *typically* and *symbolically*.

Here it is important to distinguish between the essential and the incidental, between the substance of the revelation, and its garb, for the one is permanent, and the other is incidental.

4. That such prophecy has both a *primary*, and an *ultimate* fulfilment.

The prophets spoke to their own age, and much of what they said related to events which took place afterwards, sooner or later, during Israel's history. But often these prophecies went beyond the circumstances and the time of Israel of old, to a distant future, and an ideal fulfilment (see Isaiah vii.-ix.).

5. That such prophecy *often went beyond the understanding of the prophets*.

This is clearly stated in 1 Peter i. 10-12, and it is easy to see how inevitable it was; for 'God spake in old times to our forefathers through the prophets, little by little, and in different ways' (Heb. i. 1), and they were unable to apprehend, as we now can, the fuller significance of what they were inspired to say, or write.

THE COVENANT

When mankind as a whole failed to respond to the purpose of God, He turned from them, and called a man who would apprehend His revelation (Gen. xi. 1-9; xii. 1-3). When Abram responded to God's call and covenant, history took a great leap forward. The Covenant which God made sovereignly with Abram is the root of prophecy, and is the foundation of His government of the world.

'Now the LORD said unto Abram:

"Get thee out of thy country, and from thy kindred, and from thy father's house, unto the land that I will show thee.

And I will make of thee a great nation.

And I will bless thee and make thy name great; and be thou a blessing.

And I will bless them that bless thee, and him that curseth thee I will curse.

And in thee shall all the families of the earth be blessed".'

Conditional only on faith and obedience, Abram received a promise of fourfold blessing—personal, family, national, and universal; and it is this Covenant which is historically developed in the whole of the Bible from this point. As it necessarily includes the coming of Christ and all its results, the Covenant is essentially Messianic in character. It took national form at the time of the Exodus, and in Christianity it is taking universal form. To eliminate the Covenant would be to eliminate Israel as the medium of God's redemptive purpose.

THE KINGDOM

The idea of the Theocratic Kingdom occupies a central place in the religious consciousness of the prophets; but it inheres in the whole history of Israel from the time of the Exodus.

First of all the Kingdom was *Theocratic*, that is, God was Israel's Ruler, mediating His rule through Moses, Joshua, and the Judges.

Then the people, wishing to be like other nations, asked that one of themselves might be their king, and they were given Saul, who inaugurated the *Monarchy*, which lasted for over 500 years. The greatest of the kings was David, who typifies the true Messianic King. This being so, the Theocratic idea continues in the Monarchy, for the kings of Judah were, ideally, Jehovah's representatives. During the time of the Babylonian captivity of 50 years (B.C. 586-536) God's people were under alien rule for penal and disciplinary purposes; after which, from the time of the return under Zerubbabel and Joshua, the people were again under a Theocracy mediated by priests.

It is, therefore, easy to understand the Kingdom outlook and onlook of the prophets. But the glaring discrepancy between the prophetic promises, and the actual experience of the people, set their eyes and hearts on the coming of the King who would fulfil all the promises, and make the ideal actual.

Hence the many references to the Messiah King who is yet to come, and Who will establish a Kingdom which shall be universal and abiding.

'The LORD of Hosts shall reign in Mount Zion, and in Jerusalem'
(Isa. xxiv. 23).
'Thy God reigneth'   (Isa. lii. 2).
'The LORD shall reign over them in Mount Zion'
(Mic. iv. 7).
See also Psalms ii.; xx.; xxi.; xlv.; lxxii.; lxxxix.; cx.

Expositors are not agreed in their interpretation of these promises. There are two distinct views: (a) that the promises will be literally fulfilled, and that the Messiah will again return to the earth and establish a visible universal Kingdom which shall have a reunited Israel for its medium, and Jerusalem for its centre; and (b) that the promises must be fulfilled spiritually, and are now being so fulfilled in the Christian Church.

This is not the place to discuss these views, but it will be seen that the first view necessitates a break in God's dispensational dealings with Israel, a break coextensive with the Christian Age; and that the second view regards His dealings with Israel as continuous, only with the temporal and material features of the promises sublimated. What is clear, however, is that the whole Kingdom conception is Messianic in character.

THE SACRIFICES

Sacrifice was in the warp and woof of the religion of Israel, and the New Testament warrants the belief that it was Messianic in character, though the Israelites themselves did not know this; for, to them, the Messiah was a Sovereign, and not a Sufferer; they believed that He would rule, but it never entered into their thought that He would die. The nearest approach to this is in Isa. liii. 10, but this does not mean that the whole sacrificial system was understood as foreshadowing that event.

Paul regarded the sacrifices of the Old Testament as types of the true Sacrifice which Christ made (1 Cor. v. 7); and the author of 'Hebrews' has not a little to say about the true significance of the Old Testament sacrifices, looked at in the light of Christ's death (chs. ix., x.). Christ Himself accepted the whole sacrificial system as of Divine origin (Matt. viii. 4), but He taught that the ethical transcends the ceremonial. He spoke of His 'blood of the covenant which is poured out for many' (Mk. xiv. 24; Matt. xxvi. 28; Lk. xxii. 20).

32

We, therefore, must read the Old Testament revelation in the light of the New Testament interpretation. From the first blood-shedding, in Genesis (iii. 21; iv. 4; Heb. xi. 4; xii. 24), sacrifice is traceable throughout the Primeval, Patriarchal, and Israelitish periods; and from the Exodus its fullest expression was in the Passover and the Levitical Offerings. The sacrifices were not observed to any extent in the wilderness, as it was impracticable (Amos v. 25); and they were entirely suspended in Jerusalem during the fifty years of Babylonian exile; but on the Return the first thing that was done was to build an altar (Ezra iii. 2), and from then on the Sacrifices were again offered.

But 'in the end of the age Christ appeared to put away sin by the sacrifice of Himself', and now 'there remaineth no more a sacrifice for sins' (Heb. ix. 26; x. 26). The whole sacrificial system therefore leads to and ends with the Messiah.

TYPES

Not only are there many Messianic types in the Old Testament, but the whole history of Israel is typical. The Apostle Paul, speaking of the Exodus, says:

'These things became for us types (*tupoi*)'
'Now all these things happened to them (as) types (*tupoi*), and were written for our admonition in whose days the ages have reached their climax'   (1 Cor. x. 6, 11).

Because some claim to see types where they do not exist, is no reason for denying them where they do exist. An inspired Apostle says, speaking of the rock in the wilderness:

'They drank of that spiritual rock that followed them, and *that rock was Christ*'   (1 Cor. x. 4).

And again:

'*Christ our Passover* is sacrificed for us'   (1 Cor. v. 7).

But numerous types are evident which are not expressly declared to be such; and the types are of many kinds.

1 TYPICAL PERSONS

ADAM: type of Christ as Federal Head (Rom. v. 12-21)
MELCHISEDEC: type of Christ as Priest-King (Gen. xiv. 18-20; Ps. cx. 4; Zech. vi. 13; Heb. vii.)
JOSEPH: the most perfect type of Christ, as Beloved Son, Suffering Servant, and Gracious Sovereign (Gen. xxxvii.-l.)

MOSES: type of Christ as Prophet (Deut. xviii. 15, 18; Luke
                vii. 16)
DAVID: type of Christ as King (2 Sam. vii. 12-17; Rev. xi. 15;
                xii. 10; xix. 16)

2 TYPICAL THINGS

THE TABERNACLE:
                type of the manifestation of God bodily-wise among men
                (John i. 14: 'dwelt' is 'tabernacled')
THE ARK: type of Christ as God-Man (Exod. xxv. 10, 11; John
                i. 1-14)
THE MANNA: type of Christ the true Bread from heaven (Exod. xvi.;
                John vi. 48-51; Rev. ii. 17)
THE BRAZEN SERPENT:
                type of Christ 'lifted up' to die for our healing (John
                iii. 14)
THE RENT VEIL:
                type of Christ rent that there might be a free way of
                access for us to God (Exod. xxvi. 33; Mk. xv. 38;
                Heb. x. 20)

3 TYPICAL ORDINANCES

THE PASSOVER: (Exod. xii.; 1 Cor. v. 7)
THE OFFERINGS:
                types of Christ who satisfied every requirement of God,
                and perfectly met every need of ours.
                The MEAL Offering tells of His unblemished life; and
                the BURNT, PEACE, SIN, and TRESPASS Offerings represent
                various aspects of His vicarious death for us.
THE DAY OF ATONEMENT:
                Ritual of the 'two goats' (Lev. xvi).
                The slain goat, type of Christ our *propitiation* (1 John
                ii. 2):
                the scapegoat, type of Christ as the believer's *substitution*
                (2 Cor. v. 21)
THE TWO BIRDS:
                The one slain: Christ in *death*; the one liberated:
                Christ in *resurrection*.

There are also typical Places, Numbers, and Colours; but special
attention should be given to:

4 TYPICAL OFFICES

Of these there are three outstanding, the *Prophet*; the *Priest*; and the
King; and the need for these is deep-seated in us, as the following Chart
shows:

CHART 112

THE MESSIAH

	OLD TESTAMENT				NEW TESTAMENT		
	EXPECTATION				REALIZATION		
	ANTICIPATION				ACCOMPLISHMENT		
	LONGING				SATISFACTION		
	THE HUMAN NEED				THE DIVINE SUPPLY		
Office	Function	Type	Reference	Antitype	Office	Time	Reference
PROPHET	To Reveal because of Blindness	MOSES (Deut.) xviii. 18	Oral and Written Prophecies	CHRIST	PROPHET	Past (Luke vii. 16)	The Gospels
PRIEST	To Represent because of Sinfulness	AARON (Heb. v. 1–5)	Leviticus		PRIEST	Present (Heb. iv. 14–16)	The ACTS and EPISTLES
KING	To Rule because of Wilfulness	DAVID (2 Sam. vii. 12–17)	David's Reign and Psalms		KING	Future (Rev. xi. 15; xii. 10; xix. 16)	The REVELATION

Bishop Marsh has truly said: 'To constitute one thing the type of another, something more is wanted than mere resemblance. The former must not only resemble the latter, but must have been designed to resemble the latter. It must have been so designed in its original institution. It must have been designed as something preparatory to the latter. The type as well as the antitype must have been pre-ordained; and they must have been pre-ordained as constituent parts of the same general scheme of Divine Providence. It is this previous design, and this pre-ordained connection (together, of course, with the resemblance) which constitute the relation of type to antitype'.

PSALMS

We do not here discuss whether or not there is in the Psalter an element of Messianic prediction, but we assume the fact of it, and the inevitability of it. That applications have been made to the Messiah of sayings in the Psalms which do not really refer to Him in no way invalidates the many references which do refer to Him, some of which have the sanction of our Lord and His Apostles.

Bishop Horsley has said that Messianic prediction is nowhere more perspicuous than in the Psalms, yet this fact is largely overlooked, and in some quarters is denied. It is not an exaggeration to say that the Psalter is full of Messianic prophecy, which sometimes is objective, sometimes subjective, sometimes typical and sometimes mystical. We have Christ's own warrant for looking for Him in the Psalms, for He said: "All things must be fulfilled which were written in . . . the Psalms concerning Me" (Luke xxiv. 44), and on several occasions He interpreted of Himself passages in the Psalter. For example: "Did ye never read in the Scriptures, 'The Stone which the builders rejected the same is become the head of the corner'?" (Matt. xxi. 42; Ps. cxviii. 22). "Have ye never read: 'Out of the mouth of babes and sucklings thou hast perfected praise'?" (Matt. xxi. 16; Ps. viii. 2). "Hosanna to the Son of David. Blessed is He that cometh in the name of the LORD! Hosanna in the highest" (Matt. xxi. 9; Ps. cxviii. 26).

The Apostles made a like use of the Psalter. For example: Peter said, "This is the Stone which was set at nought of you

builders, which is become the head of the corner" (Acts iv. 11;
1 Pet. ii. 7; Ps. cxviii. 22). "His disciples remembered that it
was written, 'The zeal of Thine house hath eaten Me up'"
(John ii. 17; Ps. lxix. 9). "That it might be fulfilled which was
spoken by the prophet, saying, 'I will open my mouth in parables;
I will utter things which have been kept secret from the foundation
of the world'" (Matt. xiii. 35; Ps. lxxviii. 2).

There are at least 36 Psalms in which Messianic references can
be found, namely: ii., viii., xvi., xviii., xx., xxi., xxii., xxxi.,
xxxv., xl., xli., xlii., xlv., l., lv., lxi., lxviii., lxix., lxxi., lxxii.,
lxxviii., lxxxix., xci., xviii., xcvi.—xcix., cii., cix., cx., cxviii.,
cxxxii., cxlii., cxlv., cxlvi.

These tell of Messiah's Manhood (viii. 45; Heb. ii. 6-8); His
Sonship (ii. 7; cx. 1; Heb. i. 5; Matt. xxii. 42-45); His Deity
(xlv. 6, 11; Heb. i. 8); His Holiness (xlv. 7; lxxxix. 18, 19;
Heb. i. 9); His Priesthood (cx. 4; Heb. v. 6); His Kingship
(ii. 6; lxxxix. 18, 19, 27; Acts c. 31; Rev. xix. 16); His Conquests
(cx. 5, 6; Rev. vi. 17); His Eternity (lxi. 6, 7; xlv. 17; lxxii. 17;
cii. 25-27; Heb. i. 10); His Universal Sovereignty (lxxii. 8;
ciii. 19; Rev. xix. 16); His Sacrifice (xl. 6-8; Heb. x. 5-7); His
Zeal (lxix. 9; John ii. 17); His Obedience (lxix. 9; Rom. xv. 3);
His Betrayal (xli. 9; Luke xxii. 48); His death (xxii. 1-21; the
Gospels); His Resurrection (ii. 7; xvi. 10; Acts xiii. 33-36);
His Ascension (lxviii. 18; Eph. iv. 8); His Coming to Judge
(xcvi-xcviii.; 2 Thess. i. 7-9).

(From the author's "PSALMS", Vol. 1, p. 35).

The most remarkable of all Messianic predictions in the
Psalter is Psalm xxii. Peter refers to "the sufferings of Christ,
and the glory that should follow" (1 Pet. i. 11), and it is just this
that the Psalm forecasts. Verses 1-21 tell of Christ's sufferings,
and verses 22-31 tell of His glory, yet to be manifested, for not
yet have all the ends of the world turned to the LORD; not yet do
all the kindreds of the nations worship before Him; not yet is
the Kingdom the LORD'S, but this prophecy will be fulfilled.
At the name of Jesus every knee shall bow, and every tongue
shall confess that He is LORD. The kingdoms of the world
shall become the Kingdom of our Lord, and of His Christ; and

He shall reign for ever and ever (Phil. ii. 9-11; Rev. xi. 15; xii. 10).

But this conquest is by suffering, and so the first half of this Psalm (xxii. 1-21) is a minute description of what took place at Calvary, and it is the sufferer who is represented as speaking. The cry of Jesus (1), the mockery of the bystanders (7, 8), the pitiless beholders (12. 13), the agony of crucifixion (14, 15, 17), the piercing of the hands and feet (16), the disposing of the garments (18)—all this is detailed, and could not have been true of any human being other than Jesus. Two omissions in the description are noteworthy: there is no reference to the sufferer's father (9, 10), and none to the piercing with the spear, which took place after the victim's death, and so could not be described by Him.

PREDICTIONS

That Christ Himself is predicted throughout the Old Testament cannot, surely, be seriously questioned. These predictions relate to His Human Pedigree; His Redemptive Programme; and His Divine Person.

1 CHRIST'S HUMAN PEDIGREE

To be the Woman's Seed (Gen. iii. 15; Matt. i. 18)

To be born of a Virgin (Isa. vii. 14; Matt. i. 22, 23)

To be of the Line of Abram (Gen. xii. 7; Gal. iii. 16)

To be of the Tribe of Judah (Gen. xlix. 10; Heb. vii. 14; Rev. v. 5)

To be of the House of David (2 Sam. vii. 12, 13; Rom. i. 3)

2 CHRIST'S REDEMPTIVE PROGRAMME

(i) THE YEARS OF PREPARATION

To be born at Bethlehem (Mic. v. 2; Luke ii. 4, 15)

To be called Immanuel (Isa. vii. 14; Matt. i. 23)

To be worshipped by Gentiles (Isa. lx. 6; Matt. ii. 11)

To have a Forerunner (Isa. xl. 3; Matt. iii. 1-3)

(ii) THE YEARS OF MINISTRATION

To Heal and to Save (Isa. lxi. 1; Luke iv. 16-19)

To be Deserted (Zech. xiii. 7; Matt. xxvi. 31)

To be Spat Upon (Isa. l. 6; Matt. xxvi. 67)

To have Vinegar given Him to Drink (Ps. lxix. 21; Matt. xxvii. 34)

To be Pierced with Nails (Ps. xxii. 16; John xx. 25)

His Garments to be Distributed (Ps. xxii. 18; John xix. 23, 24)

No Bone of Him to be Broken (Ps. xxxiv. 20; John xix. 33-36)

To be Buried with the Rich (Isa. liii. 9; Matt. xxvii. 57)

(iii) THE DAYS OF CONFIRMATION

To Rise from the Dead (Ps. xvi. 10; Acts xiii. 33-35)

To Ascend up to Glory (Ps. lxviii. 18; Eph. iv. 8)

3 CHRIST'S DIVINE PERSON

The Eternal Son (Ps. ii. 7; Acts xiii. 33)

The Suffering Servant (Isa. xlii. 1; Phil. ii. 7)

The Morning Star (Num. xxiv. 17; Rev. xxii. 16)

The Sovereign Sceptre (Num. xxiv. 17; Rev. xix. 15)

The Great Prophet (Deut. xviii. 15, 18; Acts iii. 22)

The Divine Redeemer (Isa. lix. 20; Eph. i. 7)

(From the author's *Christ the Key to Scripture*)

But this outline by no means exhausts the revelations of the Messiah. He is predicted as: Messiah the Prince (Dan. ix. 25); Wonderful Counsellor; The Prince of Peace (Isa. ix. 6); The King (Zech. xiv. 16); The Redeemer (Isa. lix. 20); The Holy One of Israel (Isa. xlix. 7); Witness, Leader, Commander (Isa. lv. 4); The Stone, tried, precious, sure (Isa. xxviii. 16; Ps. cxviii. 22); The Branch—as King, Servant, Man and God (Jer. xxiii. 5, 6; Zech. iii. 8; vi. 12; Isa. iv. 2); Man of Sorrows (Isa. liii. 3); The Shepherd (Ezek. xxxiv. 23; Zech. xiii. 7);

The Rod, and the Root (Isa. xi. 1, 10); The Sun of Righteousness (Mal. iv. 2); Shiloh (Gen. xlix. 10); Wisdom (Prov. viii. 12, 22); The Angel of the LORD (Judg. xiii. 18, and often); The Captain of the LORD's Host (Josh. v. 15); The 'I Am' (Exod. iii. 14; John viii. 24); The Lamb of God (Isa. liii. 7).

If all references to the Messiah in the Old Testament were eliminated, it would be fatally mutilated, and many passages in the New Testament would be left finally unexplained. Let it be said again that such passages are read in the light of the New Testament, and not from the standpoint of the prophet's understanding.

Here, then, is the central feature of the UNFOLDING DRAMA OF REDEMPTION.